IP. 1500
9a

D0762259

BROTHERHOOD
OF POWER

1st executive council (1918) Afrikaner Broederbond

Standing L. to R.: D.H.C. du Plessis, J. Combrink, H. le R. Jooste.
Sitting: L.J. Erasmus (sec.) H.J. Klopper (chair.) Rev. Wm Nicol (V. chair.), J.E. Reeler (treasurer).

BROTHERHOOD
OF
POWER

AN EXPOSÉ OF THE SECRET AFRIKANER BROEDERBOND

J.H.P. SERFONTEIN

Indiana University Press
Bloomington & London

Copyright © 1978 By J. H. P. Serfontein

All rights reserved

No part of this book may be reproduced or utilized in any form
or by any means, electronic or mechanical, including photocopying
and recording, or by any information storage and retrieval system,
without permission in writing from the publisher. The Association
of American University Presses' Resolution on Permissions constitutes
the only exception to this prohibition.

Manufactured in the United States of America

Library of Congress Cataloging in Publication Data
Serfontein, J   H   P   1933-
  Brotherhood of power.
  Includes index.
  1. Afrikaners — Politics and government. 2. Broeder-
bond. 3. South Africa — Politics and government — 20th
century. 4. South Africa — Race relations. I. Title.
DT888.S47 1978 366'.0968 79-2604
ISBN 0-253-19473-3 1 2 3 4 5 83 82 81 80 79
(Previously published by Rex Collings Limited
under ISBN 0860 360 93 8)

Contents

Preface

With this book I intend to give the reader a glimpse into the workings of the secret Arikaner Broederbond. It will hopefully provide insights into the machinations of Afrikaner Nationalism, its power structure and the crucial role played by the Broederbond, perhaps the most important factor responsible for the remarkable unity of Afrikanerdom and of the ruling National Party.

The book is based on Broederbond documents which I have obtained over the years, and also on my own personal investigations, covering over two decades, into the organisation. For 15 years I was the only South African journalist who specialised in the machinations of the Bond – a subject about which little was known until the early Sixties, when I started my inquiries.

Material used includes information collected during the Second World War by the Smuts Government; authentic Broederbond documents of the periods 1939 to 1942; and from the Fifties until the mid-Seventies. These include circulars, study documents, minutes of the executive council and management committee.

The 1939 – 1942 documents have never been published before. Some of the other documents were published in the early Sixties and Seventies when I wrote a series of exposés of the organisation, that appeared from time to time while I was employed in a freelance or full-time capacity by the Sunday Times.

In writing the book I have largely confined myself to the contents of these documents, explaining and analysing where necessary; but I have also recorded the personal part the Broederbond has played in my life.

The major difficulty is that a history of the Bond is a history of Afrikaner Nationalism from 1918 onwards. So general knowledge of Afrikaner politics might thus be helpful in fully understanding the role of the Broederbond throughout this period.

In dealing with the study documents of the Broederbond, on a whole I have not bothered to print their full contents; what is overwhelmingly of interest is the scope of their topics, and the fact that they steered the thinking of Bond members in a certain pre-determined direction. The language of the documents – turgid and tortuous – adds to the problems of translation.

In some respects the book cannot be complete. Because Dr Beyers Naudé, is banned in South Africa, I am precluded from quoting his fascinating statement in November 1963, when he explained why, as chairman of a Broederbond cell, he had made documents available for scrutiny to a fellow theologian after his conscience led him to decide that as a Christian he could no longer belong to such an organisation.

And since the book is not intended as a massive work of academic research, it had to be kept to a readable length. So it was not possible to deal in any detail with the infighting in the Forties and Fifties between the Broederbond and its offshoot the Afrikaner Orde. In a book intended for an international audience the facts are too parochial and the individuals relatively unknown outside Pretoria, even in South African circles.

Unfortunately I cannot thank those who have given assistance to me over the years, either as journalist or while I was writing this book. The simple reason is that divulging my sources would be too dangerous for the persons concerned. When it comes to revenge, there is no more ruthless organisation than the Broederbond. From past experience I know that families will be hounded and ostracised; contracts will be cancelled; jobs might be lost.

While I cannot mention names, my personal gratitude to those who have over the years helped, given information, tips and documents in abundance. Often the most helpful of all has been the benefit of their experience and evaluation of situations.

I know that each of my sources had his own motives, personal or political. Some were HNP supporters, others verkrampte Nationalists; some Vorster supporters, others verligte Nationalists.

Regardless of their motives they have helped reveal to the South African public the intricate workings of the world's most secret political organisation, operating in their politics, church, schools and very neighbourhoods. They have helped write history.

To my one sparring partner on Afrikaner politics for the last 10 years – who has spent hundreds of hours of discussing, arguing and analysing the Afrikaner and Broederbond scene – my special word of thanks.

Without the support of my wife and children, not only throughout the writing of the book, but during the years of tension and personal anxiety for all of us as my exposés appeared, I could not have gone on. They, perhaps more than myself, have been at the receiving end of this ruthless machine.

A letter I received from a Cape Nationalist in 1972, who was anonymous to me at the time but who was to reveal his identity later, perhaps sums up best of all why a book of this nature had to be written about the Broederbond.

He wrote: "I will have to remain anonymous. Suffice to say that I am a leading Afrikaner figure in the area where I live – this you must believe. I have read your book "Verkrampte Aanslag" for the third time, especially after your revelations concerning the Broederbond.

"Please, do you not want to write a documented book about the Broederbond? You must especially again provide the revelations and names which your newspaper published during the Beyers Naudé episode.

"Among Afrikaners, especially Nationalists who have already been hurt by this evil movement, there is great interest and concern about the Afrikaner Broederbond.

"They must be exposed – ruthlessly and mercilessly.

"Give us a book about them. It will be a bestseller among the ordinary Afrikaners who are not privileged to be an AB elite.

"By the way, last Sunday you reported that Mr Jannie Loots was not a Broederbonder. You have made a mistake. He was suspended when he became a United Party candidate. He has been reinstated as a member.

"This you can accept on authority. I can at a later stage, when the time is ripe, again write to you an provide you with information."

32 Marathon St. Malvern Johannesburg where the Broederbond was launched on the night of June 5 1918. The residence at that time, of Mr. D.H.C. du Plessis who later became General Manager of the South African Railways & Harbours.

PART I

Introduction: The Broederbond and I

The all-male Afrikaner Broederbond is a secret organisation unique in today's world. In the Western democracies to which the Afrikaner regards himself as inseparably bound, there can surely be no comparable body.

Certainly, secret and semi-secret organisations exist in many countries, but the Broederbond goes beyond absolute secrecy in its all-embracing and far-reaching influence from the highest national levels to the smallest local structure.

For an Afrikaner who defects, or opposes the Broederbond, the price is terrible – total excommunication. He will be ostracised from Afrikaner society, and the man in business faces economic destruction. Small wonder, therefore, that the Bond has been the most powerful and influential organisation in South Africa for the past 40 years.

It was founded on the evening of June 5, 1918, in Malvern, Johannesburg, by a handful of young Afrikaners. Since the early Thirties it has played a decisive role in shaping the history of Afrikaner nationalism. Indeed, to understand the true character of Afrikanerdom, to interpret the very soul of Afrikaner nationalism, it is essential to have knowledge and understanding of the Bond's nature, philosophy, actions and machinations.

Only such knowledge can provide a key to many crucial questions being asked throughout the contemporary world.

Will the Afrikaner change his political course and his policy of apartheid or separate development?

Will the National Party eventually split between the so-called verligtes and verkramptes? If not, what is holding the Nationalists together?

And, of crucial importance, will foreign pressures and Western threats of sanctions – or even their implementation – succeed in forcing the Nationalist Government to abandon its racial policies and steer the country towards majority rule?

What then is the Broederbond? Membership (kept an absolute secret) numbers some 11 000, organised in about 800 cells (called *"afdelings"* – "divisions"). These people represent what is regarded as the cream of Afrikaner nationalism.

So, firstly, the Broederbond is an elitist organisation, representing the vast majority of Nationalist Cabinet Ministers and Parliamentarians, as well as leaders in the church, education, cultural movements, newspapers, labour, police, government services, universities and the farming community. It links these leaders from Parliament to church councils and local village committees in the smallest centres.

They are knit tightly together, each cell receiving regular directives from head office in Johannesburg. At monthly meetings these directives, study material and other instructions are intensively discussed, so forging the members into a cohesive nationwide unit. A common approach to issues and problems is created so that public opinion can be masterminded and moulded by the secret body.

Over the years the Broederbond has become shrouded in a mystical haze. Legends and myths have developed; half truths and untruths been spread as facts. This is largely the result

11

of absolute secrecy. In 60 years the organisation has officially reacted to public attacks fewer than six times.

Nothing is to be found about the Bond in Afrikaans books on history and politics, while the pro-Government Afrikaans newspapers have over the years – with the odd exception – never reported its activities, unless to react to reports in the English-language newspapers. These are usually dismissed as inaccurate or twisted.

Some books written by overseas scholars do contain substantial references to the Broederbond, but the information dates back to the war years when the Smuts Government unearthed valuable facts about the organisation. The result is that few people, probably including many Broeders themselves, have any conception and appreciation of the Bond's true nature.

There are two popular, but contradictory myths surrounding it.

Firstly, for anti-Broeders, including many Nationalists, the body has become a caricature of evil influence, seen as a "Mafia" dictating policy to the Government, the National Party, the churches, the schools and the newspapers on all important issues. So, for these people, the Broederbond is seen as governing South Africa.

Secondly, its supporters – and indeed some English-speakers – claim that it is an innocent cultural organisation confined to non-political activities, and that it plays no other role.

Both beliefs are false, as this book will demonstrate.

It is necessary to understand the Bond's limitations before its power and influence, often subtle but very real and effective, can be understood in their correct perspective.

Here I must inject a personal note. The Broederbond has played an important and often decisive role in my life. It was directly responsible for a complete change in my career, and for the fact that I entered journalism in 1965. I was engaged full-time in politics at that time, and had trained as a lawyer, so journalism was the very last profession I had ever had in mind.

Since early childhood, in a staunchly Nationalist household, I had been extremely politically conscious. I hated everything that was non-Nationalist, English and pro-Government, praying for a German victory which would liberate South Africa. There was hardly a book on South African political history which I had not read by the time I reached high school.

I became aware of the Broederbond as a boy of 11 in the war years. This was the time when the Smuts Government had forbidden all civil servants to belong to the organisation, dismissing those who remained members.

It so happened that my father was a senior civil servant, pro-Nationalist, but a moderate, originally a follower of General Hertzog in the Fusion years in the Thirties. I was somewhat disappointed to discover that he was *not* a Broeder.

He later told me that he had in fact been approached by Nollie Bosman of Volkskas, one of the super-Broeders in the Thirties and Forties, but had turned down membership for two reasons.

Firstly, he simply did not believe in belonging to secret organisations at all. Secondly, he felt that his Afrikanerskap did not depend on whether he belonged to a secret, elitist organisation or not.

As a first-year university student in 1950 I was an excited witness of a libel action brought by Dr W. Nicol, then Moderator of the Nederduits Gereformeerde Kerk (NGK - Dutch Reformed Church), against Senator A.M. Conroy, a former member of Smuts's Cabinet.

The Broederbond featured prominently in the case as Dr Nicol was a senior member and a former chairman of the UR (*"Uitvoerende Raad"* – "Executive Council").

At this time my father – who was very friendly with many civil servants who were Broeders – told me that political murder had been the result of the betrayal of secrets involving Afrikaner organisations such as the Broederbond and the Ossewabrandwag (the "Sentinels of the Ox Wagon" – a para-military organisation).

He referred to the murder of one Lotter – shot one night in front of his house in Pretoria in 1944 – and speculation about the mysterious disappearance of George Heard in 1945. Heard was then due to take up the appointment of editor of the *Sunday Times* and had written about the Broederbond some years before.

Then, and for some years afterwards, I was a Broederbond admirer, though knowing very little about it. My view was simply that of many non-Broederbond Nationalists: a secret organisation that represented the cream of the Afrikaner leadership, including many highly respectable Afrikaner leaders, and which was constantly attacked by the enemies of the Afrikaner, had to be a "good" organisation. It was "on our side" and working for the "interest of the Afrikaner cause."

In the early fifties I was very active in the Nasionale Jeugbond – the youth organisation of the National Party in the Transvaal. I also participated in some Afrikaanse Studente Bond debates sponsored by the Rembrandt organisation – headed by Dr Anton Rupert, the Afrikaner industrialist. The theme of these debates involved the role of the Afrikaner in the economy, which in the early Fifties was almost 90% in non-Afrikaner hands.

In 1954 I was approached by a senior member of the Rembrandt organisation in the Transvaal. He sounded me out on whether I would be prepared to join a *"vertroulike"* ("confidential") organisation of leading young Afrikaners whose "hearts were in the right place."

The body was to be formed in the near future and its purpose would be to do "constructive work for the Afrikaner cause in a quiet, unobtrusive manner".

Instinctively I knew this had something to do with the Broederbond and enthusiastically said yes, I would be interested.

This approach apparently formed part of the preparations to launch the Ruiterwag (Guard of Riders) a few years later, which became the youth wing of the Broederbond.

Had I been asked on the spot to join the Bond, I probably would have done so, although I had already had reservations about a secret Afrikaner body which often arbitrarily decided who should be included in the inner circle and who left out in the cold.

But I was never to be approached again because of my clash with the National Party leadership at the 1955 Transvaal Youth Congress on the issue of the removal of the Coloureds from the common roll. And, undergoing a political change of heart, I eventually joined the Progressive Party in 1962.

In the years after 1955 I gathered as much information as I could about the Broederbond, most of it second-hand, or by way of deduction. It mostly involved the role the Bond was playing in the church, and its opposition to moderate and "liberal" Afrikaans theologians who had serious scriptural objections to the racist apartheid policies of the government.

But the watershed year was 1963. After that the Broederbond and South Africa would never be the same again and my own career and life took a dramatic and unexpected turn.

In January 1963 I was informed in the utmost confidence by Charles Bloomberg, then political reporter of the *Sunday Times,* that he had made a major breakthrough. He had obtained valuable information about the Ruiterwag and Broederbond, and would soon receive some Bond documents.

It is true that under the Smuts Government the investigations of the Special Branch and Military Intelligence during the Second World War produced considerable information on the Broederbond. Methods used included telephone tapping, and bugging of meetings, and the interception of documents. But the new information was far more thorough-going.

For one thing, General Smuts had forbidden disclosure of the contents of a report by Dr E.G. Malherbe, later Rector of the University of Natal, and suppressed the names of members revealed at the time because he was afraid of upsetting the Afrikaans churches.

Since 1958 I had become what is known in journalistic circles as a "contact" of Bloomberg's, who was deeply interested in developments in Afrikaner Nationalist circles. He was in touch with me regularly and often used to see or phone me to discuss a specific development or to evaluate a certain situation in Afrikaner ranks. This was why he contacted me again in January 1963.

It is important to note that Joel Mervis, who took over the editorship of the *Sunday Times* in 1958, was directly responsible for the new focus on Afrikanderdom. He, more than any other editor of the English-language Press before or after him, fully understood the importance of concentrating on the Afrikaner, purely as a vital source of news.

Mervis, too, understood that however angry Afrikaners became over exposés in his newspaper of situations directly involving the Afrikaner – about which the Afrikaans Press would remain silent for many years – they would still read the *Sunday Times* with a certain grudging respect and admiration.

As a *"Boere Jood"* from Kroonstad he understood the Afrikaner better than most of the English editors, some of whom remain uninformed and still today adhere to the totally false notion that certain subjects concerning the Afrikaner are "sacred" and untouchable and should, journalistically speaking, be toned down – or, better still, ignored or avoided. His approach led directly to a change in journalism in South Africa as other English-language newspapers gradually accepted the importance of Afrikaner news, and the Afrikaans newspapers were forced to write more openly about Afrikaner affairs which for years had been hushed up.

In 1963 I was the full-time public relations officer of the Progressive Party in Johannesburg. In our discussions in January of that year Bloomberg stressed that there were three immediate objectives.

First, to collect as much information as possible on developments involving the Broederbond in the Afrikaans churches. Here he had an excellent contact (not Geyser) in the Bond – somebody closely connected with the church. Later I learned the name of this person, who was never exposed. Indeed, to this day he is still generally regarded as a loyal Afrikaner Nationalist in Johannesburg.

Secondly, arrangements were to be made to get information from inside the Ruiterwag and Broederbond annual congresses to be held in April 1963.

And, finally, shortly after the congresses, the contents of the Broederbond documents – including monthly circulars of 1962 and *"studiestukke"* ("study documents") of that year – should be revealed in the *Sunday Times*.

Bloomberg had to go to Cape Town in February. He asked me to see a senior diplomat at a specific embassy and ask him whether he would be prepared to give "technical assistance" to bug the congresses!

This diplomat was a friend of Bloomberg's. I went to see him in Pretoria. Although I explained to him the importance of the Broederbond, its reliance on absolute secrecy and the political implications and benefits if the lid of that secrecy could be lifted, he remained non-committal and neutral.

Other enquiries by Bloomberg in the world of electronics, including contacts with private detectives, also did not prove successful. In fact he feared that if he passed on too much detail, they might renege on us and tip off the Broederbond.

We knew that the Bond's annual conference was scheduled to take place during the second week of April in the ATKV Hall in Braamfontein, a venue often used over the years.

Two weeks before the meeting we visited a third-floor flat directly opposite the hall, hoping to use this as an observation post during the two-day conference and to photograph people entering the hall.

On the whole I must admit that in our youthful enthusiasm we went about matters in a very amateurish way. We did not have a full appreciation of the enormity of the task we were tackling and of how formidable and even dangerous an organisation the Broederbond could be when cornered.

My wife warned us that we were looking for trouble and would be found out – warnings which we simply laughed off.

However, the *Sunday Times* investigations were indeed discovered by the Broederbond. How I do not know. But in the light of subsequent information about the Bond's close ties and co-operation with the Special Branch, and later with BOSS, it is obvious that the SB – a State agency – was used to sniff out any anti-Broederbond plots. Bloomberg at least must have been under observation.

Before the congress the *Sunday Times* published detailed information about the Ruiter-wag, and reports about uneasiness in the Afrikaans churches about the Bond.

As a result the congresses of both the Ruiterwag (planned for April 6, at the Vryburger Hall in Linden, Johannesburg, with 160 delegates expected) and the Broederbond (planned for April 9 and 10 in the ATKV Hall with nearly 400 delegates expected) were cancelled at the last minute.

On April 21, 1963, the *Sunday Times* carried a report headlined: "Broeders, Ruiters cancel talks: Traitors scare," stating: "South Arica's two secret societies – the 8 000 member Broederbond and its junior wing, the 2 400 member Ruiterwag – this month cancelled their annual congresses because of a traitor scare. Both congresses were called off at the eleventh hour after an exposé of the Ruiterwag in the *Sunday Times*.

"An urgent meeting of the Broederbond's UR – its executive – decided to cancel both meetings to avoid further leakages.

"Last year's congress was also cancelled because of fear of leakages.

"In a top-secret circular sent by registered post last August to all branch chairmen, the Broederbond said: 'The UR has received information from an absolutely reliable source that certain English-language newspapers have instructed some of their officials to obtain as much information as possible about our organisation.

"The UR has therefore decided that no Bondsraad will be held this year, but one will be held next year at the same time as the next Rand Show in Johannesburg.'

"An intensive investigation is being carried out by both societies into the source of the *Sunday Times*."

The Secretarial Report of the UR for the period March 1, 1963, to February 28, 1964, later lifted the veil on Broederbond counter-strategy at the time.

It said: "After it was already decided to hold the Bondsraad congress on April 9 and 10 of that year and all arrangements and notices had been completed, we received confidential information that the date and venue of the meeting were known to the hostile Press and other persons. Together with it information was received that irresponsible actions by hostile persons could not be excluded. The UR thus had to cancel the annual meeting with the utmost haste and notices had to be sent by express post and in some cases telegraphically to all corners of the country to inform delegates that the meeting would no longer be held.''

Years later I discovered that the postponed Bondsraad was held as a one-day meeting amidst the greatest secrecy and special arrangements on May 21 at a farm near Bapsfontein, not far from Johannesburg.

With hindsight there is no doubt that if it had been possible to obtain expert assistance we could have successfully listened in on proceedings as did the Special Branch in 1943.

But it was obviously not a job for amateurs.

Nonetheless, we went full steam ahead with the plan to expose Broederbond activities by publishing the contents of the circulars and study documents which Bloomberg had obtained over a period of time.

By then I knew that the documents came from Professor Albert Geyser, then professor in biblical studies at the University of the Witwatersrand. Two years earlier he had been de-frocked by the Nederduitsch Hervormde Kerk (NHK) when professor of theology at the University of Pretoria.

Geyser was not a Broeder, although he had been a member of Trekmaats – a semi-Broederbond youth organisation in the early Forties.

Early in 1963 he was given a number of 1962 Bond circulars, including several study documents. Some of these involved the church. The source was the Ds Beyers Naudé, then Moderator of the Southern Transvaal Synod of the Nederduits Gereformeerde Kerk (NGK) and chairman of a Broederbond cell. He had been a member for 22 years.

Naudé was soon afterwards to launch *Pro Veritate,* mouthpiece of the later established Christian Institute (both now banned, as is Naudé). He was at that time involved in a crisis of conscience about the influence of the Bond on the church, and the slavish pro-Government attitude of the NGK on the race problem.

Towards the end of 1960 he played a leading role at the famous Cottesloe ecumenical conference in Johannesburg, attended by leaders of all churches in South Africa. He and other NGK leaders supported a statement which repudiated basic aspects of the Government's racial policies. As will be shown later, Government and Broederbond pressures resulted in the Synods of the NGK later repudiating their own leaders.

Naudé gave the documents to Geyser – a brilliant theologian – to enable him to advise Naudé on the question of whether he should break with the Broederbond and the NGK's pro-apartheid policy. He knew only too well that the Broederbond was not a body from which one simply resigned. Although it was possible to do so in terms of the Bond constitution, in practice it often meant ostracism and victimisation – especially if the individual concerned was in an influential leadership position.

The documents were given to Geyser in confidence. However, as he said in a public statement seven months later, Geyser soon realised that the church was being abused by the Broederbond for political purposes, and he was convinced that the contents would eventually have to be made public.

Moreover, he was aware that the majority of the church tribunal that de-frocked him were Broeders, and that the contents of the documents could help him in the Supreme Court, where he had put his case for reinstatement.

So Geyser gave Bloomberg a complete set of the documents to be copied. Bloomberg then passed on to me copies of each document for evaluation.

16

On Saturday, April 20, 1963, the first historical report was prepared by Bloomberg and myself in a secluded office on the fith floor of the old Sunday Times offices in Main Street, Johannesburg. I translated relevant documents used in that report from Afrikaans to English. It was also decided for security reasons to ask the editor not to byline Bloomberg's reports, as is customary. We did not know that it was already too late. The Bond was closing in on Bloomberg.

On April 21, 1963, the *Sunday Times* published the first in a series of exposés that were to continue for over a year.

Published on page three, the headlines reported a "Secret Broeder plan to oust new dealers. Direct link between Broederbond's decisions and church policy."

A second headline read: "Photostats of authentic Broederbond documents."

There were extracts from documents revealing the Broederbond attitude on developments in the church; a circular which revealed that Dr Piet Koornhof, until then undersecretary of the National Party (NP) in the Transvaal, had been appointed chief secretary of the Broederbond, although officially he would be known as Director of Cultural Guidance of the FAK (Federasie van Afrikaanse Kultuurverenigings) the Broederbond cultural front organisation; and another which contained names of prospective members on a *"keurlys"* ("selection list").

These historical revelations shook the Broederbond to its foundations. Referring to the *Sunday Times* article the abovementioned U R Secretarial Report said that "it commenced a series of exposés about our organisation unequalled in our history . . . It was clear that somewhere treason was being committed. The big question that arose with everybody was WHO. It is not necessary to dwell here upon everything. It will remain indelibly in the memory of each Broeder."

It was with a feeling of triumph that early on Sunday morning, before six o'clock, I bought a copy of the *Sunday Times* and saw the headlines.

We had to leave early that day for a family gathering at the Potchefstroom house of an uncle – a Broeder. I found it rather amusing when a younger uncle – a non-Broeder Nationalist – called me aside before church and gleefully said: "Did you see, the Broeders have been exposed. I wonder what (and he mentioned other family Bond members) they are saying now?"

I simply smiled, not replying to what was a typical reaction of many non-Broeder Nationalists who resented the club of self-appointed super-Afrikaners, leaving others out in the cold as second-class Afrikaners.

At that time, with the exception of Mervis, Geyser, Bloomberg and my wife, nobody knew of my involvement in the exposé.

Significantly, in the following week Dr H.F. Verwoerd, as Prime Minister, launched a vicious attack in Parliament on the *Sunday Times* in an attempt to discredit it, claiming that it printed more "untruths" than any other newspaper.

The SABC, headed by Dr Piet Meyer, gave these remarks extensive publicity. Not surprisingly, Dr Verwoerd had served on the UR for many years and Dr Meyer was at the time actual chairman of the Broederbond.

The following Sunday, April 28, 1963, the second exposé was splashed in the *Sunday Times,* again without Bloomberg's byline.

Referring to circulars by Piet Koornhof about the importance of maintaining absolute secrecy, the headline read: "Top Broeders' warning to members. 'Whispered voices also audible,' says Koornhof."

17

But that Sunday morning was to provide a major shock to those of us involved in the anti-Broeder campaign.

Dagbreek en Sondagnuus, then the only Afrikaans Sunday paper, published a front-page story splashing the following headlines: "Burglary attempts at certain offices in the golden city. Broederbond disclosures: Police have clues." The story said:

"It is authoritatively learned that the recent publication of copies of so-called official documents of the Broederbond have provided valuable clues to the Special Branch, regarding an investigation with which they are concerned.

"This investigation arose from the fact that there was a recent attempt to break into certain offices in Johannesburg, as well as nightly visits and threats to people whose names appeared on a membership list of a certain organisation published some years ago in an English-language newspaper.

"The police are also aware that the movements of a few leading Afrikaners have recently been carefully followed by unknown persons . . .

"It is learned that the reports in the Press about the affairs of the mentioned organisation represent the policy of certain English-language newspapers to attack Afrikaans organisations inside and outside politics.

"However, the police investigation is aimed at an altogether different target: namely the underground onslaught of Communism against the security of the Republic, which is conducted in a reckless manner and in which subversive forces make clever use of the so-called revelations about the mentioned organisation.

"This onslaught against the Broederbond by subversive forces is stamped with the Communistic pattern of sowing suspicion and/or condemning the church and religion in South Africa.

"*Dagbreek* was told that in this manner attempts are made to weaken the resistance and unity of action of the community against Communism."

This blatant nonsense was obviously necessary to provide an excuse for Special Branch – and not ordinary police – involvement in the whole affair. Thus was effectively demonstrated the close bond between the Broederbond and the N P Government.

At that time John Vorster (Broeder 3737) was Minister of Justice, and fellow-Broeder Colonel Hendrik van den Bergh head of the Special Branch. Those of us involved in the Broederbond exposés saw the *Dagbreek* article as false. Whether it was a clever ploy of the Bond and the Government to bolster Broeder morale, I do not know. And whether the unnamed police informant believed his own information; whether it was blatant false propaganda; whether in fact somebody had really tried to burglarise a Broederbond office; or whether the Broederbond was simply nervous, one would not know either.

The fact is, that I know of no attempt to follow people, or of any attempt to burglar an office. We had obtained the documents legally, and had a Broeder informant (*not* Naudé).

However, the Broederbond was convinced that an attempt had been made, and would be made again, to break into their offices.

In the Broederbond Report of 1963-1965 the following was asserted: "Because there were indications that attempts would be made to break in at our offices, and since there was in fact definite evidence that a former office of our organisation was burglarised, arrangements had to be made to guard our offices.

"In this regard we made use of the good services of several Broeders. But Broeder G.F. Rautenbach of the division (General Maritz) in particular provided special services by sleeping every evening in the offices over a period of more than 10 months."

18

If the report in *Dagbreek en Sondagnuus* was intended to create panic among us, it succeeded. It must be remembered that it appeared very shortly after the Terrorism Act was passed and the introduction of the diabolical 90 days' detention regulation.

I argued that if the Government and the Broederbond were busy with a massive cover-up designed to frame us at a time of anti-Communist hysteria, it might also be desperate enough to take action against us.

Within minutes of buying *Dagbreek en Sondagnuus* I was busy in my backyard burning some of the documents. This was done in an empty dustbin. But what I had not foreseen was that the process would cause a considerable smoke column to soar lazily into the air. The next 20 minutes felt like 20 hours, with me not knowing whether the smoke column would attract the attention of hidden observers.

Shortly afterwards I left home. Firstly to see a member of the Progressive Party – a prominent businessman – who I requested to look after my family should something happen unexpectedly to me. I did not disclose what my anxiety was about.

Then I deposited the remaining documents with another party member – without disclosing what they were.

Thirdly, that afternoon I went to see Advocate Johan Kriegler (now SC) at his chambers in town. He was then working on the Geyser case against the Nederduitsch Hervormde Kerk.

I told Kriegler that I wanted him to act on my behalf should anything happen to me. I assured him that whatever was said, or whatever charges were laid against me, I was not involved in anything illegal or subversive. Nor was there any question of sabotage.

But again I could not tell him what it was all about.

This might all sound highly melodramatic today; however, it only reflected the fear syndrome which had become symptomatic of a South Africa which was then slowly but determinedly embarking on a course towards a police state.

A second consequence of that traumatic day was that Bloomberg shortly afterwards unexpectedly left South Africa for Rhodesia. He had been receiving threatening phone calls and strange visits late at night at his flat.

A few weeks later, after receiving a note from him through an indirect channel, I drove at night, accompanied by my wife and two small children, to Lobatsi, to meet Bloomberg coming down on the night train from Rhodesia.

He then informed me that he was leaving for England, where he wanted to continue his university research on Christian Nationalism, as the basic philosophy underlying Afrikaner Nationalism.

As I had a complete set of Bond documents, it was up to me to continue the exposés in the *Sunday Times*.

And 10 days later Joel Mervis summoned me. He offered me Bloomberg's former job of political reporter, but I turned it down.

Journalism was definitely not for me for a number of reasons.

There was the financial aspect; I could not write; English was in any case my second language; and I was determined to complete my LL.B. and go to the Bar.

He then asked whether I would not be prepared to freelance, and to do reports from time to time on the contents of the documents. Mervis had nobody else who understood their contents and their political and journalistic importance.

That was the beginning of my journalistic career.

It was to lead to a long association, of 12 years, with one of the shrewdest and most out-standing editors in the history of South African journalism.

He was a hard task-master. The very first story I wrote he tore to shreds with his red pencil, dissecting my highly emotional and politically slanted report on how Broeders helped each other to obtain jobs.

But the following week the story was duly accepted and published on May 26, 1963, under the headline: "This is how Broeders help each other to get jobs."

Obviously it had no byline, merely stating that it was written by a *"Sunday Times* reporter."

For the next 20 months I freelanced for the *Sunday Times*. Few people knew that all the Broederbond reports of that period, including those on the Afrikaans churches and fights inside the Afrikaanse Handelsinstituut, were written by me.

I dealt directly with Mervis. Early on Saturday mornings I would go, to his office. The only person on his staff who knew was Miss Rose Lewin, who had to re-type the stories from my handwritten copy after Mervis himself had sub-edited them.

The strategy was to stretch the exposés over a long period so as to obtain the maximum effect; to keep them guessing what we still had; and simply to work on their nerves. I knew that nothing could be more devastating to the Bond's efficiency than the constant exposure of its membership, strategy and structure.

However, with the full machinery of the State and the Broederbond co-operating to dis-cover our sources it was clear they would not rest until they traced the leak.

From Broederbond records of that period it was clear that originally they had no idea of how the *Sunday Times* had obtained the documents. Yet they soon knew that at the very least we had all the circulars dated between August and December 1962.

In handling the material and reproducing photostatic copies of the documents we were careful to erase all incriminating marks or handwritten comments. For example, docu-ments that had the names of new members in handwriting were specially reproduced and re-written by a *Sunday Times* staff member.

I had an uneasy feeling at the time – it was too good to be true that nothing happened. With Mervis overseas on long leave, I warned the late Lesly Welch, then acting editor, to ensure that his set of documents was kept in a safe place.

He replied that it was locked away in a safe. I was not too happy about this and wanted it off the premises. But Welch simply thought I was suffering from a persecution complex. Unfortunately, I was not.

The Broederbond Head office in Johannesburg asked the secretaries of all cells to return all minutes and other documents of the affected period. But matters were to go further than this.

On October 1, 1963, the police struck. Captain Van der Westhuizen of the Hospital Hill police, accompanied by three other detectives, raided the offices of the *Sunday Times*. In the absence of Mervis they served a search warrant on Welch.

Then they removed photostatic copies of the Broederbond documents.

According to a public statement by Major-General Van den Bergh, head of the CID, the raid followed charges laid alleging the theft of Broederbond documents.

Which Bond official made a statement, under oath, alleging that the *Sunday Times's* Broederbond exposés had involved the crime of theft is not known to this day. The charge was a false statement; by that time it ought to have been clear to the Broederbond itself that there was never a theft or burglary.

A week before the raid a news-magazine quoted Mervis as denying that the *Sunday Times* had been involved in any burglary.

After the raid it was only a question of time before the source of the information was traced. The marks on the seized copies were compared with those on the documents of that period sent back by each of the 350 cells, and the cell from which the leak emanated was discovered.

From Bond documents of the time it is clear that the leakage was a major point of discussion at UR meetings. At a lengthy meeting held on August 22 and 23, 1963, in the Sasbo Building, Johannesburg, it was decided, according to the minutes, "to go ahead and leave no stone unturned to trace the source of the leakage."

According to the minutes of the UR meeting of Thursday, November 7, 1963, in Johannesburg, it was decided to approve of an expense of R200 to trace the source.

And on Tuesday, November 12, a special UR meeting was convened in the TO Building in Braamfontein, to announce that the source – Beyers Naudé – had been discovered.

Significantly, the meeting was attended by Col Hendrik Van den Bergh, then head of the Special Branch.

The minutes of that meeting revealed that Naudé, as chairman of the Emmarentia division in Johannesburg, had collected the documents from the wife of a Broeder living in the house of the secretary of the cell, who was on leave in March 1963.

Naudé was subsequently questioned by Col Van den Bergh, and then had a confrontation with Dr Piet Meyer, the Bond chairman. He told both men what had happened and why.

Naudé issued a statement containing correspondence between him and the Broederbond. The first was his letter of resignation in March of that year; the second was dated November 12, after he had been visited by Col Van den Bergh the previous day. It transpired that Naudé had handed the documents to a "fellow theologian" to enable him to discuss his problem concerning his, Naudé's, membership of the Broederbond and the racial policies of the Government. The "fellow theologian," unknown to him, made the documents available for publication.

That same day the UR issued a statement giving their version of what had happened, and stressing that it could make no apology for the fact that it had fully supported the apartheid policy since its inception.

That night regular programmes on both services of the SABC were interrupted when statements by Naudé and the UR were broadcast in a special 15-minute session. This departure from regular programming was hardly surprising in view of the fact that Meyer was head of both the SABC and the Broederbond. But it was a blatant abuse of a public corporation to further the sectional interests of a secret organisation.

The next day, November 21, a statement was issued by Professor Geyser in which he revealed that he had photostated Naude's documents and given them to a journalist. The documents made it clear that the church was being used for political purposes by the Broederbond and he had decided that the only counter was to expose them. He, and not Naudé, gave the documents to the Press.

He also announced that he had been visited by SB officers after they had seen Naudé, and he questioned the merits of an investigation of a matter which did not concern the security of the State and where there was no question of theft.

Geyser said that if it was a crime to force the Broederbond into the open, "then I am as guilty of the same offence as Generals Hertzog and Smuts." If the Broederbond had nothing to hide, let it reveal all its documents.

21

The same Thursday morning a third police visit was made, this time to myself. At 9.30 a.m. Captain Van der Westhuizen of the CID called at the Progressive Party offices in Rand Central, Johannesburg.

According to the *Rand Daily Mail* of Friday, November 22, 1963, I said at the time: "The police captain, who was from the Hospital Hill station, questioned me for 20 or 30 minutes. He said he was making general inquiries into the matter.

"I refused to give any statement because I regarded the police action as political intimidation and because I had no knowledge of any theft or any other criminal matter.

"I told him, however, that I was not a party to any criminal action and that I had no documents in my possession."

The report appeared on the front page under the headlines: "Broederbond drama. Two new names."

It stated that the Broederbond sensation had taken a surprising turn when it was revealed that Charles Bloomberg, former political reporter of the *Sunday Times,* was the journalist involved, and that the police had questioned Hennie Serfontein, 30-year-old public relations officer of the Progressive Party on the Witwatersrand.

Apart from the ensuing great drama, with both attacks on and praise for Naudé, there followed a public outcry because of the Special Branch involvement. This led to a most curious explanation by Lieutenant-General J.M. Keevy, then Commissioner of Police. Of course as Broeder no 8 125 he had a special interest in the outcome of the case.

According to *Die Transvaler,* a pro-Government Johannesburg morning newspaper, Gen Keevy said that Col H.J. Van den Bergh acted as an "ordinary" policeman when he investigated the alleged theft of the Broederbond documents, not in his capacity as head of the SB.

Gen Keevy stated that a charge had been laid, alleging that Bond documents had been stolen. Col Van den Bergh was regarded as the best man to investigate certain aspects of the case, and in the course of his investigations he regarded it as necessary to interrogate Mr Naudé. Keevy stated that Van den Bergh "thus acted in the specific case merely as a policeman and not as Security Branch chief."

This dramatic period in the history of the Broederbond (and of my own life) was followed by several threats and some abusive letters.

One letter I still remember very clearly, if it could be called a letter. Written on a piece of paper smaller than a post-card, it contained only a few sentences. The gist was as follows: The Afrikaner never forgives or forgets treason. Traitors will be dealt with by the Afrikaner volk.

It was signed by Wynand Viljoen, an attorney whom I knew in Pretoria.

Geyser and Naudé received a considerable number of death threats.

Suffice to say, this police investigation lead to no criminal charges against anybody.

It did have an aftermath in Parliament the following year, when Sir de Villiers Graaff – then leader of the Opposition – called for a judicial commission of inquiry into the Bond. Dr Verwoerd later reacted by appointing a judge as one-man commission to investigate the Broederbond – but also the Freemasons and the Sons of England, two semi-confidential organisations. All were exonerated from exercising undue influence in public affairs.

As a result of the Broederbond episode I continued freelancing for the *Sunday Times* until I was appointed political reporter, commencing as a full-time journalist on January 1, 1965. This was a period of infighting in the National Party between the so-called verkramptes and verligtes. In particular, I investigated the activities of the Hertzog group, the verkrampte faction of the NP which was resisting the slow "liberalisation" of government policy under the premiership of John Vorster.

The Broederbond was largely involved in this struggle because its leadership under Dr Piet Meyer was by its very nature ultra-conservative, and sympathised with Dr Albert Hertzog, then a Cabinet Minister, who was on the UR for many years.

In 1967 I wrote a series of exposés about the infighting between the Hertzog group and the pro-Vorster factions. In the middle of 1967 the Hertzog group narrowly failed to take over the powerful SA Akademie vir Wetenskap en Kuns, and Dr Meyer suddenly "emerged" as the "peace-maker." Shortly afterwards I wrote about a meeting between the Prime Minister, John Vorster and Dr Meyer.

On August 11, 1967, Vorster, in typical fashion, stormed into the arena and denied the infighting, describing it as a "holiday episode"; he denied in his characteristically hair-splitting fashion that he had seen Dr Meyer on the day and place I had mentioned; launched a scathing attack on myself; and threatened that very soon he would take action against the Press publishing "ascertainable lies."

Little more than two years later Vorster had to swallow his words when virtually all the personalities mentioned in my reports broke from the NP to form the new HNP.

In June, 1968, I could report that the anti-Hertzog group had won an important battle when it was decided to disband the Afrikaner-Orde, a secret organisation within the Broederbond of which Hertzog was the spiritual leader.

It was in that year that I had one very narrow escape. I was visiting a Broeder contact – a well-known person – in Pretoria, at his home. He was anti-Hertzog, hated Piet Meyer, whom he accused of quietly co-operating with Hertzog, and had just informed me about the disbandment of the Afrikaner-Orde, which was regarded as a victory for the Vorster supporters.

Unexpectedly, Meyer, with whom he had been friends for years, arrived on the scene. I was pushed into a large empty cupboard in my contact's study. And there I was, a mere few feet away from Meyer, the man I had been exposing for years, listening to their conversation. However, it was a mere social call and with some excuse that he had an important appointment elsewhere, my friend got rid of Meyer. Fortunately for me, I had parked my car a block away.

At the end of 1969 and the beginning of 1970 I could reveal more Broederbond secrets which came to light after the HNP break-away. I reported how Vorster had confronted some HNP leaders at a special meeting at Bapsfontein near Johannesburg and how a special Broederbond delegation went to see the PM at Libertas in October 1969 to swear allegiance to him.

And in my book *"Die Verkrampte Aanslag,"* published at the end of February 1970, I revealed for the first time the contents of a speech by Dr Meyer in October 1966 which spelled out in the clearest terms the policy of Afrikaner domination and imperialism.

1972 was a most important year. In April Dr Andries Treurnicht, arch-verkrampte, succeeded Dr Meyer as new chairman of the Broederbond. A month later, I disclosed the names of the 11 newly-elected members of the UR. This was purely the result of a hunch, and proved that in journalism luck plays a major role.

I had a persistent feeling that I had to leave my Cape parliamentary tasks and go to the Transvaal. I felt certain I could obtain more information about the Broederbond there, so I asked my Johannesburg office for permission to come up for a few days, informing them that I had a tip-off – which, of course, was not correct.

23

But that trip proved to be highly successful. From a contact – not a Herstigte Nasionale Party member – who had never given me information before, I got the names of the executive in a mere 10-minute discussion.

My three days' trip was worth it and the following Sunday we could print the names of the full UR.

On this trip I was warned by two separate sources – one Broeder and one non-Broeder – that I was being watched and followed and had to be careful as the UR was determined to stop leakeages to me.

Later that year came the split in the Broederbond, when they axed all HNP members, thus completely abandoning the pretext that the Bond was a neutral non-political cultural organisation.

Obviously it was somewhat easier to obtain hard news now, but not as easy as some people might imagine. The oath never to divulge Broeder secrets is in effect eternal, and is as binding after resignation or expulsion as during one's membership. It is very seldom that people are prepared to talk, and often they only tell you what they want you to know.

While I was reporting this unfolding drama in 1972, Dr Treurnicht told a Broederbond meeting in Natal they were hot on my track and would reveal my source soon. Of three names mentioned, however, all were wrong.

One was the name of a man in the Western Cape, Theunis Visser. At that stage I had never met him. But, highly significantly, Dr Treurnicht told the Bond audience that it was known that on one day I had phoned him twice.

This happened to be correct. I did phone Visser – an HNP member – on two occasions one day from the Cape Town office of the *Sunday Times,* asking whether I could come and see him on his farm at Worcester. However, although he agreed during the first call, he later cancelled the meeting. This confidential journalistic event was known to Dr Treurnicht.

The second suspect was Sakkie Smit, then an organising secretary of the FAK. Not strangely, he was also suspect because I telephoned him when I was in Johannesburg in May that year.

The third was Beaumont Schoeman, editor of the *Afrikaner,* mouthpiece of the HNP, with whom I had often had discussions over the years. (Unlike some other people serious political differences have never interfered with my personal relations with others – whether they are from the left or the right).

On the last night of our stay in Cape Town in June 1972, my car was sabotaged. Some white chemical was put into the ventilators of the car. The effect was that of tear gas, and the eyes of the whole family streamed with tears for the first 200 miles of our return trip to Johannesburg.

And a week before our departure the car of a woman neighbour new, and in impeccable condition, parked next to our garage, mysteriously caught fire one morning.

Back in Johannesburg I immediately left for America on a six weeks' trip. On my return in August the HNP and National Party confrontation in the Broederbond was coming to a head. I could virtually give a move-by-move description, how circulars were sent by special couriers, with instructions on how to deal with the dissidents, and that one courier was Etienne le Roux – a well-known Pretoria attorney.

During this time mysterious cars would stop and park on the pavement outside my house in the evening for a few hours; also, cars would enter my drive-way, switch off their lights and drive off again after a few seconds.

We were living in an area without street lights.

There was no doubt that this was a process of subtle intimidation. The worst part was the affect on my children. Although my wife and I tried to remain non-commital, they were quick to spot that something unusual was up, and the first to report that "that car is parked again."

Eventually I reported the matter to Joel Mervis, who promised that if it continued the office would provide a guard for my house, particularly when I was away.

However, the intimidation abruptly stopped a few weeks after it began. Perhaps a telephone discussion had something to do with it. In a rage one day, because of the blatant attempts to intimidate my family, I told a friend that I would throw bricks at the next car parked on the pavement without asking who it was. Those responsible quickly got the message – an obvious advantage of having an "open line."

In fact, years later an impeccable source gave me details of this campaign of intimida-. tion. It had been carefully planned and instructions came from very high quarters – the names of the Government men involved are known to me.

A year later there was another fascinating development. I had an offer out of the blue – not directly from the Broederbond – that if I would be prepared to reveal my sources and undertake never to write again about the Bond, I would be paid an amount sufficient to pay off the bond on my house – which was R35 000 at the time.

The initiative for this offer ame from an individual who had high Government authority to negotiate with me.

For a struggling journalist always in financial debt, it was a fascinating offer. I knew, of course, that acceptance would have meant that journalistically I would be a corpse.

At one stage it was even said that the money would be given in cash to avoid payment by cheque. Obviously nothing came of the talks.

My next encounter with the Broederbond was real drama. In view of the tremendous security involving Broederbond meetings, especially regional gatherings or annual congresses, what happened, I can in all modesty say, was unique in the 60-years' history of the Bond.

The date was Saturday, August 24, 1974. I was in Durban attending the Natal congress of the NP. Before I went a contact told me he might have news for me, and early that afternoon I got a message from my Pretoria office saying that a certain person had phoned. He tipped me off about a Broederbond meeting in Pretoria that night, and said he would phone back to ascertain the time of my arrival at the airport. The name given was a cover, so I was not sure which one of two persons had made the call.

I told my office I would be arriving at seven o'clock that night. Since I have a tremendous fear of flying, I was busily working up some Dutch courage, without which I often cannot fly.

On my arrival I spotted the person who had phoned and followed him to the basement parking garage where he told me that the meeting was scheduled to start at 7.30 p.m. at the Langenhoven High School in Pretoria. It would be attended by all the cells in Pretoria and was being addressed by no less a personage than the Prime Minister himself!

I rushed to Pretoria, following him after having alerted the office to get two staff members to wait for me at the Burgerspark Hotel. There, in fact, I met Hertzog Bierman, formerly SA Foreign Information officer in London, and Ken Slade, who was working for the *Rand Daily Mail* and for the *Sunday Times* on Saturdays.

We rushed off to the school at full speed. The schoolgrounds are directly opposite the Petoria Zoo at the bottom end of Paul Kruger Street.

Biermann was with me in the car. All the way to the grounds I could hardly believe the news, although my contact had never been wrong before.

A meeting of the Broeders of Pretoria and surroundings in itself was important. But with the Prime Minister flying up from Cape Town, where he was settled for the parliamentary session, meant that it was a very special occasion indeed.

We arrived at the grounds at about 8.30 and, yes, there were cars, plenty of them. I very slowly drove through the gate, with only my parking lights on, expecting at any moment to be stopped by guards. But there was not a soul in sight.

I drove inside past the cars, round a circle, which was very close to the front entrance, and then slowly out again. Then I reversed back close to the entrance.

I was worried that somebody could come up at any moment. Therefore I drove from car to car illuminating their number plates and reading them out aloud for Biermann to scribble them down on a piece of paper. For this purpose we kept our inside lights on.

We got the numbers of some 15 cars. Then I drove into the grounds, and around the circle for a second time with my lights full on. Some people suddenly made their appearance and I rushed back to the hotel with the paper's early deadlines in mind. I urgently requested a photographer, hoping to be able to take pictures as the Broeders emerged.

It took half an hour to get the story through. Then I rushed back to the grounds, only to discover that no photographer was available. Biermann and Slade were waiting in a car outside the gate in Paul Kruger Street.

The meeting must just have ended because as I arrived the first cars were driving out of the gate. And there I was in my car, a mere four yards from the entrance, waving as they streamed out.

As is usual with these meetings there were three to four Broeders in each car – and plenty of Mercedes Benzes. The astonishment and consternation on their faces was something to watch. Coming out slowly, they were clearly amazed to see a car waiting, and as they came past us would accelerate when I waved at them and they realised they had been observed.

In retrospect I always wondered what would have happened had I got out and entered the hall. I had considered it. But I simply did not believe it to be possible to enter the hall unobserved and thought it better to collect as many car numbers as possible.

There was in any case an early deadline to meet in order to get the report in as many editions as possible. Moreover, I knew that sooner or later I would get a full report on what happened inside.

Yet, looking back, I suppose it would have been the experience of a lifetime to walk into such a meeting. Or perhaps it would have been a case of fools rushing where angels fear to tread.

And as so often and so frustratingly happens with newspapers, most of the trouble was in vain. Because of technical problems the final edition carried only a small report on the front page, and even missed the Pretoria area.

However, the next week full coverage of the meeting *was* given, reporting on aspects of Vorster's speech, publishing the car numbers and the names of the registered owners.

This meeting had an important sequel. In March 1975 I obtained more information about the Prime Minister's speech that August night in Pretoria. Broeders were by then astonished and surprised at his dètente moves with Zambia on Rhodesia. Because in his speech that night – only two months before the first public overtures to and from him and Kenneth

Kaunda – he came out with a strongly verkrampte, pro-Rhodesian line, welcomed by the conservatives.

I then wrote a report setting out in full the theme of Vorster's speech, pointing out the importance of his remarkable change in attitude. But by then the *Sunday Times* had a new editor, Tertius Myburg. Only two paragraphs of a long report were used.

Myburgh told me the Broederbond was no longer a force, if it ever was one; that its importance was completely exaggerated; that I had sensationalised the Broederbond issue in the past; and that it no longer had news value.

In this period I had a tip-off from a key government source to the effect that they "knew" the *Sunday Times* had changed its editorial policy and no more of my Broederbond stories would be printed.

At a later stage, however, in February 1976, Myburgh was indeed to express considerable renewed interest in the Broederbond. That was when *Rapport* carried a front-page report stating that the Western Cape Broederbond division had come out in favour of Coloured representation in Parliament. He then suddenly wanted a story on the new image of the Broederbond – as a verligte movement! Obviously I did not write it. Three months later I resigned from the *Sunday Times*.

It was a pleasant surprise when the *Sunday Times,* in early 1978, published fresh Broederbond exposés, providing valuable and updated information. There must therefore have been a welcome change in editorial policy and thinking on the importance of the Broederbond at the *Sunday Times*.

However, there are some puzzling aspects surrounding the Sunday Times exposé. I understand that the two reporters involved obtained the most comprehensive set of documents ever by any outside individual, newspaper or organisation in the history of the organisation. It is said to include 5 000 names.

The newspaper published reports on four consecutive weeks in January and February 1978 – and then suddenly stopped. There were two reports later. These were clearly only the tip of the iceberg.

In view of the fact that the most devastating blow the Broederbond can receive is publicity about its activities, organisation and membership, it is strange indeed that the newspaper did not then fully expose the organisation. Of course it can still do so at a later stage.

The latest *Sunday Times* reports constitute the fourth major breakthrough on the workings of the organisation.

First came the investigations during the war years, not much of which was made public directly at the time.

The second was the Beyers Naudé episode of 1963.

The third came during the period 1968 – 1974 when the *Sunday Times,* under Mervis, gave maximum publicity and coverage to Broederbond exposés – which, according to Broederbond documents of the period, caused havoc in their ranks.

For 12 years (1963 – 1975) I was closely involved in reporting about the Broederbond in the face of the most bitter resentment of the Afrikaner establishment. Nobody is more despised and hated than the "traitor," who has "betrayed" the cause of Afrikanerdom.

True, physically nothing has happened to me or my family. But there was a price to be paid: total ostracism in every sphere and spectrum of Afrikaner society. This is an experience which the liberal English South African, secure in his comforts, can and will never understand.

One "small" example: in 1965 we were refused permission to baptise our daughter.

One of the objections officially raised by Ds A.W.L. Smal was my friendship with Beyers Naudé. As a result of an argument with him when he made the formal objection, Smal, after pressuring the church council, laid a charge against my wife for "insulting" the representative of God.

This led to lengthy and protracted proceedings in terms of which my wife was censured when she refused to face the church council without me being present.

We went on appeal to the regional authorities. The scribe of the area – a Broeder – privately admitted that we were right, and church law was on our side; that Smal and the church council had acted illegally. But he admitted openly that my *Sunday Times* connections, and my friendship with Naudé, made all the difference.

The irony is that when he served on a special committee of three ministers to hear our case on appeal he was silent. One of the other two members was Ds D.P.M. Beukes – for many years a member of the UR.

As a journalist and an Afrikaner who had the opportunities, I pressed ahead with my exposés – knowing the consequences. I believe that this secret organisation is one of the main reasons why the Afrikaner Nationalist finds himself today in a spiritual bondage, chained and fettered behind an iron curtain built by the Broederbond; and why the Afrikaner, once known for his individualism and independence, has become a herd animal.

The basis of its organisation; the methods of its operations; the ruthlessness with which it deals with those who resign; its philosophy of Christian Nationalism coming close to being merely a modern day version of Hitler's "herrenvolkism"; its real objective of Afrikaner imperialism and domination; its reliance on fear, fear for the loss of Afrikaner identity and fear for the consequences of defying the values it has laid down for the Afrikaner tribe – all this has woven it into an organisation that will drag the Afrikaner down to his doom in a Gotterdämerung spirit of last-ditch defiance.

PART II

The Beginning: 1918 – 1940

A. Motivation and Birth

"The Afrikaner Broederbond was born out of the deep conviction that the Afrikaner volk has been planted in this country by the Hand of God, destined to survive as a separate volk with its own calling."

So said Dr J.C. van Rooy and Ivan Lombard, respectively, chairman and secretary of the Broederbond, in a statement to *Die Transvaler* on December 14, 1944.

In other words, the Bond's primary motivation was to prevent the disappearance of the Afrikaner volk as a separate political, language, social and cultural entity. The identity of the Afrikaner had to be ensured at a time when, economically and culturally impoverished, he was faced with the threat of being swamped and absorbed by the stronger English group, which at that time regarded this as an inevitable process.

"The Afrikaner Broederbond was born out of the need (*uit die nood van*) of the Afrikaner volk." This is how the Broederbond itself described the original motivation for its establishment in a 16-page document circulated in 1968 at its jubilee celebration, giving an historical review of the Bond's development. The author was Professor A.N. Pelzer, for many years Professor of History at the University of Pretoria. His report is of paramount importance.

It is crucial to examine the circumstances prevailing in 1918, when the Bond was launched.

Although the constitution of the Union of South Africa entrenched the language rights of both white groups, and although in law members of each group enjoyed full equality, in practice the Afrikaner was in many ways a second-class citizen.

Historical and other reasons had ensured that the English-speaking section completely dominated the civil service, commerce and industry. Many Afrikaners were still struggling to find their feet, having been impoverished by the second Anglo-Boer war, which ended in 1902 when Lord Kitchener and his troops applied a scorched earth policy, destroying thousands of Boer farmsteads, with 26 000 women and children dying in British concentration camps.

More bitter for the Afrikaner than the fact of physical inequality was the English attitude of superiority, arrogance and contempt for the Afrikaner and his language.

At that stage Dutch was still the only other official language, and would only be replaced by Afrikaans in 1926, although it was in practice the language of the Afrikaners.

It was the time when there were very, very few Afrikaans schools in the whole of South Africa; when the language of instruction in the schools was either English – or, in many cases, dual-medium instruction, with some subjects taught in either Afrikaans or English.

It was the time when many an Afrikaans school-child came home with tears in his eyes because he had been punished by the unilingual English teacher for daring to speak Afrikaans on school grounds. Such punishment not infrequently included walking around with a board slung on your neck which read: "I am a donkey. I spoke Dutch."

29

And the English often referred to the upcoming and virile Afrikaans language as a "kitchen language."

The process led to thousands of Afrikaners, ridden with an inferiority complex, becoming Anglicised – absorbed by a world language and culture.

Politically, the Afrikaners were divided between so-called "moderates" and "extremists": the followers and supporters of Generals Botha and Smuts in the South African Party on the one hand, and those of General Hertzog in the National Party on the other.

The Botha-Smuts policy after 1910 was known as "conciliation" in contrast to Hertzog's "two-stream" policy.

In December 1912 Gen Hertzog, then also a member of the SAP, was kicked out of Botha's cabinet for his famous De Wildt speech with its theme of "South Africa First" and its rejection of the English jingoes whose ultimate loyalty was to England and the Empire.

Botha and Smuts fell over backwards to accommodate what they regarded as moderate pro-South African English-speakers for fear that extreme jingo elements could seize control. In the process they appeared to be prepared to abandon demands for legitimate Afrikaner rights and the redressing of legitimate grievances.

In 1914 came the establishment of the National Party, the outbreak of the First World War, and a clash between Botha and Hertzog because of Botha's active support for Britain.

For 50 years the political and constitutional relationship between South Africa and Britain would be a major bone of contention in South African politics. A badly planned rebellion broke out in 1914 with former comrades in arms of Botha and Smuts such as Generals De Wet, Kemp and Maritz deeply involved. It was however short-lived and fizzled out early in 1915.

It left a legacy of hate nonetheless – not just between Afrikaner and Briton, the latter's kith and kin obviously deeply involved in fighting Germany; but also between Afrikaner and Afrikaner.

For more than 60 years these divisions would dominate the white South African political scene.

The jingoism of the English-speaking South African; his lip service to a language in practice scorned; his arrogance and contempt for the cultural struggle of the young Afrikaner volk to attain its rightful goals – all this provided the fertile ground in which the Afrikaner Broederbond found its roots.

In short, jingoism and imperialism were directly responsible for the Bond.

If it were not for the hypocritical attitude to the equality of the two language groups, the Broederbond would probably never have been established.

Its establishment and basic aims could therefore be historically justified. It was only later, in the pursuit of honourable aims, that it deviated from its original goals and degenerated into a power-hungry organisation whose major aim was Afrikaner domination of South Africa and the Afrikanerisation of all the Whites.

Over 60 years the full circle from English jingoism to Afrikaner imperialism would be encompassed.

Henning Klopper, for many years Speaker of the South African Parliament and the first chairman of the UR, summed up the events leading to the establishment of the Bond as follows, when he addressed the jubilee festival of the Broederbond on October 1, 1968.

He said: "The years 1914 to 1917, culminating in the establishment of the Broederbond in 1918, were years of struggle for the Afrikaner, years of dissension, years of scattering (*verstrooiing*), years of frustration. This was the decade after the English war in which we were destroyed. But we felt that we could not remain lying down; by the grace of God we had to stand up."

An incident on the evening of April 13, 1918, sparked off a series of events which would lead to the establishment of the Broederbond on June 4, 1918.

Dr D.F. Malan, then editor of *Die Burger,* and leader of the National Party in the Cape, addressed a meeting in the Selborne Hall in Johannesburg. Ivan Lombard gave a lively description of what happened that night, and what ensued, when he addressed the quarter-century celebrations of the Broederbond on December 13, 1944, at its Bondsraad in the Visser Hall at the Normal College in Bloemfontein.

He recounted the story from the diary of one of the foundation members, H.___ Merwe, who was also present at the Selborne meeting, and who was asked by ___ stand up amidst the wide acclamation of the delegates.

A special agent, with the unlikely cover name of A. Mann, had bugged the ___ for the Smuts Government and produced a full report on the events, including ___ speech in which he dealt with the history of the Broederbond and the situation in ___

Lombard told the congress: " . . . it was at this moment in the life of the nation ___ moment when the Afrikaner soul was sounding the depths of the abyss of despai___ movement was born which was destined to watch over the destiny of this heroic ___ 25 years of success and failure, of disappointment and renewed hope; in other w___ Afrikaner Broederbond was born."

The Mann report mentioned that Lombard then referred to Van der Merwe's diary. ___ report continued: "The English flag at the back of the hall was removed by Van der Merwe himself and torn to shreds. This was observed by an Englishman and a mob of English people gathered outside the hall singing *Tipperary,* etc. Dr Tom Visser, chairman of the meeting, warned that the English were waiting for them outside the hall, but the audience dauntlessly went out and a free fight ensued, as the audience had decided to do the manly thing and face their antagonists although they were few compared to the English. An assault was made on the National Party club when Dr A.M. Moll's motor car was burned. The brawl was witnessed by Van der Merwe, H.J. Klopper and Bertie Naudé from a balcony.

"Lombard, taking extracts from time to time from Van der Merwe's diary, showed how this scene had impressed Klopper and Van der Merwe, so that they discussed the situation with D.H.C. du Plessis, but they always took the precaution of holding their discussions in the veld, as they dared not take the risk of being overheard in a country where to think in Afrikaans was dangerous, let alone speak it. Many discussions took place among Van der Merwe, Klopper, Du Plessis, Ds Naudé, etc.

"They all came to the realisation that the Afrikaner must not be anti-anything, he must be pro-Afrikaner. Gradually, after many discussions the idea came to these young Afrikaners that they should form an organisation which would be above the usual party political questions, and would strive only for one thing, the Afrikaner. This organisation was called Jong Suid Afrika ('Young South Africa').

"Faith in Afrikanerdom must be engendered and this organisation, based on the brotherhood of Afrikaners, seemed to these young men the only way. A meeting was held at the house of Ds Naudé in Roodepoort and the framework of Jong Suid-Afrika worked out, with a membership of 14 young men, on the 24th of May 1918."

Klopper became the first chairman.

31

The Naudé mentioned was the father of Dr Beyers Naudé. In 1902 he was one of only six of the 60 Boer delegates at the Vereniging peace conference who refused to agree to the unconditional surrender of the two Boer Republics.

On the evening of June 5, 1918, the members of Jong Suid-Afrika held a meeting at the house of Danie du Plessis in Malvern. This date is officially recognised by the Broederbond as the day on which it was founded.

Klopper was elected chairman and Du Plessis secretary. Among the original members present were P.H. van Wezel, Erasmus, Otto, Steyn and Swart.

Paragraph 32 of the Report of the Commission of Enquiry into Secret Organisations (RP 20/1965) – the commission appointed in 1964 to investigate the Broederbond, the Freemasons and the Sons of England and headed by Judge Botha – said that in the bitter climate of that time 14 railway clerks, clergymen and policemen "formed an organisation in which Afrikaners could find each other in the midst of great confusion and disunity and be able to work together for the survival of the Afrikaner people in South Africa and the promotion of its interests."

According to the Mann report Lombard explained its objectives as follows: "It was agreed at this meeting that the salvation of the Afrikaner people lay in a brotherly attitude towards each other and faith in their cause. South Africa must be served and Afrikaner culture must be fostered and Afrikaans traditions taught to the youth. Afrikaners must help each other on economic lines and the movement must be non-political. They must strive to have their own Afrikaans language recognised everywhere. The nature of the movement must be thoroughly South African. Unity was the keynote."

According to the official minutes of the founders' meeting on June 5, 1918, Klopper set out the aims of the organisation as follows:

"Our main object is the bringing together (verbroedering) of Afrikaners who are at present spread over the whole of South Africa and are largely opposed to each other, without the least cohesive power."

On June 18, 1918, Ds Naudé was elected as the first president of the movement. At that meeting there were 27 members. The name of the organisation was changed to the Afrikaner Broederbond (AB) with the prime object of fostering brotherly love.

According to its first minutes some of the aims of the Bond were formulated as follows: "The welding together of Afrikaners . . . Differences of opinion about national problems must be removed and a healthy progressive society and uniformity of purpose must be achieved . . .

"The interests of Afrikaners must always be served . . .

"To carry the Afrikaner volk towards its sense of identity (selfbewussyn), to inspire self respect and to encourage and to cultivate love for his language, history, land, volk and law . . .

"Pure, original South African culture and art must be promoted in every regard . . .

"The society must be purified (veredelmoedig) with the maintenance of its old pure morals and characteristics, such as hospitality, democratic conviviality, and readiness and generosity to stand by each other in bitterness or need . . . ."

It concluded by saying: "We build our future on the Rock of Christ."

The two cornerstones were thus: the promotion of the Afrikaner ideal and identity out of which the later philosophy of Christian Nationalism was to grow; and the fostering of a common, unbreakable brotherhood among its members.

As Lombard explained it according to the Mann report:

"The Bond would work for the fusion of all Afrikaners, embracing all the interests of the Afrikaners, transforming them into a self-determining democratic nation, with a love of their own language. Cultural and economic aspects of Afrikaner life should be given full and careful consideration, a clean and moral life should be led, self-sacrifice be their watch-word when the Afrikaner cause called. They should help each other to obtain promotion in the civil service or any other field of activity in which they worked, and the foundation of the whole organisation must rest on the rock of Christ. The subscription was 5/- per annum, strictly in advance. On account of a speech delivered in Johannesburg by Professor J.H. Hofmeyer about this time, it was decided that no man could become a member if his parents and grandparents had not been born in South Africa. This rule was later rescinded.

"Reading from the manifesto issued by the Afrikaner Broederbond in those early days, Lombard said that it was decided that nationalisation (i.e. the bringing to a national consciousness) of the youth must take place in order to combat the immigration into the country which took place after the 1914-1918 war. The Afrikaner Broederbond was then open to all Afrikaners, irrespective of religion or political leanings."

In a later chapter the aims, objectives and philosophy of the Broederbond over 60 years will be more fully discussed.

It took the Broederbond more than two years to become the organisation its founders had intended it to be. Pelzer in his review made it very clear that the Bond was supposed to become a very special organisation, as indeed has happened over the years. On page one he said: "For understandable reasons it was difficult to clearly state the aims of the Broederbond from the outset. The result was that initially people were admitted to the organisation who regarded it merely as yet another cultural organisation."

According to Pelzer this "initial uncertainty" largely ended on September 21, 1920, when the Fundamental Rules *(Grondreëls)* of the Afrikaner Broederbond were finally accepted.

L.J. du Plessis, (not the Professor) at one stage secretary, told *The Star* on October 12, 1948, that in its early years "it was little more than a semi-religious organisation" with little purpose or direction.

The Fundamental Rules of 1920 provided for a Bondsraad and the UR, though the body at that time comprised only one cell.

On September 21 a majority of the members meeting in the old Carlton Hotel, Johannesburg, decided that the Broederbond would be a secret organisation. From then on the Bond also began to concern itself with matters such as "the native question, immigration, profiiteering, home language education and library affairs." (From *"Die Afrikaner Broederbond,"* section V, paragraphs six-eight, Hofmeyer Papers.)

Ironically, the first person to address the Broederbond was Jan Hofmeyer, then rector of the University of the Witwatersrand and later the leading liberal in the Smuts Cabinet.

The very first Bondsraad was held on November 25 and 26, 1921, in the Grand National Hotel, Johannesburg. The first UR was then elected and until 1932 the UR was elected annually at the Bondsraad. However, from 1932, the constitution was changed and the UR only elected at every second meeting.

The first chairman of the UR was Henning Klopper, from June 5, 1918, until June 26, 1924.

As will be seen later, the chairman of the UR and the UR itself played a key role in the activities of the Broederbond.

Between 1918 and 1921 there was also a president who wielded great powers and could even remove the chairman of the UR if he performed his job unsatisfactorily.

The first president was Ds J.F. Naudé, regarded as "the spiritual father" of the Broederbond. He was president until August 19, 1919, when he moved to a congregation in Graaff Reinet. He was succeeded on January 18, 1921 by Ds L.J. Fourie. However, after the first Bondsraad meeting of November 1921, the all-powerful position fell away.

It is significant that the first two persons occupying the presidency were church ministers. This symbolised the inextricable link over the years between the Bond and the Afrikaans churches.

The holding of the first Bondsraad in 1921 is regarded in Broederbond circles as the end of the first chapter in its history. Pelzer described it as follows on page six: "Only from then onwards could serious attention be given to the main task which its founders had in mind for the Afrikaner Broederbond, namely to protect the Afrikaner by means of an efficient organisation against vilification, humiliation and oppression. In view of these onslaughts the Afrikaner had to be united and all the contradictions in his existence had to be bridged."

In the years 1922 to 1939 the Broederbond actively involved itself secretly in every sector of Afrikaner society. It laid the foundations of its organisation and created the many front organisation that enabled it to get an octopus-like grip, first on Afrikaner nationalism, and later on the government structure itself.

The first phase coincided with the first National Party victory in 1924; the official recognition of the Afrikaans language; the maintenance and promotion of Afrikaans in the schools, public life and the commercial world; and the promotion of mother tongue education and Afrikaans literature.

The biggest achievement of this period was the establishment in 1929 of the FAK *Federasie van Afrikaanse Kultuurverenigings* – Federation of Afrikaans Cultural Associations.)

By 1930 the Broederbond had thus consolidated its total grip on Afrikaans culture.

Pelzer, on page seven, summarised the second phase, which ended in 1939, as follows: ". . . it coincided with the problematic situation of our volk in those years in the social, economic and political spheres, and was characterised by the lead taken by the Afrikaner Broederbond *inter alia* with regards to the organising of the Kimberley Volkskongres in 1934 on the Poor White problem; the creation of an Afrikaans bank, Volkskas; the organising of the Economic Volkskongres in 1939 and arising from it the Reddingsdaadbond; Ekonomiese Instituut and Handelsinstituut; the establishment of the National Institute for CNE, (Christian National Education) and of the Instituut of Social Welfare (*Volkswelstand*) and the establishment of Afrikaans worker organisations to combat Communistic and other denationalised influences among the workers."

B. Organisation

To tackle this all-embracing task a nationwide organisation was needed. By the end of 1921 there were only two cells, Rand Central and West Rand. Though there followed the establishment of the East Rand cell on March 3, 1922, the Broederbond remained an urban organisation confined to the Reef.

During the next few years, however, new cells sprang up on the platteland – the Potchefstroom cell, for example, which with its strict Calvinistic philosophy was destined to play an influential role for decades, was formed on April 11, 1923.

34

By 1925 there were eight cells with 162 members.

On October 23, 1927, the first cell outside the Transvaal was formed in the small eastern Free State village of Memel. In 1929 the first cell was founded in Natal in Newcastle and by 1930 there were 23 cells with 512 members.

On May 20, 1931, the first cell in the Cape was established in Cape Town and by 1935 there were 80 cells with a membership of 1395. The Broederbond was spreading its tentacles all over South Africa.

In 1939 the Bond actually crossed the borders of South Africa when a cell was formed in Daisyfield, Southern Rhodesia, on July 15. By 1940 there were 135 cells with 1980 members.

The process of expansion would be completed when on March 29, 1949, a cell was formed in Windhoek; and on December 12, 1949, in Lusaka, in present-day Zambia.

In the Twenties the Broederbond had teething problems in the process of consolidation. There seemed to be some confusion about its goal.

Pelzer on page five described it as follows: "Because a conception, which among a small circle achieved an early ripeness, had to be carried out to a larger group, it can be understood that during the early years people were admitted to the Afrikaner Broederbond who did not comprehend the spirit of the organisation and who could consequently also not give voice to it. Therefore it was necessary in the early Twenties to intervene drastically on several occasions and to deny a comparatively large number of members their privileges . . .

"Because of a lack of understanding about the nature and character of the Afrikaner Broederbond it was even necessary to dissolve the West Rand division in 1926."

According to the Mann report this is how Lombard saw the situation. "There was a gloomy period during 1923 – 1924, when dissensions took place in the ranks of the Afrikaner Broederbond and the future prospects of the organisation looked exceedingly gloomy. However, things brightened up in 1925, and it was then that the members of the Afrikaner Broederbond learnt to get together and to find common ground . . . A period of consolidation and expansion followed and it was decided at this time to scrutinise the *bona fides* of intending Afrikaner Broederbond members before admitting them to Afrikaner Broederbond deliberations.

"Lombard then went on to discuss the procedure to be adopted by members if they were to be really *broers* in the full meaning of the term. Members must seek close acqaintance with each other, and try to help themselves and each other in every walk of life. In 1927, the Afrikaner Broederbond decided to take an active part in the life of the community and that no avenue could be neglected.

"At this time the Afrikaner Broederbond sponsored Afrikaans-medium schools, and the use of Afrikaans on South African coins. An Afrikaans bank with Afrikaans capital must be fostered by the Broederbond. Assistance, financial and otherwise, should be given to candidates approved by the Broederbond who stood for Parliament or for the Provincial Council. Members should try to enter the government services, such as the post office, railways, etc, to as great an extent as possible, with a view to working themselves up into important administrative positions, and in this respect all members should help each othher."

By the early Thirties the Broederbond was thus properly and powerfully established.

As a fully-fledged and highly secretive organisation it naturally had its own symbols, though efforts over the years to design a distinctive flag were not successful.

Although Kloppers had proposed in 1920 that the Bond's colours should be ash-coloured, green and gold, this has not been accepted in later years.

Since 1922 the Broederbond has established secret signs of identification. A special handshake, for example. And when writing to a person without knowing whether he was a Broeder, there had to be special marks on the letter to inform the receiver, if indeed a Broeder, that the writer was one too.

However, because the secret signs were discovered in due course by non-Broeders, all members were informed on September 3, 1963, that they were no longer in use.

In 1927 the Broederbond accepted an external recognition sign *(herkenningsteken)*. Broeder J. Retief of the East Rand was responsible for the design – a triangle with the three sides bound together by a circle (band). The triangle and the circle together form the letters AB, recognisable only to the initiated.

On September 5, 1931, the UR accepted the following symbol devised by Ivan Lombard: "The symbol of the Bond is a triangle as sign of strength, enveloped by a circle as a sign of unity. The triangle is within a circular rim (rand) with the inscription: The Afrikaner Broederbond on top and the founding year 1918 underneath. This circle is embroidered with a cord as a sign of the close bonds of brotherhood. The outward badge *(kenteken)* of the Bond consists of the symbol with the exclusion of the circular rim, inscription and cord."

In 1925 a competition was held for a Bondslied (Song of the Bond). Eventually, in 1928, one of the three songs submitted was effectively accepted. It was written and composed by Ivan Lombard. In 1957 the Bondslied was composed anew by Broeders Stephen Eyssen, former headmaster and MP, and Broeder Jan Pienaar of Pretoria. (See Annexure A.)

Other points about the Bond:

Since 1920 its motto has been *"Wees Sterk!"* ("Be strong!"). Membership fee on admission is R15 and the annual fee R7. Over the years, especially among members, it has come to be referred to as the "AB", the abbreviation of "Afrikaner Broederbond."

On the question of secrecy Lombard said, according to the Mann report, "Even at this time (1921 – when the second cell was formed) it was decided that no communication on AB matters would be sent through the post and that secrecy must be vigorously observed."

C. Culture

Since its inception the Broederbond has concentrated much of its work in the Cultural sphere. According to Pelzer (page eight), by the end of the Twenties there was "an alarming superficialisation" in the cultural sphere: ". . . with a mere 12 cells and only 263 members" it was clear that the AB could no longer fulfil the cultural task alone. A public arm was necessary through which larger numbers of culturally aware Afrikaners could be employed to further Afrikaans language and cultural tasks.

"What made the position so much more urgent was that, together with superficialisation, an organisational fragmentation of forces in the cultural sphere had set in.

"It was as if the need *(nood)* was sensed from all sources *(oorde)* and that people without insight or consultation, separate from each other and often in opposition to each other, started to launch one or other cultural organisation. There was an urgent need for a co-ordinating body in the cultural sphere."

So it happened that the Broederbond took the lead in 1929, with Lombard as its energetic chief secretary. An invitation was sent to all the recognised cultural bodies in the country to serve on a steering committee to make the arrangements for a nationwide conference.

The aim would be to establish closer co-operation between all the Afrikaans cultural institutions; to discuss methods to maintain the cultural and linguistic independence of the Afrikaner; and to work out a programme of action which could be implemented by a vigilance committee on a federal council.

The steering committee met on August 24, 1929, in Bloemfontein. As a result, the planned national language and cultural conference was held on December 18 and 19 in Bloemfontein under the auspices of the SA Akademie vir Taal, Lettere en Kuns (SA Academy for Language, Literature and Arts).

It was decided "with an eye on joint and, where necessary, simultaneous action regarding the maintenance and promotion of the Afrikaans language and the protection of other related matters, to form a federation which will be known as 'Die Federasie van Afrikaanse Kultuurvereninginge!"

Thus the FAK was born. The name means Federation of Afrikaans Cultural Societies and its motto was *"Handhaaf en Bou"* ("Maintain and Build" – or "Vindicate and Cultivate").

Lombard became its first secretary, whilst remaining secretary of the Bond.

Since then most intimate links have existed between the AB and the FAK. The latter was its official front and could over the years provide a cover for most of its activities.

For example, Broederbond officials would for outward appearances be employed as FAK officials whilst in reality they were working for the Bond.

"cultural" sphere – and since 1929 every Afrikaans cultural body, however important or unimportant, has been affiliated to the FAK. Thus, by 1978, far more than two thousand such bodies, including church councils, were linked to the FAK.

D. Economics

Once the FAK was in full control of the cultural sphere, the Broederbond could concentrate all its attention on the poor economic situation of the Afrikaner.

Dr Piet Meyer, in his address to the 1968 Bondsraad during the jubilee celebrations, emotionally and vividly described that period in Afrikaner history.

He said that the Afrikaner volk had not only been humiliated in schools and shops but that "it was more oppressive in our daily existence as members of an all-embracing socio-economic whole, of an impoverished platteland and British-Jewish-dominated growing urban complexes. We were the poor and the Poor Whites, the Boers without markets and without capital; the lowly-paid unskilled workers in the mines and the factories; we were the civil servants in the inferior jobs, on the railways, in the post office, in the police.

"When the great drought came, we were the first who had to toil merely to live; and when the Great Depression came, we were the first unemployed. Brotherhood did not escape this all; it was in it and struggled with it . . . ."

On July 26, 1930, the UR decided to accept as policy for the forthcoming year "development in the economic sphere." As a result, on November 14, 1931, an extraordinary Bondsraad was held in Johannesburg. It became known as the Economic Bondsraad.

Immediate attention was given to the establishment of an Afrikaans commercial bank because the banks of the time exercised a "power grip", especially over the farmers. So, after investigations by a series of commissions, Volkskas (Koöperatief) Beperk, the first Afrikaans commercial bank, was established on April 3, 1934.

The founding meeting was attended by 55 Broeders and took place under the chairmanship of Professor J.C. van Rooy, then Bond chairman.

In truth, therefore, Volkskas was a Broederbond bank and to this day is regarded as such. The capital of Afrikaners, and of Broeders in particular, could be mobilised to provide financial backing for Afrikaans business undertakings.

In the same year the Broederbond also organised a volkskongres on the Poor White problem in Kimberley where, according to Meyer, "the Afrikaans churches took the lead to provide, together with the State, charitable services for our impoverished people . . ."

In 1938 the UR decided to use the new enthusiasm generated by the Voortrekker centenary festival for the economic interests of the Afrikaner. As a result the FAK, on the instructions of the UR, organised an Economic Volkskongres on October 3 – 5, 1939. It was in Bloemfontein and coincided with the Bondsraad meeting.

A number of Broederbond organisations arose out of that congress. The most important was the Economic Institute which, as a steering committee, had to see that the decisions of the congress were implemented.

The Economic Institute met for the first time on December 1, 1939, in Bloemfontein. It established the Reddingsdaadbond (RDB), an organisation which collected money to assist Afrikaners in economic difficulty, and also to assist with the financing of Afrikaans business undertakings. By 1943 it had more than 50 000 members across the country.

The congress also led to the establishment of Federale Volksbeleggings Beperk (FVB), whose aim was to weld together in one company a portion of Afrikaner capital and to make it available for the establishment or taking over of commercial and industrial enterprises.

In August 1942 the RDB launched the Afrikaans Handelsinstituut – the counterpart to the English-dominated Chamber of Commerce. It was a non-profit making company to promote the interests of Afrikaner businessmen.

The Handelsinstituut, in October 1942, took over the magazine *Volkshandel* – in existence since March 1940 – as its official organ.

It is clear therefore that the Bond played a major role in the mobilisation of Afrikaner capital and enterprise, and in initiating the establishment of Afrikaans enterprises in spheres which until then had been closed to the Afrikaner. So it is not surprising that a relatively large number of Afrikaner businessmen have over the years been Broeders.

In the wider cultural field, the Broederbond in those years (according to Lombard) "was instrumental in having the Bible translated into Afrikaans; made attempts to have Van Riebeeck Day and Kruger Day recognised as public holidays"; was responsible for the "conversion of the University of Pretoria into a 100% Afrikaans institution . . . and gained recognition for *Die Stem van Suid-Afrika* as the Afrikaans national anthem."

E. Education

From its inception the Bond devoted much attention to education. And, closely linked with it, the question of equal language rights for Afrikaans.

The education-cum-language issue has been one of the two important factors in the emergence of Afrikaner Nationalism in the Twentieth Century, and for the creation of the National Party in 1914. The other was South Africa's relationship with Britain and its Empire.

In 1903 the Afrikaans churches formed private CNE schools to counter Lord Milner's deliberately announced policy of Anglicising the Afrikaners, with English education for Afrikaner children an important factor. In 1906 General Hertzog clashed with the English jingoes when he wanted equal education rights for both langugage groups in the Free State. In 1912 his "South Africa First" speech lead to his break with the South African Party and even by 1920 there were virtually no Afrikaans-medium schools.

Lombard, in his 1943 Bloemfontein speech, told the Bondsraad: "On May 17, 1921, the Afrikaner Broederbond decided to take up the sword on behalf of the question of Afrikaans-medium schools. It was decided that propaganda for Afrikaans and for all Afrikaans ideals was to be made directly and indirectly."

Over the years the Broederbond initiated public agitation on the issue, culminating in a Volkskongres on educational matters on July 6 and 7, 1939.

As was only to be expected, it was organised by the FAK. Following the by now established Broederbond pattern, a steering committee was formed to implement congress decisions. It was called the Nasionale Instituut vir Opvoeding en Onderwys (NI00 – National Institute for Upbringing and Education).

According to Pelzer (page 10): "Because the FAK was increasingly placed in charge of the handling of educational matters, the AB in a certain sense disappeared into the background."

As will be seen in a future chapter, during the war years the Broederbond would again champion the cause of mother-tongue education, and through the FAK initiated a congress on the subject in 1944.

F. Politics

In terms of section 88 of its constitution, the Broederbond has officially nothing to do with party politics. In practice, however, the situation has always been somewhat different. For most of the 60 years of its existence there has been a very very close relationship between the Broederbond and the NP.

However, in the earlier years the situation was not so clear cut, and indeed was somewhat confused. The reason probably was that the Afrikaners were largely divided between Smuts and Hertzog.

Not until the early Thirties were there direct links with the top party leaders.

The first serious problems in the Broederbond between 1923 – 1925 concerned politics. This was thanks to the Pact between the Afrikaans National Party and the predominantly English Labour Party which brought General Hertzog to power in 1924. The Pact partly sparked off a purge and the expulsion of some members at the time.

The second big crisis in the Bond was the result of General Hertzog's famous attack on the organisation in a speech at Smithfield, his Free State constituency, on November 7, 1935.

Important political events in the late Twenties and early Thirties had preceded the attack.

At the Imperial Conference in 1926 the Balfour Declaration made the sovereignty of the dominions clear beyond all shadow of doubt. On his return from the conference Hertzog declared that the constitutional aims of his party had been largely satisfied and that he would abandon the republican demands.

The young hot-heads in the party were horrified, since they all believed passionately in the republican ideal. South Africa becoming a republic would visibly demonstrate its constitutional independence and separate nationhood.

Dr N.J. van der Merwe, a rebel Free State MP, in 1930 established a formal republican pressure group within the party. It was called the Republikeinsebond.

He did this in consultation with Professor L.J. du Plessis and Dr J.C. van Rooy of the Dopper University of Potchefstroom, which dominated the Broederbond at that time. Prof du Plessis was UR chairman from 1930 – 1932 and Prof van Rooy from 1932 – 1938 and 1942 – 1951.

The 1933 coalition and the Fusion in 1934 between the National and South African Parties, which merged to form the United Party, heralded a new era in the affairs of the Broederbond. It became ever more closely involved in party politics.

Dr D.F. Malan, Cape leader of the National Party, broke away to lead 27 MPs in opposition to form the Herenigde Nasionale Party (HNP – Re-united National Party). In January 1934 Dr Malan was wavering whether to join General Hertzog in the Fusion with Smuts, or not. A Broederbond deputation was sent from Potchefstroom to the Cape for urgent consultations with Dr Malan, to dissuade him from taking the fatal step. It would not be in the interests of the future of Afrikanerdom, he was told. Malan was also under pressure by some of his own Cape followers, so this visit had a decisive intended effect.

Advocate J.G. Strydom, later Prime Minister, was also persuaded by Potchefstroom's Broederbond not to go along with Hertzog. Ds W.J. de Klerk, of the Gereformeerde Kerk (Reformed Church), father of the later Senator Jan de Klerk and grandfather of F.W. de Klerk, the present Minister of Posts and Telegraphs and Social Welfare, spent virtually an entire night persuading Strydom not to take the step.

De Klerk was to become Strydom's father-in-law.

Thus, during the Fusion years, there were considerable Bond infighting between *"Gesuiwerde"* (Purified) Nationalists and *"Smelter"* (Fusionist) Afrikaners of the United Party.

However, there was no doubt where the leadership of the Broederbond stood. They were firmly behind the HNP, and with its secret activities in the schools and churches did much to promote the philosophy of a narrow, exclusive Afrikanerdom.

The AB rejected Hertzog's belief that the Afrikaner had attained his political goals and his desire for a two-stream approach; and also his conception of one Afrikaner nation – which would include English-speaking South Africans on a basis of absolute equality between the two groups.

In fact the Broederbond was then already plotting its strategy of Afrikaner imperialism and domination.

Dr Piet Meyer, chairman of the UR from 1960 to 1972, described this greater political ambition in his speech in 1968 at the jubilee celebrations: "For our Brotherhood a resurrection out of our Afrikaner political humiliation was not conceivable without the restoration of our republican independence. To give decisive support to this aspiration in times of political uncertainty, since about 1934 Afrikaans Nationalist political leaders were recruited as members of the AB; General Hertzog had not been asked in the past because the AB had from the beginning not linked itself to any political party.

"Among the first Nationalist MPs who became AB members were D.F. Malan, C.R. Swart, J.G. Strydom, N.J. van der Merwe and H.F. Verwoerd." (Verwoerd was in fact at that time still a Stellenbosch University professor who would become first editor of *Die Transvaler* in 1937, and a Senator in 1950.)

"Since then the coming into being *(totstandkoming)* of our Republic was one of the most important aims of our Broederbond . . . Because of our active participation in the realisation of our republican ideal, the AB had in practice linked up more closely with the national organising of the political struggle . . ."

In theory, lip service was paid to party political neutrality; but in practice there was full commitment to the broad ideals of Afrikaner Nationalism, although differences between Nationalists on how to attain these ideals caused serious problems within the organisation over the years.

The cry for Republicanism – a quite legitimate poltical aim- would be the cloak to camouflage the Bond's true aim of Afrikaner domination.

Soon Broederbond activities and propaganda would come into direct conflict with General Hertzog. On January 16, 1934, a circular was issued by the UR, signed by chairman J.C. van Rooy and the chief secretary Lombard.

The key sentences were: "Let us keep constantly in view the fact that our chief concern is whether Afrikanerdom will reach its eventual goal of mastery *(baasskap)* in South Africa. Brothers, our solution for South Africa's maladies is that the Afrikaner Broederbond shall rule South Africa."

General Hertzog was provided with all the available inside information on the Broederbond by one of its high-ranking officials, who had fallen out with the body. This was what led to his Smithfield attack, in which he exposed the whole organisation, its aims, its strategies and its influence in education and the civil service.

Sketching the existence of the Broederbond, of which nothing had previously been publicly known, he referred to the abovementioned extract from the 1934 UR circular and exclaimed: "Magnificent isn't it? Flattering to the soul of a Dutch-speaking Afrikaner, such as you and I! But there is one great flaw – the flaw that must necessarily lead to the destruction of Dutch-speaking 'Afrikanerdom' itself, if it goes on persisting in this sort of Afrikaner-jingo self glorification – and that is the overlooking of the fact that there are also English-speaking Afrikaners who have a right to a place in the Afrikaans sun. When will that foolish and fatal idea cease to hold sway over some people – the idea that they are the chosen of the gods, destined to rule over all the others? The English-speaking section tried it, and did not succeed in ruling over the Afrikaans-speaking group. The Afrikaans-speaking group have also tried and failed, in connection with the English-speaking section. Neither the one, nor the other, will ever succeed in attempts at domination; and when Potchefstroom fanaticism is trying to hurl 'Afrikanerdom' – my people – this: Has South Africa not suffered sufficiently in the past from Afrikaner quarrels and discord? Are our language, our freedom, of so little worth and meaning to us, that, from sheer racialism and fanaticism, we are more prepared to imperil everything?"

Referring to the close ties between the Broederbond and the then – HNP he said: "There is therefore no room for doubt that the secret Broederbond is nothing other than the 'purged' Nationalist Party secretly busy in an underground capacity and that the 'purged' Nationalist Party is nothing other than the secret Afrikaner Broederbond, pursuing its objective openly. Between them the unity of 'Afrikanerdom' is being bartered away for a Republican-cum-Calvinistic Bond!"

Dealing with its influence in education he said: "Can it be tolerated, that teachers, – paid by the State to educate the children of the nation – be permitted to misuse the opportunity given them of contact with the children for purposes of provocative political propaganda? And what is more: is it right that teachers should be permitted – by their membership of

41

the Broederbond – to declare their hostile disposition towards the English-speaking section of the parents whose children have been placed in their care, and who – as much as the Afrikaans-speaking parents – pay their salaries?

"The teacher, now cringing in the darkness, must come into the light of day. There is nothing that needs the full light of day more urgently for its continuing health, than education."

He went on: "What I have brought to your attention today reveals a state of affairs which must raise in the minds of all who love South Africa and have a sense of responsibility. the question: where are we going?

"Has the Afrikaner nation sunk to such hopeless depths that it must seek its salvation in secret conspiracy aimed at promoting race hatred, national disunity and civil war? Is no higher goal, no nobler task, to be held up to the Afrikaner boy and girl than racial strife and disunity? Can our children attain no higher ideal than that of racial domination – of racial mastery?"

Hertzog concluded: "Any doubts that might thus far have lingered concerning the motives that impelled Dr Malan and his 'purged' National Party followers to refuse their co-operation at the inauguration of a United Afrikaner nation, are now finally dispelled, with the revelation of his secret association with the Afrikaner Broederbond and the secret conspiracy between the Broederbond and the 'purged' National Party.

"The purged National Party, with its 'purged' leaders, now stands forth openly in all its racial nakedness, adorned with only one fig-leaf: SECRECY." (See Annexure B for the full text of Hertzog's speech.)

Pelzer (page six) referred to the consequences of the attack. He said: "Immediately afterwards it became obvious that it was no longer possible to reconcile within the AB the divergent political views which originated after Fusion . . .

"A number of members resigned voluntarily whilst disciplinary action was taken against a large number of others . . . In itself it was a pity, but for the Bond not unprofitable. In a confidential organisation (vertrouensorganisasie) it is a good thing periodically to engineer a purge in one way or another."

With this attack General Hertzog sealed his political doom. Through its control of the FAK and related organisations such as the ATKB, " – " which in 1938 organised the symbolic ox-wagon trek during the Voortrekker centenary festivals, " – " Hertzog, as Prime Minister, was excluded from the final celebrations on December 16, 1938, at Monumentkoppie outside Pretoria.

Yet Dr Malan and other HNP leaders addressed celebrations at other venues in the country.

There was perhaps no more important single event in the rise to power of the Afrikaner then the 1938 Ox Wagon centennial. It commemorated the Great Trek of the Voortrekkers a century earlier – when they set out with Bible and gun from the Cape to settle in the Orange Free State, Transvaal and other northern areas. The roots of the unexpected 1948 election victory and the majority for a Republic in the 1960 referendum can be traced back to the emotional fervour of 1938.

The AB can claim the credit for all the social, cultural, economic and political changes which emanated from the symbolic Trek; the UR took the enabling decision, though even they probably never foresaw the successes that were to flow from the event.

The leader of the Trek was Henning Klopper, an ATKV official and the first AB Chairman. There were nine ox wagons, representing different historical Treks. They all set out from different towns – Cape Town, Durban, etc, – all moving towards Pretoria where the cornerstone of the Voortrekker Monument was laid on December 16, 1938.

Pulled by oxen – with the "Voortrekkers" of each wagon dressed in the clothes of a century ago, the men with broad hats and beards, the women in long flowing costumes – the slow procession crossed the fields, plains and mountains of SA. As it passed through towns and small villages it attracted tens of thousands of additional followers.

The arrival of each wagon at each stopover point – whether town, village or small railway siding – was a special celebration; there were speeches and national and religious songs. The treks, which each lasted several months, sparked off an emotional wave among Afrikaners throughout the country, causing a new national revival and new interest in Arikaner history and culture.

In itself there was nothing wrong with this, until one realised that since it was an AB-organised festival, Afrikaner supporters of General Hertzog's UP – still more than 40 per cent of all Afrikaners – were frequently excluded from playing a leading role in the festivities.

The most tragic case in point was Hertzog himself – a man who has done more for the upliftment of the Afrikaner than any other leader. Though Prime Minister he was was prevented from laying the foundation stone at Monument Hill.

The organisers were obviously too shrewd to adopt a blatant HNP stance – but with all the stress on the historical achievements of the Afrikaner, the event was subtly exploited in such a way as to counter the broader South African nationalism of Hertzog's UP.

This mobilisation of Afrikaner nationalism helped create the atmosphere for the successful economic Volkskongres of 1939, and the launching of the Reddingsdaadbond which sought the economic upliftment of the poor whites.

Although the differences between Gen Hertzog and his erstwhile followers were patched up in 1939 when he broke with Smuts on the issue of South African neutrality during the war – when he lost the premiership – it was short-lived.

Efforts in 1940 to reconcile Hertzog and Malan followers in a new poltical party failed disastrously. Hertzog walked out of the Free State Congress when Malan's extremists rejected his proposal to entrench the equality of the English language together with Afrikaans in the constitution.

Thus a man who first fought for the rights of his own people was later rejected by them when he insisted on the same treatment for the rights of the former enemies.

Another semi-political Nationalist organisation was soon to emerge. The Ossewabrandwag was formed in 1939. Impressed by the rise of Hitler in Nazi Germany, distressed because of political strife between Afrikaners and disillusioned by the party political system, it was founded to propagate a South African National Socialism aimed at a one-party republic.

The Ossewabrandwag was soon to develop into a mass organisation. At its peak in 1942 it had some 400 000 members.

There would be a conflict of interest between the Ossewabrandwag and the HNP in the political sphere, and between the Ossewabrandwag and the FAK in the cultural sphere.

Many Afrikaners belonged to both the Ossewabrandwag and the HNP. In this conflict of interest, discussed in the next chapter, the Broederbond was deeply involved.

The leader of the Ossewabrandwag, Dr J.F.J. van Rensburg, was a prominent Broeder, whilst other Ossewabrandwag leaders such as Professor L.J. du Plessis were on the UR.

Thus, although the Broederbond existed totally independently, did its own research and studies of political problems, and on several occasions in its history – 1940 to 1954 – initiated action on the republican issue, the links with the Nationalist political leadership remained inseparable. Both had the same goal and were part of the same all-embracing movement of Afrikaner Nationalism.

G. The Youth

Out of the 1938 centenary festivals here was a new surge of enthusiasm for the "Afrikaner cause." In that year the UR appointed a commission to investigate establishing a Broederbond youth organisation.

It was accordingly decided to establish one on the same basis as the Bond and this was done in 1939.

The new organisation was called Trekmaats. By October 1940 it boasted 30 divisions and 270 members. A few senior Broeders were involved in leadership positions to keep an eye on its morals and progress.

However, because of disturbances in the war years, and internal friction in the Broederbond over the youth body, Trekmaats was disbanded in 1944 and its members incorporated in the Bond itself.

When the Voortrekker movement was established as a counter to the English Boy Scouts, the Broederbond was not directly involved. But it was consulted in advance. The UR gave its blessing and, according to Pelzer (page 11), cells were "encouraged to attend the founding congress on September 30, 1931, in Bloemfontein and to encourage other organisations to take an active interest."

H. Labour

In the early years the Bond's "assistance" on the labour front consisted of support for some organisations which had originated separately, but in which it had "confidence."

It would not be before the late Fifties that the Broederbond would establish its own workers' organisation.

In 1934 a railway workers' union, the Spoorbond, was founded by Henning Klopper. Out of this, three years later, developed a savings bank – Spoorbondkas. Although the latter later went bankrupt, it initiated the first Afrikaans building society, Saambou.

After the 1936 Bondsraad and FAK Congress, another Broederbond front organisation was formed to channel cultural activities with the aim of organising railway workers. This was the Nasional Raad van Trustees (NRT – National Council of Trustees).

It was established on October 4, 1936, and the founding members were all Broeders. There was Dr Albert Hertzog, son of the General, later a Cabinet Minister and first leader in 1969 of the breakaway Herstigte Nasionale Party; Dr Nico Diederichs, on a number of occasions chairman of the UR and later the State President; Dr Piet Meyer; and Frikkie de Wet, then manager of Volkskas.

On May 7, 1937, two founder members of the NRT attended a meeting of the UR to, according to Pelzer (page 12), "exchange ideas about the establishment of Christian Nationalist trade unions. After questions were asked from both sides the UR gave its blessing to the organisation and promised it its strongest support."

Shortly after these discussions the UR sent a special circular to all cells announcing that it was supporting the idea of establishing Afrikaans trade unions.

After 1938 the NRT was linked to the Pieter Neethling Fonds, a fund created by a wealthy Stellenbosch farmer who was Hertzog's maternal uncle.

44

In 1944 a labour organisation separate from the Broederbond was established on the Witwatersrand by the then-HNP. It was partly a response to a "labour front" formed for the Ossewabrandwag by Dr Meyer and was called the Blanke Werkersbeskermingsbond (White Workers' Protection Society).

According to Pelzer (page 12), "its existence was brought to the attention of the UR by Broeder H.F. Verwoerd. When the UR was asked to support the organisation financially, it was decided immediately to make R400 available to it.

"However, the matter was not left there . . . the existence of the new organisation was shortly afterwards brought to the attention of the divisions."

I. "Non-White" Affairs

From its inception the Broederbond – given a membership of which a relatively large proportion are academics, teachers and ministers of religion – has given much attention to the racial problem. There were many discussions on blueprints for the future, before and after the NP attained power in 1948.

Without doubt the Bond played a vital and important role behind the scenes in influencing and shaping the views and policies of the political leaders. So it is important to take note of what Pelzer (pages 13 and 14) and Meyer, in his jubilee speech on October 1, 1968, had to say.

Pelzer: "By 1935 the AB had already formulated a policy which . . . can be regarded as its confession of faith in this respect.

"Because of the importance of this document, it is fully quoted here: " 'Total mass segregation should not only be stated as the ideal, but should also be the immediate practical policy of the State. At suitable places on the borders of the Union suitable and sufficient ground should be purchased . . . which would be set aside for occupation by native families and tribes which today are still scattered throughout the country on farms and in kraals and small reserves.

" 'The opportunity should exist for different tribes to be gathered in separate regions. Then it should be made compulsory for the already mentioned groups of natives to move to these areas. They can then become jointly or separately land-owners there. But the ground ought to be bought from the State through a form of tax such as a hut tax or through a form of leasehold.

" 'In these areas a greater measure of self-government can be granted with the lapse of time, which as far as possible should take into consideration the pre-history and traditional form of government of the native. Areas of or sub-divisions of it should be under the supervision of white commissioners who have been specially trained for the job and who will be directly responsible to the Minister of Native Affairs.

" 'Here the native can then develop and realise (uitleef) himself in a political, economic, cultural, religious, educational and other spheres. In these areas whites will not be able to become land-owners, and Whites who go there to settle as traders, missionaries, teachers, etc., will enjoy no political rights.

" 'Natives who have reached a certain fixed age will be allowed, with the permission of his tribal Chiefs and the commissioner, to go temporarily to the area of the White to work on his farms, or in the towns or cities, but they will not be allowed to go with their families.

" 'With regard to the de-tribalised urban natives, they must be encouraged as far as possible to move to these native areas. Those who cannot do it ought to be housed in separate locations where they will enjoy no political privileges and may own no property because

45

they must be regarded as temporary sojourners who are living in the White areas as employees for their own advantage and from their own choice. Unemployed natives ought all to be compelled to leave these locations after a reasonable period of job-seeking, and to live in the native areas.' ''

So the foundations of NP policy, which the Government would relentlessly implement more than 40 years later at the end of the Seventies, were laid down.

Pelser continued: ''After this viewpoint was established, the AB made it its task to convey the viewpoint of the Afrikaner to the Bantu. Apart from influence through education, direct contacts would be created to do this. In this regard useful work had equally been done by the Randse Onderlinge Hulporganisasie for non-Whites (the Reef Mutual Aid Organisation – a body which co-ordinated the work of various charitable organisations which was established by the AB).

''In order to be able to make a useful contribution to the long-term solution of South Africa's racial problems, as early as 1940 the UR became convinced that an expert body should be established to handle the racial problem on behalf of Afrikanerdom. As a result the UR gave instructions to its racial problems commission to consider the creation of such a body and to advise it about the possibility of organising a Volkskongres on these matters.

''A few months later the chairman had a discussion with representatives of the Afrikanerbond for Racial Studies, as a result of which the UR decided to instruct the FAK to appoint the commission for race relations which would consist largely of members of the UR's own commission and members of the Afrikanerbond for Racial Studies. This commission should organise the planned Volkskongres, if necessary in conjunction with an ordinary FAK Congress, at which occasion a permanent Institute for Racial Affairs would be formed.

''After the commission was composed, the UR transferred its leadership regarding racial matters to the FAK, dissolved its own racial problems commission and would thereafter for more than seven years maintain complete silence on the matter.''

Meyer, on page six of his speech, described the role of the Broederbond in racial affairs as follows: ''Since about 1933 our brotherhood has tackled another task which will become one of our main endeavours in our national political aspirations – namely the healthy arrangement of the relations between White and non-White in our country for the preservation and advantage of each separate race group (volksgroep).

''In 1935 the Bondsraad accepted a policy document in which separate development was principally and logically enunciated, and the implementation of it laid down and planned in advance, not only in broad terms but with a remarkable vision of future developments with the coming into being of various autonomous Bantu homeland governments.

''It also served as a guideline for Broeders inside the National Party . . . Later the AB established SABRA to investigate this policy in a scientific manner and to propagate it.''

Thus the Broederbond was not merely close to the most important decisions affecting the lives of millions of ''non-Whites'' for decades, it was in fact an inextricable part of that decision-making process.

J. The Churches

Throughout its history comparatively little of the Broederbond's time has been devoted to the three Afrikaans churches. This was not because the churches were not involved in Bond activities. The contrary was the case. The churches were very much part and parcel of the Broederbond structure, activities and organisation. So no special attention was needed.

The only two presidents in the Bond's history were church ministers: Ds William Nicol, later a NGK Moderator and Administrator of the Transvaal, became UR chairman in the Twenties; and Ds J.C. van Rooy, a GK leader, was chairman twice in the Thirties and Forties.

Moreover, the whole philosophy of the Broederbond has a powerful religious basis; the philosophy of Christian Nationalism forms its very foundations. The Broederbond and Afrikaner religion and the church have over the years been inseparable.

K. Octopus

By the early Forties the foundations of the octopus like structure of the Broederbond were completed, giving it immense influence even while the Smuts Government was in power, and enabling it, after 1948, to get a total grip on South Africa.

Based upon a hard core of carefully selected members – 2 811 in 183 cells in 1945 – it extended its influence through directly-controlled front organisations in the cultural, educational and economic fields.

Indirectly, it extended its power by infiltrating the civil service. It particularly dominated education. And there was extremely close co-operation and consultation with political leaders in organisations such as the Ossewabrandwag and the HNP.

In 1943 Dr E.G. Malherbe, then head of SA military intelligence, who had made a thorough investigation of the "subversive" activities of the Broederbond in the war years, described it as functioning as an inter-locking directorate.

The Bond's strategy in those early years was explained as follows by Lombard in a 1943 speech: "The AB decided that, in cases where the organisation as a whole could not exercise influence, members of the organisation should act individually in whatever capacity would be most suitable for the cause, and in this way the AB achieved several things through individual action on the part of their members."

He concluded by saying (Mann report, page 16): "All these things had been achieved because the AB tackled each problem systematically and methodically, and shown patience where necessary until its goal had been reached." Lombard spoke eloquently on the great value of brotherhood among members and showed how the AB had weathered all storms because the Broeders were imbued with brotherly love and that love of volk which alone could spur them on.

Pelzer (page eight), in summarising the activities and achievements of the Bond over 50 years, gives this description of its activities: "In a certain sense the AB can be called a meddlesome body which pays attention to everything in which the Afrikaner has an interest, and therefore it can be stated with frankness that few things of any importance happened to the Afrikaner in the past half century in which the AB did not have a share . . .

"Perhaps it can be said the greatest activity of the AB was implied in the quiet influence which went out from the movement – an influence which had a formative effect on its members, which gave stability and certainty to his activities and thoughts . . . an influence which is radiated through its members to the whole of Afrikaans society, and increasingly is also penetrating into English-language society – *an influence which cannot be measured, weighed or described."*

PART III

The War Years: 1939 – 1945

South Africa delcared war on Germany on September 6, 1939. This had important internal political repercussions and would prove a severe test for the Broederbond.

The Fusion Government split apart when Hertzog's neutral stance was defeated in Parliament and a proposal by his deputy, Smuts, that South Africa declare war was accepted.

Hertzog and his former bitter political enemies – the Purified Nationalists – were together again, though not for long. A few days after Hertzog's defeat a mass meeting organised by the Broederbond was held at Monumentkoppie just outside Pretoria. It became the scene of an emotional reconciliation between Hertzog and Malan before audiences of more than 50 000 Afrikaners.

For a short while Hertzog was the official Opposition leader. But problems arose when his followers had to merge into one party with those of Malan. Hertzog was to walk out into the political wilderness when his proposal that both Afrikaans and English were to be recognised was rejected by Nationalist hot-heads such as C.R. Swart, later the first State President, and a Broeder.

Before this re-unification the Broederbond had been involved in a smear campaign against General Hertzog, claiming that correspondence between him and the Freemasons had been discovered – a blatant untruth.

The result was that soon in 1940 the nationalist-minded groups were split into three political parties – the HNP of Dr Malan, the Afrikaner Party lead by Hertzog's trusted confidante, Klasie Havenga, and the Nuwe Orde (New Order) lead by the brilliant Advocate Oswald Pirow, which supported a programme of National Socialism.

And outside Parliament there was the Ossewabrandwag, with members from all three political parties belonging to it.

The Ossewabrandwag was soon in conflict with the political parties, and also with the cultural organisations, – a split in Opposition ranks reflected in the Broederbond itself, which had members in all four organisations.

And precisely then the Bond, which had just completed the arduous process of establishing itself on all fronts involving Nationalist Afrikanerdom, became faced with a double crisis of survival.

Firstly, the strife, dissension and conflict among the broad masses was reflected within the organisation at a time when it was desperately attempting to solve the escalating crisis.

Secondly, it came into conflict with the Government, particularly on the language question in schools, and the issue of mother-tongue education *vs* dual-medium education.

Nonetheless, while fighting on these two fronts, it continued as normal to expand membership, hold meetings, study particular issues and was still actively involved behind the scenes in promoting anti-Government actions on a wide front.

I will first discuss its early general activities, then its attempts to reconcile the various Afrikaner factions, and finally its confrontation with the Smuts Government.

1. Bondsraad Meetings

On October 2, 1939, the 18th Bondsraad was held in the Kinderhuis Hall in Bloemfontein.

According to the minutes Ivan Lombard, the chief secretary, told the congress that it was "a fruitful year" for the Broederbond: "Everything shows that the Bond is healthy to the core."

Item 14 of the minutes dealt with an Angola Investigation Fund. The purpose was to investigate the position of Afrikaners living outside South Africa, such as those in Angola, and also to keep in touch with Afrikaans students studying overseas and to promote their organisations since this "contributed to the national moulding of such members."

Items nine and 15 dealt with the need for a more solemn *(plegtige)* installation of members – a topic to which much time was devoted over the years. Broeder Albert Hertzog demonstrated a new method when he installed aspirant Broeder P.G. Viljoen of the Monument division (Bloemfontein).

After the ceremony there was considerable argument for and against it. Objections were that the ceremony was alien to the nature of the Afrikaner because it contained mystic elements. (Unfortunately details of the installation ceremony were not revealed.) However, others claimed that the mystical element was to be found among all nations and that the Afrikaner, because of a lack of "formalism" *("formalisme")* and an exaggerated soberness or level-headedness *(nugterheid)* was driven to laxity.

The 19th Bondsraad was held on October 4 and 5, 1940, also in the Kinderhuis Hall. As always it was opened and closed by prayers and readings from the scriptures.

Draft resolutions included matters such as the following: speakers at Dingaansdag celebrations should stick to a single theme; Afrikaners should be encouraged to become chemists and doctors; propaganda must be made for an Afrikaans medical faculty (until then only the English-language universities had medical faculties.); Afrikaans businesses to be established by the RDB should be conducted on a strictly commercial basis.

Reports on the various front organisations were submitted. Professor L.J. du Plessis reported that the fund of the Ekonomiese Instituut was already £30 000 strong. Dr N. Diederichs reported on the RDB and its fund. According to the minutes he especially stressed the organising of Afrikaner buying power, a beginning had been made – 160 branches of the RDB already having been established. Real attempts had also been made to organise the free time of the volk in its own interests.

Dr T.E. Donges, later Minister of Finance, acting Prime Minister and President designate, reported on Federale Volksbeleggings BPK and revealed that the preferential shares of £100 000 had almost been fully subscribed.

Reports were also submitted on Trekmaats, the Institute for Social Welfare, and the Nasionale Raad van Trustees, the Kopersbond (a business organisation), the National Institute for Upbringing and Education and a planned institute for racial affairs.

Item 24 of the minutes read: "Nasionale Raad van Trustees. Dr A. Hertzog gave a short exposition of the battle of the Afrikaans minorities on the Reef. Because of the recent strike the State promised a commission of inquiry into existing irregularities."

Item 25: "Die Kopersbond. Dr J.H. Pienaar informs us that more than 25 businesses are already purchasing *(inkoop)* through the Kopersbond . . . It has already been proved that it is advantageous to purchase through the Kopersbond."

Item 28: "Radio section, FAK. The assistant secretary informs us that the radio section of the FAK has been extended to make provision for individual members. Advocate

J.F. Marais has been nominated as full-time radio organiser of this division. An appeal is made to the Bondsraad to give its active support to the renewed efforts to defend and promote Afrikaans interests in the broadcasting service."

This represented the beginnings of the Bond's aim to gain control of the SABC (South African Broadcasting Corporation). The SABC was to become not only a blatant Government organisation, but in the first place a mouthpiece of Broederbond philosophy.

Marais is today well known as Kowie Marais, Progressive Federal Party MP and the ex-judge who in the Forties was interned with Vorster in Koffiefontein.

Item 29 is most significant. It deals with the Freemasons, regarded by the Broederbond as one of its main enemies. This subject has regularly come up for discussion.

After a discussion of a resolution from the Oudtshoorn-De Rust, Hartebeestfontein and Paul Roux cells that the Broederbond rejected the Freemason movement and double membership of both the Bond and the Freemasons, the minutes state: "From the discussions it is clear that the Bondsraad was opposed to Freemasonry, especially its imperialistic character in South Africa. The matter is left in the hands of the UR. The Bondsraad, however, expressed itself against members of the Bond who are Freemasons being persecuted for that reason. But it is further urged that this movement be thoroughly investigated."

At that Bondsraad a new UR was elected, as at every second meeting. Dr N. Diederichs (No 560) was elected with an absolute majority as chairman and Professor J.C. van Rooy vice-chairman. The other UR members who were elected were T.E. Dönges, Prof L.J. du Plessis, Dr H.F. Verwoerd, later Prime Minister, Ds C.R. Kotze, Dr Albert Hertzog (No 456), L.W. Hiemstra (of Nasionale Pers), and J.H. Conradie, then a Nationalist MP and later Speaker of Parliament.

In his presidential address, Nico Diederichs dealt with the three components of the Bond's freedom ideal: spiritual, economic and constitutional freedom. In dealing with practical political problems he stressed, according to page six of his address: "We must always keep in mind that the AB as such does not operate in public, but always through the channels which it has created for a specific purpose."

Referring to the republican ideal of the Bond and its plan for a new constitution he announced (page seven): "A number of Broeders have already been busy for a considerable time working on the form of the desired Boer State." Diederichs also emphasised the political role of the Bond and stated (page nine): "The legend of a strict division between culture, economics and politics has fallen away. We will no longer be blinded by it. The volk is an organic whole. Its different parts are closely connected with each other and cannot be separated."

The 20th Bondsraad was held on October 6, 1941, once again in the Kinderhuis Hall.

Item 11 of the minutes noted that it had been decided, in view of the extraordinary situation prevailing at the time, to temporarily suspend the regulations of the Broederbond constitution and that the UR would be free to take any action it deemed in the interest of the Broederbond.

The theme of Dr Diederichs' chairman's speech was *"Die Republikeinse Toekoms van die Afrikaner"* ("The Republican Future of the Afrikaner").

At the time, the Policy Committee of the Broederbond had drafted a constitutional blueprint. The contents were published prematurely as ostensibly a document of a few individuals, and caused great public controversy.

Dr Malan and other Nationalist leaders disassociated themselves from it, although it in fact conveyed their secret aims. The document was an undisguised blueprint of Afrikaner imperialism, laying the foundations of a State where the Afrikaner would predominate and Afrikaans would be the only official language. It was the very basis on which the later HNP would formulate its policies in 1969.

In the discussion that followed Diederichs' speech, the new republican constitution was also debated, though no formal decision was taken.

A motion thanking the UR and its policy commission for its work in drafting the constitution was passed.

2. UR Meetings and Circulars

On November, 3, 1939, only two months after the outbreak of the war, the UR met in Johannesburg. Present were Dr N. Diederichs (chairman), L.J. du Plessis, J.C. van Rooy, L.W. Hiemstra, A. Hertzog, J.W. Potgieter, I.M. Lombard (chief secretary) and P.J. Meyer (assistant secretary).

According to the minutes, Item five dealt with the possible resignation or elimination of Broeder M.C. Botha, a very prominent public figure. Botha was Secretary of Education and then Rector of the University of Pretoria. He was a great Hertzog supporter and in 1948 would unsuccessfully oppose P.W. Botha in George in the general election.

Botha was the father of Professor M.C. Botha, a member of Chris Barnard's famous heart team, André Botha, a Pretoria judge, and Jan Botha – news editor of the *Argus*.

Botha had been elected to the UR two years previously. The affair was to drag on for another two years until of his own accord he resigned.

Item six revealed the uncertain war situation for the Broederbond. It noted: "Members in the civil service will be informed that their position as AB members is not threatened and that the work must be continued with the greatest circumspection . . ."

Item 28 dealt with Trekmaats, the youth organisation. Differences of opinion about its field of operation had arisen, especially between Albert Hertzog and Professor Du Plessis.

Hertzog wanted it to concentrate on trade unions and professional bodies, which should be infiltrated through a cell system.

"Broeder Hertzog explained his viewpoint and pointed out the necessity for the trade union and civil service organisations to be conquered and retained for our volk by means of secret reform organisations."

However, L.J. du Plessis said that the Nasionale Raad van Trustees (in which he was a key figure) should lend itself to the promotion of industrial labour organisations and that the civil service should be left directly to the Broederbond.

It was decided that Trekmaats would remain a general body like the Broederbond, and would not be transformed into a professional organisation. "Broeder Hertzog is free to establish secret reform organisations inside the trade unions. He is instructed to work out a scheme to do this and to submit it to UR for its approval and support."

Du Plessis, Hertzog and Meyer (as convener) were appointed to a commission to investigate the situation of civil servants and to submit recommendations concerning "the necessary action to the UR."

Other matters discussed at this meeting included the propagating of Afrikaans newspapers, the strategy of the Ekonomiese Instituut and its various sub-committees, the establishing of an all-embracing "volksorganisasie", the Reddingsdaadbond, and books and historical novels which should be recommended to schools.

Item 38, concerning prescribed books, noted that the AB secretariat had been instructed to work "through suitable Broeder teachers in the various provinces."

Item 33 dealt with the question of the unification of the three Afrikaans churches – NGK, NHK and the GK. Basically, they had no fundamental doctrinal differences. It noted: "The AB continuously uses its influence to promote the necessary co-operation between the Afrikaans churches."

On February 2 and 3, 1940, the UR met in Cape Town. Present were Broeders N. Diederichs (chairman), T.E. Dönges, A. Hertzog, W. Louw, J.C. van Rooy, L.W. Hiemstra, L.J. du Plessis, J.H. Conradie, I.M. Lombard and P.J. Meyer.

Much time was devoted to the RDB and its Fund. The FAK's suggestion that Diederichs become full-time "organisational leader" of the RDB was approved, after L.J. du Plessis had questioned the appointment.

In discussing the desirability of establishing an organisation to study the racial problem from the Afrikaner viewpoint, it was decided to appoint Broeder W.J. Snyman of Pietersburg – a teacher and later a senior official in the Transvaal Education Department – to the Asiatic committee, of which Verwoerd was convener.

Then, in circular No 8/39/40 of February 7, 1940, a special programme of action was set out to laungh the RDB Fund, with each district in the country set a target of £1 000. Branches were to be established across the land, and a list of all Afrikaans businessmen drawn up.

Item five of the circular recommended a book by Dr G.D. Scholtz, then a journalist on *Die Transvaler* of which he later became the editor. It was *"In Doodsgevaar,"* and dealt with the Anglo-Boer War; it "ought to be read by every Afrikaner."

The minutes of the management committee *(dagbestuur)* of the UR met in Johannesburg on March 2, 1940. A major point at issue then was the position of the Broederbond in the prevailing war situation. The committee held discussions with a deputation from the Springs, Brakpan and Boksburg divisions, involving the fears of some members of infiltration and betrayal.

"A suitable private meeting place" had to be found because of certain investigations into the Bond's membership; publication of members' names could lead to their losing their jobs. It was stressed that, general policy cell meetings should continue. However, "divisions should recommend that members who are a danger to them should be eliminated."

The minutes of the UR meeting of May 12 revealed that attention was given to the question of more Afrikaans trainee chemists and the lack of an Afrikaans handbook for music teachers – two matters which were constantly discussed in these years.

Item 11 stated: "An amount of £50 was voted for legal costs to protect the AB as regards the court case P.J. Kock – De Vos."

Item 12 dealt with another matter also frequently discussed over the years: that of brotherhood, one of the two important principles on which the Broederbond was founded. It noted: "Broeder Louw stressed the exercising of brotherliness in cases of friction between Broeders. Especially as regards the introduction of new Broeders, the characteristic of brotherhood should be kept in mind."

The dangerous general political situations for the Bond was again raised at the UR meeting in Johannesburg on August 14 and 15. It was reported that the UR head office had been informed in May and June, by at least 30 cells, that they were, for the moment at any rate, no longer holding meetings. There was fear of "local persecution."

At the UR meeting on October 4, 1940, in Bloemfontein it was confirmed that the FAK had appointed the following commission to investigate the racial problem: Professor

G. Cronje (convener) Prof J.A. Engelbrecht, C.W. Prinsloo; N. Diederichs, Prof A.J.H. van der Walt; Prof P.J. Schoeman; Dr J.H. Greyvensteyn, Prof Wolmarans; and Dr B.F. Nel.

Cronje was then a professor of sociology and during and just after the war years produced a number of popular books on racial matters. Prinsloo was an official of the Department of Native Affairs; Schoeman an Afrikaans author and anthropologist from Stellenbosch; Greyvenstein and Wolmarans two NHK theologians.

In the subsequent circular No 2/40/41 of Otober 16, 1940, it was announced that a regular item, called *"Help-mekaar"* ("Help each other") would be appearing in future circulars. Under this heading would be included, "openings or vacancies in one or other profession for which there are good prospects." Members were advised to ensure in advance that their candidates would be assured of local support.

For almost the next 40 years this method would be used to get Broeders into vacancies on the platteland, and later in the cities, in jobs ranging from the local schoemaker to posts in city councils. It was the beginning of one of the most effective aspects of the Broederbond machinery: how to get their own men into influential positions.

Item six of that circular dealt with Sunday sport – quite naturally a matter to which much attention was devoted – and methods were discussed on how to oppose this "evil." A six-point plan of action was proposed. Ministers of religion were to be "requested" to raise the matter at synodal and other church meetings, and in their sermons; MPs must be asked to introduce legislation; and speakers on national holidays should condemn it.

The prospectus of FVB was discussed and the directors approved – including men such as Dönges and Professor C.G.W. Schumann of Stellenbosch. Item six noted that "one of our members, Mr A.J. Coertze, is appointed as chief organiser of the company and is already busy making the necessary arrangements for the subscription of the necessary capital." Members were asked to give him the necessary support "in this great task . . . (of) becoming economically independent."

At the UR meeting of October 25, 1940, the appointment of Ivan Lombard as director of Uniewinkels was approved.

Item 10(f) returned to the Freemasons. It was noted that, "Members who are Freemasons are advised to resign . . . The UR accepts as policy no recruitment of active Freemasons in the AB. Divisions will be personally asked to warn young men not to join the Freemasons."

Item 21 raised the question of Jewish doctors on the platteland. As a counter. "it is felt that Afrikaner doctors must be encouraged to establish themselves on the platteland."

Radio matters, the establishment of municipal voters' organisations and of Afrikaans nursery schools, were discussed at the UR meeting of January 30, 1941, in Cape Town.

Item 18 mentioned the concern of the Brandfort cell about the "excessive use" of strong liquor at dinners. The UR, however, piously decided that "such abuse did not happen at AB events."

Another item dealt with the campaign to have Kruger Day declared a public holiday. The strategy to be employed gives a useful insight into the Broederbond. A proposal of the Linden cell was accepted, namely "that all AB divisions are instructed to approach public bodies in their areas on this matter in order to start a nationwide campaign. The public bodies which are to be considered are, e.g. school councils, school commissions and municipalities."

Item five of the minutes of the management committee of the UR of March 8, 1941, noted a request for advice from Broeder Ds Lourens of the Carolina cell as to whether he should join the Army as a chaplain. In the event there would be no objection from the Broederbond, as it was necessary to look after the spiritual needs of the Afrikaner in the Army. It is important to note that in the war years, and for some time thereafter, there were very strong political feelings in the Bond against the Defence Force – which was seen as politically controlled by Smuts.

At the UR meeting of May 3, 1941, Item 33 once again revealed the extremely close link between the Broederbond and the churches. Dealing with the Freemasons it noted: "The synodal Commission of the Nederduits Gereformeerde Kerk, Cape Province, as well as Broeder Dr Badenhorst will be requested to send the reports on Freemasonry to the head office for distribution."

Item 36, on Volkskas, noted a request of the Johannesburg divisions as well as the directorate of Volkskas to appoint a Broeder as the Johannesburg manager of Volkskas.

The security problem was still causing great concern. Confidential messages would be conveyed by special visits.

According to Item 44, Professor H.P. Wolmarans would be asked to attend a management committee meeting to discuss the question of co-operation with the NHK. The NGK and Gereformeerde churches had in the past been far more involved in politics, the leadership being pro-Nationalist and some of them active on the UR and in other Broederbond activities.

In Nationalist and Broederbond circles in those years the NHK was regarded as being pro-United Party, with many of its leaders sympathetic to General Smuts. One reason was that the NHK, which is very small, always had aspirations to become once again the State church – as was the case in the old Transvaal Republic.

Under the item *Helpmekaar* in circular No 8/40/41 of June 4, 1941, the Broederbond was looking for an Afrikaans attorney in Dewetsdorp, and an Afrikaans dentist in Brandfort.

At the management committee meeting of June 6, 1941, a discussion took place with Ds H.P. Wolmarans and Ds A.J.G. Oosthuizen, two NHK leaders. Their differences with the other Afrikaans churches were discussed and it was agreed to arrange a subsequent meeting between four NHK leaders and members of the Inter-Church Commission – representing the other two churches – who were Broeders.

Following a representation made by the Johannesburg divisions the UR decided at this meeting what steps would be appropriate in the event of the Broederbond being banned.

Circular 1/41/42 of August 1941 had several interesting *Helpmekaar* items. Jamestown had a vacancy for an Afrikaans "garage man," and J.H. Pansegrouw, the local MPC, could be contacted; Fouriesburg had a vacancy for an Afrikaans doctor and H.A.J. du Toit of the high school could be contacted; Wolmaransstad had a vacancy for a dentist and A. Burger, the RDB organiser, could be contacted; Pietersburg had a vacancy for an Afrikaans dentist and W.J. Snyman of the primary school could be contacted.

Circular 2/41/42 of September 5, 1941, warned members that the average age of Broeders was very high. They were urged to give preference to young Afrikaners between the ages of 25 and 35.

Item six of circular 7/40/41 of September 8, 1941, dealt with the question of *"Taalhandhawing"* ("Language Maintenance"), an issue which came up innumerable times in these years in minutes and circulars. It noted that the maintenance of Afrikaans on the platteland and in several big cities was unsatisfactory, and that at many shops, hotels and garages the personnel were unwilling to speak Afrikaans. It regretted the fact that platteland Afrikaners for the most part did not mind whether they were served in Afrikaans or English and did not give preference to businesses using Afrikaans.

The circular made the following appeal: "We are on the eve of great developments in the industrial sphere and it is essential that the divisions should urgently investigate the language situation in their own area and to try and improve it . . ."

Thirty-seven years later many Afrikaners believe that the language battle has not yet been won. But, ironically, in the Seventies those Afrikaners who employed militant and aggressive tactics to enforce Afrikaans language rights were accused of being "extremist verkramptes" by their fellow Afrikaners. This is one battle in which the Broederbond has not scored total victory over the years.

Item eight of the minutes of the UR meeting of September 15, 1941, recorded a report by Hertzog about a strike at Grootvlei – it was won by the mineworkers and saved 1 500 from unemployment.

Item nine contained a report by L.J. du Plessis about co-operation with the NHK. The latter had agreed to join the Inter-Church Commission and the other two churches had agreed to recognise the NHK. Thus the Broederbond had succeeded in bringing the three major Afrikaans churches together.

Circular No 5/41/43 of November 3, 1941, revealed a Broederbond tactic which has helped make it such an influential organisation.

It involved tactics for getting Broeders elected to top bodies without the other members realising that there was in fact an organised campaign going on behind the scenes for the Broeder candidate – whose membership of the body was obviously unknown.

Item two dealt with the election of the Council of the University of South Africa and "informed" Broeder members across the country of the following: "Soon there will be an election for four members of the Council of the University of South Africa. Please inform former students and others eligible to note that Dr A. Hertzog, Professor W. Arndt, Professor J.C. van Rooy and Dr N. Diederichs have been nominated.

But, according to item nine of the minutes of the UR meeting of January 23, 1942, held in Cape Town, the Broederbond failed in its campaign to have Broeders elected to the council. It noted: "In order to begin earlier and organise better on a future occasion, Broeder L.W. Hiemstra is requested to keep a watchful eye on the matter."

Item 11 of the management committee meeting of December 1, 1941, recorded a long discussion of an editorial in *Die Transvaler* in which its editor, H.F. Verwoerd, apparently criticised Diederichs for retaining his job as a full-time paid official of the RDB, though still retaining the leadership of the movement.

Both Diederichs, as chairman of the Broederbond and Piet Meyer as its assistant secretary, objected to the article. Verwoerd, who was a member of the management committee, and Diederichs gave explanations of their actions. It was eventually decided "to accept" the good faith of the Broeders concerned, and to leave the matter there.

The question of assistance to the families of men detained in camps for political reasons was also discussed.

Item 23 noted that £25 had been made available to the family of Broeder Stephen Eyssen, then a headmaster, and later an MP, while assistance to other families was looked into as well.

In a circular of April 16, 1942, Broeders were asked to provide head office with information on the situation of families of interned Broeders.

The minutes of the UR meeting of April 24, 1942, noted that Broeders detained in camps or jails included J.C. Neethling, D.J. Erasmus, J.H. Pienaar, J.F. van der Merwe, P.J.R. Hendriks, C. Neethling, A.J.L. Joubert and P.W.R. Zerwick.

Attention was also given to the question of education. This would soon bring the Bond into conflict with the Government. Item 18 noted that the National Institute for Upbringing and Education – a Broederbond front organisation – must urgently be asked to prepare a paper stating the case for single-medium schools against duel-medium ones, as there had been a new emotional escalation in favour of the latter.

There were complaints about the laxness of many cells for not holding regular meetings, for failing to keep in regular touch with head office, and for failing to return compulsory forms to the office after each meeting – an indication that the war situation had severely affected the AB.

According to the minutes of the UR meeting of April 24, 1942, the Broederbond would support the establishment of an Afrikaans-medium school in Daiseyfield, in Southern Rhodesia, and would provide £500 for an emergency fund. This event was the culmination of a long series of discussions over the previous two years.

An interesting incident took place in this period, showing a bitter clash between Verwoerd and Broeder J.G. (Kaalkop) van der Merwe, the well-known Heilbron farmer businessman.

According to the minutes of the management committee meeting of May 30, 1942, a letter of Verwoerd (who was absent) was tabled in which he complained that Van der Merwe had "made *'ondermynende'* ('subversive') remarks about him."

Verwoerd alleged that at a meeting Van der Merwe had branded him as a *"godloënaar"* ("atheist"). The chief secretary was investigating the matter. At the UR meeting of August 1, 1942, it was decided to ask Van der Merwe to attend the next UR meeting. Unfortunately, the records of what transpired then are not available.

At the August 1 meeting the question of establishing an Afrikaans medical faculty was again discussed at length. The UR had requests from five cells to do something positive.

Item 14 of the minutes noted that the UR would recommend that the Bondsraad make a donation of £1 000 to start a fund for the formation of a faculty, and that the secretariat would investigate establishing a study fund for Afrikaans medical students.

Study documents circulated in the early Forties give some indication of the priorities of that period. They included the following: *"Ons Republiek"* ("Our Republic"), the controversial constitutional blueprint for a future Afrikaner republic; "Ten Years' Uphill Battle" – a five-point programme to enable all Afrikaners to live positive lives in the interest of the volk; *"Monumentkoppie"* – a statement by the very revered Professor J.D. du Toit (Totius) at the end of 1941 in which he bewailed strife and dissension amongst Afrikaners; and a pamphlet on how a sincere Afrikaner ought to *"Handhaaf en Bou"* ("Maintain and Build") – a list of 19 do's and dont's for Afrikaners; "The Afrikaner does not get his Rightful Part of the Union's Commerce and Industry" – a copy of a speech by Dr Dönges in Parliament on April 15, 1941; how a sincere Afrikaner ought to *"Handhaaf en Bou"* in the economic sphere; – "The Afrikaners and Local Government" – obviously written by Dr Hertzog, advocating the reason for the involvement of Afrikaners in local government, and detailing methods and tactics to conquer local town councils by establishing taxpayers' organisations or by taking over existing ones; "Bilingual Music Examinations" – an attempt to get more Afrikaners involved in the music profession because of the influence of British musical institutions in South African musical examinations; and two documents dealing with trainee chemists which pointed out the practical aspects and problems of getting more Afrikaners trained as chemists – a profession virtually dominated by non-Afrikaners then.

3. Broedertwis and the Bond

When the Bondsraad of October 2, 1939, took place in Bloemfontein the emotional *"Volksvereniging"* ("National Reunion") of the followers of General Hertzog and Dr Malan at Monumentkoppie outside Pretoria was still fresh in memory.

Totius, the famous and revered Afrikaans national poet, had specially drafted for that occasion a *"volksverklaring"* ("national declaration"). At the mass gathering 70 000 Afrikaners approved the ideal that Afrikanerdom would never again allow itself to split.

Thereafter there was an optimistic belief that the differences – as much personal as philosophical – had been finally and permanently bridged.

According to Item 18 of the minutes of that Bondsraad Ds D.P. Ackerman, referring to the *"Volksvereniging,"* said: "It bore witness *(getuie)* that God had a plan for his volk. We are beginning to see light for the future. Like the Ossewatrek and the Torch processions (of 1938), the *Volksvereniging* meeting at Monumentkoppie on September 9 was an inspiration of God."

Ackerman then thanked Broeders H.B. Stegmann, I. Lombard and P.J. Meyer for organising that occasion. The chairman then asked all the Broeders to stand up. The *"volksverklaring"* of September 9 was read "in a solemn silence" and the vow taken with uplifted hands.

The Broederbond thus played an important behind-the-scenes role in getting the different Afrikaner factions together once more. Apart from the abovementioned men, Professor E.C. Pienaar apparently also played a major role, since he was later specially thanked by the UR for the work he had done.

However, there were obviously many problems still to be overcome, as is evident from the minutes of the UR meeting of February 2, 1940.

Item 17 (b) noted: "The divisions will be encouraged to continue working for the *'hereniging'* ('reunion') of Afrikanerdom, which has as yet only partly been attained. Broeders N. Diederichs and L.W. Hiemstra will draft the circular."

The obstacles remained. For one thing, Item 12 of the minutes of the management committee noted that the meeting had been informed by Diederichs and Hiemstra that they regarded it as "undesirable" to draft such a circular on *"volksvereniging."* The apparent reason was the attitude of "a particular political party." Permission was then granted for the drafting of a circular about the prevailing national situation.

Rivalry between the Ossewabrandwag and the HNP and the FAK about its activities in the political, cultural and economic spheres caused continual tension. Acording to Item 13 of the same minutes Du Plessis, who was to become a senior Ossewabrandwag leader, gave an exposition of the movement's aims. He claimed that it deserved the support of Afrikanerdom because it operated in a sphere not covered by other cultural organisations.

He especially had in mind the "disciplining of the volk and the organising of *'volksfeeste'* ('folk festivals')."

The committee decided to investigate the purpose and aspirations of the Ossewabrandwag.

But the OB was expanding on a wave of emotionalism, strengthened by growing disillusionment with the party political system, which was blamed for the increasing political fragmentation of Afrikanerdom, and encouraged by the sweeping Nazi victories in Europe.

With Dr van Rensburg acting as a Führer, backed by his *"generaals"* – including one John Vorster – the Ossewabrandwag considered itself indestructible, and felt the future belonged to it.

Naturally, this strengthening of its muscles brought it into conflict with the Broederbond, which believed that it alone had mapped out the areas of responsibility for each Afrikaner organisation.

At the UR meeting of May 12, 1940, it was decided that in view of the tremendous expansion of the Ossewabrandwag, and the role of Broederbond members in its promotion, it was important for the Bond to express more than a strictly neutral attitude.

The issue of the Ossewabrandwag cropped up again at the UR meeting of August 16, 1940. After discussions dealing with the organisation a special committee was appointed to investigate three matters in particular. These were: reunification of Afrikanerdom; the Ossewabrandwag itself; and the republican aspiration. Shortly afterwards the Transvaal executive of the Ossewabrandwag informed the UR that it would not expand its activities to the "economic or general cultural spheres" – which were to be left to the FAK and RDB – and would not link up with any political party. But through its own political links it would exercise influence on the acknowledged political leaders of the Afrikaner in the promotion of the republican ideal.

In practice things worked out differently, with hundreds of thousands of members, of both groups, inevitably over-lapping on the spheres of established organisations. Worse still, the Ossewabrandwag had a "foreign" ideology – that of National Socialism – which caused additional friction with those Afrikaner Nationalists who believed in "Boer democracy."

The uneasy political alliance between Hertzog and Malan – which would finally collapse in November 1940 – and the simmering conflict involving the Ossewabrandwag was reflected in Diederichs' speech at the Bondsraad meeting in Bloemfontein on October 4. Discussing the political situation he said that several divisions had approached the UR to take a lead. There was a feeling "that the volk did not always get the leadership it desired."

Diederichs assured the Bondsraad that the UR had done much more on the political front than was generally realised, but he admitted that "the present crisis has caught us unprepared."

The Broederbond as such had no organisation in the political sphere, as had been created in all other spheres for the volk. Because the Bond was precluded from party political activities in terms of its constitution it would fulfil its task much better if it stood "outside and above narrow party politics and gave its leadership."

Describing the Broederbond's wider political role, he said that it performed two functions: it arranged for co-ordination between big organisations in the political field; and it saw to it that the necessary leadership was given when necessary.

Diederichs stressed that the strict divisions between culture, economics and politics had lapsed and that the Broederbond could not adopt a neutral attitude towards political matters. In fact, this was "never the intention of the AB."

However, it was not necessary for the Bond to directly involve itself in active party politics. Just as the AB could not interfere directly in church matters, it could not do so in political matters.

Then, significantly, he spelled out the political role that it should really play: "It should

58

live in the closest contact with everybody, see to it that they give the necessary leadership. And only when they fail in their duty, leading to a situation dangerous for the volk, must the Bond intervene.

"In a certain sense the AB must be the axle round which turn the different aspects of the volk; or rather the authority that stands above them, which co-ordinates them with a view to a unity of direction and action."

The ambition of the Broederbond was stated in the clearest terms: it had to become the super-body above all other organisations – not only the watchdog of all Afrikaner interests, but in the final instance its highest authority.

The history of the activities of the Broederbond is the history of the struggle to achieve this over-riding ambition.

Diederichs closed his speech by appealing to the members to give the newly elected leadership the necessary confidence "to actively serve the whole *'volksaak''* ('cause of the volk') according to the best of their abilities." This was not to be done for the sake of the Bond itself, but for the sake of "our volk as a whole . . . one indivisible being."

Then in a climactic crescendo he summed up the rationale for the very existence of the Broederbond and its highest ideals:

". . . This volk *will* not go under . . . You and me . . . *will* be assured of the everlasting future existence *('voortbestaan')* of a separate totally free Afrikaner volk, with its own language, own culture, and an own fatherland and God-given calling."

The minutes of the Bondsraad noted that Diederichs had urged the members and the cells to keep in close contact with the UR and the head office in cases of serious matters concerning the volk.

After his speech the Bondsraad decided that the UR must prepare itself for "possible future eventualities. It instructed the UR to appoint an expert commission which can provide . . . the desired co-ordination of activities, and to provide real leadership."

This committee was called the Committee for Policy Matters.

With the clash between General Hertzog and Dr Malan's Free State Broeders at the November 1940 Bloemfontein congress, leading to Herzog's resignation from public life, the uneasy Nationalist parliamentary front broke into three factions – the old HNP; the Afrikaner Party; and Pirow's New Order – with the extra-parliamentary Ossewabrandwag adding to general political confusion in Afrikaner Nationalist ranks.

Amidst this growing chaos the AB tried desperately to reunite the factions.

On May 3, 1941, the UR met in Johannesburg. For the first time the meeting was attended by Dr J.F.J. van Rensburg, Commandant-General of the Ossewabrandwag. It had been agreed to invite him to attend UR meetings "in an advisory capacity."

Item 27 of the minutes of that meeting referred to the report of L.J. du Plessis as Chairman of the general Policy Commission designed to bring the warring factions together.

It noted that Dr Malan did not like the idea of a *"volksvergadering"* ("peoples' meeting") which, as a first step towards consolidating the volk, was intended to get the leaders of the different organisations to issue a joint "consolidating statement."

The UR nonetheless said the statement would be issued at the "appropriate time." It also granted the committee finances from its reserve fund to use when "it really becomes necessary."

A month later, on June 6, the matter was once more discussed by the management committee. Item seven of the minutes noted that Du Plessis expressed the view that the efforts of the Broederbond to consolidate Afrikanerdom should be made public. Matters were not being correctly reported and he was concerned that the position of the OB was not being factually reflected.

Meyer stressed the importance of carrying the Bond's task of consolidation further "through systematic propaganda."

The meeting decided to tackle the question of propaganda "as soon and as effectively as possible" via the divisions. Implementation was left to Diederichs and Verwoerd and £1 000 was made available for urgent work of the policy committee. This would back the efforts of the *"Eenheidskomitee"* ("Unity committee"), the Broederbond-inspired public body designed to achieve unity. However, the major problem facing the committee was that it was divided amongst itself. Thus the UR meeting of August 16 became a battlefield of the debate raging outside within the rank and file and the conflicting organisations.

With Diederichs in the chair, the groups were lined up as follows: Dönges, Hiemstra and Verwoerd for the HNP; Van Rensburg, Du Plessis, Meyer and Ds C.R. Kotze for the Ossewabrandwag; and Van Rooy, Lombard, H.J. Herbst (the treasurer) and M.S. du Buisson (minute-keeper) respresenting the others.

Du Plessis explained the activities of the *Eenheidskomitee,* which consisted of three members of the HNP and Ossewabrandwag each, and two of the FAK and RDB.

He revealed that the HNP was furious because the contents of the draft constitution – written by the policy committee – was contained in an Ossewabrandwag circular sent out by "Generaal" J.A. Smith of the Cape.

The HNP resented Van Rensburg's propaganda for a republic, and his "interference" in the clash between the HNP and Pirow's New Order, in which he gave the impression of supporting the latter.

A lengthy discussion ensued, interrupted only by the lunch break. Van Rensburg explained that the Ossewabrandwag would welcome National Socialists if they were Afrikaners and republicans, and explained his recent speech which had so annoyed the HNP hierarchy.

Verwoerd rejected Van Rensburg's claim that the body politic could be separated into party politics and *volkspolitiek* – and resented its refusal to accept the political leadership of the HNP, whose "sole right" in the political sphere should be recognised.

Diederichs attempted to mediate, claiming that the OB and the HNP did not want to split, but "that the volk did not want to make a choice and that the largest part of the problem was due to a misunderstanding."

The UR decided to arrange a meeting between Van Rensburg and Malan on August 20. It would be attended by Du Plessis as chairman of the *Eenheidskomitee,* and Van Rooy on behalf of the UR.

It was also agreed to invite Dr Malan to attend future UR meetings in an advisory capacity.

The UR meeting was followed by several others involving the leaders of the various groups under the auspices of the *Eenheidskomitee.*

In a September 9 circular, Diederichs made a special plea to members in Item nine. This immediately led to further clashes at the subsequent UR meeting, since it was seen as reflecting on his impartiality as chairman, and on the role of the Broederbond in the Ossewabrandwag-HNP dispute.

Diederichs said it appeared that "the worst danger seems to have been warded off" and that matters would soon be "normal" again.

Members' duties were two-fold. Firstly they should remain "calm," and should refrain from "unnecessary and damaging actions." Secondly they should not in advance "make a firm decision in one or the other direction."

Diederichs said there was no conflict between Afrikaner and anti-Afrikaner, but between two volks-movements with the same "love for the fatherland."

He then added that Broeders should not "become nervous about the so-called National Socialism of certain leaders and groups . . ." These National Socialists were merely "ordinary Christian Afrikaners who were in strong reaction against the liberalism of, or especially strongly longed for deliverance from, British Imperialism." Diederichs stressed that all the organisations and leaders who co-operated in the *Eenheidskomitee* had accepted a basis "which was basically Christian National and at the same time anti-liberalistic and anti-imperialistic."

At the UR meeting of September 15, the sparks flew. Chairman Diederichs came under fire, especially from Verwoerd and Hiemstra. Verwoerd objected to the references to "National Socialism" and to the fact that Broeders were asked not to make a choice between the HNP and the Ossewabrandwag. This gave the impression that the Bond was sympathetic towards groups hostile to the HNP.

Hertzog and Du Plessis defended the phrase "National Socialism" while Verwoerd thought that it should be rejected as "a foreign term."

Another lengthy debate followed between the two factions, with Verwoerd and Hiemstra defending HNP interests; Van Rensburg and Du Plessis defending the Ossewabrandwag; while Hertzog and Van Rooy adopted a conciliatory position, attempting to elevate the Broederbond to a political position above the various conflicting groups.

But the deadlock remained. Verwoerd refused to budge one inch from his attitude that the HNP had the political monopoly and that the Ossewabrandwag should accept its political leadership.

Finally, the UR was unable to take a final stand. Diederichs was instructed to retract his circular and to stress at the next Bondsraad, in October, the Bond's positive aspects.

Meyer's position also came up for discussion. An assistant secretary of the Broederbond, and an official of both the RDB and the FAK, he had also been appointed chief information officer of the Ossewabrandwag. It was decided to defer a decision pending the reaction of Dr Malan, but that he could also offer his services to Malan as an information officer of the party. Obviously he would then be in a key position of influence matters one way or another.

The very next day Diederichs sent out his new circular, stressing that it was not his intention to be "protective" towards one or other of the groups involved in the dispute, or to defend the doctrine of National Socialism. He explained that he merely wanted to counter possible gossip sowing suspicion against members – as had happened before when it was said that a large number of Broeders were Freemasons.

At the Bondsraad meeting in Bloemfontein on October 6, the differences again came up. Du Plessis submitted a report on behalf of the Policy Committee (which no longer existed). The chairman made it clear he was delivering it in his personal capacity as chairman of the *Eenheidskomitee*. He first explained that the republican constitution was the brain-child of the disbanded policy committee. Then, immediately after he had delivered his report, Dönges, supported by J.H. Conradie (the other HNP MP), proposed that further discussions be abandoned and that the Bondsraad leave it to the UR to take the steps necessary to prevent the threatening division within the volk.

Thus a major debate which could split the Broederbond itself wide open was averted. In his word of thanks the chairman expressed the hope that "through the Broederbond the unity of the Boerevolk will be maintained."

Less than three weeks after the Bondsraad, the delayed clash took place on October 24, at the UR meeting in Johannesburg. Van Rooy reported efforts by certain Johannesburg Broeders to reach reconciliation. The plan was to summon Dr Malan as the *"volksleier"* ("leader of the people"), and to establish a Policy Council consisting of representatives of the Ossewabrandwag, the RDB, HNP and the FAK. Malan, however, favoured a National Committee.

A lengthy debate followed, involving a clash between Du Plessis and Dönges, in which the latter was accused of distorting Du Plessis' report at the Bondsraad.

Du Plessis regarded the Ossewabrandwag as an extension of the Broederbond and compared the attacks on the OB with those on the Bond in the Thirties by General Hertzog.

Finally, the UR appointed a committee consisting of Diederichs, Van Rooy, Van Rensburg and Verwoerd to discuss with Dr Malan the various proposals. Should Malan agree, this committee, with Malan as chairman, should work out a plan and submit it to the UR for approval.

At the management committee meeting on December 1, it was reported that the committee had met Malan in Pretoria, but that he was not yet prepared to act as chairman. There was some public correspondence about the matter in the Press. Matters were certainly not finalised yet.

By the beginning of 1942 it was becoming clear that the task of reconciliation was beyond the Broederbond. At a meeting of the UR on January 23, 1942, a proposal of Verwoerd, seconded by Hiemstra, was accepted. It stated that the UR committee had failed to achieve the necessary co-operation; that the UR should not continue with its work of intercession; and that cells be asked to avoid contentious issues.

The UR thanked the HNP for accepting the Broederbond republican constitution – that it had tabled a republican motion in Parliament – and thanked Verwoerd and Du Plessis in particular for their work on the constitution.

The pendulum was also swinging against the Ossewabrandwag in the Broederbond. A decision of the UR was noted in Item 25 of the minutes, as follows: "It is decided that paid officials of the AB may not occupy any responsible positions in the . . . Ossewabrandwag."

This was a blow indeed for Meyer and his aspirations to promote the ideals of the OB while retaining his AB position.

At the March 6 management committee meeting there was a clash between Verwoerd, Diederichs and Meyer. Verwoerd objected that the last circular had not contained all the UR resolutions of the previous meeting, especially those favouring the HNP and the one affecting Meyer.

The decision of the UR to abandon its efforts to mediate was met by a stream of protest from a large number of cells. No less than 14 resolutions from cells and regional meetings were sent to head office between February and April, to be put to the next UR meeting.

These resolutions, along with a brief summary of their main points, were discussed at the UR meeting of April 24 – 25. Some of them were that: the UR did not provide leadership; its members took a lead in fraternal quarrels; UR members participating in the public conflict should resign; the Broederbond, as a binding factor, ought not to withdraw from the conflict; the UR should persuade the various national leaders to abandon sharp attacks on each other; a special Bondsraad should be held; and it was up to the UR to draw up the basis for unity.

That UR meeting took a crucial decision. Declining to hold a special Bondsraad, it admitted its failure and decided that the unity of the Bond itself was of paramount importance – not to be endangered by any efforts at mediation. Survival, again, was the watchword.

It was decided "that the first consideration of the UR is the preservation of the Broederbond as an embodiment of Afrikaner unity and also as a common home for groups which . . . find within the Broederbond a basis for unity."

Moreover, the desire for unity could not at the moment be found on an organised basis. The existing organisation should avoid unnecessarily sharp clashes and any outward unity between organisations should not be forced.

The resolution called for public action against detention without trial, against Communism, on the attaining of a "Christian National republic within legal channels" – a swipe at the para-military activites of the Ossewabrandwag.

This UR decision was conveyed to the Broederbond in circular No 9/41/42 dated May 4, 1942.

The dramatic split in Afrikanerdom clearly demonstrated the political limitations of the Bond. It had enormous influence, but only up to a point. The ultimate political power lay in the hands of those politicians who were *also* Broeders – who would fight it out between the HNP and Ossewabrandwag as to which body had the political monopoly over the Afrikaner.

Diederichs discussed the events in full in his chairman's speech to the Bondsraad on October 2, 1942. His theme throughout was that the unity of the AB was all-important. He described the Broederbond as the core of the volk; from the core would go out the healing powers: "We are the core and must be prepared to accept that responsibility, because we comprise the elect, those who regard ourselves as the best in the volk . . .

"If the AB should split it will be a sad day in the history of our volk. It would mean that the forces of disintegration had finally conquered the forces of unity. It would mean that the rift in the whole of our volk had penetraded to the core."

4. Smuts and the Broederbond

With the 1935 Smithfield attack by General Hertzog on the Bond, public attention was for the first time truly focussed on its existence and strategy. But, because of its secrecy, and because respectable Afrikaner leaders were known to be members, many people in government initially did not regard it at all seriously, rejecting the Broeders as a bunch of fanatics who would never win widespread public support.

Hertzog himself is reported to have changed his mind about the Broederbond only shortly before his death in 1942. A Broeder deputation apparently gave him a "true" picture of the Bond, providing him with "new" information, and Broeder sources claimed that he changed his assessment. However, in view of his bitterness, and tragic isolation – he was at the time shunned by the majority of both Afrikaans and English-speakers – this belated change of attitude has not been taken seriously, not even by the Broederbond which for many years ensured that his important role in the Afrikaner cause was deliberately played down in public.

Key people in government – in Military Intelligence and the Special Branch – kept a close watch on the Bond's activities throughout the war years. The Government's war effort against Nazi Germany was actively or tacitly opposed by all the Afrikaner Nationalists, although from 1941 onwards they were disunited and fragmented in groups and parties such as the HNP, the Afrikaner Party, the New Order, the Ossewabrandwag, the Greyshirts and the Boerenasie. All they wanted in common was a republic.

The concern of the Smuts Government over the Broederbond was due to the following: it was a secret organisation; its narrow exclusivism was in direct conflict with Smuts's philosophy of one united nation of Afrikaans and English-speakers; a number of Broeder members had close ties with Germany and held Nazi sympathies; and members of the Ossewabrandwag were physically involved in subversive activities like sabotage.

While the organisation's leadership included prominent OBs such as Dr Hans van Rensburg (co-opted to the UR for a while); Professor L.J. du Plessis and Ds C.R. Kotze (both UR members); and Dr Piet Meyer, a paid official – it was blatantly undermining the Government's new educational policy of dual-medium schools.

In 1943 it planned a schools boycott. The AB had infiltrated the civil service and there were fears that Broeder members in key positions would actively sabotage or delay the implementation of government policy.

The concise 25-page report of Dr E.G. Malherbe, Military Intelligence Chief, written on March 29, 1944, and other earlier and subsequent reports submitted to General Smuts during and after the war – as well as regular reports of certain government bodies such as the Controller of Censorship, for example on "Subversive influences in Training Colleges and Schools" – give valuable insight into the thinking and assessment of the Broederbond by the Smuts Government.

Smuts's first concern was obviously the Nazi influence. There were the ties with Germany, and the fact that prominent Broeders like Diederichs, Meyer and Van Rensburg had visited Germany before the war to make a close study of Nazi techniques of propaganda, manipulation of public opinion and infiltration of public bodies.

Malherbe, on pages seven and eight of his report entitled the "Afrikaner Broederbond," noted: "ever since the arrival of the first Nazi agents disguised as scientists, educationists, etc., the AB has become immensely interested in the Nazi system.

"Dr Diederichs and a specially selected Stellenbosch student were sent over to study National Socialism. Both of them qualified as Quislings in the Nazis' Anti-Komintern training school."

The Smuts investigators regarded the Broederbond and the Ossewabrandwag as one, and believed that the OB was a direct product of Broederbond planning designed to take over government through unconstitutional means.

It also believed that basically the ideological differences between the Ossewabrandwag, the HNP and the Broederbond were few, and that they came down to a question of different strategies designed to achieve the same end.

Thus in 1941 a judge found that Dr Verwoerd, as *Transvaler* editor, had "made himself the tool of Nazi propaganda in the Union – and he knows it."

The Government was also alerted by a clerk who had worked for the Bond for three years under Lombard. According to a special report to Smuts on November 4, 1941, this man "discovered its true aims and thereupon resigned in disgust . . ."

According to pages four and five of the report he stated: "I told him (Lombard) quite frankly that I could not continue working for him, as I considered his activities to be subversive and anti-Government. I felt I was a traitor to the country by working there. My work was entirely connected with the Broederbond and, at the commencement, it appeared that the aims and objects of the organisation were to further the interests of Afrikaners in so far as promoting the use of the Afrikaans language, etc. But I eventually discovered that their real aims were to enrol as members officials who were in key positions in the Police, Railways, Post Office, Education and other Government departments and, at the opportune moment, to overthrow the Government and form a republic.

"I used to type the minutes of the meetings at which these resolutions were adopted . . . The Executive Council consisted of nine members. After war was declared they did not meet for some time, because they were afraid that they were being watched; but with the invasion of France, a feeling of reassurance again prevailed and with great rejoicing the meetings continued."

The republican constitution, drafted by the Broederbond in 1941, and which – as has already been mentioned – was prematurely published, was regarded by Smuts's investigators as a blueprint for a republic controlled by an Afrikaner dictatorship. According to them it was "purely Nazi in letter and spirit."

Page 11 of the report warned: "It must not be thought that this constitution is merely a toy of the academic mind. When our informant, previously quoted, left the Bond offices, he states: 'There was a minority in the Broederbond who wanted a republic and were prepared to resort to any means to attain their objective. This minority comprised the younger element and it is felt that if they were to come into control, they would resort to any lengths to obtain their objectives.'

"The young hotheads have evidently been curbed; but only because older heads know that violent measures at present would fail to secure their aims."

The report also contained an extract from a speech by Diederichs made before the war in which he "explained this to a great gathering of important Nazi officials in Goering's Grand Aviator's House at Berlin. He concluded a long address on the constitutional development of the Union by saying, 'that there were three groups of politicians in South Africa today; the first was of the opinion that the development towards a republic had already gone too far and should be forced backwards; the second group held that the present position should be maintained, but that any further development was not desirable; and the third group considered that the present position was only a step towards absolute independence. Now it was difficult to say which of these three was in the right, but one could in any case take it that a nation and a State could never complete their development in a couple of decades. For the Afrikaners in this respect the old German saying: *We don't give away, we fall!* might well be considered to hold good.'

"This is only one example of the close contact maintained between the Broederbond and the Nazi Government before the war. There is a long chapter dealing with this in my full report."

The report continued by referring to conducted tours of Germany by the ANS (Afrikaanse Nasionale Studente), formed by Piet Meyer as the counterpart to Nusas in the Thirties. These were under the leadership of Meyer "with the most cordial co-operation of the Nazi Government."

On page 13 it reported information given by an informant to the effect that even before the war Van Rensburg had planned a new State with Pirow at the head, Van Rensburg Minister of Justice and Defence, Diederichs for Cultural Affairs, with Marais, then a teacher at Grey College, Bloemfontein, also in the Cabinet.

According to the report, Van Rensburg and Diederichs "imported a specially trained German student named Gerlach to convert and organise South African students on Nazi lines. Gerlach had been trained by the 'Anti-Komintern' organisation in Berlin " – " supposedly an anti-Bolshevist body, nominally under the control of a well-known Swede. It was in reality the secret training school for Nazi Quislings.

"Gerlach, who stayed at my informant's house, proved a failure. He was too robot-like and could only deliver set anti-Bolshevik speeches learnt by heart at his school. Diederichs lost patience with him and sent him back.

"Then Diederichs took leave and himself went to Berlin, nominally to study 'Staatsphilosophie', but in reality to qualify at the Anti-Komintern. He returned not long before the war broke out."

That early 1941 report continued to warn about the role of the Broederbond in education, the civil service and the church as well as in other spheres of life. Illustrating its influence in the church, it reported an incident at an international missionary conference held in Durban in 1941.

Ds William Nicol, a founder member of the AB in 1918, and Moderator of the NGK in the Transvaal, was to have been chairman. But when the Bond discovered that Indians and other "non-Whites" would be attending they told Nicol to abandon the chairmanship.

On page 19 the report came to the following conclusions:

"1. The Afrikaner Broderbond, with its fanatical racial aims, and with its offspring, the Ossewabrandwag as action front, has become a formidable subversive force.

"2. The parent is much more dangerous than the child. The Ossewabrandwag, which sprang up in the night like a toadstool, could do so only because the soil had been prepared for it by the Broederbond. Its leaders had been in close contact with the Nazis and had copied their methods wholesale.

"The Ossewabrandwag has waxed with the rise of the Nazi power; It will wane with it. The Broederbond will outlive both, because its policy is much more patient and insidious.

"3. The Broederbond has obtained a strangle-hold on education, which will enable it, in sober truth, 'to govern South Africa' within a few decades. Its members have studied the history and methods of the Jesuits to good purpose. (Diederichs and M.C. Botha are typically Jesuit in outlook and action.)

"4. Some thousands of servants of the State, more especially teachers, are bound by inclination and by oath to carry out the subversive plans of the Broederbond, and to scorn and flout the authority of our Government, which is pledged to racial co-operation and a vigorous prosecution of the war.

"5. In sum, the Broederbond is a malignant cancer in our body politic, and only the knife can remove it."

Malherbe, the author of that report, was to submit several more on the AB.

Other factors strengthened the belief that the Broederbond and its various sponsored and supported organisations were pro-Nazi. For example, since 1937 the Transaal National Party – its leadership dominated by Broeders – had a clause forbidding Jews to become members – and this was not scrapped until nearly 30 years later.

This policy was largely due to the influence of Dr Verwoerd. He was editor of the *Transvaler,* and heavily involved in a public campaign to stop the South African Government accepting Jewish immigrants.

At the 1943 Jubilee meeting of the Broederbond in Bloemfontein, Verwoerd – who was born in Holland – expressed virulent anti-British and anti-Semitic sentiments and demanded that *"the Afrikaner Broederbond must gain control of everything it can lay its hands on in every walk of life in South Africa. Members must help each other to gain pro-*

motion in the civil service or any other field of activity in which they work with a view to working themselves up into important administrative positions."

In the field of education the Broederbond was involved in a head-on confrontation with the Government. Indeed, throughout its history education was perhaps the most important issue of all for the Bond.

This long-term policy laid the foundations of the 1948 victory and led to the absolute entrenchment of Afrikaner domination with the assistance of generation after generation of pupils brainwashed by Christian National Education.

But in the early Forties it was still an uphill battle. In 1943 the Smuts Government – enjoying the support of many Afrikaners – decided to embark on a dual-medium educational policy. This involved the eventual abolition of single-medium Afrikaans and English schools, to be replaced by schools where some of the subjects would be taught in Afrikaans, and other in English. It was all part of a policy to foster a broader South Africanism. The emphasis was on national unity, with separate sectional and language interests protected – but relegated to a secondary position.

So the policy ran in direct conflict with that of the Broederbond, which sought to protect Afrikaner interests, to redress injustices and grievances, and to use the fight for Afrikaner equality as part of its long-term strategy for eventual Afrikaner domination and the "Afrikanerisation and nationalisation" of the English sector.

To achieve this a policy of single-medium education was vital to ensure the separate, total indoctrination of Afrikaner youth. Once that succeeded, the future was assured because the Afrikaners were numerically the strongest of the White groups.

Whatever the real merits and demerits of the two systems from an educational point of view, ideological and political considerations were decisive in Broederbond strategy and thinking.

As noted earlier, General Hertzog had as early as 1935 questioned the right of teachers – whether members of or influenced by the Bond – to stir up hostile feelings against English speakers.

By 1943 a large number of teachers – 500 of them or nearly 25 per cent of the AB membership – were Broeders. While Smuts was ruling South Africa, the Broederbond controlled and influenced education in the Transvaal, the Free State and the Cape. Its members occupied key positions like Director of Education, heads of schools, and other jobs at Afrikaans universities and training colleges.

Moreover, it concentrated on capturing control of school boards and committees. The latter appointed new teachers and on this basis it was ensured that the "right" teachers were appointed.

A special report of the Smuts Government dated August 1, 1943, warned: "The Broederbond is by far the strongest and most influential organisation working for racial disruption. It may be recalled that General Hertzog exposed the aims of this body and threatened to take action if the teachers themselves did not protect their profession from Broederbond infiltration. No action has been taken either by the teachers' associations or otherwise and the Broederbond now has an intensive grip on the educational machinery. About 30 per cent of its members are teachers and probably over 50 per cent of the members are in a position to influence schools and children either by being teachers or by serving on school boards or committees.

"The Broederbond is spreading rapidly and selects its new members for the influence which they may exert in the community.

67

"How strict this discipline is, is reflected in the case of a schoolteacher who tried to resign from the Broederbond but subsequently asked to be allowed to withdraw his resignation on the ground that his colleagues who were also members of the Bond would make his position in the school intolerable.

"Thus if the control of education has not yet passed out of the hands of the constitutional authority to a secret society it has gone a long way in that direction. The position is at present that the Government pays the piper while in many schools the Broederbond calls the tune."

It became known that teachers who supported the Government were not promoted. Constant intrigue went on to discover the political views of a teacher before he was appointed. In many cases where young children expressed political views contrary to those of their pro-Smuts parents, they were traced back to the influence of the school, or the activities of a particular teacher.

In this period, as also in later years, the Broederbond paid careful attention to the recruitment of teachers. A Bond letter intercepted by the Government recommended a schoolmaster as a member because of his "rich experience in silent propaganda."

Another teacher was recommended as a member since he would be able to assist in capturing the town council, the school committee and the library committee. But a third was rejected because he "will be retiring soon and will therefore not be in a position to use his position to influence the children."

History teachers in particular were fervent Broederbond converts. They gave a Christian National slant to the subject. Sometimes parents removed their children from a particular school because of political animus displayed by the history teacher.

During the anti-dual-medium campaign one headmaster complained that it would hamper teachers in teaching one section incidents offensive to the other – thus admitting that two different versions of history were being taught in South Africa. This would inevitably cultivate greater language division.

A report of January 12, 1944, warned: "It is plain therefore that the approved policy in education will not be carried out unless a) teachers who act under political duress are freed from that compulsion; b) teachers who act with racial or political animus are restrained; and c) an adequate flow of qualified men and women inspired with the wide ideals of humanity are forthcoming from the training colleges and universities."

From mid-1943 onwards the Broederbond was involved in a nationwide campaign of opposition to the Government's dual-medium educational policy. The two organisations it employed for this purpose were the FAK and the RDB. The body directly involved in planning and organising the campaign was the N100, also called the Pretoria *"Onderwysraad"* ("Educational Council") an affiliated body of the FAK.

M.C. Botha, later Minister of Bantu Administration and Development, was the secretary of the N100 and of the Afrikaanse Kultuurraad. The campaign had the full backing of the NGK and Gereformeerde Kerk and a number of minister – all Broeders – were employed either full or part-time to organise the campaign. They were Ds L. Botha of Ladysmith in Natal, Ds Worst of Potchefstroom and Ds E. Greyling of Bloemfontein.

The details of this educational battle are to be found in Malherbe's outstanding book *"Education in South Africa: vol. II 1923 – 1975"* and is also discussed in his famous report to Smuts.

One of the steps taken was the organising of a strike of pupils and students, in conjunction with teachers and Afrikaans churches, to protest against the introduction of dual-medium schooling in the Transvaal. A joint memo of the Afrikaanse Kultuurraad of Pretoria and the N100, signed by M.C. Botha, was sent to Broeder members to organise the strike. This memo gives a remarkable insight into Broederbond thinking and strategy.

Paragraph five of that memo stated that, "The true objective (of the dual-medium policy) is simply the sacrificing of Afrikanerdom on the alter of British-Jewish Imperialism."

Through the FAK, the Moderature of the three Afrikaans churches in all four provinces were to be approached to make statements encouraging their flock to keep children at home. "The presbyteries should come together to do the same, and where a minister is unsympathetic a strong personality in the church council or congregation should take the lead."

Others to be approached included the school committees, school boards, MPs, MPCs, farmer associations, arts and cultural bodies, the Voortrekker movement and newspapers. It was stressed that the "strike had to last long enough in order to bring the Government to its senses."

On page 55 of his book Malherbe observes: "The strike did not, however, materialise as the plan was exposed before it got under way. The way it was motivated illustrated once more the almost paranoic persistence with which the Broederbond was always looking for some enemy or threat with which to galvanise Afrikaner Nationalist forces into some form of militant unity."

The next step was to organise a *"volkskongres"* ("national peoples' congress") on mother-tongue education under the auspices of the FAK. The congress was held in December 1943, immediately after the Broederbond's Jubilee conference, with many Broeders attending.

(It was standard practice over the years to hold the Broeder annual congress at the same venue immediately before or after another major congress, e.g. on education or culture.)

After the congress the N100 took charge of the campaign. It put into practice the well-established Bond strategy of manufacturing public opinion by arranging via the FAK's innumerable *"skakelkomitees"* ("liaison committees") for deputations, telegrams, letters, protest meetings, etc., to be held and sent across the land.

Not even the results of the provincial elections in early 1944, with the UP convincingly winning control of three provincial councils, leaving only the Free State in Nationalist hands, could deter the Broederbond campaign; yet the elections were fought mainly on the school language issue itself.

Optimistic about long-term prospects and the effective infiltration of the school system, a Free State Inspector of Schools stated at one of the Broederbond conferences of the period: "The Afrikaans teachers will demonstrate to Afrikanerdom what power they possess in their teachers' organisations for building up the youth of the future republic.

"I know of no more powerful instrument. They handle the children for five or more hours daily for five days a week, while at the hostels and boarding houses the contact is continuous for long periods."

Thus a generation of Afrikaner schoolchildren grew up for whom Paul Kruger, President Steyn, General Christiaan de Wet and Jopie Fourie, the 1914 rebel, were the only real heroes to be remembered at national festivals. Louis Botha, General Hertzog and General Smuts were regarded as renegades, traitors to the cause and not *"ware Afrikaners"* ("true Afrikaners").

In this battle the leaders of the NGK and Gereformeerde Kerk fully backed the Broederbond initiative. The sole exception was the small NHK, which at the time refused to get

69

officially involved in political action. In fact the Synod of the NHK had refused to accept the resolutions of the FAK language conference of December 1943.

As pointed out by Malherbe (page 47) a different, but significant, development was taking place outside the South African borders among tens of thousands of South African soldiers at war – a substantial number of whom were not only Afrikaans but also pro-Nationalist.

As Afrikaans and English-speakers were thrown together for the first time, a new South Africanism was emerging. Many English-speakers recognised for the first time that the Afrikaans language and culture was part of their own wider South Africanism. A survey conducted among soldiers showed that 93 per cent wanted children of the two language groups to go to one school; and 81 per cent also wanted the teaching of some subjects through the medium of the second language, though most subjects were to be taught in the home language. This was all contrary to Broederbond doctrine and philosophy.

Thus we find that the Government kept a watchful eye on the December 1943 visit by Broeders Ds William Nicol and Ds A.J. van der Merwe, respectively the Moderators of the Transvaal and Cape NG Churches, to the troops in North Africa. Men like Malherbe were anxious about the real purpose of the visit because of the close involvement of the NG Church and its leaders with opposition to the Government's educational policy. The security services were also anxious.

At this time Nicol had said this about the "threat" of mixing the two language groups: "It would be fatal to religion, and it cannot be tolerated by us . . . to have children of the Afrikaans churches under the same roof as the children of other churches."

The men wanted to visit the Afrikaans community in Eldoret. General Theron, head of the South African forces in North Africa, was warned about this by the security services in a confidential note dated December 20, 1943.

"I frankly must confess that I cannot see how friendly relations and close co-operation between states in Southern Africa and the Union will be furthered by a mission of intriguers like these two," it read in part.

And on December 21, 1943, Louis Esselen – Smuts's chief political adviser – was also warned about the Nicol-Van der Merwe visit, by Malherbe: "If one could be assured that General Smuts's prestige with the Dutch Reformed Church and the so-called *ware Afrikaners* would be enhanced by the rather vicarious generosity on his part (in allowing the visit), one would derive some consolation.

"I do not think, however, that such appreciation will be forthcoming. On the contrary I am sure that they will cash in on it as hard as they can."

And D.G. Forsyth, the Secretary of External Affairs, was warned in a confidential note: "Of course secretly they are pleased because he (Smuts) has made it possible for them to promote their sinister schemes in a way that could not have been improved upon by even a Nazi organisation."

Whatever the religious purposes of the trip, the two Broeder ministers clearly also had political motives in mind. (It must be remembered that at this period troops wearing uniform were not welcome in many NG churches, and that there were many incidents of soldier families being forced to leave Afrikaans churches.)

On page 43 Malherbe says of the Nicol trip: "He went under the guise of ministering to the spiritual needs of the Afrikaans-speaking troops. When, however, he started preaching the Broederbond doctrine of separate-medium schools, he ran into quite a storm of indignation from his audiences."

70

In North Africa, Nicol and Van der Merwe drafted two reports. The one which was made public was innocuous and contained generalised, friendly statements about their generous treatment by the authorities.

The second, secret report was far more contentious. However, they naively sent it home from Jerusalem, not realising that all post was censored. On February 11, 1944, Malherbe informed General Theron – who up to then had expressed misgivings about the critical attitude in official circles regarding the NGK's political role – about the second report.

Discussing the visit Malherbe wrote: "I am sure that their visit among our men did them a lot of good and I hope that it will lead to the appointment of further padres from our church, provided, however, they are not selected for an ulterior purpose. Daily I receive more evidence which increases my misgivings regarding the motives of these people. An order of the day has gone out through the Broederbond that they must openly fraternise and create a good impression among the English-speaking section in order to disguise their real motive of building up a complete Afrikaner bloc within this country which is strongly anti-English."

He added: "The other report is a confidential one, not for publication. Here their true impressions and fears are expressed. The second report, which is to my mind the important one, can be fairly summed up as an expression of fear of proselytising by other denominations and of *'verengelsing'* in general. In urging that more ministers be sent north, they stress particularly that no general call for volunteers among the predikants of the three churches should be made, but that, instead, certain predikants should be approached directly and personally and asked to volunteer. This can only be in order that these new recruits will be trusted 'Broeders', I consider this dangerous. There should be a public call by the UDF for a dozen more chaplains and applications should be carefully (but secretly) vetted before appointment."

Nicol had also complained about the presence of "non-Whites" among the White troops and said that at the appropriate time voices from the church should be heard against the recruitment of "non-Whites" for war purposes.

Malherbe concluded his letter as follows: "At the same time I must point out that we have to do with a very clever organisation . . . the very charm and affability of men like Rev. Nicol make them all the more dangerous customers to deal with.

"I write to you of these matters in no uncharitable spirit towards these men or our church, but because I feel outraged that under the guise of religion other motives actuate people who have had every facility from us. Actually, the position is much more serious than I am able to explain to you in this letter and I am really worried about the situation. Field Marshall Smuts has been given a full statement outlining their machinations and it is up to him to make the necessary revelations at an opportune time."

A shaken Theron – who in the meantime had been profusely thanked for all his kindness by Nicol and Van der Merwe – replied to Malherbe on February 15, 1944, as follows: "What you say about the two reports is certainly a revelation to me, and a very distressing one indeed. I, in my soldierly innocence, certainly should never have thought that anyone wearing the cloth could excel in such double dealing! On top of it I send for your information a copy of a letter which was addressed by one of the gentlemen to Duxbury and is in rather a different strain to the comments in the secret report on the proselytizing of *'jong lidmate'*."

Smuts's advisers were thus fully aware that behind the benign, affable appearance of many Broeder leaders was hidden the ruthless ambition to achieve, not Afrikaner equality, but Afrikaner domination. And, to attain this, it was important to keep the two language

71

groups at arms' length – not only in school but also in bed! Thus we find Nicol actively engaged in mid-1944 urging Afrikaners not to inter-marry with English people.

On August 14, 1944, Verwoerd, as a UR member, contacted Advocate G.F. de Vos Hugo, a Broeder and later a judge, then Pretoria chairman of the Kruger Day Committee in charge of the national celebrations on October 10. Verwoerd suggested that a symposium be held on that day on the theme of the preservation of the identity of the Afrikaner volk, and of the undesirability of inter-marriage from the sociological, educational, religious and legal points of view.

Hugo informed Verwoerd that Nicol had suggested that "you should elaborate on this theme of the undesirability of inter-marriages in an editorial in *Die Transvaler.*" Verwoerd agreed, provided Nicol mentioned the topic again in public.

And the Smuts men, from their observations, also knew that there was a difference between the public utterances and assurances of Broeder leaders and their private ambitions. This was particularly true concerning Afrikaner-English relations. Take this discussion between Verwoerd and Willie Maree, then an HNP organiser, and later a Cabinet Minister, on September 1, 1944.

Maree reported criticism from Potchefstroom intellectuals because Dr Malan had stated that Afrikaans-English co-operation was an important principle for him. Verwoerd replied that many of the younger Nats, such as himself, often felt that Dr Malan was too honest in his desire for equal rights for English and Afrikaans. Some English people had become assimilated by the Afrikaners – e.g. the Nicols, Murrays and MacDonalds – and Malan hoped to see a united nation one day with joint traditions. Younger Nationalists like Verwoerd would prefer to see Afrikaans becoming the predominant, and eventually the only language in South Africa.

"Malan decreed equality of rights and would stand by it, but if Verwoerd and his younger Nat friends could do anything about it they would seek predominant Afrikaans influence rather than the assimilation of *races* that Malan constantly preached . . ."

It is against this background that Malherbe reached the following conclusions in his report. On page 24 he said: "As this policy of Afrikaner dominance creeps into the various spheres of employment, and particularly into the higher professional and State services, those who are not that particular brand of *ware Afrikaner* required by the AB, will be more and more pushed into the background to posts of secondary importance. Professional men and particularly teachers who are now in the army and who have thrown in their lot with the Government will thus have scant chance of future advancement. It is already beginning to worry them though most are not yet aware of the power operating against them. It works so cleverly behind the scenes . . . nearly always just within the regulations.

"What chance, we may well ask, has the Government, under such conditions, to effectively carry out its demobilisation plans in so far as they impinge on spheres impregnated by Broederbond influence? Broederbond officials are constantly present (a prominent one figures in demobilisation); there are innumerable methods of subtle obstruction calculated to create annoying delays leading to subsequent disillusionment . . . detrimental to the Government, and valuable to the Opposition."

Referring to General Hertzog's 1935 warning he added (page 26): "Today, with the bitter experience of the Broederbond's evil influence on the war effort, and its stranglehold on South African public life, the need for action is much more urgent. If we are to live together in peace and amity in South Africa, the Broederbond must be destroyed.

"If the AB is not simultaneously immediately exposed and its stranglehold eradicated root and branch – in particular its insidious hold on education – it will at its present rate of growth destroy South Africa within a few years.

"In this way the Nazi system, also starting with a small but powerful underground group, gained ultimate control, dragging the entire world into the most devastating war of all time.

"The potentialities, in the case of South Africa, are more dangerous. Germany's nemesis came in the form of a humble and poorly educated housepainter. South Africa's equivalent is a university professor." Before he acted Smuts waited many months. He respected the Afrikaans churches and was wary of their political influence. Because of the close ties between the Broederbond and Afrikaner religious bodies he refused until the end to publish named Broeders, although Malherbe had carefully prepared a campaign to expose all their activities.

Thirty years later Malherbe told me that the Smuts Government would have been far more effective than it was if it had emulated the *Sunday Times'* formula of the Sixties and Seventies in publishing everything known about the AB. The only way to reduce a secret organisation's power is to expose it absolutely.

Smuts acted only at the end of the 1944 – eight months after receiving Malherbe's recommendations. In the preceding months a barrage of public attacks on the Broederbond appeared in Government newspapers; and there was criticism by leading United Party politicians.

In a tough speech opening the UP congress in Bloemfontein in December 1944, Smuts announced that all civil servants would be prohibited from Broederbond membership in the near future.

However, the Broederbond as such was thus not banned. Smuts noted that the Bond had flouted his earlier warning about its activities at the October 11 Transvaal congress of the UP. He mentioned a special meeting of civil servant Broeders held in Pretoria shortly after this speech, attended by UR executives who advised members not to resign from the Bond but to continue doing the "good work" in the civil service and teaching profession.

Smuts had clearly come to the conclusion that the Broederbond differed radically from other secret organisations. It was in a position to control and influence entire sectors of Government – so in many respects constituted a State within a State.

Smuts then said: "It is unnecessary to emphasise the dangers of such a secret organisation. It is quite undemocratic, and in conflict with the outlook of the South African people. Secretly the public was deceived by people whom they had no reason to distrust. There were people who had joined the Broederbond years ago, thinking that it was an innocent organisation, but later they discovered the truth. They were kept silent by a strict oath.

"Is this not a dangerous state of affairs which every decent person must deplore? Why the strict secrecy, if it is not a sinister organisation? Let the Broederbond state what their membership is and what their aims are, so that the public can know where it stands.

"I warn the people that here is something in their amidst which conflicts with our better feelings and customs, affects the ethical character of our society, and in the long run is going to pollute our society. A small secret minority, or oligarchy, is working itself into a position of power. It is clear that the Broederbond is a dangerous, cunning, political, Fascist organisation of which no civil servant, if he is to retain his loyalty to the State and administration, can be allowed to be a member.

"Public interest demands that the public service and the teachers be protected against this danger. It is, therefore, the intention to declare the Broederbond a political body, membership of which will be a contravention of the law and punishable as such. We know that it is the declared policy of the Nationalist Party to fill every board, every organisation in the country, public or private in the State or in the church, with their followers.

"We ask that it should be done openly, and not secretly by treachery and intrigue. We see to it that our civil service and teaching profession, which belong to the people, are not dragged into the mess and exploited by a sectional movement of a secret nature by a sort of Gestapo."

For the next few months the Broederbond dominated the news. Events occurred in rapid succession. One effect of Smuts's attack was that it forced the Bond into the open for the first time in its 26-year history.

On December 17, 1944, the UR issued a brief Press statement stating that it would call on the volk as the highest court. It said: "As a result of the unfair and untruthful attacks which have recently been made on the Afrikaner Broederbond, the Executive Council of this body has resolved to call on the highest court which it can approach – the Court of the 'Volk'.

"The Executive Council, therefore, intends shortly to take the Afrikaner people into its confidence and openly inform them of its history, aims, activities and objects. The people will thus be enabled to undertake further investigations to judge for themselves that the Bond is interested and sincere in the service of the highest ideals of the people in a manner that can withstand all tests."

A series of four lengthy Press statements followed on December 14, 1944; and on December 20 and 30. All were published at considerable length. (See Annexure C).

But on December 15, the Broederbond was curbed in a special *Government Gazette*. All civil servants and teachers were prohibited from belonging to the secret body. Should they refuse they could be fined R200; their rank or salaries be reduced; or they could simply be dismissed from the civil service. In consequence 1 090 members resigned from the AB – though 870 rejoined after the 1948 Nationalist victory when the Malan Government naturally lifted the ban with immediate effect.

The Press statements regarding the aims and aspirations of the Broederbond preceding the ban were given in the most idealistic terms, with no indication of its real power and influence.

The communiques stated the following:–

"The Afrikaner Broederbond was born out of the deep conviction that the Afrikaner nation was planted in the country by the hand of God and is destined to exist as a nation in its own right and with its own mission;

"The secret character of the Afrikaner Broederbond is comparable to that of a Cabinet meeting;

"The reason why the confidential nature of the Bond is being attacked by the enemies of the Afrikaner volk is that in their secret councils they themselves seek to make plans to break Afrikanerdom economically. But at the same time they want to prevent young Afrikaners from meeting for the purpose of drafting plans for the economic advancement and happiness of the volk and thus for our independent existence."

These statements made no secret of the fact that the Broederbond had political objectives. Indeed, they divulged a seven point programme:

1. The independence of South Africa;
2. The abolition of Afrikaner "inferiority" and that of the Afrikaans language;
3. Strict segregation of all non-Europeans;

74

4. An end to exploitation of South Africa and its people by "aliens";
5. Rehabilitation of the farming community and the creation of social security through work and more intensive industrialisation;
6. Nationalisation of credit, and a planned economy;
7. The Afrikanerisation of public life and education in a Christian National sense, leaving the internal development of all sectors free as long as this did not militate against the safety of the State.

The first six points were also embodied in the social and economic programme of the HNP, drawn up for it by the Broederbond's professors and other experts. But it is most important to note that point seven – the question of Afrikanerisation – was excluded from the HNP's public programme. Obviously this secret aim – the most important in the whole programme of the Broederbond and the Afrikaner establishment – was deliberately kept out of the party's programme of action in order not to unnecessarily alienate the English vote. But it was a logical sequel to the 1934 circular in which Van Rooyen and Lombard spelled out the AB's ambitions for its future rule of South Africa. This ultimate goal would never be publicly revealed, and never outside the limited circle of those Broeders who saw themselves as custodians of Afrikaner Nationalism.

It was therefore with a notable hypocrisy that the Nationalists of 1969 objected to the programme of Afrikaner domination put out by the second HNP (Herstigte Nasionale Party) formed then by Dr Albert Hertzog.

In response to Smuts's attacks, the Nationalist newspapers, with Verwoerd leading the field, churned out a series of highly indignant articles, describing the anti-Broederbond movement as a direct attack on the Afrikaner volk itself.

Dr A.J. Stals, MP, and Dr Gerard Moerdyk, the well known architect who designed the Voortrekker Monument – both prominent Broeders – issued public statements. And Dr Malan himself, as the political leader of Afrikanerdom, rallied to the defence of the Bond.

An additional demand by the Government, that all Broederbond members who resigned had to send copies of their resignations to their civil service chiefs, was flatly rejected by the AB leadership after special legal advice had been obtained.

Naturally, not all the Broeders resigned. A number refused outright and were charged with contravening the emergency war regulations. They appeared before a magistrate in a departmental inquiry and were defended by such illustrious advocates such as Oswald Pirow, and Victor Hiemstra – another Broeder.

These hearings received considerable Press publicity and angry letters appeared in the Nationalist newspapers. The upshot was that those involved emerged as heroes and martyrs, and the impact of Smuts's action was defused.

The affected Broeder civil servants were top, outstanding men. They included Wentzel du Plessis, a secretary in the Department of the Prime Minister; Dr H.O. Mönnig, a world-renowned scientist, and Professor Avril Malan, both of Onderstepoort; Nollie Bosman, an under-secretary of the Department of Commerce and Industry; Jan Combrink, secretary of the Housing and Planning Commission; Jan Cloete, senior clerk in the Department of Finance; B.J. de Klerk, inspector of agricultural education in the Department of Union Education; and B.G. Venter of the Department of Agriculture.

Ironically, three years later du Plessis was to defeat Smuts in a shock result in the Standerton constituency.

Malherbe – whose advice to publish all information about the Bond, and indeed to have its offices raided, was rejected by Smuts – wrote of this period as follows (page 678): "This measure, as General Smuts himself later admitted, was a tactical mistake on his part. It did not weaken the Broederbond. On the contrary." Referring to the public controversy caused by the action against the civil servants he added: "They, of course, had in the meantime been taken care of by their 'brothers' and later on, when the National Party came into power, these same men rose to even greater prominence than before in the public service."

So the Bond survived this crisis though its was obviously a major blow, which cost it more than one third of its members. It carried on determined to persevere with its long-term plans for Afrikaner domination. In the short term the first priority was the 1948 general election, three years away.

Discussions at the UR meeting of May 11, 1945, a few months after Smuts's action, made it clear they were not abandoning any plans. They went full steam ahead to create a wide Afrikaner Nationalist front, involving the churches, the workers, the political parties, the Ossewabrandwag, the RDB and business. It was an overall strategy for their eventual election onslaught.

The meeting, which lasted for two days, was attended by men like Van Rooy, Verwoerd, Diederichs, Hertzog, Dönges and Lombard.

The following main points were discussed:

1. The co-ordination of the movements initiated by the Ossewabrandwag and the Nationalist Party for the purpose of getting control of trade unions, under a Broederbond-controlled organisation to be known as the "Blanke Werkers Beskermingsbond" ("White Workers' Protection Union"). To obtain financial support from the churches for this organisation it would be pointed out to church leaders that the trade unions were in the hands of Communists and that there was a burning need for them to be based on a Christian National foundation.
2. The Medical Faculty at Pretoria had to be supported. Watch had to be kept over it so that it developed in accordance with Broederbond aims.
3. The apppointment of Broeders as directors of companies sponsored by the RDB was desirable.
4. An attempt to bridge the gulf between the National Party and the Ossewabrandwag had to be made. It was stated that the quarrel was due to Dr Hans van Rensburg's attempts to intrude into the "political front," whereas he should confine himself to the "action front."
5. German children needed to be brought into the Union.
6. A relief fund to assist Holland and Germany was to be established.
7. University posts for dismissed civil service Broeders were to be secured.
8. Broeders should be (radio) broadcasters.
9. The secretary was to communicate with Broeders and point out that they had nothing to fear from Smuts's Government since it did not know enough of the Bond's activities to persecute them further.
10. The Hervormers (reformed) organisation within the Mine Workers' Union should be brought into the White Workers' Protection Union of the Broederbond.
11. It was reported that the Parliamentary Caucus of the NP had decided that no member should admit to being a Broeder, except Dr T.E. Dönges.

The overall feeling was that as soon as the emergency regulations fell away, the National Party would soon take over the government.

(Smuts obtained a verbatim report of these discussions.)

Dönges had the gathering in hysterics when he explained how he had convinced UP members of Parliament that the Broederbond was not in the least a dangerous organisation.

During the discussions Verwoerd said that however distasteful to other Broeders, he thought it useless to think of overthrowing the Government by force. The route to power was by the ballot box. So by this time the HNP had gained the upper hand in the infighting with the Ossewabrandwag. After the 1943 election the party emerged as the only parliamentary body for Afrikaner Nationalists, although Smuts gained many seats in three-cornered contests where the HNP was opposed by Afrikaner Party or New Order candidates.

Tens of thousands of Ossewabrandwag members also returned to the HNP fold after Dr Malan's ultimatum that no HNP member could belong to the OB. However, the rift between the Ossewabrandwag and the HNP was causing concern in Broeder circles. After all, in the 1948 election, every vote would count. So at that UR meeting a deputation of Broeders once more urged their leaders to form a united Afrikaner front. In replying to them Van Rooy significantly explained that the Broederbond had "engineered the formation of the HNP," had initiated earlier agreements between the OB and the HNP, and had formed several "eenheids" ("unity") committees. The UR made it clear that the HNP was "the best instrument to bring about the republic."

It is important to note that at this meeting a full half day was spent in discussing the OB-HNP differences – yet not once was it suggested that these differences were ideological. What was basically at stake was a struggle between the HNP and OB for the political leadership of Afrikaner nationalism. Any ideological differences that might have existed were of secondary importance.

In the process of building up a united political front against Smuts, bitter infighting took place in the UR itself. Beaumont Schoeman in his book "Van Malan tot Verwoerd" (page 21 onwards) gives a vivid description of how the Bond tried to keep peace in this period.

The UR meeting of May 1945 was preceded by the Bondsraad of October 1944, when it was decided that the UR should again attempt to achieve reconciliation between the OB and HNP. Two of the UR men who were foremost advocates of reconciliation were W.J. du P. Erland (the writer Eitemal), and T.E.W. Schumann, the well-known scientist.

At a UR meeting at the beginning of 1945 Dönges and Verwoerd, on behalf of the HNP, rejected the move. They said the OB had no right to exist, that the party could get on quite happily without it, and that the Broederbond should not keep the Ossewabrandwag alive artificially. However, Diederichs, Schumann, Erlank and Hertzog maintained that reconciliation was vital for the HNP. It could not afford Afrikaner divisions.

With such sharp internal differences the meeting achieved nothing. Dönges and Verwoerd were simply not prepared to agree to a formal reconciliation with the OB. Shortly afterwards, Van Rensburg and L.J. du Plessis, in discussion with UR members, suggested the creation of an OB political front to put up candidates in the 1948 election. Du Plessis proposed men such as Piet Meyer, Phil Bothma, Prof. G. Cronje, Nollie Bosman, and H.O. Mönnig as members of the proposed front. In the end nothing came of it.

Efforts by the UR and individual members to reconcile the differing factions continued. At a UR meeting towards the end of 1946 Erlank, Hertzog and Schumann took considerable pains to persuade the obdurate Verwoerd that the HNP had no chance of winning the election if there was no reconciliation between the OB and Klasie Havenga's Afrikaner Party – made up of followers of General Hertzog who broke away from Malan in 1941.

77

At the same time two leading Pretoria Broeders, Hertzog and Avril Malan, approached Advocate Strydom, the Transvaal HNP leader, and Havenga. They submitted a plan which later formed the basis of the HNP-Afrikaner Party alliance which made all the difference between defeat and victory on May 26, 1948.

In terms of the Hertzog-Malan proposals the Afrikaner Party leaders would be given some safe seats. Moreover, doubtful marginal constituencies would be contested by the Afrikaner Party. Due to Havenga's moderate image they would be able to draw English and Jewish votes, which the HNP would never get.

Early in 1947 Malan and Havenga met secretly and reached agreement. However, inside the Broederbond the issue remained highly controversial and continued to cause considerable friction. Schoeman (pages 24 and 25) describes how Verwoerd (at a UR meeting later in 1947) sharply criticised the Bond for involving itself in political matters. He accused the members of being novices in politics and said that the HNP had been presented with a *fait accompli* because of the negotiations between the OB and the Broederbond. Verwoerd added that without Bond involvement, both the OB and the Afrikaner Party would have disappeared because of dwindling membership.

Notwithstanding the resistance of Verwoerd and Strydom – who even wrote a letter to Malan prior to the 1948 election stating that he would resign from politics afterwards – the Malan-Havenga agreement went ahead.

The OB was politically incorporated into the Afrikaner Party, but it was stipulated that their candidates could not be nominated if they were OB officers. So John Vorster's candidature for the Afrikaner Party in Brakpan was vetoed by Ben Schoeman, the HNP Witwatersrand chairman, because Vorster was still an OB general.

The Ossewabrandwag-HNP friction continued until the 1948 election and remained an issue within the Broederbond. At a UR meeting in Potchefstroom shortly before the election Van Rooy announced that Van Rensburg, through Professor H.L. de Waal, had asked to meet some of the Pretoria Bond leaders to discuss the OB-HNP situation. Van Rensburg subsequently met the Pretoria Broeders, including Avril Malan, De Waal, Mönnig, W.A. Bührmann, J.C. Combrink and M. Cilliers. Van Rensburg told them that on May 1 the "Groot Raad" ("Big Council") of the OB had decided that its members would vote for HNP candidates on condition that discrimination against OB members would cease.

The Broederbond – or at least a very influential section of it – can thus with justification claim most of the credit for the narrow five-seat victory of the HNP/Afrikaner Party pact on May 26, 1948. Several seats were won by the smallest of margins. Their constant efforts, against great odds, to create a united Afrikaner Nationalist front – however shaky – paid dividends in the end. It made possible the unexpected victory at the polls, and paved the way for the official unification of all Nationalists into the National Party. The HNP and the Afrikaner Party disbanded in 1951, so heralding three decades of uninterrupted Afrikaner rule under the NP.

A significant factor in the 1948 triumph was the AB involvement with the trade unions. By 1948 the vast majority of Afrikaners lived in urban areas and were workers; six Witwatersrand seats were for the first time captured by the Nationalists. This was largely the result of the activities of Albert Hertzog and other Pretoria Broeders, though the NRVT ("The National Council of Trustees") which since the late Thirties had concentrated on the trade unions, particularly the Mine Workers' Union, previously entirely under non-Nationalist control.

Early in 1947 the Bond became involved in a behind-the-scenes campaign to warn the public about the visit of the Royal Family to South Africa. The Broederbond fervently believed that Smuts had invited the King to South Africa to consolidate his own internal political position. UR member Erlank drafted a pamphlet and several other UR members supported it financially – as individuals. Dönges and Verwoerd, as HNP members, were doubtful, fearing that the HNP might suffer political damage.

Nasionale Pers refused to publish the anti-Royal pamphlet. However, Verwoerd, as editor of *Die Transvaler,* did not publish a single news report about the visit. A copy of the pamphlet was sent to teachers and ministers of religion for their "guidance."

The infighting among Afrikaners deeply affected the Broederbond. On August 17, 1946, the UR discussed the question of recruiting new members. The general feeling was that the volk appeared to be without inspiration. Pelzer commented on this phase as follows: "The war years did the AB no good. By 1946 many Broeders were not happy about how things had gone and all kinds of criticism were levelled against the Bond. The Bondsraad viewed the situation in a serious light. They attributed the state of affairs to the 'spirit of the times' *('tydsgees')* and sought the solution in a new dedication. And for that reason, in prayer, they asked the Almighty for leadership."

5. Personalities

A list of UR candidates at the 1941 Bondsraad gives an indication of their fields of interest, and their influence.

They were: Ds D.P. Ackermann of Bethlehem; P.J. Badenhorst, medical doctor of ·Ceres; M.J. Beukes, Railways official of Linden, Johannesburg; S.J. Botha, teacher at Pretoria East Primary School; Ds C.B. Brink of Witbank, later to become Southern Transvaal Moderator; W.S. Bruwer, a missionary of Middelburg, Transvaal; J. Combrink, civil servant of Pretoria; J.H. Conradie, advocate, MP and later Speaker, of Cape Town; Professor G. Cronje of Pretoria; J.J. Dekker, a lecturer of Bloemfontein; Ds H.J. de Vos, Langlaagte, Johannesburg; C.F. de Wet, civil servant of Zastron and later well-known as a Johannesburg city councillor and businessman; N. Diederichs, RDB leader, later State President; T.E. Dönges, advocate of Cape Town; Ds T.F.J. Dreyer of Standerton; Professor L.J. du Plessis, Potchefstroom; N.J. du Plessis, headmaster, Klerksdorp; S.J. du Toit, school inspector, Bloemfontein; G.D. Geer, teacher, Ventersdorp; J.H. Greybe, headmaster, Benoni, later MP and leader of the Voortrekker youth movement; Ds E. Greyling, Bloemfontein; P.J. Hattingh, headmaster, Krugersdorp; A. Hertzog, advodate, Pretoria; L.W. Hiemstra, journalist, Bloemfontein; Ds H.M. Hofmeyer, Stoffberg Gedenk School; D.M. Hoogenhout, teacher, Zeerust; J.A. Jooste, inspector of Boere Saamwerk, Port Elizabeth; Ds C.R. Kotze, OB general of Bloemfontein; D.J. Kritzinger, teacher, Paarl; Ds J.J. le Roux, Bethlehem; W.H. Louw, architect, Paarl; D.D. Malan, teacher, Wellington; J.P. Malan, headmaster, Lichtenburg; P.J. Maree, teacher, Nylstroom; D.J. Mostert, official of the ATKV, Hartenbos; Professor E.C. Pienaar, Stellenbosch; J.W. Potgieter, headmaster, Germiston; J.A. Pretorius, headmaster, Steynsburg; T. Radloff, medical doctor, Klerksdorp; Ds C.W. Retief, Paul Roux; J.J. Scheepers, headmaster, Johannesburg; T.E. Schlebusch, headmaster, Linden, Johannesburg; T.E.W. Schumann, civil servant, Pretoria; Ds W.J. Snyman, Venterstad; Ds S.J. Stander, Hartbeestfontein; H.A. Steyn, headmaster, Johannesburg; J.J. Styger, farmer, Aliwal North; Ds D.G. van der Merwe, Bloemfontein; Dr G.S. van der Merwe, Pretoria; J.G. van der Merwe, attorney, Heilbron; Ds J.P. van der Spuy, Reitz; Professor A.J.H. van der Walt, Potchefstroom;

Ds S.P. van der Walt, Johannesburg; Professor D.J. van Rooy, Potchefstroom; Professor J.C. van Rooy, Potchefstroom; S.S. van Straaten, teacher, Springs; S.P. van Wyk, teacher, Boksburg; Ds W.F. Venter, Krugersdorp; H.F. Verwoerd, editor, Johannesburg; F. Viljoen, teacher, Johannesburg; P.D. Zeeman, agent, Germiston.

The town of Potchefstroom, centre of the Doppers (the Reformed Church with its strict Calvinist doctrine) played a major role in these years, out of all proportion to small Doppers' membership.

Joon van Rooy was twice chairman, from August 13, 1932, to October 6, 1938; and then again from October 3, 1942, to February 23, 1951. Van Rooy in this period was also chairman of the FAK.

A most interesting AB personality was L.J. du Plessis, who was chairman from September 6, 1930, until August 13, 1932. An ambitious man, he played a great role in the early Forties in the attempts at reconciling the various Nationalist factions. As an OB member he used his position as chairman of the UR unity committee to the benefit of the OB. In the early Thirties, shortly after his term as UR chairman had expired, he had himself appointed as the AB's political *kommisaris*. His functions were never clear, but he gave the impression of wanting to determine the political course of the Broederbond and to eventually emerge as a major political leader.

When General Hertzog launched his 1935 attack on the Broederbond, Du Plessis' position was abolished because of suspicions by other Broeders about his ambitions.

Du Plessis and Verwoerd could not stand each other and had furious clashes in the UR in the Forties. In the late Fifties Du Plessis broke openly with Verwoerd, criticised his racial policies in public and called for a coalition government.

The first names of Lombard, full-time secretary of the Broederbond and the FAK for many years, were Ivan Makepeace – highly unlikely ones for an anti-British, frontline Afrikaner fighter.

Piet Meyer, assistant Broederbond secretary in the early Forties, was closely aligned with Du Plessis. He used the Bond to promote the Ossewabrandwag, so bringing him into direct conflict with Dönges and Verwoerd, who represented the interests of the HNP. Meyer was also involved in the early attempts to take over the Mine Workers' Union and in this campaign he began to realise the importance of the post of secretary in a trade union. He often in private discussion emphasised that Stalin could only have out-manoeuvred Trotsky because of his key position as secretary of the party.

Other senior Broeders noticed how he had succeeded in securing the position of secretary of several Bond-controlled organisations and in private he boasted of how he had managed to steer the UR in his direction. Apart from being assistant Broederbond secretary, he became secretary of Trekmaats and of the FAK; and was later appointed, as noted earlier, propaganda chief of the Ossewabrandwag.

Meyer was separately paid by each organisation, and was thus in a very strategic position to steer opinion in favour of the OB. However, junior Broeders and pro-HNP Trekmaats began a campaign against him. At the 1941 Bondsraad P.K. le Roux of Oudtshoorn, later a Cabinet Minister, asked serious questions about Meyer's position.

Dönges and Verwoerd were later to clip his wings. They proposed that in principle key Bond positions should be occupied by separate persons. In the end Meyer had the choice of being either assistant Broederbond secretary or secretary of the FAK. He opted for propaganda chief of the OB, banking on a National Socialist take-over in South Africa.

A junior official at the Bond head office and at the FAK was Hennie Coetzee, later a professor at the University of Potchefstroom. In the late Fifties he joined his fellow Broeder Dopper, Du Plessis, in publicly attacking Verwoerd, who was in constant conflict with the Potchefstroom intellectuals. He resented their aversion to Dr Malan, as a background to which were the accusations by the Doppers that Malan was a "liberal" theologian.

Also, the Potchefstroom group joined the OB in large numbers and came up with new constitutional and philosophical theories of how politics should be conducted. Verwoerd referred to them as the "theorising professors of Potchefstroom."

In 1947 Verwoerd clashed with Hertzog on the question of worker organisations. With an election looming he had realised the importance of the role played by labour, and wanted the Broederbond-backed NRVT, where Hertzog held a key position, to merge with an HNP-controlled labour body. He was backed by Dönges on the UR, but Hertzog held back.

Verwoerd's constant obsession was with the party. Everybody had to belong to the HNP. According to his fellow Broeders he was prepared to fight for this to the bitter end, even at the cost of great friction and disharmony. To him the party was the rock on which Afrikaner Nationalist unity had to be founded.

Out of the UR of those years came Diederichs, Cabinet Minister and State President; Verwoerd, Prime Minister; Dönges, Cabinet Minister and President designate; Hertzog, Cabinet Minister and leader of the breakaway right-wing HNP in 1969; and Meyer, chief of the SABC which he was to convert into the most powerful and effective propaganda machine the country had ever seen.

PART IV

Thirty Years of Broederbond Influence

A Broeder member, who later resigned, was years later to describe how shortly after the 1948 victory Verwoerd addressed a Bond meeting in Johannesburg. Verwoerd stressed that the major task of the Broederbond was to entrench the NP Government in power and to see that it never lost it.

The 1948 victory was a victory for Afrikaner nationalism, for Afrikaner Nationalist power, for Afrikaner Nationalist ethnicity. Apartheid, race issues, and post-war grievances were all of secondary importance. The election showed that a reconsolidation of scattered Afrikaner Nationalist groups had occurred. Thanks to the educational and "cultural" white-anting of the Broederbond a fresh generation of brainwashed Afrikaner youth had been delivered to the Nationalist Party. And Smuts was losing his grip on his old traditional Afrikaner supporters, who were weaned away by the Bond's drive for Afrikaner unity.

Non-Afrikaans votes accounted for a fractional percentage of the total Nationalist vote. So the AB had achieved a major breakthrough towards its ultimate goal of an Afrikaner-dominated Republic outside the British Commonwealth.

Within weeks of the unexpected victory the new rulers demonstrated their ruthlessness. Their first priority was to destroy all evidence linking the Ossewabrandwag and many of its Broeder members with subversive activities and with the defeated Nazis.

Malherbe describes vividly (page 683) how in July 1948 the new Minister of Defence F.C. Erasmus – a Broeder – entered the office of the then – Director of Military Intelligence, Colonel Chas Powell, gave him 24 hours' notice of dismissal, and removed "masses of secret files dealing with information which the military authorities had obtained during the 1939 – 1945 war concerning the subversive activities of certain people – members of the Ossewabrandwag and the Broederbond.

"The present writer, who was Director of Military Intelligence during the war, had also been in charge of the Union War Histories Section and in 1948 was still chairman of the Prime Minister's War Histories Advisory Board. He personally remonstrated with Dr D.F. Malan, the then-Prime Minister, over this rape of the official War History Archives by one of his Cabinet Ministers. Dr Malan said that the Minister of Defence was within his rights in dealing with official documents. Dr Malan, however, was not prepared to give any undertaking that these documents would be restored to the Archives of the Union War Histories Section."

Thus all traces of Broeder involvement with Nazism were wiped out and the Broederbond and the Nationalist Broeder rulers were spared any later embarrassment.

Throughout the next 30 years the Bond went through various phases. The first was a period of uncertainty over its role at a time when its political members were actually ruling the country; this lasted until 1956.

The second period saw preparations for a Republic in 1961. Then came what can be called its classical period, from 1960 – 1966, when it was actively, though covertly, involved as a co-partner in government. It was no coincidence that throughout this era Verwoerd headed both the Party and the Government while Meyer, the SABC chief and a professional ideologist and propagandist, headed the Broederbond.

The fourth phase, from 1966 – 1972, saw the AB reflecting the growing split in the National Party, an event similar to the internecine quarrels of the war years. And during its fifth period to date, the Broederbond became a secret instrument in the hands of the dictatorial Vorster.

Here follows a short discussion of these five phases, with more details of specific aspects of the changing Broederbond to follow afterwards.

A.   1948 – 1956: "No vision"

Pelzer (page six) observed that after the 1948 takeover many Broeders wrongly thought that the Bond was growing passive, and that the NP would fulfil all the needs of the Afrikaner. This uncertainty about the AB's role when it was no longer in the opposition camp came out, for example, at a meeting of the 1951 Bondsraad, held in Cape Town. Albert Hertzog, backed by people such as Gert Beetge, Schalk Botha and Hartman van Niekerk, then FAK secretary and later MP for Boksburg, told the meeting about the problems facing Nationalists in the trade unions. Existing legislation made it possible for the Communists, who had a foothold in many trade union organisations, to out-manoeuvre Nationalist attempts to take over the workers' bodies.

Hertzog said that even after the NP had held power for three years, the situation in the trade unions was from its point of view more critical than ever. A Ds Coertze, of the Gereformeerde Church, Cape Town, wanted to know why it was necessary for a Member of Parliament to ask the Bondsraad for assistance when the UR chairman – Diederichs – was also an MP and the NP was in power.

This illustrated the dilemma of the Broederbond in these years. It was widely regarded as unthinkable that the Bond should apply pressure on its own Broeder-led Government. Men such as Diederichs, Hertzog and others, however, believed that while the Broederbond was above party politics – that it was the body protecting Afrikaner interests on all fronts – it nonetheless should, when necessary, use its influence on Broeder politicians.

The majority belief was that the Government was in "safe hands" and that the Broederbond should concentrate on cultural and economic matters; and discussions of long-term goals such as the Republic.

This attitude was described as paralysis by some. The situation had arisen because men on the UR such as Dönges, Verwoerd and Conradie had constantly taken the pro-Party line of saying "hands off" to the Broederbond in the war years.

In 1948 Dönges and Conradie – who became Speaker – resigned from the UR, followed by Verwoerd in 1950 when he became a Cabinet Minister. When, in 1952, a new UR was chosen, Hertzog and Diederichs were the only remaining politicians. The rest included Professor H.B. Thom of Stellenbosch as chairman; Dr. T.E.W. Schumann of Pretoria as vice-chairman; Dr Herman Mönnig (sacked by Smuts in 1945); Piet Meyer, then PRO for Anton Rupert's Rembrandt Tobacco Corporation; Ivan Lombard; Karel Wilcocks, and Professor S. Pauw, later Rector at Unisa.

Wilcocks, Meyer and Hertzog were the men who then endeavoured, without much success, to strengthen the Broederbond's super political role. They believed that the cells across the country should be mobilised to apply pressure on the Government to implement

Nationalist policy far more boldly, and in particular to take action in curbing the influence of non-Afrikaner "big capital" – an old bugbear.

It must be remembered that the first two post-1948 Prime Ministers – Malan, from 1948 to 1954, and Strydom until April 1958 – were not really Broeder activists like Dönges, who became vice-chairman, and Verwoerd (although they were of course members).

Schoeman revealed in *"Van Malan tot Verwoerd"* (page 120) that Strydom was adamant in 1955 that the Broederbond should not establish a special parliamentary and civil servant cell of Broeders during the six months when Parliament was sitting in Cape Town. He argued that MPs who were not Broeders would hear of it, and that the Bond should keep out of policy and party matters and that it should confine itself to establishing business undertakings like Volkskas and Uniewinkels.

Strydom told a UR deputation consisting of Thom, Diederichs and Hertzog that the Broederbond should not involve itself with problems dealt with by the Party as this would only lead to clashes and unpleasantness.

Ironically, informal meetings of Broederbond Parliamentarians – there were 75 in 1954 – were used by the pro-Strydom faction, which included Diederichs and Hertzog, to win support for them in the battle for the premiership expected between Strydom and Havenga after Malan retired.

Hertzog, supported by his two colleagues, felt that one of the most important aims of the Broederbond was to ensure that "the Government of the Afrikaners always remained on the course which was in the interest of Afrikanerdom and which could ensure the survival of Afrikanerdom."

Pelzer (page seven) lists among the achievements of the AB in this period attempts to bridge the "ideological confusion" which arose in the war; the formulation of a republican policy; the strengthening of the "public arms" of the AB which had been hampered in the war years by hostile government action; active organising for the inauguration of the Voortrekker Monument in 1949 and the third centenary Van Riebeeck festival in 1952; and the establishment of SABRA as an authoritative Afrikaner body to give the lead in race relations.

In 1950 the Bondsraad launched out in a new direction when it provided cells with study documents on fundamental matters prepared by experts. Nonetheless, the uncertainty about its real role under a Nationalist Broeder Government continued and led to accusations of "sluggishness" against the UR.

In April 1956 a Potchefstroom cell sent a deputation to the UR in Johannesburg. It consisted of Professor Fanus du Toit, Professor Dirk van Rooy, Ds Beyers Naudé and Professor H.L. Swanepoel.

Professor Du Toit told the UR that there was a general feeling that the Broederbond had "no task any longer and no vision." He said the UR was too scared to touch matters involving the Government or a Minister. The Broeders were hamstrung by the Party and Potchefstroom was frustrated by the Party. He warned that many were losing their interest since it seemed as if no Broeder could do or say nothing critical of the Government.

B.   1957 – 1960: The Republic

The Broederbond played an important role in the late Fifties in the growing clamour and demand for the political leaders to tackle head-on the problem of achieving a Republic. Much of the agitation came from speeches and articles by Broeders in the academic, cultural and political fields.

The 1954 Bondsraad was devoted largely to the republican issue. Papers were delivered by Professor A.J.H. van der Walt, Piet Meyer, Strydom, Advocate Van Wyk de Vries, Frikkie de Wet, former UR member and businessman, and R.C. Hiemstra then a Colonel and later chief of the Defence Force.

As a direct result a special study document dealing with the republican policy of the Broederbond was sent to all cells in 1958. It is interesting to note that this document was only circulated after the death of Strydom, and four years after it was discussed at Bondsraad level. Schoeman notes (pages 120 and 121) that Strydom was totally opposed to the Broederbond initiating a series of public discussions on the possible forms a new Republic might take.

The proposal was made by Piet Meyer in 1957, and Thom subsequently discussed it with Strydom who warned against clashes over the form of the Republic and again urged the Bond to stay out of politics.

Strydom reiterated that the AB should confine itself to economic affairs and should assist in capturing the profession of attorneys for the Afrikaner. Just as the church should not involve itself in politics, the Broederbond should also stay out.

But under Verwoerd the situation changed. As an active Broeder, previously holding a key position, he understood the Bond's importance and influence. He realised that a closer alliance between the Government, Party and Broederbond could be of great advantage to himself and strengthen his leadership. As long as the ultimate political leadership remained in his hands, the Broederbond could play a vital role in moulding public opinion, and in influencing Afrikaner Nationalist and other White public opinion on a national scale.

At an early stage Verwoerd took the Broederbond into his confidence on the republican issue. In mid-1959, six months before his Parliamentary announcement in early 1960 that there would be a referendum on the Republic later that year, he informed a Bondsraad meeting that the Broederbond should "accept co-responsibility for the establishment of a Republic."

This was the first time that a Prime Minister had ever attended a Bondsraad meeting.

In the UR secretariat report for the period July 1958 to June 1960 Thom, as chairman, and J.P. van der Spuy, as secretary (and later a Minister), gave details of the Broederbond republican policy document and its involvement in the subsequent referendum campaign. The UR, aided by several committees, and "expert Broeders" and "Broeders in responsible positions", conducted a survey as to what extent the civil service, the Defence Force, the Police, the transport and communications system, the Press and radio, the financial world and utility companies would support the republican ideal in the short term; and the implementation of apartheid as a long-term policy.

A memo was drafted, the matter discussed with those "responsible people in Government," and the UR duly reported to the 1959 Bondsraad. In his report (page seven) Thom stated that after Verwoerd's referendum announcement in Parliament "each Broeder had to help in the registration of pro-republicans as voters, canvass support for the republican form of Government, with the accompanying build-up of large election funds."

All in all the Broederbond secretly spent at least R30 000 on the republican referendum to assist the NP in its campaign. It provided money for a country-wide republican competition organised by the ASB (Afrikaanse Studentebond) and provided money to the SA Academy of Science and Arts for a republican musical composition.

In 1958 the Broederbond formed its youth wing, the "Ruiterwag" ("Guard of Riders"). However, shortly after this the *Rand Daily Mail* published a series of exposés, having obtained original documents when the first Ruiterwag branches were set up in Pretoria. The leak involved at least one interesting incident. One of the founder secretaries was apparently standing in a street, chatting beside his car after a meeting one night in an eastern suburb of Pretoria. He had placed an envelope containing documents – mostly handwritten – on the roof of his car, and simply forgotten about it. When he drove away it fell off – to be picked up shortly afterwards by a non-Nationalist Afrikaans student. Realising the importance of the documents he handed them to a post-graduate student, today a well-known professional man in Pretoria.

The latter then suggested that they should be handed over to the *Sunday Times*. When the student arrived at the SAAN building in Main Street, Johannesburg, the first person he met belonged to the *Rand Daily Mail* – who immediately said he would pass it on to the *Sunday Times*. (The *RDM*, *Sunday Times* and *Sunday Express* all belong to the SA Associated Newspapers' group – which is not to say there is no rivalry between the different papers. On the contrary.)

So the historical documents were intercepted by a sister newspaper, and appeared first in the *RDM*.

Thom said in his report that the dragged-out publicity about the Ruiterwag had "caused great embarrassment." Indeed so.

Apart from the Republic, matters with which the UR also concerned itself included the maintenance of racial segregation in State hospitals; the repatriation of Angola-Afrikaners; the procedure at State funerals; the organising of language festivals; and the position of Afrikaners outside the borders of SA and SWA.

Thom (page 19) reflected the uncertainty at that time in Broeder ranks about the organisation's role. He said that the announcement of a republican referendum had "the fortunate result that there was less speculation . . . on the direction of the Afrikaner Broederbond."

It was a time of uncertainty about the future of apartheid. The "homeland" policy had still to unfold and there was a tremendous debate among Nationalists and Broeders on the position of the Coloureds, with a very small but influential group of ultra-liberals advocating direct representation for Coloureds in Parliament.

The list of tasks with which the local cells were involved (as given by Thom) reveals much about their activities and scope of influence. It included the "composition of school committees, school councils, (educational) controlling bodies, hospital councils, town and city councils, divisional councils, the SA Nursing Council . . ." And so on.

In simple words, each Broederbond cell attempted to control all these particular bodies in its area by either getting Broeders elected to their ranks, or securing Broeder-nominated candidates.

For the two-year period ending June 1960 the UR consisted of H.B. Thom (No 1773), chairman; P.J. Meyer (787), vice chairman; H.J.J. Bingle (1663), Rector of the University of Potchefstroom; R.C. Hiemstra (4152), a senior army officer; Avril Malan MP (2285); S.J. Naudé (788), a church official; Professor S. Pauw (1448); Ds H.J.C. Snijders (1917); A.D. Wassenaar (3947), a well-known Cape businessman; Ds P.M. Smith (3219), a NH Church leader; Dr G.F.C. Troskie (2855) of Kroonstad; W.H. Delport (4572) a Port Elizabeth businessman; and J.F.W. Haak (2916), then an MP and later a Cabinet Minister.

The officials included J.P. van der Spuy (2985), chief secretary; T.J.N. Botha (6159), under-secretary; C. Du P. Kunn (6158), under-secretary; J. Combrink (4); and J.H. Swart (1843), both travelling secretaries.

In addition four women occupied clerical positions.

By June 30, the Broederbond had 5 760 members organised in 409 cells.

C. 1960 – 1968: Full Partnership and Crisis

This period was marked by two major historical development.

Firstly there was the much greater direct involvement of the Broederbond in the affairs of the State, Government and Party politics. In his speech at the jubilee Bondsraad meeting on October 1, 1968, Meyer explained that "because of our active participation in the realisation of our republican ideal, the AB aligned itself closer in practice with the national organising of the political struggle . . ."

State, Party and Broederbond formed the closest alliance possible, forming an intertwining part of an inter-locking Afrikanerdom with Verwoerd as political leader and Meyer leader of its secret foundations. Verwoerd, the visible national leader, and Meyer the "ghost" leader, formed a partnership which enabled Meyer (via the SABC) to submit the South African public to a slow but insidious process of ideological brainwashing.

Secondly, in 1963 there occured the first major large-scale public exposés of the Broederbond in the *Sunday Times;* the first public denouncement of the Broederbond by an ex-member (Beyers Naudé); and the subsequent judicial commission of inquiry into the Bond, the Freemasons and the Sons of England. The latter event shook the organisation to its foundations and led to "two years of crisis" according to anguished remarks in circulars and minutes of UR discussions.

The politicising of the Broederbond after 1960 did not of course mean that it had never been political before then. But it took the Broederbond 12 years after 1948 to work out a "constructive" political role with its elected Broeder politicians. It is true that the 1959 Bondsraad can be regarded as a turning point. According to Pelzer's history the subject of discussion was "The task, work methods and organisation of the Broederbond in view of the prevailing demands." But, to my mind, the radical change was directly attributable to the fact that Verwoerd became Prime Minister in September 1958 and Meyer Broeder chief at the end of 1960.

It is important to note that Verwoerd and Meyer were personally very close – and Verwoerd was a man who had very few confidantes. So it was as much a personal as a political and ideological alliance. The clashes on the UR during the war years – with Verwoerd fighting for the NP and Meyer for the Ossewabrandwag – were forgotten.

The closeness of the Meyer-Verwoerd relationship is illustrated by the fact that when Verwoerd was lying seriously wounded in a Johannesburg hospital after an assasination attempt in April 1960, the only outsider allowed to see him that night with his wife was Meyer – and it would be some time before one of his Ministers managed to get to him.

Verwoerd had a feeling, understanding and appreciation of the power of the Broederbond which Vorster was never to have. It is significant that when he took over as Premier, Verwoerd immediately included Hertzog and Diederichs in his Cabinet – both former UR comrades-in-arms.

Apart from Meyer, Hertzog was one of the very few other people who could be regarded in any way close to Verwoerd.

Until Meyer became chief, the Broederbond had been largely culturally orientated, though obviously pro-Government and pro-National Party. The greater direct involvement in government led the 1961 Bondsraad to appoint 14 expert task groups; and another three were formed at the 1963 Bondsraad. Eventually they were expanded to 19 in the late Sixties.

The field covered by these groups and the composition of the membership of each committee gave them the status of secret watchdogs over every aspect of public life. It was never a question of the Broederbond and its committees crudely dictating to the various government bodies and departments – in all cases influential men on these committees included key men in government and public life. The committees – basically a government within a government – monitored the following areas: "non-White" affairs; the Coloured group; the Indians; technical and scientific matters; youth affairs; planning; Press matters; economics; agriculture; Africa; education; religion; defence; relations with the English; the "Jewish problem"; Sports; Immigration; Communism; liberalism and Freemasonry; and group inter-relationships.

In the special study documents circulated to all cells, and in the regular monthly circulars, the findings of the committees were divulged. Advice to Broeders on any subject concerning the State or politics was given.

Details of the individuals involved in these task groups and of the Broederbond involvement in government will be discussed later.

Although Verwoerd knew that as Prime Minister and Party leader he had absolute power, he never showed it in his dealings with the Broederbond, accepting the organisation as a co-partner by directly involving it in government affairs. In so doing he actually strengthened his own position, since he knew he had the absolute loyalty and support of the Broederbond leadership. The secret body was his second line of defence, to be used when other methods or channels failed to achieve certain objectives.

The Beyers Naudé incident, with all its implications, was the most dramatic in the history of the Broederbond. It mirrored wider turmoil and anxiety among Afrikaner Nationalists about the existence of the Bond and its activities, and about the moral and Christian justice of apartheid.

From the end of the Fifties onwards, searching questions about this racist policy were asked in Afrikaner Nationalist, academic and church circles.

At the end of 1960 the famous Cottesloe ecumenical conference took place in Johannesburg. Leading ministers of the NG and Gereformeerde Churches – most of them Broeders – supported resolutions which rejected basic aspects of government policy regarding the Coloureds and the urban Africans, though they accepted that in principle a policy of just separation and ethnic differentiation complied with scriptural demands.

However, the Broederbond machine soon got into operation, and at subsequent Synods the respective churches rejected the proposals which their own leaders earlier supported.

One point on which NG theologians attending the Cottesloe conference agreed was that the Afrikaans churches should take the initiative in forming a new ecumenical body. However with the political storm engineered by the Broederbond over Cottesloe, most got cold feet. It was left to Beyers Naudé, and a few others – who regarded loyalty to the demands of the scriptures of greater importance than loyalty to the Broederbond, Afrikaner unity and the interests of the NP – to push ahead.

Accordingly, in 1962, *Pro Veritate,* an ecumenical monthly, was established. Naudé was the first editor while still a minister of the wealthy Northcliff Aasvoëlkop congregation and Moderator of the Southern Transvaal Synod. In August 1963 he was to become the first director of the Christian Institute, a position he occupied until his banning on October

19, 1977. Thus the Institute was in the first place the direct result of the ferment in the Afrikaner churches in the early Sixties.

In Afrikaans church circles there was considerable soul-searching on the issues Naudé was facing. There were demands by various ministers and congregations that the position of the Broederbond be investigated: could one be a Christian and a Broeder? Was apartheid just?

Moreover, it was a period of anti-Communist hysteria in South Africa – and "Communist" could mean "liberal". A number of Communist ANC leaders and saboteurs were arrested or fled the country. In public statements, speeches and articles, "liberalism," "humanism" and "internationalism" were regarded as a danger comparable to Communism, indeed, as part of the same process.

It was against this background that the events involving the *Sunday Times,* Naudé, myself, and the publication of Broederbond documents, took place in April 1963.

I have mentioned that Naudé gave Bond documents to Geyser, a fellow NH Church theologian; that Geyser, without Naudé's knowledge, passed them on to Bloomberg; that Bloomberg, with my assistance, published the first documents on April 25, 1963; and that at the beginning of April the Broederbond cancelled at the last minute its annual Bondsraad and that of the Ruiterwag.

There followed seven anxious months for the Bond leadership when they attempted – with the assistance of the Special Branch – to find and plug the leak. Publicly and privately the AB claimed that the reports were part of the Communist and liberal onslaught against the Afrikaner. The attack on the Broederbond was seen as being the first step in the destruction of Afrikanerdom.

In the Bond circular of May 4, 1963 – No 1/63/64 – Piet Koornhof, then chief secretary, discussed the *Sunday Times'* disclosures under the heading "A new Challenge." Piously, he claimed: "The latest onslaught against the Afrikaner Broederbond clearly carries the Communist pattern of suspicion-sowing . . . of subverting Afrikanerdom and its holiest spiritual possessions." Koornhof claimed that because the Broederbond "has been most intimately interwoven with the cause and task of the Afrikaner, it can obviously be accepted that the Communistic powers threatening South Africa would direct their onslaughts at us."

On May 21, 1963, the postponed meeting of the Bondsraad was held on the farm Tweefontein, belonging to Broeder P.A. van Wyk, near Bapsfontein, between Johannesburg and Pretoria. This was the first Raad not held in a city. Special security measures were accordingly taken, delegates were not even informed where it would take place. They had to meet at pre-determined places, from where they were transported to the farm.

In all, 344 delegates representing 379 divisions and 142 "visiting members" attended. Only 59 cells were not represented.

Meyer, as chairman, assured the members that the UR knew which *Sunday Times* staff member was responsible for the reports; what his links with leftist groups were; and how he would set about to obtain further information. Ironically, however, Bloomberg was already out of the country, and it had been decided that I would continue the exposés – quietly, underground, anonymous, not in the light of day, in fact in the best Broederbond tradition.

The Bondsraad meeting took place on the very day that I left Johannesburg to meet Bloomberg in Botswana.

Members were urged to take special precautions to ensure the secrecy of the Bond.

They were threatened that any contravention of the extremely strict secrecy regulations would lead to summary expulsion. After the meeting a special ceremony was performed around a campfire; stones were stacked upon each other, as at other historic occasions, and the Broeders pledged themselves to continue the struggle, singing the national anthem while they were at it.

One extremely important decision was taken: it was agreed to collect R1 m. within the next five years, the task to be completed by 1968, when the AB would celebrate its fiftieth anniversary. The fund would be the Broeder response to the *Sunday Times* revelations – a direct reply to the "new onslaught" on the organisation. It would enable the Bond to intensify its activities during a period of crisis and embark on various new projects. And it would finance the task force committees; the watchdogs would have monetary teeth.

After this Bondsraad the Broeder exposés continued, until Van den Bergh and his Special Branch discovered the sources and the *Sunday Times* was raided. Naudé, Geyser and myself were questioned, culminating in dramatic statements by Naudé and Geyser; and by Meyer on behalf of the Broederbond.

These three statements are of great historical importance. Naudé's is a moving document of a man explaining a great personal crisis. However, because Naudé is banned today this statement, which was broadcast along with that of Meyer by the SABC, can no longer be quoted.

Meyer concluded his statement by saying: "From its foundation to the present day, as Mr Naudé well knows, the Bond has, by means of well-motivated appeals to the leaders concerned, fought all attacks, on whatever terrain, which were intended or aimed at the destruction of the independent survival of the Afrikaner nation as a Christian Western nation with the God-given task; while it occupied itself in the main with the cultural and moral enrichment and strengthening of this nation . . .

"The Bond does not apologise for the fact that it has, since its foundation, wholeheartedly supported and actively propagated the apartheid policy of our country and is still doing so. If this has now become a bone of contention to Mr Naudé, the executive council is sorry that he waited 22 years to fight it in the way he is doing now.

"Finally, this – the members of the Bond are Christians who do not regard themselves as better than others but who, on the grounds of ability and their undertaking to live in harmony with others, are prepared to sacrifice more, to give more, and work harder for the future of South Africa as a whole with its great variety of ethnic groups . . . without expecting honour or compensation and without striving for honoured positions or self-interest."

Geyser's full statement appears as Annexure D. Reference to it has already been made in the introduction.

As a result of this publicity, at the end of November 1963 Naudé and Geyser received a number of death threats.

The whole issue of the Broederbond got a thorough airing in the Press. Laurence Gandar, the brilliant editor of the *Rand Daily Mail* stated this in an editorial on November 22, 1963: "The Broederbond has become a cancerous growth in the living body of South Africa. It is an arrogant self-chosen elite, operating by stealth and intrigue, its early cultural aspirations swamped by neo-Fascist ideas on race and colour. By refusing to face the facts of the 20th Century, it is driving this country to its destruction. It is an evil that must be rooted out before it is too late." (See annexure E for the full text). Gandar dealt with the manner in which the SABC – a public corporation – was used to defend the interests of "a completely faceless organisation."

And two days later the *Sunday Times,* in an editorial entitled "The Great Broederbond Burglary of 1963," referred to a statement by Japie Basson, then a United Party MP. "As a result of Broederbond pressure, the Special Branch police are becoming the Gestapo of South Africa," he said. (See annexure F.) Mentioning its own role in the affair and the absurdity of the burglary allegation, *the Sunday Times* spoke of "this phantom burgalry, this figment of a fevered Broeder's imagination . . ." And as far as a Communist conspiracy is concerned, this deserves no comment, apart from noting the tragic fact that the Broeders actually believed this fiction.

The minutes of the special UR of November 12, 1963, when the sources of the exposés were revealed, show the uncertainty and anxiety the crisis had caused in Broederbond ranks. Special "visitors" attending the UR were H.J. van den Berg and one D.J. Malan.

The following important points were noted:

- "Any semblance of a church split should be fought with the available information."
- "The UR relies on the Afrikaner volk to make known the whole course of events in the best possible manner in order to reveal the methods of Communistic infiltration," – perhaps a reference to the subsequent role of the SABC in the affair?
- "The influence of Beyers Naudé and his soulmates should not be under-estimated."
- "If details are revealed by us and they lead to an action for libel, the whole functioning of the AB could be revealed. In a criminal case this will not necessarily happen."
- "Any reference to church matters in our documents must be treated with great care."
- "Thanks are expressed for the work done by Broeders in *responsible circles* in solving the case."

This last remark could only have been a reference to the Security Police. In fact, at the next Bondsraad in 1964, a special medal was awarded to Van den Bergh, together with one to Broeder P.A. van Wyk whose farm was used for the 1963 Bondsraad. This meeting also noted that "there was concern among Broeders in responsible circles about an apparent increasing hostility in certain circles within the National Party against the AB." This hostility went so far that in Smithfield in the Free State as well as in some places in the Transvaal, Nationalists formed an organisation called the Nasionalistebond to fight the Broederbond within the Party.

The Nasionalistebond was initiated by Koos de Wet himself, a Broeder. However, in 1964, the organisation petered out when the Broederbond privately "persuaded" De Wet to abandon it.

In 1963 and 1964 the *Sunday Times* gave great prominence to the movement. Although never very strong it reflected a widespread feeling among many Afrikaner Nationalists who were bitter at being excluded from the elite.

In circular No 7/63/64 of December 2, 1963, chief secretary Koornhof said that "1963 will be known in our history as the year in which the enemies of our volk launched a most subtle onslaught against us." However, the future of the organisation "is in the hands of Him who guides the destinies of people and nations."

1964 would prove equally tough for the Broederbond. The constant Press attacks, and those by Opposition politicians, culminated in major debates in Parliament.

On January 21, 1964, Sir de Villiers Graaff, leader of the United Party, demanded in the no-confidence debate that Prime Minister Verwoerd should resign from the Bond. Graaff said any secret organisation involved in public life was unhealthy.

Verwoerd refused. He defended the Broederbond by saying that all sorts of organisations held secret discussions. Even the Oppenheimer group's directors held secret talks, he said. He had been a member for 25 years, dismissed Graaff's challenge as "stupid," and denied that his membership meant that he could not fulfil his duties as Premier satisfactorily.

Verwoerd said that if Graaff proposed it he was prepared to investigate the affairs of not only the Broederbond, but of other groups which conducted their affairs in secret, such as the Freemasons, the Sons of England, and certain financial and other groups like the Oppenheimer organisation.

Four days later Graaff and Verwoerd clashed, causing an uproar in the House of Assembly. Verwoerd adamantly refused an exclusive investigation into the Bond and insisted that Sir De Villiers include the other groups in any investigation; he said the onus lay with Graaff.

Sir De Villiers: "I think it is necessary as regards the Broederbond and I think there is a *prima facie* case against that organisation. I do not think there is a *prima facie* case against the Freemasons or the Sons of England and I do not have enough knowledge to make a decision on the Anglo American Corporation." (Laughter.)

Dr Verwoerd: "You don't dare propose such an investigation."

Sir de Villiers: "As regards the Freemasons, there are 38 books in the library and the Prime Minister can even buy a calendar on the meetings of their various lodges from a bookseller. I have sought in vain for such material on the Broederbond . . ." He went on: "The Prime Minister made an offer to me and I accept it. I did not even see it as a challenge."

Dr Verwoerd: "But accept my challenge as I put it."

Smiling broadly at the Prime Minister, who throughout the exchange shifted uneasily in his seat, Sir De Villiers once more welcomed a commission of inquiry into the Broederbond, adding that if Dr Verwoerd wished to include any other organisations he would agree. But he emphasised that his complaint was specifically against the Broederbond. When it became obvious that Verwoerd would not accept these terms, Graaff indicated that the Opposition would take the matter further at a later stage.

Verwoerd had clearly made one of the biggest tactical blunders of his career. In the parliamentary duel Graaff dramatically gave the Government a free hand to investigate any secret society or other body it wished – provided it investigated the Broederbond as well.

Broeder Verwoerd was most reluctant to allow any such investigation. And an inquiry into Anglo American – the biggest financial enterprise in South Africa – which would be basically of a political nature could have serious international financial repercussions.

That week also brought to light more information about the Government's view of the publication of the Broederbond documents in the *Sunday Times*. Vorster, as Minister of Justice, said in Parliament on January 22 that the police had evidence that five attempts had been made to break into the offices of the AB.

Asked by Marais Steyn (UP Yeoville) whether a charge had been laid about the alleged theft of the documents, the Minister said a charge had been laid. To which Steyn replied: "Then it is a false charge." Vorster challenged Steyn to repeat the statement outside the House and went on to say that what General Keevy had said about the matter was perfectly true. Every member of the Security Branch was a policeman – and any member of the police force could be used to investigate any case.

92

Verwoerd's attempt to avoid investigating the Broederbond brought into the open the intimate connections between the State, the National Party and the Bond.

On January 26, 1964, Mervis, in a brilliant analytical article, dealt with the Government's arguments. He claimed that the debate appeared to prove two things:

1. The Broederbond revelations, backed as they were by documentary proof, had thrown the Government off balance; and 2. Sir De Villiers Graaff had spoken the truth when he said that Broeders (including the Prime Minister) had a first loyalty to the Broederbond and a second loyalty to their country.

On February 2, 1964, Bloomberg hit back in a statement to the *Sunday Times* from London, where he was then studying. He said that Vorster's allegations about the theft of Bond documents were a South African version of Hitler's Reichstag Fire plot.

He said that allegations that one Kodesh, a named Communist, had conspired with him to burglarise the Broederbond offices were false. He was not part of any Communist plot or conspiracy. "Mr Vorster, protected by parliamentary immunity, alleges that Kodesh and I offered money to procure the theft of Broederbond documents. I emphatically deny that I conspired with Kodesh to obtain documents, or that with him I offered payment for a burglary or any other purpose. Kodesh had as much to do with my inquiries into and reporting of Broederbond matters as the man in the moon."

Pointing out discrepancies in the Government's claims he added: "Linked with the Communist plot story is the contemptible charge that the *Sunday Times* disclosures were an attack on the Afrikaner nation. Since when has the Broederbond become the proprietor of Afrikanerdom?

"This is akin to saying that critics of the John Birch Society are slurring America's national honour, or that an attack on the Nazi Party is an insult to German culture.

"What the revelations did was to expose the Broederbond's racially divisive role; its extensive behind-the-scenes grip on the administration; and its suffocation of independent thought among Afrikaners."

Years later, in 1976, Bloomberg returned to South Africa – and no action was taken against him.

On April 27, 1964, it was announced in Parliament that Graaff and Verwoerd had agreed that a thorough-going investigation would be launched into the activities of the Freemasons, the Sons of England and the Broederbond. Details would be announced later.

Significantly, Verwoerd had dropped all mention of Anglo American. Later, however, he was to initiate his own secret Broederbond-based inquiry into Anglo.

Opposition members and newspapers expressed the hope that the investigation would be a public judicial inquiry, but on June 9, 1964, Verwoerd announced that the one-man commission of inquiry into the three secret organisations would in fact itself be conducted in secrecy.

Mr. Justice D.H. Botha of the Appelate Division would investigate whether any of the societies were guilty of:

a) Any form of subversion, treason or intrigue, directed at obtaining for itself domination of or unlawful influence over the people or the State, or any of its organs such as the central government, the provincial authorities or the administration of justice;

b) Anything which might weaken the determination and will of the people of South Africa in the fight for their survival;

c) The acquisition of funds from hostile sources, or the use of its own funds, for the financing of subversive action against the authority of the State, or of threats to the security, peace and order of the people; or for the overthrow of the Government by impermissible and undemocratic methods;

d) Nepotism or interference in appointments and promotions in the public service, the Defence Force or the police in such a way that people were appointed or promoted for reasons other than merit;

e) Attempts to subvert the relations between the English and Afrikaans- speaking people with the object of bringing about strife and national discord, and of undermining national unity;

f) Improper or objectionable activities which harmed, prejudiced or undermined the rights, liberties or interests of persons or groups; or which aimed at controlling other organisations in an irregular manner;

g) Subversion, in any form, of the morals, customs and way of life of the people of South Africa by circumventing or transgressing the country's laws, or by any other means;

h) Becoming a serious danger to peace and order in the body politic by exerting influence in an impermissible manner in the economic and cultural spheres;

i) Attempts to dominate the Prime Minister, Ministers, administrators or any other persons in authority in an effort to use him or them in the service of an organisation in such a manner that, as far as the performance of his or their official duties was concerned, loyalty was in the first place shown to the organisation and not to the State.

In a Press statement on June 9, 1964, Graaff completely rejected the commission, "because it amounts to a secret inquiry into a secret organisation." In a special statement the Opposition leader said: "In some respects the terms of reference are wide and extravagant, in others they are so narrow that many of the charges against the Broederbond cannot be brought to the attention of the commission."

Sir De Villiers added: "I have the highest regard for the appeal judge who has been appointed, but it should be remembered that he will not be sitting in a court. It appears that he will have to be detective, inquisitor, advocate and judge at the same time – no easy task for any man to combine all these functions."

Discussing the "extravagant" terms of reference, Sir De Villiers said: "They seem to ensure that a verdict of not guilty will be returned . . . Dr Verwoerd's proposals are utterly unsatisfactory. As the inquiry will be in secret it will not have the manifest appearance of justice."

The *Rand Daily Mail* said in an editorial on June 10, 1964, entitled "Why in Secret?": "The Prime Minister's reasons for having the inquiry held in secret are not convincing. He says, for example, that there was no indication that a crime had been committed. Yet one of the terms of reference relates to secret organisations obtaining funds from hostile sources or using their own funds for subversive activities. Clearly Sir de Villiers Graaff is right when he says that the public should have been given the opportunity to know the nature of the evidence laid before the commission and to observe the process of justice in action."

And in another statement to the *Sunday Times* on June 14, 1964, Graaff said: "I stipulated that the commission should be open to the public as our courts normally are. Neither Dr Verwoerd nor anyone else on the Nationalist side contested this at the time of our public debate. Furthermore, our law as it stands makes no provision for a commission in secret and is being changed by the Government during the coming week to make this possible.

"The terms of reference are Dr Verwoerd's alone. They are so wide that they include a

94

number of crimes of which none of the organisations have, so far as I am aware, been accused – for example, treason and the use of funds to undermine the authority of the State.

"In some respects the terms of reference are hopelessly narrow. Thus, any hold or influence the Broederbond may have on the SABC and on other important public and semi-public bodies cannot be investigated.

"I have the highest regard for the judge who has been appointed to undertake this task. But I feel that handicapped by these terms of reference and deprived of the assistance of either assessors or fellow judges, he will be labouring under very great disadvantages.

"So many tasks impose a very great burden on one judge, even in an inquiry into limited matters, largely of a personal nature. They are quite inappropriate for the vast tasks designated here, particularly where the relationships of our Afrikaans-speaking people with each other, and the relationships between the two great sections of our people are also vitally affected.

"Such a situation requires a hearing in public in accordance with our commission law and, in addition, it requires . . . speedy, yet complete investigation of the facts.

"The existence of the Broederbond, Dr Verwoerd's membership of it, and its suspected activities, are to me today one of the main stumbling blocks on the road to national unity."

On June 21, 1964, the well-known *Sunday Times* political commentator, Stanley Uys, raised the most important objection of all. Verwoerd had appointed a commission to investigate a secret organisation of which he, by his own admission, was a member. Uys wrote: "The Prime Minister should have recused himself from the whole situation. He should not have appointed the judge, defined the terms of reference, or stated the conditions under which the commission should operate."

The upshot was that all public interest in the inquiry was lost. The UP and other Bond critics announced that they would not testify.

On July 31, 1964, chief secretary Piet Koornhof submitted a 24-page memorandum with 20 annexures stating the Broederbond's case. He included circulars and study documents of the period August 1, 1962, to June 30, 1964; brochures given to all new members; and the findings of various church Synods which had cleared the Bond of misdemeanour.

On March 6, 1965, the commission gave its findings – the Broederbond, and the other two organisations, were not guilty of any of the possible accusations. Malherbe's comment (page 682 onwards) is important. He said that the commission had "interviewed a number of heads of departments in the public service. These witnesses apparently assured him that there was no nepotism . . . this evidence the commissioner apparently accepted, because he stated in his report: 'If individual members of the Broederbond did favour Broeders in promotion to posts, the organisation as such cannot be blamed for it.' Furthermore, the commissioner stated that he could 'find no indication of party political matters, or of any subversive activities, or of anything which could render the organisation guilty of any conduct referred to in the commission's terms of reference . . . It was only for reasons of efficiency that the Broederbond had to work in secret.' He also could find 'no evidence for the grounds on which the Government, in December 1944, had banned officials in the service of the State from being members of the Bond or from participating in its proceedings.'

"Apparently the furthes back into the history of the Broederbond that the commissioner went was to refer to the series of articles which appeared in the *Transvaler* in December 1944 protesting against the injustice perpetrated by the Smuts Government in 'banning' such a worthy organisation.

"As already pointed out these articles were written by the chairman of the Broederbond,

Professor J.C. van Rooy and I.M. Lombard, secretary of the Broederbond. For the benefit of the general public they set out at length the aims and aspirations of the AB. According to these statements the Bond was an organisation 'in which Afrikaners could find each other in the midst of great confusion and disunity and be able to work together for the survival of the Afrikaner people in South Africa and the promotion of its interests . . . Although it is not unimportant for the realisation of its aims which political party is in power, it does not arrogate to itself the function of a political party by its fixed aims. The Bond is a service organisation intended to serve the Afrikaner, and its field of operations is the sphere of work of the Afrikaner people as a separate historial Protestant, Christian cultural community.'

"Apparently the furthest back into the history of the Broederbond that the commissioner went was to refer to the series of articles which appeared in the *Transvaler* in December 1944 protesting against the injustice perpetrated by the Smuts Government in 'banning' such a worthy organisation.

promotion of good relations between the Whites and non-White groups of South Africa . . . Assistance to one another which envisages preferential treatment is not tolerated by the Bond.' The commissioner also found no evidence that the Bond had 'worked for the formation of a solid anti-British bloc.'

"Referring to the 'banning' of the organisation the commissioner stated that "little information is available regarding the grounds for banning . . . since most of the documents of the Defence Information Service which could possibly have thrown some light on the question were destroyed a few years after the end of World War II . . . Under the circumstances no inference whatsoever can be drawn to the detriment of the Bond on the strength of the fact that the ban was in fact imposed.'

"It seems clear that the Commissioner did not have before him as evidence the record of the speeches made on the occasion of the secret silver jubilee meeting of the Broederbond held at Bloemfontein in 1943, when the achievements of the Broederbond were recounted to the accompaniment of the most blatant anti-English sentiments directed also against English-speaking South African citizens. This record General Smuts had in his possession together with other evidence of the Broederbond's intrigues during the war, e.g. its secret organisation of a nation-wide strike by school-children and students.

"Further, the commissioner made no reference to the persistent and wide-spread efforts of the Broederbond and its affiliated organisations such as the Federasie van Afrikaanse Kultuurvereniginge and the Nasionale Instituut vir Opvoeding en Onderwys during the 1940s to sabotage the implementation of the Government's dual-medium policy in the schools.

"The strangest blind spot of all in the commissioner's report is the fact that nowhere did he make any mention of the very serious strictures made by General Hertzog in 1935 strongly condemning the Broederbond's party political intrigues and its infiltration into the schools. It is difficult to understand how such a public pronouncement by a great Afrikaner on the Broederbond's activities could have been so completely ignored by the commissioner.

"It seems that the commissioner simply accepted the Broederbond's own version of its record as a noble enterprise with motives as pure as driven snow, and declared it to be nothing more than 'a vigorous and dynamic organisation' designed to further the interests of the Afrikaners."

Laurence Gandar, in a special front-page editorial on March 6, 1965, commented:

"What an astonishing document is the report of the one man Commission of Inquiry into certain secret societies, notably the Broederbond! Its conclusions are completely at variance with those that any reasonable reading of the published evidence about the Broederbond over the years will produce . . ."

What of the Broederbond and the Government in this period? Schoeman (page 184) says that Verwoerd had acted virtually without consulting Meyer or the UR when he spoke out in Parliament in January 1964. When he hinted in the no-confidence debate of a possibility of an investigation into the Broederbond which might also include Anglo American, the Freemasons and the Sons of England, he apparently did so independently of other Bond leaders. Verwoerd only afterwards contacted Meyer to find out whether the AB would have any objection to this.

According to Schoeman, "The UR then informed him that it could not agree to such an investigation. Verwoerd then wrote a letter to the UR in which he said that he, as a member of the Broederbond, totally abided with the decision of the highest body of the organisation.

"So the fact that Verwoerd later continued with the appointment of a commission suggested that he had persuaded the Broederbond to agree to it."

It is important to note that none of the facts in Schoeman's highly controversial book were ever seriously disputed at the time of publication.

Meyer and other UR leaders were apparently most upset when it appeared that Verwoerd might agree to an inquiry. At the end of April, 1964, Meyer held a discussion with Verwoerd on the issue.

Later, Meyer told other UR members that Verwoerd would not permit an inquiry into the Broederbond – only an investigation into particular charges carefully formulated by the Prime Minister himself. Meyer had also made it clear that the Bond would refuse to divulge its membership to any commission of inquiry.

This apparent prior agreement between Verwoerd and the AB leadership, before the actual appointment of the commission, is confirmed in Broederbond documents. In circular 3/64/65 of May 5, 1964, Koornhof said of the investigation that "the struggle does not in the first place involve the AB as such . . ." It was designed to "Break Afrikanerdom" and to bring about Verwoerd's fall. And he assured members that "the UR believes that an investigation into the activities and aims of the organisation does not mean that membership must be revealed . . ."

Significantly, he added: "The UR records its conviction that the Prime Minister will only allow an investigation on such conditions as will be to the advantage of our country in the present difficult world situation. *He will not do something which will lead to the destruction of, or render powerless our organisation and our volk.*"

The circular warned against the danger of a wedge being "driven between the Government and the AB." It concluded by making "a serious call to all members to be calm and *to have the necessary confidence in the UR and the Prime Minister . . .*"

Meyer further explicated the relationship between the Broederbond and the compliant Verwoerd when he addressed the Bondsraad late in 1964. Prior to the appointment of the commission Verwoerd had discussed the whole matter with him as a fellow Broeder. He could therefore say in confidence: "*We await the report of this commission without worry or concern.* We are convinced that the finding of the commission, like those of our Afrikaans churches, will put an end to the organised liberalistic and Communistic attempt to use the AB as an instrument . . . to divide our church and our volk and to cause political division among national Afrikaners." So "one of the most dramatic" phases in the Bond's history drew to a close.

Apart from increased political activities through the task force committees, special attention has been given to combatting Communism. In April 1964 a massive volkskongres on Communism was held in Pretoria. It led to a hysterical campaign against liberalism, regarded as the forerunner of Communism. In 1965 the Broederbond founded and sponsored the National Council against Communism. This organisation became a stronghold for super-conservatives such as Ds J.D. Vorster, the Prime Minister's brother, Gert Beetge and Adriaan Pont – the latter two later to become HNP leaders.

On March 10, 1964, a special circular informed members that those who wished were free to resign. But those who remained had to sign a document reaffirming their membership, and a pledge "to maintain the confidential nature of the organisation and to regard all your promises *(beloftes)* as binding until death." They also had to pledge that they were not members of any other secret or semi-secret organisation.

Only eight members resigned. They were: Professor J.J. Muller of Stellenbosch; Ds J.W. Hanekom of Darling; Dr O.W. van Niekerk, a medical doctor, of Mafeking; Bill de Klerk, the famous writer, of Paarl; A.M. van Wyk, scientist, of Hermanus; Ds T. Botha, of Johannesburg; J. Maarschalk, a teacher, of Pretoria; and D.J. Brand, a missionary, of Dordrecht.

The UR for the period 1963 to 1965 consisted of:

Chairman	**P.J. Meyer (787)**
Vice Chairman	**J.S. Gericke (1999)**
Members	**D.P.M. Beukes (2735)**
	H.J.J. Bingle (1663)
	J.P.V.S. Bruwer (5022)
	R.C. Hiemstra (4152)
	S.J. Naudé (788)
	J.H. Stander (770)
	A.P. Treurnicht (4240)
	G.F.C. Troskie (2895)
Co-opted:	**S.P. Botha (4418)**
	F.D. Conradie (4765)
	J.A. Hurter (3298)
	P.E. Rosseau (2712)
	P.M. Smith (3219)

The executive council had eight full-time secretaries and organisers, and seven women as clerical assistants and by February 28, 1965 there were 6 966 members in 484 cells.

Meyer and Naudé Botha, who became chief secretary when Koornhof went to Parliament at the end of 1964, concluded triumphantly: "The AB continues to prove that it is still the organisation which exercises the greatest influence among Afrikaners."

D.   1966 – 1970 Strife and Dissension

John Vorster took over as Prime Minister on September 13, 1966, a week after Dr Verwoerd's assasination. This signalled the beginning of a new era in the fortunes of the Broederbond. There would come about a gradual, subtle alteration in the Broederbond's status – from being a co-partner of the National Party, to becoming only a *"stut organisasie"* ("support organisation").

The situation arose because of infighting within the NP centred on the person of Dr Albert Hertzog, former UR member, and a Cabinet Minister under Verwoerd and Vorster.

On August 14 and August 21, 1966 – prior to Verwoerd's death – I wrote two major articles in the *Sunday Times* on the emergence of an undercover conservative faction within the National Party, known as the Hertzog Group, so called after its spiritual leader.

At the time my articles were discounted by Afrikaans and English newspapers alike; and Vorster attacked me publicly at Koffiefontein in April 1967 as a person not to be taken seriously. Yet in October 1969, when the Hertzog Group came into the open, the names of the Nationalists – many prominent public figures – involved in the new party, the HNP, had almost all been mentioned in those first two reports.

The basis of the Hertzog Group was yet another secret organisation – the Afrikaner Orde (AO). Hertzog founded it in 1929 and was to manipulate it throughout its existence. The leaders of the Afrikaner Orde were all Broeders, and from the Fifties onwards two of its executives were appointed by the Broederbond while a Bond official reported on its activities to the UR.

This secret organisation within a secret organisation was based largely in Pretoria, and by 1966 had some 600 members. Its existence had all along been a source of friction between Hertzog and his fellow Broeder leaders, the latter fearing that he might use it for his political ambitions, and that a rival secret organisation might weaken the exclusive AB itself.

Until my articles only the initiated were aware of the existence of the Hertzog Group and the Afrikaner Orde. The AO operated very subtly, through its own front organisations, or infiltration of Broederbond and other Afrikaans Nationalist front and cultural bodies.

The Hertzog Group was small, but extremely influential. Its direct supporters or fellow travellers occupied many influential key positions. They were to be found in Parliament, the churches, academic and cultural bodies, rate-payers' associations in Pretoria, labour organisations and newspapers.

In the early Sixties it was the Hertzog Group, together with Piet Meyer and other Broeders, who organised the Congress to Combat Communism and involved themselves in the campaign against liberalism.

By 1966 its basic theme was one of outspoken conservatism. Its prime fear was that Verwoerd and later Vorster were diluting the sound policies of racial separation, and that the position of the Afrikaner as a separate entity might be endangered. From then on the struggle within the NP gathered momentum, first covertly, then publicly in cultural bodies – ostensibly on matters not directly related to politics.

Ironically, Hertzog Group MPs were largely responsible for getting Vorster elected party leader and Prime Minister, above the old stalwart Ben Schoeman.

The issues that rankled the Hertzogites under Vorster included the liberalisation of the sports policy (on this very issue the Hertzog Group MPs broke away in September 1969 to form the HNP); immigration, with tens of thousands of foreigners seen as a threat to Afrikanerdom; Vorster's so-called "outward policy" in Africa; the possibility of Black diplomats and independent homelands; and the new policy of closer English-Afrikaans co-operation.

In October 1966 Wimpie De Klerk, editor of *Die Transvaler,* the National Party mouthpiece in Johannesburg, coined the famous phrases "verlig" and "verkramp" to categorise the opposing groups of Nationalists. ("Verlig" – liberal or enlightened; and "verkramp" – narrow-minded, ultra-conservative).

Over-simplification of the conflict was inevitable. The Hertzog Group supporters were labelled verkramp, and the Vorster supporters verlig. The fact, of course, is that the vast majority of Afrikaner Nationalists were and are verkramp, and only a small minority verlig.

Moreover, the clash really turned on the style and strategy of Afrikaner survival and dominance. Ultimate objectives remained common cause. Many observers, like myself at the time, tended to regard the differences as rather more fundamental – a view strengthened by the fact that Vorster was not a Verwoerd-style ideologue or party philosopher, but a pragmatist – naturally within the framework of apartheid.

The details of these three years of NP infighting are to be found in *"Vorster se 1 000 Dae"* (*"Vorster's 1 000 Days"*) by Beaumont Schoeman, a former senior journalist with *Hoofstad* and *Dagbreek* and later editor of *Die Afrikaner,* mouthpiece of the HNP. Schoeman views the battle from the Hertzog viewpoint. And there is my book: *"Die Verkrampte Aanslag"* (*"The Verkrampte Onslaught"*).

The NP infighting and Afrikaner dissension and strife were naturally reflected in the Broederbond. It found itself in a Forties-type situation, desperately attempting to keep peace between various Afrikaner Nationalist political groups. But this time the fight was within the party itself. A profound conviction of all Afrikaner Nationalists, whether verlig or verkramp, was that a major split would "play into the hands of the enemy," that however deep the differences the political machine should be kept intact.

The vast majority of Afrikaner Nationalists were sympathetic to the conservative ideals of the Hertzog Group, although the latter often weakened their case by taking too extreme a line. On the other hand, Afrikaner Nationalists instinctively followed the party leadership and would frequently accept a policy or adjustment simply for this reason, and not because they were necessarily in agreement.

In the Broederbond there was friction at all levels. Moreover, at least two UR members, Meyer and Treurnicht, were strong supporters of Hertzog, while men such as Koornhof and Ds J.S. Gericke, Moderator of the NG Church, were strong Vorster supporters. The political divisions were a major point of discussion.

Significantly, Vorster and the UR went into the matter on several occasions.

Meyer, as Broeder chief and SABC chairman – with Treurnicht as a newspaper editor and UR member – meant that the Hertzog Group gained considerable, influential support. Together with other Broeders they publicly resented the verkrampte tag given to the Hertzog Group, first by the *Sunday Times* and later by Afrikaans newspapers. Accordingly they became involved in public clashes and direct confrontations with the Broeder editors of some Afrikaans papers who supported Vorster against Hertzog and who had unleashed an onslaught against Hertzog's supporters. The two editors most deeply concerned were Piet Cillie of *Die Burger* and Schalk Pienaar of *Beeld,* then a Sunday newspaper.

Cillie, Pienaar and others publicly questioned the concepts of "conservatism" and "Christian Nationalism" as explained and expounded by Meyer and other diehard verkramptes. So this was a period of alienation and tension between Bond and party, and the disturbed relationship between the two was openly discussed in 1968 for the first time. The spark was the result of the Swellendam parliamentary by-election on April 25, 1968, when hundreds of Nationalist voters abstained. During the campaign they openly accused the Rapportryers and Broederbond of interfering in the nomination struggle between the Nationalist candidates.

History was made when National Party newspapers openly blamed the Bond for the setback. On April 27, 1968, Dawie, political columnist of *Die Burger* asked: "Is the relationship between the National Party, the Broederbond and the Rapportryers in all respects correct? Or can the United Party achieve success against the Government at places other than Swellendam, merely by fighting against the Broederbond and the Rapportryers?''

On May 6, 1968, P.W. Botha, Minister of Defence and the NP's Cape leader, made a significant speech at Wellington. He made it clear that the party would not permit itself to be dictated to by any other power when it came to policy, organisation and authority.

Both Botha and Dawie stressed that the Broederbond and Rapportryers were *"buite organisasies"* ("outside organisations") and not political bodies. This was remarkable; it was the first time since the war that a Nationalist Cabinet Minister – and a Broeder – had, even by implication, criticised the Broederbond.

The reason for the new line was that the Hertzog Group – aided and abetted by Broeders such as Meyer, Treurnicht and others – was sheltering behind the Broederbond while continuing its political strategy of subverting Vorster's leadership. Vorster supporters were convinced that Meyer's ostensible efforts to preserve Afrikaner unity clouded the fact that he was using the Broederbond to help the Hertzog Group to prevent Vorster from "liberalising" aspects of government policy.

The relationship between Meyer and Vorster was precisely the opposite of that between Meyer and Verwoerd.

Meyer and Verwoerd had a clear-cut political philosophy, were Broeder comrades-in-arms for many years, and together ruled South African for six years in amicable AB-NP partnership.

Meyer did not enjoy the same relationship with the pragmatic Vorster, and soon became disillusioned with Vorster's leadership. He made a secret Bondsraad speech in October 1966, spelling out the Broeder philosophy of widespread Afrikaner domination. This served to strengthen the Hertzog Group's initial position and was in direct conflict with Vorster's policy of greater Afrikaner-English consultation. Vorster, while not in disagreement with Meyer's sentiments, feared that his efforts to woo English voters into the Nationalist camp could be hampered.

Schoeman tells the remarkable story of how Meyer gave a party at his house for Broederbond officials in December 1967. During discussion of the political ferment Meyer explained the role of the Broederbond, baldly stating: "Our most important task is to get rid of John Vorster." And he was to repeat this statement in later discussions with politicians.

Schoeman also tells of how on September 20, 1967, Meyer was bitterly disappointed after an argument with Vorster. Afterwards he drove from Johannesburg to Pretoria to discuss his disenchantment with Hertzog, his old Broeder colleague, and made scathing remarks about the Prime Minister. This incident clearly indicates the close relationship between Meyer and Hertzog. At the time Hertzog was still a Cabinet Minister – and Vorster's biggest threat, though nobody mentioned this unpalatable fact in any Nationalist newspaper. Certain Nationalist newspapers did refer to his supporters as "obstructionists" – but no names were mentioned. The dispute was still in the family.

Within a few months after Vorster's takeover the Broederbond was forced to smooth things over. In circular 3/67/68 of May 3, 1967, it assured its members that, following talks, the UR had "ascertained at the highest level" that "our traditional sports policy will be applied as strictly as in the past."

In circular 5/67/58 of August 19, 1967, Broeders were asked "not to classify or categorise each other, especially not with superficial generalisations like verlig and verkramp. The sooner these terms disappear the better." Since only the pro-Hertzog camp and other conservatives objected to being called verkramp, this circular represented a subtle defence of the Hertzog Group by Meyer.

On August 2, 1967, a special circular entitled "We and our political leaders" reported on discussions between the UR and Vorster after the parliamentary session. There were warm thanks for what the Prime Minister and other NP leaders were doing. There was mention of the fact that some politicians had complained that branches of certain Broeder cultural bodies had interfered in the election of party office-bearers. The circular stressed that Broeders ought only to participate in politics as individuals.

This was a clear reference to party objections to the activities of the Rapportryers. The circular urged members not to sow suspicion against each other, but to solve problems dispassionately.

Circular 8/67/68 of November 11, 1967, contained another report on a lengthy discussion between the Prime Minister and the UR. Members were assured that Vorster had dealt satisfactorily with all matters raised by the executives. Broeders were urged not to "gossip" about political and cultural leaders. It was stressed that the Bond would not flinch in opposing all "deep rooted policy differences" which might arise, and efforts to divide "our volk on that basis."

In 1967 the UR discussed the question of "sensational" reporting in Afrikaans newspapers. Pelzer, a UR member, was appointed to discuss the matter with individual editors – in particular, Pienaar and Cillie, who as journalists broke the Nationalist tradition of covering up differences in Afrikaner ranks. The *Sunday Times* exposés had forced them into the arena.

The minutes of the UR meeting of August 7, 1967, contained a lengthy report of a discussion on "the present situation." This was just after Vorster's Koffiefontein speech.

Vorster had attacked S.E.D. Brown, editor of the obscure right wing monthly publication *The SA Observer*, which had labelled as liberals prominent Broeder Nationalist businessmen like A.D. Wassenaar, Anton Rupert and Etienne Rousseau. In the early Sixties the Broederbond had recommended the *Observer* to its members, though there was no financial support.

These turbulent events were followed by a special UR meeting on August 17, 1967, which continued its business on August 20. The seriousness of the situation was revealed by Meyer. The minutes state that "he (Meyer) felt that if the roads of the AB and the National Party should part . . . it would be a disaster for the volk. The co-operation between the two organisations should be maintained and expanded. The AB will go out of its way to maintain strong co-operation for as long as possible. The organisation will do everything in its power to help the Government."

After a lengthy discussion involving Gericke, E.J. Marais, Rector of the University of Port Elizabeth, P.E. Rousseau, A.N.P. Pelzer and S.P. Botha (now a Cabinet Minister), it was decided to send a deputation to see Vorster and to hold talks with Cillie, P.A. Weber (chairman of Nasionale Pers), as well as Broeders engaged in journalism in Johannesburg.

In this period Broeder supporters of Vorster had conducted their own separate enquiry into the Afrikaner Orde. Under pressure from Vorster the UR decided that the AO, which was indirectly under its control, should be disbanded.

According to the minutes of the UR management committee of September 19, 1967, it was noted that Meyer would meet the management committee of the AO on October 6, 1967, to inform them of this decision, and that its members would be incorporated into the Broederbond.

The wrangling dragged on until mid-1968 when the AO was finally disbanded and hundreds of its members absorbed into the Broederbond. Beaumont Schoeman, who as a political editor of *Hoofstad* had earned the wrath of Vorster, was one of a large number of AO members who were black-balled and not accepted by the Bond.

At the UR meeting of March 21, 1968, some pro-Vorster UR members like Koornhof and Ds Gericke expressed alarm about the incorporation of AO members. Koornhof thought the incorporation could "aggravate the present ferment in Afrikaner ranks." He and Gericke were also afraid that the large influx of AO members could lead to a Trojan horse situation in the Broederbond.

Circular 2/68/69 of April 8, 1968, admonished the newspapers for campaigning against nameless "obstructionist" – once again a subtle defence by the AB of Vorster's conservative opponents. It re-affirmed that in no circumstances would South Africa's participation in African or world affairs lead to the abandonment of apartheid. The circular contained details of the incorporation of the AO members into the AB in Pretoria; at that time the Bond there consisted of more than 1 100 members in more than 50 cells.

A report by the chief secretary of the UR meeting of June 26 – 27 complained about a report in the *Sunday Times* of June 2. In it I had revealed for the first time that Vorster had achieved an important victory with the disbandment of the AO, and that large numbers of its members had been black-balled by the Broederbond.

The article was said to be aggravating matters – and it revealed "a serious leakage."

In fact my source is to this day an active Broeder member. Once when I visited him in Pretoria, Meyer arrived unexpectedly – as I mentioned in the introduction.

The tension in Broeder ranks was building up. On July 29, 1968, a deputation of Pretoria cells met the executive of the Pretoria *Streekraad* ("Regional Council") to discuss complaints about the direction of government, and the attitude and role of newspapers and editors.

Pretoria was a bastion of the Hertzog Group and most of these Broeders were either supporters or sympathisers. A nine-point "charge" sheet was drafted as a basis for discussion with the UR. It mentioned the "unrest" in Afrikaner circles; the uncertainty about the application of government policy on sport; "non-White diplomats" in White areas; the outward policy; job reservation and immigration.

Objections were lodged that "liberalistic elements" were given full opportunities while the conservatives were continually hamstrung. Complaints were made about Cillie and Pienaar.

The "charge" sheet said that certain Broeders propagated and did things detrimental to the identity of the Afrikaner.

The Pretoria Regional Council also urged the UR to intervene and to give a direct lead so as to avoid the prevailing confusion. A deputation of the council handed the "charge" sheet to Meyer, who promised to investigate. Schoeman reports (page 38) that during this interview Meyer remarked: "A thing clicks or it does not click. With Verwoerd it clicked, but with Vorster not." He asked for time to put matters right.

The internal problems of the Broederbond and NP were discussed at the Bondsraad meeting of October 1, 1968, when the Bond celebrated its fiftieth anniversary. Special arrangements were made to ensure absolute secrecy and to prevent anybody coming near the meeting, held on the farm of P. van Wyk near Bapsfontein.

The minutes of the management committee of July 26, 1968, note that Broeder L. van der Walt (later a BOSS official) was "requested to take specific technical measures with regards to confidentiality." Documents indicate he had a "special responsibility" in the AB.

In his report for the period March 1965 to February 29, 1968, Meyer referred to internal dissension in the Broederbond. On page 13 he said that the ferment which developed in 1967 in Afrikaner ranks had at times threatened to lead to an open split, and stressed that the aim remained to strive for "the necessary co-operation and solidarity among Afrikaners without abandoning principles." Support for the National Party had been stressed on some occasions. This was in fact a deviation from the traditional political aloofness of AB.

The report stated that the statements and articles of Broeders in which suspicion was cast against conservatism contributed to the fact that it was only with difficulty that the UR could control the ferment.

In his chairman's speech on the theme of "Fifty years of Brotherhood" Meyer dealt directly with the political differences within the Broederbond. He explained that "because of our active participation in the achievement of the republican ideal, the AB forged closer links . . . with the national organisation of the political struggle . . . ." The differences and divisions which continued to exist in the political sphere had been reflected in the Bond.

Spelling out the Broederbond's "neutrality" in this situation Meyer said: "Whilst the AB as a non-party political cultural organisation is in an increasing measure giving its support to the political aspirations of the National Party, it is at the same time part of our Brotherhood to prevent political differences leading to divisions within our own ranks, and to simultaneously help control divisions in the national-political sphere." When there were political differences it was the task of the Broederbond to "bind Afrikaner Nationalists together and keep them together." The AB therefore never identified itself with either side of any dispute.

Vorster, who attended the Bondsraad, dealt at length with the various points of dispute. He vigorously defended himself against right-wing criticism, claiming that much of the doubt and uncertainties had been deliberately instigated. He criticised the fact that "liberalism" was used as a swear word against (verligte) Afrikaners and by implication took a swipe at Meyer by claiming that a volkskongres against liberalism planned in 1966 was actually aimed against Verwoerd; some Broeders had been discussing the question of a new party at the time. Significantly, Meyer backed a revival of this congress idea in 1967. The idea was eventually abandoned.

Vorster also attacked the editor of *Hoofstad* – though without mentioning Treurnicht's name – for publishing a report claiming that Vorster had said that Maori rugby players could come to South Africa. This apparently trivial racial issue eventually led to the split in the NP.

In private discussions at this time Treurnicht expressed disappointment about Vorster's leadership. The internal disputes led the UR to send a special directive to cells on what procedures to follow in ironing out differences.

In the period of 1965 – 1968 the UR consisted of:

Chairman	**P.J. Meyer (787)**
Vice Chairman	**J.S. Gericke (1999)**
Members	**D.P.M. Beukes (2735)**
	H.J.J. Bingle (1663)
	J.P.V. S. Bruwer (5022)

	J.H. Stander (770)
	A.P. Treurnicht (4240)
	C.F.C. Troskie (2895)
	J.A. Hurter (3298)
	P.G.J. Koornhof (6844)
Co-opted	S.P. Botha (4418)
	P.E. Rousseau (2712)
	A.J.G. Oosthuizen (362)
	A.N.P. Pelzer (3381)
	F.D. Conradie (4765)
	E.J. Marais (4955)

Head office personnel comprised the following:

Chief Secretary	T.J.N. Botha (6159)
Secretaries &	
Organisers	F.J. Beyleveldt (5749)
	M.J. Kruger (6086)
	I.A. Meyer (8410)
	A.J.O. Herbst (7663)
	J.H. Swart (1843)
	F.P. le R. Retief (4071)
	H.S. Hattingh (7231)
The female staff	
were:	A. Retief; M. Radyn; F. Terblanche;
	B. Beyleveldt; S.E. van der Walt;
	M. Grobler and E.M. Louw.

By the end of February 1968 there were 560 cells with a total of 8 154 members.

Amidst turmoil and strife the Broederbond celebrated its fiftieth anniversary in 1968. Naturally the October 1 Bondsraad was a special occasion. Earlier in the year – on June 5, the actual anniversary date – nation-wide celebrations had been held. Each cell met that night to follow a special programme worked out by head office. Each chairman read from the same text, briefly explaining the Bond's history, and exhorting members to bravely face the future. Hymns were sung during the ceremonies.

But the National Party was moving to an inevitable split. Circular 3/69/70 of May 1969 warned against the ''irresponsible possibility'' that a new political party might be formed. It stressed that the NP provided channels for discussion, and that ''there was no justification whatsoever for the establishment of a new party.''

The break came in September 1969 when Hertzog and three other MPs clashed with the party on the sports policy and broke away to form the HNP (Herstigte Nasionale Party). On September 25 the UR met Vorster informally at Libertas, his official Pretoria residence. According to circular 7/69/70 of Otober 7, 1969, Meyer had assured Vorster that the ''AB does not interfere in the domestic matters of the party.'' It noted that the UR accepted the assurance of the Government that in the implementation of the sports policy there would be steps to ensure that ''our traditional apartheid policy'' would not be subverted.

Vorster said that he sincerely welcomed and appreciated the co-operation of the UR.

In my book *"Die Verkrampte Aanslag"* I mentioned that at this meeting Vorster bluntly asked the delegation, which included conservatives such as Meyer, Koornhof and F.D. Conradie, the Cape MEC, whether they supported him. The atmosphere was apparently tense and electric. Treurnicht, with whom he had previously been on first-name terms, was addressed formally. Meyer also stressed that he stood by the party.

By this time Meyer and Treurnicht had abandoned the Hertzog Group. In fact, the large majority of Nationalist Bond members – who in fact sympathised with Hertzog – opted in the end for loyalty to the NP, which meant that it retained its basic conservative foundations.

The "unity at all costs" principle applied and the conservatives were prepared to swallow a few liberal adjustments of racial policies as long as the dominant position of Afrikaner nationalism was not affected. So they retained their power base within the NP.

Men like Meyer and Treurnicht are basically concerned with survival, and in this respect are no different than so-called verligtes like Koornhof, who believe that as long as you remain inside you are in a position to influence the course of events.

Meyer survived a determined onslaught by Vorster supporters to destroy his position in the Bond. At the October 1968 Bondsraad Meyer decisively beat Gericke, a Vorster confidante, for the position of chairman. The architect of this victory was Daan Goosen, who played a leading role in 1967 as secretary of the Akademie vir Wetenskap en Kuns when there was a Hertzog Group plot to take over the Akademie, which narrowly failed.

At this Bondsraad meeting Meyer employed a clever strategy. In his chairman's speech he praised Vorster – the very man he wanted to get rid of – and his policy. The man who touched Vorster, he said, touched Piet Meyer and the Bondsraad. After all, they had both been members of the Ossewabrandwag in the war! Meyer had not previously been known to hold Vorster in such esteem.

In October 1969 Daan Goosen was one of the key figures in the launching of the HNP.

In the weeks between the UR's meeting with Vorster and October 25, when the HNP was established, Broeder leaders such as Meyer made frantic appeals to Hertzog and his sympathisers to abandon their plans of forming a new party, which would split Afrikanerdom. All in vain.

But these Bond pressures did produce some results, and the HNP suffered early casualties. Professor A.B. du Preez – who at a public meeting in Pretoria North early in October 1969 actually proposed the motion to form a new political party – and Ds A.J.G. Oosthuizen, ex-moderator of the N H Church, who had agreed to open the HNP inaugural meeting with prayers, withdrew their support at the last moment after being "persuaded" by "influential" people that this was in the best interests of the volk.

On Friday, October 24, when a meeting to establish the HNP began in Pretoria, a special circular was sent to all cells dealing with "the AB and the present political situation." It stressed that the UR had given special attention to political turbulence and "continually strived to avoid serious divisions."

But, admitting failure, it went on: "When brothers differ from one another . . . the struggle must take place between brothers, as Christian believers. How we differ from each other is for the AB more important that the fact that we differ." The circular referred to the unity after the schisms of the Forties. It again assured Broeders that the sports policy of the NP would not affect the traditional apartheid policy.

The conflict between verligte newspapers like *Beeld* and *Die Burger* on the one hand and verkrampte Broeders on the other reached such a stage in 1969 that Phil Weber, chairman of Nasional Pers (the publishing company of these newspapers), wrote a letter in early 1969 to the Bond head office. In it he warned that unless attacks by cultural leaders on *Beeld,* obviously inspired by Meyer and Treurnicht, did not cease, the Nasionale Pers group would be compelled to retaliate and attack the Broederbond.

Although Meyer had in the past clashed with Hertzog on the position of the Afrikaner Orde, he could not have been too happy about its dissolution since it would only serve to strengthen Vorster's position. In 1969, for example, he told senior Broeders that claims by Vorster supporters – including Cabinet Ministers – that the AO had subverted Verwoerd (an issue first raised in my articles in August 1966) were rejected by Verwoerd himself in a discussion with Meyer shortly before his death.

In May 1969 Vorster strengthened his position *vis à vis* the Broederbond when he appointed J.S. van der Spuy (formerly Broederbond chief secretary before Koornhof) to the key position of Minister of Cultural Affairs and Education. Vorster wanted to counter Meyer's influence – and Van der Spuy and Meyer did not get on well in the Broederbond. It was privately said that Van der Spuy was close to Thom, the previous Bond chairman, and an opponent of Meyer.

From the end of 1969 onwards the Broederbond gradually shed all pretexts of neutrality; and in October 1972 it officially became a mere tool of the National Party, vindicating General Hertzog's 1935 claim that the Broederbond was the secret extension of the NP.

Vorster took the offensive on Saturday afternoon, November 8, 1969. The occasion was in Broeder Van Wyk's farm near Bapsfontein – in a barn. Vorster was not scheduled as a speaker, but he appeared unexpectedly a few minutes before the conference began. This caused quite a stir since it was obvious that Professor P.F.D. Weiss – conference chairman, a director of the Africa Institute, and a founder member of the HNP – was taken by surprise. Clearly, he had not been informed that Vorster would attend.

Weiss, anticipating a possible discussion on the political clash between the NP and the HNP, specifically referred to the Bond's constitution in his opening speech. He stressed that the AB was not entitled to become involved in party politics. Weiss then asked Vorster whether he would like to address the meeting and at this stage Vorster declined.

Although Vorster was a member of the Broederbond, and as such entitled to attend Raad meetings, it was somewhat unusual for him as Prime Minister, with heavy commitments, to be present on this occasion.

Professor Weiss then called on Wennie du Plessis – who defeated Smuts in 1948 – the former Administrator of South West Africa, ex-Ambassador in Washington, and former Secretary of Information, to deliver a paper. After this Weiss again asked Vorster, who was on the platform with Weiss and Du Plessis, whether he would speak. There were several calls from the audience by Vorster supporters who wanted to hear the Prime Minister.

Broeder Vorster then gave a fiery speech, lasting more than an hour. In defiance of Broederbond regulations and in the presence of several UR members he made a political speech, making a slashing attack on the HNP and "exposing" the activities of the Hertzog Group prior to the split. The audience sat in silence. Weiss, white-faced, sat only a few feet away, listening to Vorster attacking him and his HNP colleagues, though no specific names were mentioned.

A few days later, on November 16, I ran a front-page report in the *Sunday Times* giving the details of Vorster's amazing attack – one unique in the history of the Broederbond. This report was discussed in circular 9/69/70 of November 24, 1969, which confirmed that it was basically correct. The circular stated of the report that "the UR, together with our members, is disturbed about it and will leave no stone unturned to trace the person responsible."

In June 1968, after I revealed that the AO had been disbanded and most of its members black-balled by the Bond, Meyer threatened in a circular that he would find the "traitor." That circular also denied that the UR was divided on the political situation.

In February 1970 Vorster repeated his performance at the so-called "Grape festival," thrown by the Broederbond on the farm of Cabinet Minister Hendrik Schoeman near Groblersdal. There was an election campaign on the go. Vorster made a speech in which he attacked the HNP and its leaders (all fellow Broederbonders). In doing so he transgressed AB regulations about involvement in party politics.

In practice, of course, support had been given to the NP from 1934 onwards. In the Forties the Bond acted as a mediator between the various Nationalist factions – but in practice all non-Nationalist political parties were opposed.

Vorster's campaign against the Hertzog Group in the Seventies enjoyed considerable success. The UR refused to continue financing the Congress to Combat Communism, which had a full-time organiser and included several key Hertzogites such as Gert Beetge. The committee continued to function, but on a smaller scale and under the direct control of the head office.

The GVA *(Gemeenskap Volk en Arbeid)* – Association of Volk and Labour) a secret labour organisation which had existed as the labour wing of the Broederbond, was disbanded. This organisation was controlled by Gert Beetge.

Vorster also appeared at a cell meeting in Pretoria in 1970. There he launched a scathing attack on Weiss (who was absent) and T.E.W. Schumann, a former UR member. All had been members of the same cell. After the meeting, senior members of the cell called upon Vorster and Weiss to seek reconciliation, but Weiss apparently refused to meet Vorster.

Weiss, chairman of the cell, had been axed a month prior to this confrontation.

The *Afrikaner,* mouthpiece of the HNP, hinted for the first time on April 24, 1970, that HNP Broeders were considering court action against Vorster. The newspaper stated: "It cannot yet be established whether a court interdict will be sought against Vorster, or whether the executive of the Broederbond will be asked to prevent Vorster from addressing Broederbond audiences."

In May 1970 Piet Cillie, *Burger* editor, addressed a Broederbond meeting in the Sasolburg area. He launched a scathing attack on the HNP, singling out Hertzog and Jaap Marais, then the deputy leader of the new party, urging that they should be summarily expelled from the Bond.

A senior member pointed out, however, that the UR could not expel members; the initiative had to be taken by branches and regional bodies. The upshot was that a vigorous campaign was launched by pro-Vorster supporters in the Bond to root out the HNP members.

Meanwhile the Broederbond was struck a public blow from a totally unexpected quarter. On September 4, 1970, in the midst of a crucial parliamentary by-election in the Natal constituency of Klipriver, *Die Nataller,* official mouthpiece of the NP in the province, called upon the Bond to come out into the open.

Two weeks earlier Theo Gerdener, the former Natal Administrator and the NP candidate in Klipriver, admitted that he was a member. The result was that the Bond became an election issue, and the NP was under fire because of its relationship with the body.

The editor, Barend Venter, stated in his article that the Broederbond was endangering the national unity of the white language groups. Entitled "The Broederbonders Must Speak," it stated: "The times have gone when the Broederbonders' privacy can be respected by all Afrikaners . . . new times bring new demands, and for the Afrikaner Broederbond a time of crisis has arrived." Venter, a full-blooded Nationalist – though a non-Broeder – made these remarkable observations: "Doubt is cast upon the honesty of its stated purpose in public life, namely the true national unity of the Afrikaans and English-language groups.

"Elsewhere as well, the existence of this secret society is an embarrassment to the National Party, especially because the association has up to now not openly replied to all the allegations made against it.

"It is feared that members of the Broederbond who sit on public bodies hold private discussions and are thus not able to take their seats totally unbiased, especially in those places where it is in the public interest for them to do so.

"It is also feared that authority and discipline are being undermined in the city councils, semi-State bodies and in the private sector, by members of the Broederbond who choose to maintain contact with each other rather than follow the correct channels. Coupled with this is the fear that Broederbonders misuse their positions to give jobs to fellow members.

"Not all non-members share these fears, but it cannot be denied that they exist."

Suggesting that all Bond members should reveal their identities to counter suspicion about their motives, including that felt by Nationalist Afrikaners, he went on: "As long as the leading Broederbond members remain silent in public about their organisation, so long will the Broederbond remain under suspicion by many people . . ."

Venter pointed out that the AB limited its membership to people acceptable to each other; that there were many Afrikaners who were led to wonder whether they were regarded as weaker Afrikaners than the Broeders.

Beeld, the Nationalist Sunday newspaper, announced dramatically: "Now it is crisis time for the Broederbond," echoing *Die Nataller.* The report sparked off fresh public controversy with the United Party doing its utmost to make political capital out of the situation.

Dirk Richard, editor of *Dagbreek en Sondagnuus,* the other Nationalist Sunday newspaper of that time, cast further doubts on the Broederbond and its executive in a column on September 13, 1970, entitled: "Broederbond: No longer so untouchable?"

Richard, a non-Broeder, asked the following questions on behalf of other non-Broeders (the vast majority of Afrikaners):

• Why are we not good enough for the volk?
• Are only Broeders the cream of the volk?
• Does the Broederbond still have a right to exist?
• If the Broederbond has nothing to hide, why does it continue to operate in secret?

Richard also suggested that the AB no longer acted with its historical unity of conviction. People had to doubt whether the organisation was still the powerful factor it had been in earlier times.

An aftermath of this affair was that Venter was soon afterwards abruptly "transferred" to Johannesburg, thereafter to disappear from the national journalistic scene by joining a small country paper – one of the few visible examples of what happens if an Afrikaner Nationalist dares to question Broederbond activities.

During this period Meyer again launched a witchhunt to establish which Bond members had been leaking news to me in the preceding years. In a circular in March 1970 he pledged that he would uncover the "traitor" who had passed on confidential documents and information. I was told he was particularly furious about the publication in my book of one of his confidential speeches in which he spelled out the strategy of Afrikaner domination in October 1966. Meyer promised he would find the informant (or informants) and deal with him as the Broederbond had dealt with Beyers Naudé. In July Meyer made a similar threat in a circular after yet another *Sunday Times* report.

By September 1970 there was considerable speculation in Broeder circles as to whether Meyer would be unseated as chairman at that month's Bondsraad meeting. Thom, the previous chairman, Gericke and Ds Beukes were mentioned as possible contenders. It was also regarded as possible that Meyer would withdraw.

However, against all expectations, Meyer was not only re-elected but was unopposed.

In the *Sunday Times* of October 11, 1970, I explained this unexpected development as follows: "There can be little doubt that Dr Meyer has only been re-elected because the Vorster supporters, and probably the Prime Minister himself, have decided for strategic reasons that he should keep the job.

"The fact that he was not opposed indicated that there must have been a deal between him, Mr Vorster and men such as Mr Gericke and Prof Thom. Mr Vorster could have decided that it would be better to keep Dr Meyer in his position instead of making an open enemy of him.

"The Prime Minister, having decided to implement radical verligte policies in the next year or two, apparently wants to avoid a further split in the Nationalist ranks at this stage. The influence of the Broederbond has waned in recent years and Mr Vorster obviously feels he can handle Dr Meyer where he is.

"It is almost certain that Mr Vorster will have demanded from Dr Meyer that the Broederbond confine its activities to purely cultural matters and must not intervene in the political field, as in the past.

"The verkramptes are happy about the outcome because they are convinced that whatever pledges Dr Meyer may have made, he will never change his basic verkrampte philosophy. They hope that in a crisis he would throw he Broederbond behind the verkramptes still inside the Nationalist Party."

The secretarial report of Meyer and Naudé Botha for the period 1968 to February 1970 referred extensively to the infighting of the time. Notwithstanding an official claim of neutrality, it was clear where the real sympathies of the Broederbond lay. It said that "the knowledge that large-scale Afrikaner division could cause irreparable harm had in the end turned the scale in favour of the NP – witness the results of the 1970 general election when the HNP was crushed, with most of its candidates losing their deposits in one of the stormiest and dirtiest elections in history."

The report stated that the UR had done much to maintain "Afrikaner unity in the political sphere" and warned that "the fact that in some divisions there are members who belong to different political parties causes tension, and the matter will in an increasing measure demand the attention of the UR should friends not act with responsibility."

And then Meyer once more made it very clear where the political loyalty of the Broederbond lay. "The UR went out of its way to encourage support for the National Party and is convinced that the party is the best means of promoting our political ideals."

The Broederbond had moved a long way since Meyer's speech at the 1968 Bondsraad in which he said that the Broederbond would be "impartial" in political disputes among Afrikaner Nationalists.

The UR members for the 1968 – 1970 period were:

Chairman	**P.J. Meyer (787)**
Vice Chairman:	**J.S. Gericke (1999)**
Members:	**D.P.M. Beukes (2735)**
	H.J.J. Bingle (1663)
	J.H. Stander (770)
	A.P. Treurnicht (4240)
	J.A. Hurter (3298)
	P.E. Rosseau (2712)
	A.J. Marais (4955)
	J.B. Thom (1773)

The head office consisted of Naudé Botha as chief secretary, while the other organisers were:

Co-opted Members:	**S.P. Botha (4418)**
	A.N.P. Pelzer (3381)
	F.D. Conradie (4765)
	C.H.J. van Aswegen (4223)
	J.M.B. Faure (1256)

By February 28, 1970, there were 604 cells distributed as follows: Transvaal 269; Cape 198; Fee State 99; Natal 22; Namibia 11; Rhodesia 5. Membership totalled 8 776.

E.   1970 – 1978 Purge and Nationalist Control

By the end of 1970 the Broederbond leadership was under pressure from Vorster and his supporters to get rid of the Hertzogites. The problem was how to do so constitutionally. Party politics *per se* was not a reason for expulsion from the Bond – at least not officially. Politically motivated action would be a direct violation of the AB's constitution and could even provide strong grounds for an embarrassing court action.

The UR was apparently also careful not to take action on a massive scale against rank and file Hertzog Broeders. The strategy was apparently to hammer the leaders in the hope that the followers would abandon their support for the HNP, or at least their resistance within the Bond. So the UR had to find "legitimate" grounds for taking action against leading HNP Broeders. The dilemna is reflected in a series of letters between Naudé Botha chief secretary, and Hertzog and Jaap Marais, in which certain accusations were made in the period from October 1970 to early 1972. The correspondence had all the characteristics of comic opera; indeed, the UR committed several unbelievable blunders. But eventually events culminated in a purge of HNP members and sympathisers in October 1972.

The correspondence represented part of the final process whereby the Broederbond officially became the extensive underground wing of the National Party.

In *"Vorster se 1 000 Dae"* Schoeman discussed this fully from page 50 onwards.

111

On October 30, 1970 – shortly after the Bondsraad meeting at which Meyer was unanimously re-elected – Hertzog and Marais each received a similar letter from Botha. It mentioned that the UR had received complaints from various cells and individual members which asked "whether arising out of the court judgment against you over the use of a confidential document, what disciplinary action is to be taken against you?" The Broeders were asked whether they wished to give an explanation of the situation so as to enable the UR to consider the matter.

It must be explained that, under certain circumstances, involvement by a member in a court case can lead to his expulsion. The "confidential document" referred to dealt with the revelation of the contents of a secret government circular regarding the country's security position which was sent to certain quarters after the establishment of the Bureau for State Security (BOSS).

A press statement issued by Marais at the time contained allegations concerning the Republikeinse Intelligensie Diens (RID), the predecessor of BOSS; and of spying on conservative Afrikaners prior to the establishment of the HNP.

Jaap Marais revealed the contents of the documents – which also dealt with "bugging devices" ("meeluister apparate") – in February 1970. He spoke under parliamentary privilege in a debate in the House of Assembly just before the April general election. This led to charges against Marais in terms of the law relating to State secrets. At the trial in the Cape Supreme Court he was found not guilty by Mr Justice Van Heerden on two of the charges – but guilty on the third, ie. of revealing State secrets. Accordingly, he was fined R300. In December 1970 the Appeal Court set aside the conviction and found that what Marais had revealed was already public knowledge from Press reports.

Hertzog was never at any stage involved with the government circular or the consequent court case. Botha's reference to "the use of a confidential document" was thus totally incorrect as far as the HNP leader was concerned. This blunder would cause the UR considerable problems in its anti-Hertzog drive.

For Hertzog – a UR member for 26 years – the letter from Botha came as a complete surprise. He replied on November 16, very much tongue-in-cheek: "A few days ago I received a very strange registered letter that claims it comes from Mr Naudé Botha of the AB head office . . . I hereby enclose a copy to keep you informed."

A few days later on December 10, 1970, Botha (perhaps red-faced) confirmed in a second letter to Hertzog that the "strange" letter had in fact come from him. By this time the chief secretary must have discovered his blunder concerning Hertzog's involvement with the circular, and was equally obviously desperately scratching around for other grounds for action. He wanted to know from Hertzog who had typed his "replying" letter. Had it been entrusted to an "uninformed typist?" Botha then instructed Hertzog that he was no longer to attend Broederbond meetings until further notice. (The typist concerned had been in Hertzog's service for years and had always handled his Broederbond correspondence).

Botha's timing in taking action against the HNP leaders, so shortly after the Bondsraad, clearly suggests that an order had been issued from the top to get rid of them.

Jaap Marais replied on November 11, 1970. He demanded that those who had brought "written charges" against him should identify themselves, and said he was prepared to discuss the matter with them.

On December 10, Botha again wrote to Marais. He said the matter had been submitted to the UR; he demanded an "explanation" about the court case; and stated that it was not necessary to pass on to Marais the detailed inquiries of cells and individual Broeders. He added: "I must point out that it is the normal practice for the UR to pay attention to cases where members of our organisation are found guilty in court."

Because of Marais' "conviction" he too was forbidden to attend Bond meetings until further notice.

The UR had once more blundered. In the very week that Botha wrote his letter, the Appeal Court in Bloemfontein set aside Marais' earlier conviction in the Cape Supreme Court. So it looked very much as if the UR was guilty of double standards in using the court case to drive Marais out of the Broederbond. In fact later incidents were to cast doubt on the political morality of the Bond's action against Marais.

Fanie Botha, now Minister of Labour and then Minister of Water Affairs, appeared in the Pretoria Supreme Court in 1971, facing a libel action brought against him by Marais. The action followed allegations by Botha during the 1970 general election in which, by implication, he accused Marais of stealing the document on the controversial bugging equipment. Botha lost and had to pay the legal costs. Yet the UR took no action against Botha after the case.

In 1973 the UR came in for further embarrassment. Treurnicht – the chairman – was one of the defendants in another libel action brought by Marais. This concerned a pamphlet- referring to the "bugging" document – issued by Treurnicht in a parliamentary by-election in 1971 in the Waterberg constituency, where Marais had opposed Treurnicht. Treurnicht and the NP lost again, and had to pay damages and costs.

The UR took no action against Treurnicht.

To return to the Botha-Hertzog-Marais saga. On February 12, 1971, Marais wrote back to Naudé Botha, stating that he had won his appeal. He also took strong exception to the fact that his accusers remained nameless, that "false allegations were made behind a cloak of namelessness," and that his membership was affected "on the totally false alle- gation that I was found guilty by a court . . . ." He wanted to know whether the UR stood by its letters of October 30 and December 10.

The whole matter was obviously prickly for the UR, because Botha took a considerable time to reply to this broadside. On May 3, 1971, Marais reminded Botha of his letter of February 12. He referred to two study documents concerning sport and politics which had been sent out in the meantime, and said: "I must draw your attention to the fact that the AB should keep out of party politics, according to its constitution, and will be glad if you will convey my viewpoint to the UR and have the relevant study documents recalled."

On May 10, 1971, Botha briefly acknowledged receipt of this letter and said he would submit it to the UR.

On May 18, Marais accused Botha in a long letter of using delaying tactics on the in- structions of the UR. Adopting a threatening tone Marais said that unless he was informed before June 3, 1971, about the UR's decision he would accept that it was standing by its suspension of his membership on the grounds of "a court decision about the use of a confi- dential document."

Botha replied on May 24, pointing out that the UR would only meet next on June 24 – so the June 3 deadline could not be met. Marais replied toughly on June 1. He raised two important matters. Firstly, he pointed out that his membership had been suspended on false grounds; that the UR must know this; but that it was doing nothing to set matters right.

He made it clear that the situation was not acceptable, and hinted at further action. Marais gave the UR an extension until June 10 to give a final answer to the question of his membership. Should the suspension be withdrawn, he demanded that all cells be informed of this in a circular by June 16, 1971, and that there had been no grounds for the action taken against him.

Secondly, he referred to the Broederbond's involvement in the drafting of the Government's new sports policy (I had reported that the new "verligte" sports policy was drafted by a Broederbond committee, that it involved Treurnicht himself and that this involvement of conservative Broeders would prevent a conservative backlash inside the National Party).

Marais claimed that the suspension of his membership and that of other HNP members "was nothing else but naked political discrimination based on party political prejudices." He hinted at legal action: "If I have not heard by June 10 from the UR that my membership has been restored and my other requests complied with, I will accept that the matter has to be settled in another sphere . . ."

Nonetheless, Marais did not immediately follow up this threat when Botha informed him, on June 7, that the UR could not comply with his request before June 10. Then, on July 5, Botha informed Marais that "in view of further information obtained" the UR had decided to abandon its charges. Yet the prohibition on Marais not attending meetings was to remain in force.

This was indeed ironic and strange: the charge in terms of which Marais' attendance of meetings was prohibited was withdrawn because of a blunder concerning the facts; but the actual prohibition was not set aside. A true egg-dance by the UR.

The UR had clearly decided that Marais, as an HNP leader, would not be tolerated in the Bond.

Obviously attempting to drum up another charge, Botha added in his July 5 letter: "The question of whether your action and the spirit of your correspondence complied with the requirements of a brotherly disposition . . . is another consideration, and you will in due course again hear from the UR."

Marais immediately retaliated, writing on July 10: "Which management of an organisation with any self-respect would so drastically affect the rights of a member on grounds of totally false and libellous statements as . . . in this case?" He rejected the "brotherly" nature of the UR actions against him: "You are busy fabricating an excuse for an obvious transgression against the elementary principles of membership and justice."

Marais added that he was laying an accusation of "dishonourableness and under-handedness irreconcilable with AB membership" against the unknown members who had accused him.

Meanwhile, the Bond's case against Hertzog went the same way as that against Marais. After an exchange of letters, in which Hertzog also forced the UR into a corner, Botha wrote on July 5, 1971, that charges against Hertzog had been withdrawn; he admitted that the UR had made a mistake. But he echoed what he had told Marais and questioned whether Hertzog's correspondence had "complied with demands of a brotherly disposition." And Hertzog was barred from attending cell meetings.

Hertzog's reply came on July 31. He made scathing comments about the UR action: "It is difficult to avoid the conclusion that it was decided in advance to get rid of me for political reasons. Grounds for disciplinary action against me had to be found." He accused the UR of "fabricating" charges against him. "You come with crude unfounded charges against me and take steps without giving me a chance to defend myself. If I then dare to defend myself against such unbrotherly action, I am accused of unbrotherliness."

Deploring the fact that this action lowered the high standards and name of the Broeder-bond, he concluded bitterly: "I cannot imagine that a high-ranking member of the AB would consciously lend himself to such action. I can only ascribe the unfortunate situation to the fact that you have allowed BOSS to infiltrate the AB, and thus to carry into the AB the standards of BOSS – the standards of a body of eavesdroppers and informers created to keep specific political personalities in power in every possible manner."

Herzog was referring to claims that BOSS and the Special Branch were used in the late Sixties to spy on NP members – even parliamentarians – whose loyalty to Vorster was suspect.

On February 23, 1971, the HNP appointed a committee to investigate the matter and to negotiate with the UR. The committee – all Broeders – consisted of J.H. Jooste (chairman of the HNP); W.T. Marais (ex-MP and vice-chairman of the HNP); P.J. Malan; G.H. Beetge (HNP treasurer); N.P.C. Badenhorst; and Professor A.D. Pont of the NH Church. They were all eventually suspended as Broeder members.

Jooste had already drafted a memorandum in September 1970, to be submitted to the UR, in which he analysed the new situation inside the Broederbond caused by the establishment of the HNP.

It pointed out that Broeders were politically divided on matters such as sport and separate development, and stressed that the Broederbond should not become an instru-ment to further private party political interests. It specifically mentioned Vorster and his attacks on HNP Broeders at AB meetings.

The Jooste memorandum claimed that the UR should have spoken to Vorster after the Bapsfontein meeting of November 1969 (discussed earlier) since this would have prevented his attacks on HNP members at the subsequent grape festival. Jooste stated: "With all respect for his position, he has no claim on rights which other members do not have, and he enjoys no immunity against the regulations of the AB." Vorster, indeed, should have set an example of "brotherliness."

"That this has not happened is shocking because it shows undeniably that Vorster is subordinating the AB to his party political interests and has treated the provisions of section 88 of the regulations with contempt. This is a serious breach of the contract be-tween him and the AB and between him and each individual member. The UR should speak out and act in terms of its responsibilities and powers."

The HNP committee wrote to Botha on February 23, 1971, asking for a meeting with the UR to discuss the actions against Hertzog and Marais. A copy was sent to Meyer as chairman.

On March 4, Botha replied that the UR chairman could not comply with the request "because action has not been taken against . . . any friends as a result of membership of a particular political party."

On March 31, Jooste, on behalf of the HNP committee in another letter to Botha, once more raised the issue of Vorster's activities at Broederbond meetings.

He referred to political matters discussed in recent circulars and quoted from the secre-tarial report submitted at the Bondsraad, which stressed that the UR had gone out of its way to encourage support for the NP. Jooste denied claims in the report that the UR had held discussions with HNP members to prevent a split, and again asked for a meeting with the executive.

Botha replied on May 11, calling for a memorandum of the HNP committee to be submit-ted to the UR management committee. But Jooste's response was simply to list the matters to be discussed with the UR. These were: the lack of action by the UR against (non-HNP) members who had violated the principles of the AB; the breaking of the constitution by allowing the organisation to promote the interests of the NP – with the implication that the action against HNP Broeders was without foundation; the alleged discussions the UR held to prevent a split; and the new sports policy.

The matter dragged on. Then in August 1971 the HNP committee sent copies of the correspondence together with an accompanying letter to some 1 000 selected members of the 9 000-member Broederbond.

This led to Botha informing Jooste on September 22, 1971, that his membership had been suspended because he had circulated confidential correspondence to other Broeders.

On February 15, 1972, Botha laid a formal charge (under Bond rules) against Jooste because of this. Furthermore, it was claimed that he had refused to inform the UR, at whose request the correspondence was sent out. It was noted that, judging by reports in the English Press, the fact of the distribution was known, and the correspondence itself had probably fallen into the hands of "hostile and unreliable persons." Jooste's action did not comply with the requirements of "brotherliness," and was a serious breach of discipline.

Interestingly enough, Botha concluded his letter by requesting that further correspondence be sent by registered post to "Mr P.A. Minnaar, P.O. Box 9801, Johannesburg," because "the name of the undersigned (Naudé Botha) has already been mentioned in the newspapers and letters to the usual address may perhaps attract unnecessary attention."

In his reply on February 21, Jooste mentioned for the first time the possibility of court action against the Broederbond leadership. He referred to Press speculation on the matter – a reference to my continuing reports in the *Sunday Times* on Bond affairs.

The fact is that Jooste had already briefed lawyers and Advocate Moolman Mentz was acting on his behalf. Affadavits and other papers were prepared for an application in which the Afrikaner Broederbond was the first respondent and chairman Meyer the second.

Annexures comprising a number of Broederbond documents on political topics were to be attached.

At the time Jooste was a candidate in a by-election in Gezina, and he would ask the Supreme Court to prohibit the Broederbond from further involvement in party politics. However, because of legal advice Jooste never went ahead, although many HNP members were convinced that for the sake of publicity and strategy it ought to be done, even though the case might be lost.

The membership of other HNP members was also suspended. On May 5, Botha wrote to Marais to inform him that the UR had decided to finally terminate his membership and concluded with the sentence: "The UR of course accepts that you will maintain the promises that you made at your initiation." (This referred to the maintenance of confidentiality, even though membership had ceased).

The case of Gert Beetge, a former Broederbond official who was then HNP treasurer, is of particular interest. On July 3, 1972, he wrote to Botha, accusing him and the UR of being guilty of giving Vorster a political platform; the Broederbond had become "henchman" of the NP.

He then made the following significant revelation: "I still remember the day in your office when I told you that I objected to the AB committing itself to the Government party. *And that you answered that Mr Vorster's party was implementing the policy of the AB and that the AB therefore supported his party.*

116

"And just in case you may be tempted to believe that I went along with the AB involvement with the Vorster party, I refer you to the minutes of the Florida Park division, to which I belonged, where you will find that on constitutional grounds I objected in 1964 to the fact that the local AB division had . . . determined who would be elected to branch and divisional committees of the NP.

"These practices have increased in recent years to such an extent that the AB to a large measure must accept responsibility for the sorry state in which the National Party finds itself today."

Although Beetge is obviously biased about the NP, his inside information of Broederbond involvement in the affairs of the party is of great importance historically.

Beetge then referred to certain other events. One was "the report of a member of my division that, on the instruction of his division, he had tried to ascertain whether a certain candidate for the City Council of Pretoria was a Freemason. He had consulted a certain police officer.

"This man had told him that he would be able to find out within about 10 days – 'because BOSS has now planted a representative within the Freemasons.' Although the AB had always condemned the Freemasons on the grounds of its religious views and its *'lewens en wêreldbeskouing'* ('life and world philosophy') it has never been regarded as dangerous to the State.

"Why should BOSS spy on it? If this can happen to the Freemasons then I must assume that it can also be the fate of the AB."

The relationship between the HNP and the Broederbond reached its climax at the annual congress of the HNP on September 15, 1972, in the city hall in Pretoria North. Reacting to a resolution by the Waterkloof constituency, Jooste publicly revealed for the first time what had taken place since September 1970. He also revealed that at one stage it had been said that there were few high-ranking policemen in the Broederbond. General Van den Bergh, then head of the Security Police, consequently submitted a list of names of men in the Security Police, to be considered for membership. But Hertzog had objected.

Jooste charged that agents of BOSS had been brought into the Bond to spy on fellow members. He listed a number of examples of how the AB had become increasingly involved in the affairs of the Government and the NP in the previous year. He gave extracts from recent Broederbond circulars which announced that the organisation had asked the help of *"kundige vriende"* ("expert friends") to trace the source of the Press leaks – another clear indication that Broeders in BOSS and the Security Police were involved in the hunt.

Jooste also mentioned the names of prominent members in business and journalism, such as Anton Rupert and Schalk Pienaar.

This speech led to sensational headlines when both Afrikaans and English newspapers carried reports of Jooste's remarkable attack on the Broederbond – the first by a member since the Beyers Naudé affair in 1963.

All the leading HNP members were expelled by September 1972; and those who, like Hertzog, had been suspended were kicked out early in 1973. Vorster, of course, was the mastermind. One HNP supporter remarked some years later: "Verwoerd used the Broederbond, but Vorster abused it."

In May 1972 there was a change of guard when Meyer, after 12 years as chairman, was replaced by Treurnicht. His election was apparently a mistake, because the pro-Vorster groups wanted Professor Gerrit Viljoen, the brilliant Rector of the Rand Afrikaanse University (RAU), to become chairman. Planning, however, was poor and Treurnicht nar-

117

rowly made it. Others elected to the UR were Dr Connie Mulder, Transvaal leader of the National Party and a Cabinet Minister; Gerrit Viljoen; Prof H.J.J. Bingle, Rector of Potchefstroom University; Prof E.J. Marais, Rector of Port Elizabeth University; Dr D.M.P. Beukes; F.D. Conradie, MEC of the Cape Provincial Council; Jan Stander, former Deputy Director of Education in Natal; Prof A.N. Pelzer, of the University of Pretoria; Prof H.J. Strauss, Professor of Philosophy at the University of the Free State; and J.M.B. Faure, Deputy Director of Education in the Free State.

Subsequently co-opted as UR members were: Eben Cuyler (4580), former Johannesburg City Councillor and a Senator; Dr A.L. Kotze (8604), the Director of Education in the Transvaal; A.J. Marais (3347), a Pretoria businessman; Prof F.C. Fensham (7026) of the University of Stellenbosch; and S.A.S. Hayward (5710), MP of Steytlerville in the Cape.

It was significant that for the first time since Diederichs in 1950 an active politician was elected chairman. Moreover, the election of Mulder was curious since in the past it had been the practice for a politician to resign from the UR when he became a Cabinet Minister.

In his attack on the Broederbond Jooste used this development as proof that the AB had become a "support organisation" of the NP – as politicians Treurnicht and Mulder were bound by Cabinet and caucus decisions.

Meyer's last chairman's speech at the Bondsraad meeting of April 6, 1972, dealing with "Our Task in the Political Field," made it finally clear that the AB had abandoned all pretexts of not being a party political organisation. He stated bluntly that the primary political task of the Broederbond was to get the NP returned at the next parliamentary election with an increased majority. This speech will be discussed again. (See annexure G).

The effect of the storm round the Broederbond after Jooste's revelations was that the issue was for the first time debated at length in Nationalist circles and newspapers. Vorster had to intervene as Prime Minister, while chairman Treurnicht was forced to make no more than three public statements within a month on the crisis and on the Broederbond's role in political and public life.

Anthony Holiday (now serving a prison sentence for a conviction in terms of the Terrorism Act) reported on Treurnicht's first-ever interview with an English- language newspaper, in the *Rand Daily Mail* of September 18, 1972, as follows: "In what must be the frankest admission of Afrikaner Broederbond influence on national policy, the secret organisation's reputed chairman, Dr Andries Treurnicht, MP, yesterday defended its right to make representations to the Government.

"Asked about allegations that the Broederbond had formulated the Government's sports policy, Dr Treurnicht said: 'The policy is the responsibility of the Government. But it is the right of any organisation to make representations to the Government. If the Government thinks these are impracticable it can reject them. The Government is the responsible body,' he said."

Asked how the Broederbond went about making its representations to the Government Dr Treurnicht replied: "Now you are asking a technical question. Take the example of the Afrikaans churches, with which I have been associated for many years. They would approach the Government on a matter and perhaps request an interview. Every organisation has its own way of making such representations. Some choose to do it in a proper manner and some people choose to attempt to embarass the Government in making public statements."

Holiday suggested to Treurnicht that the latter course was not followed by the Broederbond. He replied: "No. It would seem not."

Treurnicht accused the HNP of trying to attract attention to itself by attacks on the Broederbond and said the allegation that members of the Bureau for State Security were being brought in to help trace who was leaking Broederbond secrets was untrue, but would not comment further.

Holiday noted: "Apart from Dr Treurnicht's statement there was a studied silence yesterday from the men named as new members of the organisation's leadership."

"Prof F.C. Fensham, Professor of Semitic languages at the University of Stellenbosch said: 'I am like a skeleton with a dose of Epsom salts. You won't get anything out of me.' Dr Fensham is one of the men reported to have been co-opted onto the Broederbond's executive body – the UR.

"Another man reported to have been co-opted onto the body, Mr Eben Cuyler, said: 'No comment. I am not prepared to say anything.' Other reputed Broederbond leaders were either away or had something wrong with their telephones which gave continuous engaged signals."

Rapport – whose editor, W.T. Wepener is apparently a non-Broeder – along with some other Nationalist newspapers had become highly critical of the Broederbond. It devoted the whole of its September 17 front page to the Jooste revelations, claiming that there had been an "explosion" in the organisation which had left it almost powerless.

On September 18, men like Piet Meyer and Connie Mulder vigorously defended the Broederbond in *Die Transvaler* as an "Afrikaner cultural organisation"; Mulder even said that the Broederbond "does not move in the political field." And on that Monday afternoon Treurnicht replied to accusations against the Broederbond in a question and answer interview in *Die Vaderland* (see annexure H).

Treurnicht made it clear that the organisation would not drop its secrecy and confidentiality in its task of furthering exclusive Afrikaner interests.

The unease in Nationalist Press circles about the Broederbond was reflected in a lengthy editorial on September 19 in *Die Vaderland* – whose editor, Dirk Richard, is not a Broeder – which asked: "Must the AB continue unchanged on the same pattern, or must it adapt to changed circumstances and re-plan and function on a new basis?" The Broederbond should ask itself whether it was not unconsciously damaging the Afrikaner cause.

And on Saturday 24, Vorster himself entered the battle when he addressed a National Party *stryddag* at Witbank. He strongly denied that the Bond had ever dominated his Cabinet or the Government or that he was using the Broederbond for his own political gain. A large part of his one-and-a-half hour speech was devoted to these allegations.

Vorster also condemned ex-Broeders in the HNP for breaking "an oath before God" divulging Broederbond secrets. "How high should the honour of such a person be valued?" he asked.

Every country in the world had confidential organisations: "In South Africa there are at least three – the Broederbond, the Freemasons and the Sons of England. All have an oath to protect the confidential nature of their organisations." Vorster asked why the English-language Press attacked only one organisation and not the others. The answer was simple, he said. The AB belonged to the Afrikaner and that which belonged to the Afrikaner was dragged through the mud at all times.

Ironically, while Vorster was defending the Broederbond, two Deputy Ministers shared the platform with him – Punt Janson and Hannes Rall. For some reason they have never been permitted to join the super-elite organisation – putting them among the few Nationalist parliamentarians who are not members. So while they were good enough to be

119

included in Vorster's Cabinet, they were apparently not esteemed highly enough as Afrikaners to be awarded membership of the Broederbond.

Die Vaderland of September 25 was at it again. Referring to my series of revelations in the *Sunday Times* it asked whether it was still worthwhile keeping the Bond a confidential body. "If the information of the *Sunday Times* is correct, then it means that all efforts to keep matters confidential have become useless. Apparently even the assistance of 'expert people' to trace leakages does not help. There is certainly consternation in Broederbond circles. The search for the informants has sharpened." (Naturally my revelations continued).

And Schalk Pienaar, himself a Broeder and the editor of *Rapport,* asked in his weekly column on September 25, 1972, whether the Broederbond's traditional manner of doing things – or its lack of doing things – was still meaningful in 1972, "Especially if Afrikaners are dependent on the English newspapers for Broederbond news . . ."

He asked whether the AB, through its excessive secrecy, was not responsible for much of the gossip surrounding it. The Broederbond, perhaps, had to re-assess its position in modern Afrikaner life. "Why must it . . . be an embarrassment for a member of the Broederbond when it is made known without authorisation that he is a member? It is not a disgrace to be a member of the Broederbond. Yet you are teased about it. Ask me, I know. The point is that in Afrikaner society as a whole there is a heavy questionmark hanging over the Broederbond. The rights or wrongs of the questionmark can be discussed, but the fact . . . cannot be argued away. It simply means that many Afrikaners feel that there exists an exclusive society which is really a volk within a volk. With the confidentiality as unconfidential as it has become, the question is fairly general: Who is Piet that he is seen as better than I am?"

Pienaar also contradicted Vorster on the issue of the Bond oath. Vorster said at Witbank that a Broeder "takes an oath before God Almighty." Yet Pienaar said that a Broeder merely gave an "undertaking."

In a speech a few days later at Brakpan, on October 4, Vorster said reasons for secrecy in the AB had fallen away. But, he added: "Tradition remains tradition". He angrily said that he had enough of the attacks on the Broederbond and emphatically denied that it was dictating to the Government.

Vorster asked: "Why should an Afrikaner be attacked for being a member of an Afrikaner organisation?" Jews were not attacked for being members of Jewish organisations; Greeks were not attacked for being members of Greek organisations; but if Afrikaners looked after their Afrikaner interests, they were accused. Leftists tried to create suspicion about everything that was Afrikaans, and the Bond was a favourite target.

Vorster was echoing the wild claims of 1963 – that the *Sunday Times* revelations were a Communist plot. How he could state this in 1972, when it was publicly known that Jooste and other conservative Broeders had attacked the Broederbond, is astonishing.

On October 5 *Die Vaderland,* referring to Vorster's Brakpan speech, wanted to know whether there was "still any reason for confidential organisations in South Africa . . ."

On October 8, Treurnicht declined to comment on the secrecy issue when asked to do so by the *Sunday Express:* "I do not wish to say anything on that score. I want to stress that the Afrikaner Broederbond is a cultural organisation based on Christian National ideals."

But that there was indeed a difference between the Broederbond and other organisations, contrary to Vorster's claims, was apparent from the response to a set of 15 questions put by the *Rand Daily Mail* to these secret and semi-secret organisations: the Freemasons; the Sons of England; the B'nai B'rith (a Jewish organisation); and the Broederbond.

On October 12 the *R D M* published the responses. While the other three organisations gave answers to the questions, the Bond replied to none.

Nonetheless, Treurnicht again reacted publicly, giving interviews to the *Rand Daily Mail* (two in fact) and to *Die Vaderland*. His remarks are significant in view of the known facts.

On October 16 he told the *Rand Daily Mail:* "It is time that an end was made to the suspicion and attacks on the Broederbond and that the Broederbond be allowed to continue its work. The intolerance towards the organisation and accusations of corrupt practices and sinister actions must also come to an end."

He said that the Afrikaner Broederbond was an integral part of the Afrikaner *"volksorganisme"* and therefore reflected on everything concerning the Afrikaner nation. "If the Government also acts truly in the interests of the Afrikaner nation there is no reason why the Government should not enjoy the moral support of Afrikaner cultural organisations concerning those interests.

"If there is an Opposition that only denies the rights of the Afrikaner nation it is obvious that the sympathy of the Afrikaner cultural organisations would be with the Government."

The National Party had always been regarded as the political organisation of the Afrikaner. Dr Treurnicht saw no reason why it should no longer be regarded as such. "The Afrikaner Broederbond does not dictate to the National Party and the party also does not dictate to the Afrikaner Broederbond. They are two separate organisations." But Treurnicht said that because both organisations promoted the interests of the Afrikaner, on different levels, there was obviously communication between them.

"The National Party has to, as part of its function, also protect the rights of other cultural groups. It would therefore be completely democratic and right if an English cultural organisation made representations to the Government on behalf of English-speaking people and their interests.

"The Afrikaner Broederbond will not produce an Afrikaner Somerset or Milner because what we want for ourselves we also want for others," he said.

And a day later he told Anthony Holiday that the Broederbond did not *necessarily* liaise with the Government on such matters as educational, cultural and sports policies. But, wrote Holiday, "he said the organisation gave consideration to all matters which affected the Afrikaner and consulted with, and made representations to the Government when it thought fit.

"Asked if he would concede that the Broederbond could, in certain political circumstances, have a tremendous effect on national affairs, he replied: 'It could have such an influence – just as the churches could.'

"Dr Treurnicht would not, however, confirm persistent reports that he is head of the secret organisation. 'The members of the Bond do not talk about their membership. Those who do so are disloyal to the Broederbond,' he replied."

The remarkable aspect of these remarks is that it was precisely in the educational and cultural spheres that the Broederbond's views decisively affected Government thinking. And the Bond's 1971 sports policy became official policy shortly afterwards.

On October 17 Treurnicht gave a question and answer interview to *Die Vaderland* in which he defended the Broederbond's secrecy, comparing its confidential character with that of Cabinet meetings. He described it as in the first place "a discussion body." (See annexure H).

Die Vaderland then proposed that the Broederbond could overcome the suspicions against it by doing two things. Firstly, the names of the UR and its chairman could be announced and the latter could give interviews; secondly, the AB could from time to time make known its attitude on issues of the day.

While public controversy about the Broederbond was being waged in the Press, the AB leadership made preparations for the final move against Broeders who were HNP members or supporters.

First the idea was mooted of calling a special Bondsraad. But this was soon abandoned. Then, on October 22, I wrote a front-page *Sunday-Times* report headlined: "Couriers fan out over S A with secret messages." The UR had taken emergency steps to counter the internal crisis and uncertainty caused by weeks of glaring publicity.

To ensure maximum secrecy the Bond did not dare to post the circular informing cells about the proposed plan of action. The secretaries of all cells were informed that a special circular was on the way, carried by special couriers.

I wrote: "The secretaries were told that special emissaries from the Broederbond head-quarters in Braamfontein, Johannesburg, were leaving by car and plane to distribute the circular as swiftly as possible in South Africa, South West Africa and Rhodesia. These emissaries are officers of the Broederbond, the Federasie van Afrikaanse Kultuurver-enigings (FAK), the Afrikaanse Taal en Kultuurverenigings (ATKV) and other cultural organisations controlled by the Broederbond.

"Secretaries of divisions were told to be on standby. The plan is for special Broeder emissaries to go to a number of central points. A special contact man has been appointed in each region to be the link between the special emissary and local chairman and secretaries. In Pretoria, for example, the contact man is Mr Etienne le Roux, an attorney.

"Early this week Mr le Roux was given a list of the chairman and secretaries in the Pretoria region. They have been instructed to collect personally the secret circular from Mr le Roux on Wednesday. Mr le Roux will by then have received the circular from the emissary. He will hand it to them only after they have identified themselves."

A week later, on October 29, 1972, I took the matter further with a report in which I wrote: "All divisions were instructed in a secret circular last week, delivered by special couriers throughout Southern Africa, between October 31 and November 3.

"Emergency plans will be discussed at these meetings, and a large-scale purge of 'unfaithful' and 'disloyal' elements is expected. Last week the *Sunday Times* disclosed that there was wide-spread panic and confusion in Broeder ranks. As a result, Dr Andries Treurnicht MP, the Broeder chief, and his Executive Committee or Uitvoerende Raad (UR) had sent out a special circular, delivered by hand, to reach persons at central points throughout South Africa.

"I have been told by Broederbond sources this week that this latest *Sunday Times* report caused even greater confusion and panic in the highest Broeder and Nationalist Party circles. As a result an emergency message went out at the beginning of the week, cancelling arrangements, future meetings and the delivery of circulars.

"However, this tactic later appeared to have been a smoke-screen and an attempt to shake off the *Sunday Times* investigations into Broeder secrets. A second secret order was sent out a day later, countermanding the earlier order, instructing chairmen and secre-taries to continue with the collection of a special circular at centre points.

122

"In terms of this circular the Broeder divisions were instructed to meet between October 31 and November 3 to take counter-measures to prevent a complete breakdown of morale."

The following week, on November 5, I reported that all members at these cell meetings had been compelled to sign a document – a *"plegtige onderneming"* ("solemn undertaking"). It was named the "Red Oath" by HNP supporters.

According to the document each member was to "(i) Reaffirm my dedication to the ideal of the survival of a separate Afrikaner volk as long as it may please God, and to the Christian National basis of the Afrikaner Broederbond;

"(ii) Reaffirm my solemn promise to maintain confidentiality regarding the Afrikaner Broederbond, its members and activities even if my membership is terminated;

"(iii) Affirm that I am not associated through membership or co-operation with the HNP, and that if I have been . . . I undertake to end such association immediately."

As a result of this ultimatum a number of members were excluded from the Broederbond, while some, as in 1964, exercised their right to resign voluntarily. However, I understand that these were few in number.

Thus the process which started in late 1969 has been completed. No HNP member or supporter could be a Broederbonder. Thereby the Broederbond became the official secret underground wing of the National Party, which must surely be the only political party outside Communist and totalitarian countries which uses a secret organisation above the normal party structure.

From 1972 onwards the Broederbond was effectively used by Vorster to prevent a verkrampte backlash to adaptations in race, sports and foreign policies. At the same time verkrampte Broeders such as Treurnicht and his sympathisers used their entrenched positions to delay and resist change and adaptation. In the caucus, in N P circles, and at Broeder meetings Treurnicht and his men stage-managed the long delay in the implementation of the new sports policy. But it moved from a pure multi-national policy in 1971 – mainly designed for international competition – towards a form of multi-racialism in 1978, although not accepted as such in theory.

Vorster also used the Bond to inform influential Broeders about important developments. Thus on Saturday, August 24, 1974, while Parliament was in session in Cape Town he specially flew to Pretoria to address a meeting of Broeders. With Treurnicht in the chair he attacked a move initiated by ultra-conservative Broeders to hold a volkskongres against liberalism (in fact held a month later, convened by Theo Schumann, with whom Vorster had clashed at a Broeder meeting in 1970). Vorster also explained the delicate issues of Rhodesia and Mozambique, and dealt with conservative criticism of the Government's sports and Coloured policies.

By all accounts he adopted a very conservative position, particularly on Rhodesia, making it clear that South Arica would never leave that country in the lurch as it and S A were in the same boat. In fact, some members who had contemplated leaving the Bond were so impressed by his speech that they stayed on; one right-winger told me afterwards: "I myself could not have hoped for a more conservative line."

Ironically, this was less than two months before the announcement that Vorster and Zambia's Kenneth Kaunda had been involved in dètente negotiations for several months – aimed at the establishment of majority rule government in Rhodesia and ousting Ian Smith.

The details of the Pretoria meeting were splashed in the *Sunday Times* in the following weeks and Treurnicht informally asked for the assistance of "certain government quarters" to assist in locating and plugging the leaks. I was warned that the names of a number of people I had spoken to in recent weeks had been passed on to the Bond leadership. Subsequently, on several occasions until November 1977, several people whom I knew, or who knew me, were specifically asked by certain security and BOSS agents about my possible Broederbond contacts.

Any fears Vorster might have had that the Broederbond could become a tool of verkrampte obstructionists were finally removed when Gerrit Viljoen was elected new Broeder chief, replacing Treurnicht, who only served a two-year term.

I had predicted this in the *Sunday Times* of June 3, 1974. The report stated that Viljoen was Vorster's candidate, and Meyer was blamed for Viljoen's 1972 defeat by Treurnicht on the grounds that he had not effectively planned the campaign. Vorster and his supporters wanted Treurnicht out of the way because of his obstructionism. Influential business groups like Sanlam and Rembrandt, along with BOSS and the Special Branch, were actively engaged in the pro-Viljoen campaign as early as May 1974. They made sure that the "right" delegates were chosen for the September 1974 Bondsraad.

I was told that when Treurnicht arrived and saw the composition of the meeting, he realised his days were numbered; he was not to be nominated either as chairman or as a member of the UR.

The meeting was held under tight and strict security measures. Everything was done to avoid a repetition of the "fiasco" seven weeks earlier, when the *Sunday Times* was "present" at the Broederbond meeting addressed by the Prime Minister in Pretoria. Supporters of Treurnicht claimed that the "reason" for his withdrawal was that "Vorster had offered him a deputy ministership" at the next Cabinet reshuffle, expected soon.

Piet Koornhof also played a major behind-the-scenes role in the "stop-Treurnicht" campaign; at that time he regarded himself as a contender for the Premiership and his supporters feared that a victory for Treurnicht would strengthen the position of his then archrival Connie Mulder. But, as it turned out, Treurnicht was appointed a Deputy Minister in 1975.

After the *Sunday Times* revealed that Viljoen was the new Broeder chief, *Die Vaderland* on October 7, 1974, repeated its earlier demands that the Broederbond should reveal the members of its UR and take a public stand on disputed issues.

With Viljoen in command it looks at present very much as if the Broederbond has recovered from the shocks of 1972. By the end of 1977 membership totalled 11 910. It is known that Viljoen is a believer in intellectual brain-storm sessions; he is a "think tank" man, alarmed at the failure of the Government to make use of experts in various fields outside government service on a permanent, part-time or *ad hoc* basis – as in Western Europe and the United States. He expressed these ideas in a radio interview and in Press articles in 1976. Viljoen apparently had discussions on this very issue with Vorster at the end of that year, but I am told he was totally unimpressed by Vorster's "failure to understand" the idea of strengthening government and administration by employing expert outsiders.

It can be accepted that Viljoen will push the Broederbond into taking a more assertive role than in the past, and to present the Government with clear-cut proposals on a number of issues. Viljoen is one of the most brilliant academics ever produced in South Africa. He has been compared with the late Jan Hofmeyer, of the Smuts Cabinet, who was an intellectual genius. He has a dynamic personality and is highly ambitious.

However, it is certain that after the events of 1972 the Broederbond will never again go against the Government. It will submit plans, or work in conjunction with the Government, but the National Party will hold the unchallenged political leadership.

A case in point is the contentious sports policy. On September 1, 1976, the UR sent out a monthly circular on the issue. It stated that "mixed sports should not take place at provincial or club level." Members were asked to use their influence to spread this message.

The Broederbond high command had clearly not been informed about the latest changes in government thinking. A mere two days after the circular had been sent out, the UR was invited to a discussion with Cabinet Ministers and were informed that certain new changes in the sports policy had been considered.

So an urgent circular was then sent out to recall the first one. Subsequently it was explained that the Cabinet had not been able to notify the AB sooner about the pending changes, but that they had to be accepted.

In 1977 Viljoen used the Bond to prevent a major crisis about the new constitutional proposals concerning the Coloureds, Indians and Whites. The sports issue simmered on, too.

In August 1977, Broederbonders such as Treurnicht and Professor Hannes Botha, former athletics chief at the University of Pretoria, strongly attacked Koornhof and the growing multi-racialism in sport at cell meetings. There was also strong reaction to the new constitutional proposals, the details of which were not then known. Conservative Broeders and Nationalists feared that they would ultimately lead to a multi-racial political dispensation whereby a "non-White" could be declared President and the White Parliament lose its powers.

But the Bond leadership gave its full backing to the proposals. In August 1977, just before the matter became public, a special circular dealing with them was sent to all cells. It was initiated by chairman Viljoen and members were asked to support Vorster.

Significantly, Viljoen came publicly to Vorster's rescue on the sports issue in an article in *Die Transvaler* of September 13, 1977. It was obviously written to coincide with the opening of the Transvaal congress of the NP in Pretoria, where strong resistance to the constitutional proposal – and to the sports policy – was anticipated.

' The article contained an urgent plea that the widespread dissatisfaction with the sports policy and with mixed sports clubs should not be allowed to damage the constitutional proposals, which were regarded as of the highest importance. Viljoen stressed that the first priority was the "largest possible unanimity for a constitutional framework," which would provide an acceptable solution to the Coloured "problem". This was necessary both for secure internal relations and because of increasing external pressure.

He said it would be "unwise at this stage to blow up differences of . . . a lower priority, for example, the sports policy." The article was obviously a well-planned attempt to allay fears of rank and file Nationalists on the sports issue, with which Viljoen dealt at length. Significantly, he stressed his opposition, and that of the Government, to mixed sports clubs. However, at this stage he thought that for internal and external reasons it was unnecessary to pass legislation to prohibit them in view of the small number of people involved.

But, should the situation be exploited for political reasons to promote a "common society," then: "I have no doubt that we will have to prevent mixed clubs by passing legislation." This perfectly emphasised the Bond's new role as a "support organisation" of the NP.

PART V

Organisation, Aims and Philosophy

To be able to understand the structure and organisation of the Afrikaner Broederbond it is necessary to constantly bear in mind its ultimate objective and aims.

On January 16, 1934, Professor J.C. van Rooy, the chairman, sent out a circular which *inter alia* stated: "Let us keep constantly in mind the fact that our chief concern is whether Afrikanerdom will reach its eventual goal of domination in South Africa . . . our solution for South Africa's problems is that the Afrikaner Broederbond rule South Africa."

And Verwoerd, a UR member for years, had said: "Broeders, the Afrikaner Broederbond must gain control of anything it can lay its hands on in every walk of life in South Africa. Members must help each other to gain promotion in the civil service or any other field of activity in which they work with a view to securing important administrative positions."

This is what has actually happened since 1918. In a sense the Broederbond rules and controls South Africa both directly and indirectly. Yet officially it does not exist; its name and address is not listed in any telephone directory.

In Afrikaans-English and Afrikaner dictionaries it is not referred to at all. But, after all, L.W. Hiemstra, an author of one of the standard dictionaries, was a UR member in the Forties. Its secret nature extends that far.

Meetings of the UR, Bondsraad, large conferences and cells are not only secret; special arrangements are always made to keep them so. Bond circulars contain constant warnings to members to maintain secrecy by travelling together in cars; to keep parked cars at a minimum; not to allow wives to serve tea at a house during cell meetings; and to provide realistic excuses explaining their presence if at a Bondsraad in a strange city should they bump into a non-Broeder acquaintance. Members are constantly exhorted not to discuss AB matters on the phone, and special instructions to cells lay down very strict rules regarding correspondence. The Broederbond's name, for example, must never be used in letters.

The organisation is very complex. Many bodies which may appear completely innocent to the ordinary man, and which have legitimate and admirable objectives, are in fact in the vice of the Broederbond.

The most important front organisation is the FAK *(Federasie van Afrikaanse Kultuurvereniginge)*. This is a massive umbrella body to which vitually all Afrikaans cultural organisations are affiliated.

Other front organisations or bodies within its sphere of influence include the National Youth Council and the Youth Leaders Institute; the Ruiterwag – its junior counterpart, also a secret body; the Rapportryers and Junior Rapportryers (training schools for future Broeders); SABRA (the South African Bureau for Racial Affairs); the SA Noodhulpliga (SA First Aid League); the Afrikaanse Kultuurraad of Pretoria; the Voortrekker movement (the Afrikaans version of the Boy Scouts); and the Genootskap van Rhodesiese Afrikaners (Association of Rhodesian Afrikaners) which brings together Rhodesian Afrikaners.

Other Bond-linked organisations which were disbanded because of the conflict of the late Sixties were the Afrikaner Orde; the Dirkie Uys Foundation; the Vryburgers (a secret organisation outside the AB, based largely in the Free State, which was later incorporated into the Bond); and the GVA (Genootskap Volk en Arbeid).

I will now detail aspects of the internal structure of the Bond.

A. Structure

(a) Internal Structure

According to its constitution and standing orders, the Broederbond has the following hierarchy.

- The Bondsraad or annual congress of the organisation. These are run very much on the same lines as congresses of the National Party.
- The Uitvoerende Raad. This is elected by the Bondsraad and constitutes the highest authority of the Bond.
- A Dagbestuur (management committee) of the UR, which gives attention to urgent matters arising between ordinary UR meetings.
- Streeksrade (regional councils) and Sentrale Komitees (central committees) in certain geographical areas of the country.
- Afdelings (cells) throughout the country. These consist of at least five members in a town, suburb, or in a particular country area.

It is worth examining these and associated organisations in greater detail.

1. The Bondsraad

The Bondsraad is the highest authority in the Bond, subject only to the constitution and the standing orders. It holds an ordinary meeting every year, preferably in the second half, at a place determined by the serving UR. It can, of course, also summon an extraordinary session to discuss matters of special importance. The UR is chosen every second year by the Bondsraad.

The Bondsraad is composed of members of the serving UR and representatives of the various cells. Each cell can send one delegate to the Bondsraad, though frequently two or more cells decide to send a single delegate as their representative.

Names of delegates must be handed in to head office at least 14 days before the Bondsraad. According to the standing rules, the UR can demand documents of accreditation, provided by head office, before members are admitted to the annual meeting.

The activities of the Bondsraad comprise the following:

(i) The submission and discussion of reports and recommendations tabled by the UR. A secretarial report – by the chairman and chief secretary – on the activities of the UR and the cells (excluding the year in which no UR election takes place) along with financial reports are also discussed.

(ii) The discussion of draft resolutions sent in by the cells. These cover a wide field – the total spectrum of South African public life as it affects the Afrikaner Nationalists. Everything from religion to politics, economics to foreign affairs, is discussed. (The 1966 Bondsraad, for example had 94 such proposals in the following categories: economic and related matters: agricultural matters; cultural affairs; Press matters;

youth affairs; education; politics; immigration; separate development; and domestic affairs.

The Bondsraad is thus a peoples' parliament covering matters normally raised in the House, at National Party congresses, and in cultural youth and educational bodies – and even in the churches).

(iii) The election of the UR every second year.
(iv) The determination of the business of the Broederbond for the forthcoming period and approval of a budget for the coming year. (The budget is prepared by the UR).
(v) Discussion of any matters allowed by the Bondsraad.
(vi) The determination of standing rules according to specific provisions in the constitution.

All Bondsraad decisions remain in force until they are recalled or changed after notice of review has been given. Copies of these decisions are sent to all cells.

Every full member of the Broederbond has the right to attend the Bondsraad, but only members of the UR and its official representatives may vote.

2.   The Uitvoerende Raad – UR

The UR is the highest executive authority in the Broederbond, and as such it is the most important constituent of the organisation. The period of service of the UR is two years. It consists of 11 elected members, and five others who are co-opted by the elected members. The election of members is by secret ballot. Each cell, as well as the serving UR, may nominate no more than two Broeders, and in this manner 40 or 50 names appear on a short list.

The chairman and vice-chairman of the UR are nominated in writing and elected by an absolute majority of those present entitled to have a vote. There are certain limits on the period of years which UR members may serve.

No province may have more than five representatives on the UR. When more than five such members are proposed by one province, those receiving the least votes will be eliminated. Interim vacancies are filled by the UR itself.

All UR members are eligible to vote on the understanding that they abstain when matters are discussed which affect them personally. The quorum of the UR is six; the chairman has an ordinary and a decisive vote and the chief secretary of the AB has full voting rights if a quorum can only be obtained by calling him in.

Each member is compelled to attend all meetings of the UR, and if he does not attend three consecutive meetings without providing well-founded reasons, he can, after due warning, be expelled from the UR.

Meetings are convened as often as the activities of the UR demand it – usually some five or six times a year. Members of the UR, or its representatives, may attend all meetings of all bodies of the AB in order to maintain the closest contact with the whole organisation. On such occasions they do not vote, but may advise. All books, reports, documents and articles of AB bodies are open for unhindered inspection by the UR or its representatives.

3.   The Dagbestuur

After each Bondsraad the UR appoints six of its members to form the management committee, which acts on behalf of the UR. The chief secretary serves on the committee in an advisory capacity and is its secretary. The quorum is three, and the chief secretary acts as *secondus* with full voting powers on behalf of any absent member to make up a quorum. Its brief is to deal with current affairs affecting the UR, but it also undertakes the selection of "probable applicants" *("waarskynlike applikante")* – the term used for people who have been screened for this purpose.

In important matters on which the Bondsraad or the UR have given no clear ruling, Broederbond officials act according to management committee decisions, which are submitted to the next UR meeting for confirmation. Reports must be regularly submitted to the full UR on all matters dealt with by the dagbestuur.

So the UR chairman and the chief secretary have always played key roles in shaping the affairs of the Broederbond. Since its inception on June 5, 1918, the Bond has had 11 chairmen some of whom have served more than once:

H.J. Klopper (June 5, 1918 – June 26, 1924)
W. Nicol (June 26, 1924 – March 13, 1925)
J.H. Greybe (March 13, 1925 – May 26, 1928)
J.W. Potgieter (May 26, 1928 – September 6, 1930)
L.J. du Plessis (September 6, 1930 – August 13, 1932)
J.C. van Rooy (August 13, 1932 – October 6, 1938)
N. Diederichs (October 6, 1938 – October 3, 1942)
J.C. van Rooy (October 3, 1942 – February 23, 1951)
N. Diederichs (February 23, 1951 – October 1, 1952)
H.B. Thom (October 1, 1952 – November 1960)
P.J. Meyer (November 24, 1960 – April 6, 1972)
A.P. Treurnicht (April 6, 1972 – October 1974)
Gerrit Viljoen (October 1974 to the present)

The AB has had only a few chief secretaries. I.W. Lombard occupied the position, at first on a voluntary basis but later full-time, from the late Twenties to the early Fifties. He was succeeded by J.P. van der Spuy. Then Piet Koornhof took over in 1962 followed by Naudé Botha in early 1965.

The chief secretary is assisted by two or three assistant secretaries as well as several organisers and liaison officers. So there is a full-time staff of six or seven, some running the Ruiterwag, others officially linked to the FAK to cover their Broederbond activities. There is also an administrative staff of five or six women – whose husbands all are Broeders.

For many years the Broederbond officials, together with those of the FAK and other cultural organisations, were housed in the Christiaan de Wet Building in Simmonds Street, Braamfontein, Johannesburg. Recently they have moved to a modern office block, Die Eike in Cedar Avenue, Auckland Park, Johannesburg.

Head Office employees get a salary or honorarium from the UR and provisions has been made for a pension fund, a car scheme, etc. Furthermore Bond officials are safeguuared against the consequences of any *bona fide* action, financial or otherwise, performed in the course of their duties. The large head office staff is completely separate from officials of front organisations such as the FAK, the Rapportryers and the Junior Rapportryers. However, Broeder officials often appear at public functions ostensibly representing one of these "public arms" of the Broederbond.

129

The most important link between head office and the members is the regular monthly circular to all cells.

Every three months the circulars contain a special list of "waarskynlike applikante."

4. The Afdelings

The UR can, if it regards it as desirable, establish a cell on its own initiative or when it is requested to do so. The UR may, in consultation with one or more existing cells in an area, constitute a new cell out of them, regarded as a daughter cell. A portion of the members' fees are transferred from the mother to the daughter cell.

Taking into account local circumstances, the UR determines when and where cells are established. The number of cells will be in proportion to the number of 20-40-year-old Afrikaans white males in any particular area.

The UR may also establish and administer as many cells of "Buitebroers" ("Outside Broeders" – see later explanation) as it thinks fit and name those Buitebroers who will fall under such cells.

In some circumstances a Broeder may be exempted from compulsory cell meetings. He then cannot serve in the local committee or the UR, but all prescribed regulations remain applicable to him. He still carries the full financial obligations of ordinary members and when he attends meetings enjoys the same rights and privileges of an actively engaged Broeder.

After the establishment of a new cell, where the majority are new Broeders, at least three months must elapse before the cell can propose the names of probable applicants.

The number of actively engaged members in a cell is limited to 20. Strengthening the membership of a cell to the maximum may at most be done with two initiations *(instellings)* each Bondsyear. The regulations determine that at least one of the two Broeders initiated each year must be under 35. Probable applicants older than 50 are only approved for recruitment under very special circumstances and for really convincing reasons.

A cell that exists for longer than three years may only propose members over 45 with the prior approval of the UR, unless the proposal takes place because a new cell is being hived off.

At cell meetings attempts to promote and realise the aims of the Broederbond as defined in the constitution are made; and there is the discussion *(behandeling)* of matters raised by Broeders or the UR. A cell may only contact other cells on any business undertaking or policy matter with the prior approval of the UR.

So in practice each cell concerns itself with any matter involving Afrikaner Nationalist interests in its area including religious, political, school, cultural, economic, race and town council matters. It will try and get Broeders or Broeder candidates into any public vacancies.

It will also implement any UR decision given in a circular, or advocate a specific line following a circular directive. Thus, quietly, without the public being aware of it, 12 000 people spread out in strategic places throughout South Africa, SWA and Rhodesia, will influence public opinion on any important issue of the day.

A cell meeting is held at least once a month, unless this is not possible because of special circumstances. Each month a written report is sent to the head office divulging the most important matters discussed at the meeting. A register of attendance is also kept and sent on. Thus head office has a complete record of the attendance rate of each member through-out the country. In 1968, for example, it circulated a list of members who were attending less than five meetings a year.

Each cell drafts its own domestic regulations and submits them to the UR for approval. Each cell is required to have an annual programme of action, vetted by head office.

The transfer of a Broeder from one cell to another is the responsibility of the UR. It can only take place once a Broeder has fulfilled all his financial obligations to both the cell he is leaving, and to the UR. When a Broeder moves house within a city area where there is more than one cell, he stays with his existing cell unless the UR decides otherwise because of local circumstances.

The cell committee *(bestuur)* consists of a minimum of three members (chairman, secretary and treasurer) with a maximum of eight. A new cell chooses a committee at its inaugural meeting *(stigtings vergadering)*. At the last general meeting of each Bondsyear, a new committee is chosen according to the provisions of the domestic regulations. At least one-third of the old committee remains in service for another year, and all committee members are chosen by majority vote in a secret ballot after a short list has been prepared by the cell.

It is the first task of each committee to become conversant with the contents of all official documents of the Broederbond. As in the case of the UR, all committee members are obliged to attend each meeting and face expulsion if they miss three or more consecutive meetings.

The committee is the executive authority in the cell and the Broeders who fall under it must without hesitatiion speedily implement its decisions.

5.   Streekrade and Sentrale Komitees

A number of cells can be linked together by the UR to serve common interests of a local nature, forming a regional council. This in turn may form regional committees with funds provided by the cells concerned. All financial and constitutional decisions regarding regional committees require the approval of the UR.

In the early Seventies, for example, there were regional committees for the following areas: Cape Town; Boland; Overberg; Olifantsrivier (North-Western Cape); South-Western Districts; Port Elizabeth; Border; Northern Free State; North-Western Free State; Far-Western Transvaal; Rustenburg; J.G. Strijdom (for the Nylstroom, Potgieters-rust area); H.F. Verwoerd (for the Pietersburg, Louis Trichardt area); Eastern Lowveld; Highveld; Southern Transvaal; East Rand; Natal; South West Africa; and Rhodesia.

Since then more have been established.

In some places the cells are linked together in central committees. They exist in Pretoria (including Brits), Johannesburg and Bloemfontein. Their function is largely to determine the relationships between the various cells. The powers and responsibilities of a central committee are determined by the UR.

6.   Ad Hoc Committees and Task Groups

Since the early Sixties – when it became ever more directly involved in politics and State affairs – the Bond has functioned through *ad hoc* committees and a variety of task groups, which study particular problems and issues. Thus a committee or task force has been appointed for vitually every cabinet portfolio, as well as to deal with other topics. Each committee or group has a chairman and additional members are appointed by the UR, for which they prepare study documents and reports.

Apart from the normal portfolio's such as economic affairs, labour, immigration, education, agriculture, sport, Bantu, Coloured and Indian affairs, etc., there are also specialised committees. These deal *inter alia* with film affairs, study loans, the "Jewish problem," security, legislation, the Press and cultural affairs.

7. New Members

The induction *(inskakeling)* of new members happens as follows.

Firstly, notice must be given of the intention to propose a particular person. Secondly, he must actually be proposed. Then he is approached by existing members and the UR. Thirdly, it must be determined whether he is prepared to join the Broederbond. And finally he must be initiated into the AB.

A Broeder may not directly or indirectly propose or second any person as a Broederbond candidate until he has been a member for 12 months. Nor may he propose his relations. The proposer and seconder of an aspirant Broeder must both know him well.

The following criteria must be the basis for a proposed member's acceptance:

1. Does he strive for the ideal of the eternal *(ewigdurende)* existence of a separate Afrikaner volk with its own language and culture?
2. Does he give preference to Afrikaners and Afrikaans firms in the economic, public and professional spheres?
3. Does he maintain Afrikaans in his home, in his profession and in the society as a whole?
4. Is he a Protestant?
5. Is he reliable, of firm principles and careful enough to comply with the requirements of the Broederbond?
6. Is his character irreproachable?
7. Is he financially strong?
8. Can, and will, he actively, regularly and loyally participate in all the functions and proceedings of the Broederbond?

Only when there is a strong possibility that a person will indeed join, can he be proposed. Both the cell committee and the proposers must assure themselves that any applicant is not a member of a secret or semi-secret international organisation.

A person must first be proposed in writing at a cell meeting by two members, then approved by the cell, before his name can be sent to the chief secretary for vetting by all the cells. If there is no local cell, the UR does the provisional selection *(keuring)*.

After the initial proposal the matter is discussed candidly at the next meeting. If it seems that the Broeders are satisfied, then he is proposed by two Broeders who fill in the UR's prescribed form D. But if it appears that the Broeders present are not in favour of the applicant, then his introduction *(voorstelling)* will probably be abandoned.

The local selection takes place at a third cell meeting. All the Broeders present are obliged to vote "yes" or "no". Originally one negative vote was sufficient to exclude a prospective applicant. Later the rule was changed to two dissident votes.

'A "yes" vote means that form D is sent off to the chief secretary, who circulates a selection list *(keurlys)* among all the divisions every three months. In it he gives the date on which the general selection must be completed by the cells. So there is a countrywide check on whether a person is good enough for the Bond. If a proposed person is disqualified at any level he may not be proposed again for two years.

The UR can cancel the name of a prospective applicant without him being disqualified, and in such a case he may not be proposed again within six months, unless the UR decides otherwise.

Nobody may be approached about joining until the chief secretary has been given the go-ahead by the UR. And then the applicant must apply for membership within six months, or his right to join lapses and he must be proposed and selected anew. Until a fairly late stage a proposed member knows nothing of all this to-ing and fro-ing.

The selection of approved applicants takes place by or under the control of an information committee of at least two Broeders, appointed every year by the cell committee. The unsuspecting pre-Broeder is first sounded out, preferably by a member of the information committee, on his attitude concerning joining an organisation like the Broederbond. No details of the Bond may, however, be discussed with him. Such a person must also be told that there are financial obligations involved in joining. If he indicates his preparedness, he is brought into contact with the information committee, which continues the process.

When the prospective applicant is decisively approached he must first promise to regard the discussion as confidential, whether he decides to join or not. In the selection process the canvassers must be very careful. Neither the internal workings of the Bond or the names of any members may be divulged. At this stage the constitution, but not the regulations and the AB's guidance manual, may be shown to the applicant. Some general information on the Broederbond can be communicated to him – such as the categories of person who belong to it, the financial obligations, the entry fee, the existence of a reserve fund, and the fact that the Broederbond selects its members very strictly. The *modus operandi* of selection remains a secret.

If all goes smoothly the chief secretary gives permission for initiation *(instelling)*.

The information committee of a cell is given this task. As soon as possible after the initiation the committee should inform the new Broeders about their responsibilities, and the work and nature of the Broederbond itself.

The initiation takes place according to the procedure set out in the handbook. (See Annexure I for the full induction ceremony). It is a solemn, serious, religious affair which usually takes place at the home of a Broeder, in a room darkened by dim lights or candles.

The ceremony involves a prayer, hymn singing, Bible reading, and a series of questions put to the aspirant member as he finally takes the oath to keep Broederbond secrets until his death, whether he resigns or not.

The new recruit is brought into the room by his sponsor and faces the master of ceremonies, generally either the chairman of the cell or a member of the information committee, who stands at a table with the South African flag on which the Union Jack is covered.

Other members will enter and stand behind the recruit throughout the ceremony, two of them participating, speaking in turn from behind.

Once the oral part of the ceremony is complete, the candidate turns for the first time, facing his fellow Broeders. Formal introductions takes place and he signs a document in which he affirms his pledges.

Immediately after the initiation the cell sends the statement of introduction (form G) to the chief secretary, together with that portion of the entry fee payable to the UR. On receipt of this, the person is registered as a Broeder in the records of the head office.

There are two categories of Broeders who do not normally participate in the Broeder-bond cell activities. They are the "Buitebroers" ("Outside Broeders") and "Vrygestelde Broers" ("Exempted Broeders").

These two groups are clearly distinguishable. A Broeder who is exempted from local cell obligations for well-founded reasons is known as an outside Broeder. An exempted Broeder is one who after a period of honourable and active membership is exempted by the UR from compulsory attendance of cell meetings in terms of section 36(a) of the regulations. Cabinet Ministers, judges or others who for reasons of age or work cannot be active Broeders are often found in this category.

8. The Elimination of Broeders

In the nicest possible way, a Broeder can be eliminated from his cell and become an outside Broeder. As long as he complies with the regulations of the Bond, as laid down for outside Broeders by the UR, he retains his rights of membership.

But, where it is deemed necessary for good order in the Broederbond, the UR may, using its discretion, with or without the recommendation of a cell, suggest termination of the membership of a Broeder. And where a serious charge is laid against a Broeder, the dagbestuur – or in matters of urgency, the chairman – can suspend a Broeder temporarily, pending an investigation. The Broeder concerned must be immediately informed of his suspension, and he may not attend any AB meetings during this period.

The UR can strike the name of an offending Broeder off the membership list if he:

1. Made himself guilty of conduct which the UR regards as improper;
2. Failed to meet his financial obligations for two successive years without being excused by the UR;
3. Was absent without proper notification from three consecutive cell meetings;
4. Ignored instructions of the UR;
5. Ignored the confidential nature of the Broederbond or otherwise violated his promise at induction;
6. In general neglected his duties as a Broeder;
7. Appeared to be unfit to be a Broeder;
8. Is compelled to ask for the cancellation of his membership.

Cancellation of membership takes place in a manner determined by the UR itself for each case. An affected Broeder loses all rights and privileges of membership. When somebody is cancelled (*geskrap*) as a member, it is the duty of all Broeders to take this fact carefully into account in their future dealings with him.

When a Broeder wants the membership of another Broeder to be cancelled, he must hand in his request in writing, giving full reasons, to the cell committee; or, in the case of outside Broeders, to the UR.

Reinstatement can only take place through the familiar route of introduction, selection, recruitment and initiation – with the proviso that the entry fee is not paid again.

A Broeder who becomes a member of a secret or semi-secret international organisation loses his membership.

Exempted Broeders must strictly maintain the rule of confidentiality, and regular payment of three-tenths of the normal annual fee is compulsory.

All meetings of the Bondsraad, UR, cell committees and cells are opened and closed with prayers. Broeders are expected to appear in sombre clothes at all meetings of the

Bondsraad and cells. (Indeed originally it was suggested that the cell meetings be held in evening dress!). This regulation has now been slightly relaxed, as some of the bigger Broeder gatherings in recent years have been held on farms. The Bondsraad, for example, has on some occasions been held in a barn on a farm near Bapsfontein, outside Pretoria. It was felt that wearing formal dress to such meetings would attract too much attention.

The chief secretary keeps a register of all Broeders, aspirant Broeders and probable applicants at the head office; and the secretaries of all cells keep a separate register of local Broeders, probable applicants and aspirant Broeders.

Numbers are allotted to Broeders and applicants by the chief secretary. Each month he provides each cell with a list of Broeders who have joined, and also of those who have been approved, disapproved or had membership cancelled. Each Broeder is entitled to examine the register of his cell.

When a Broeder dies the UR may provide a maximum sum of R150, which is paid to his family as a sign of sympathy.

9. Symbols and the Bondslied (Song of the Bond)

From time to time the UR determines secret signs to enable one Broeder to make contact with another, who is unknown to him. These signs are divulged after the induction of a new member. They change from time to time. For some time, for example, a Broeder would use a special handshake when greeting a stranger. If he got the right response he would know he was in the presence of a comrade.

But because it was discovered by non-Broeders, who then frequently used it to confuse Broeders, urgent instructions were issued by the UR in the Sixties that the handshake had to be abandoned.

The symbol of the Broederbond is a triangle inside a circle resembling a cord with the inscription "Die Afrikaner Broederbond" on top and the founding year "1918" beneath.

The emblem remains the property of the Broederbond and is given to Broeders on payment of a deposit and on the condition that it is sent back to head office when membership is terminated by death or otherwise. The deposit is then repaid.

The official Bondslied was composed by Dr Jan Pienaar of Pretoria, and Stephen H Eyssen with original words by Ivan Lombard.

One membership provision specifies that, wherever possible, the Broederbond should not become involved in litigation. If it does become involved, the chairman must act on behalf of the organisation.

10. Membership Statistics

From AB statistics it is evident that it has spread into almost every walk of life, in both the private and public sector. Its 11 910 members (as of 1977) represent Afrikaner Nationalists in virtually every key position in the country.

It frequently occurs that when a non-Broeder is promoted to a key position, he will soon be recruited. In other words the "cream" is skimmed off.

Significantly, education has the largest single group of members – 2 424 or 20,36 per cent of total AB membership. Farmers number 2 240 members; pensioners 1 124; businessmen 1 096; ministers of religion 848; and public servants 518. There are 390 Broeder lawyers; 309 bankers; 290 municipal employees; 265 agriculturists; 212 policemen; 201 railwaymen; 186 politicians and 165 members of quasi-State organisations.

135

Broeders in the media include 68 journalists and a further 49 in broadcasting.

There has been a steady growth in Broederbond membership. In 1965 there were 6 966 members; in 1968, 8 191; and 9 413 in June 1972.

An analysis of the 1968 figures shows that farmers constituted the largest group at that time, representing the overwhelming majority of platteland Broeders. The teaching profession ran second then with 1 691 members (20,6 per cent); clergymen 8,2 per cent (670); and the public service 5,1 per cent (419). Other groups were: commerce 10,2 per cent (838); and medical doctors 4,8 per cent (391). Of the latter group more than half came from the teaching profession.

Also in 1968 2,6 per cent (210) were in politics. They included the State President; Prime Minister John Vorster; 19 Cabinet Ministers and Deputy Ministers; 79 MPs; 28 Senators; 69 MPCs, and 18 party organisers.

The job breakdown within each profession shows that most of the top men are Broeders. Take education. Broeders in this sector in 1968 were 24 Rectors of universities and teachers' training colleges – in practice almost every Afrikaans Rector. There were 171 professors; 176 lecturers; 468 headmasters; 121 school inspectors; and 647 teachers. So the overwhelming majority of headmasters and school inspectors were members. This remains the case today.

In the Press, 22 editors were Broeders, but only three journalists were considered good enough to be elected to the elite. Sixteen managers of Afrikaans newspaper groups were Broeders. In the SABC, 15 directors and managers, four organisers, two editors, and two announcers were Broeders.

Of the 415 Broeder public servants, 59 were secretaries or assistant secretaries of government departments. With few exceptions the heads of all civil service departments were and are AB members.

In banking there were 154 managers (mostly in Volkskas), 22 accountants and 19 clerks (2,4 per ent of the membership). And there were 16 judges, 13 advocates, 156 attorneys and 67 magistrates.

In the early Sixties there were relatively few policemen, but by the end of the decade an extraordinary number of senior police officers had been recruited.

Pretoria is the city with the most Broeders. In 1966 there were already a thousand. It was followed by Johannesburg with 342; Bloemfontein with 307; Cape Town northern areas 227; Cape Town itself 159; Stellenbosch with 176; and Potchefstroom 121.

11. The Christiaan de Wet Fund

The affairs of the Broederbond are financed from a reserve fund, known as the Christiaan de Wet Fund – named after the famous Boer guerilla leader. The formation of the fund was announced in circular 7/49/50 of April 1, 1950. The main idea behind the fund was "that experience, including that of recent years, has strengthened our conviction that there awaits a large and continuous task for the Afrikaner Broederbond and that the means for the execution of the task must not be lacking.

"It is the viewpoint of the UR . . . that the activities of the Broederbond must be expanded considerably."

The circular further stated: "The Broederbond is undoubtedly the strongest and most purposeful cultural organisation of the Afrikaner, and it does not behove it to be hampered in its activities through the absence of a strong reserve fund.

"From various sides voices have been saying that the time is more than ripe to establish a fund, because once the fund exists it will hopefully not be necessary again to make further calls on members for financial support from time to time for specific matters." It was decided that interest could not be employed until the fund had reached a capital amount of R50 000. Members of the Broederbond have been encouraged to make contributions, and it was set as an ideal that each Broeder should contribute R200 during the period of his membership.

In the first 11 years (1951 to 1962) the fund grew from R30 012 to R262 218. The profits of the fund were capitalised until 1955 when it exceeded R100 000. Afterwards the profits were made available to the UR.

At the Bondsraad of May 21, 1963, it was decided to push the fund up to R1 million within five years. The decision was directly prompted by the series of *Sunday Times* exposés of the organisation which had started a month earlier. According to the minutes "this was a challenge rather than a punishment . . ."

Two full-time officials of the UR, F.J. Beyleveldt and M.J. Kruger, were specially appointed for this task and indeed reached the R1 million target shortly before the AB's fiftieth anniversary in June 1968. Today the fund stands at more than R2 million.

At Bondsraad metings reports are submitted on the income of the fund, and the Bondsraad can at all times decide how it should be used.

The Christiaan de Wet Fund was registered as a non-profit-making company. Originally the idea was that there would be 21 members, but they were later reduced to 17. The 11 serving UR members at the time, together with Dr M.S. Louw, C.F. de Wet, W. Bührman, Ivan Lombard, F.G. Lutz and Professor S. du Toit were the founder members.

UR members elected afterwards became *ipso facto* members of the fund. Out of the 17 members a board of trustees is annually appointed which handles investments and administration. So in practice control of the fund is vested in the UR and the Bondsraad.

According to the 1963 memorandum setting the R1 million target, an opportunity would be "provided whereby the AB can create a monument for the volk which can live on until the end of time, as is the case with great trust funds throughout the world, such as the Carnegie Fund, the Rhodes Trust, the Rockefeller Trust, the Eisenhower Trust and many others."

This is a very interesting comparison. Of course the one, vital difference between the Christiaan de Wet Fund and all the other illustrous funds is the fact that they – and the use to which their moneys are put – are open to public scrutiny, while the Christiaan de Wet Fund is secret, and its use far from the eyes of the general public.

The memo stated that it was a time of internal and external pressure, presenting the white nation with its biggest crisis in its 300 years of existence. So "a weapon" such as the fund could play an important role. When put to the test "financial means to counter the battle will be of immense importance . . . The AB is called upon to extend *(uitbou)* the Republic and give content to it . . ."

It was made clear that the moneys were to be spent in financing the task groups and committees. It was the "task of the AB to help initiate new things" and the fund would be put to use in the following areas: in the economic sphere, where the Afrikaner faced the "Oppenheimer group, at present busy with great efforts . . . to usurp the Afrikaner economy . . ."; in the sphere of White/non-White relations; in the cultural sphere; in the newspaper world where the Afrikaners faced a great backlog; in the industrial sector and in the trade unions; in education, especially as regards Afrikaans youth organisations; in the technical and scientific spheres, especially planning; and, most importantly, in defence.

Broeders were urged to take the offensive to "sharpen the defences of the AB."

The fund was strengthened by the donation of the farm Strydhoek in the Ladysmith district (worth R63 000) by Broeder S.A. Maree.

In the late Sixties the fund was used to finance SABRA: the GRA (the Association for Rhodesia Afrikaners); the task groups; the National Youth Leaders' Institute; the National Youth Council; the massive academic investigation and research into Afrikaner youth by Professor Pieterse of the University of Pretoria; the Voortrekker Youth Movement, the ASB; the National Council to Combat Communism; and on organising Afrikaners in the industrial sector.

12.   The UR Funds

The UR funds (excluding the De Wet fund) comprise (a) three-fifths of the entry fee of new members paid to any cell; (b) the full entry fee of outside Broeders; (c) such annual levies as the Bondsraad may impose from time to time on Broeders for the purposes of administration and organisation; (d) other funds which the UR may from time to time found through voluntary contributions for a specific purpose; (e) free gifts from Broeders and other persons; and (f) interest on investments.

The entry fee is R25 and each aspirant Broeder must pay this in full at his initiation. In addition, an annual fee of R15 a year is imposed.

The UR sees to it that all moneys received on current account are approved. Current expenses of the Broederbond are covered by annual moneys (jaargelde) and levies, and the surplus at the end of the year is transferred to a reserve fund (not the De Wet fund).

Annual fees must be paid before August 31 of each year. There is a special entry fee levy imposed on new members of 45 and older. For each year that such a member is older than 45, the fee increases by R2.

Each cell is responsible for all its financial responsibilities of whatever nature. Under no circumstances may the capital of the Broederbond be used to give financial assistance to Broeders. If a cell dissolves, its assets, after liabilities, accrue to the UR.

(b)   External Structure: The FAK

Federation of Afrikaans Cultural Associations

The FAK (Federasie van Afrikaanse Kultuurvereniginge) was established at a congress on December 18 and 19, 1929, in Bloemfontein. The motive was the tremendous cultural and economic backlog of the Afrikaner, the Poor White problem, and the mother language issue. As a secret organisation it was difficult for the Broederbond to play a direct public role in these matters; a more open body was needed.

A study document of April 1969, dealing with the FAK, states: "It was these circumstances that strengthened the belief that the AB alone could not tackle the cultural task efficiently enough, and that a public arm was needed" through which the Afrikaner could be mobilised in large numbers in the cultural field.

The main task of the new organisation was to "co-ordinate and mobilise" all Afrikaans cultural organisations under one umbrella body.

By 1969 there was no less than 2 077 bodies affiliated to the FAK. They included every kind of cultural body and even church councils. Not a single Afrikaans organisation which,

138

however remotely, is involved with some aspect of Afrikaner culture, is not controlled by the FAK. And culture is here defined in the widest possible terms, taking in virtually everything outside politics and government.

The Broederbond used the FAK to launch other public bodies, including the Afrikaanse Handelsinstituut; SABRA; the Rapportryers (both senior and junior wings); the ATKV; and the ATKB. Time and again when public action was required on an important issue, the initiative came from the FAK after specific prompting by the UR.

The first secretary was Lombard, also Bond secretary, and over the years the chairmen have always been prominent members of the UR, and sometimes the UR chairman was also the FAK chairman.

Every year a national congress is held, attended by representatives of the thousands of constituent bodies.

A Language Maintenance Committee was formed in the Sixties. Prominent Broeders who served on it were D.J. Viljoen of Bloemfontein; P. de Bruyn (SABC): Professor B. Kok (Bloemfontein); Prof J.H. Senekal (Pretoria); and Prof F.C. Fensham (Stellenbosch).

The FAK has maintained a Music Commission over the years to promote the composition of Afrikaans songs and the use of "Afrikaans" music. At one stage this commission comprised the following Broeders: Anton Hartman (former SABC orchestra conductor, now at Wits University), Dirkie de Villiers, Professor G.C. Cillie, Phillip McLachlan, D.J.J. Pauw, Chris Lamprecht and Hein de Villiers.

Specific attention has been given to the teaching of history as a vital ingredient of the Christian National policy of inculcating in children a particular concept of the past, especially as regards the Black-White conflict.

A special History Committee was founded in the Sixties to direct the holding of (national festivals *(volksfeeste)*; to stem waning interest in history at school; and to encourage respect for historical monuments.

In recent years the committee has included the following Broeders: Professor A.N.P. Pelzer (University of Pretoria) who wrote the Broederbond history and also published a book on Verwoerd's speeches; J.J. van Tonder; Prof J.S. du Plessis; J.V. Smit; Prof Marius Swart (University of Port Elizabeth and former chairman of the Rapportryers); Prof D.J. Kotze of the University of Stellenbosch; and Prof M.C.E. van Schoor of the University of Bloemfontein.

It was agitation by the Broederbond, first in its own cells in the Thirties and Forties, and later in public, to have October 10 delared a public holiday; and eventually it officially became Kruger Day. Other patriotic holidays for which it is responsible are: April 6 (Van Riebeeck Day); October 10 (Kruger Day); May 31 (Republic Day); and December 16 (the Day of the Covenant). The FAK organised major National events such as the Ox-Wagon Trek of 1938; the inauguration of the Voortrekker Monument in 1949; the Van Riebeeck Festival in 1952; and many others characterised by the narrow, exclusive Afrikaner Christian National outlook.

Taking its name from its motto of "Maintain and Build" *("Handhaaf en Bou")*, the FAK produces a free monthly circular called *Handhaaf* which propagates the spiritual objectives of the AB.

A most important aspect of its work is that among the youth. The National Youth Council *(Nasionale Jeugraad)*, originally established by the Broederbond and funded by the Christiaan De Wet Fund, is now controlled by the FAK. Through the council the FAK was responsible for several youth congresses in the Sixties. These followed on the massive investigation into Afrikaner youth by the University of Pretoria, financed by the De Wet Fund.

As a result of the investigation a report was published dealing with four aspects of Afrikaner youth: professional and economic life; leisure activities; and church and religious life.

The main findings were contained in a Bond document dealing with how to influence the youth so as to maintain and extend Afrikaner culture. The paper summarises the efforts of the Broederbond, through the FAK, to ensure that youth did not become a prey to "English deistic" philosophy, and so be led astray by international thinking which could lead to Afrikaans-English integration and a weakening in support for the policy of apartheid.

The study document made recommendations on how this could be achieved through a "positive approach," entailing the establishing of unity among Afrikaner youth, "study through cultural organisations, and through leadership."

Particular attention is given to youth leaders via the National Youth Leaders' Institute, an extension of the National Youth Council. Regular seminars and conferences are held throughout the country under the auspices of the institute for senior school-children who have leadership qualities. At these discussions specially selected Broeders give lectures on a wide variety of subjects with one basic aim – to initiate the philosophy of life contained in Christian Nationalism.

The aim is to strengthen the moral and spiritual defences of Afrikaner youth against foreign influences and ideologies. These seminars are often subsidised by the Department of National Education, which, along with all the other educational departments, is completely in the hands of the Bond.

The FAK head office is housed in the same building as the Broederbond – Die Eike, Auckland Park, Johannesburg. Nonetheless, the pretence is that the FAK is independent. Numerous Broederbond circulars warn members not to talk about Bond matters over the telephone (the FAK and the AB share the same telephone exchange, apart from the Broederbond's private number).

Members are also constantly warned not to talk about Bond matters to certain FAK officials who are not Broeders. On the other hand, some Broeder officials deliberately work for and use the FAK to provide a cover for their Broederbond activities.

These are the names of some FAK officials against whom the Broederbond has been specifically warned over the years. J.G. du Plessis; F.J. Pretorius; H.S. van der Walt; J. Taljaard; C. Young; W. MacDonald; and O.S. Smit.

B. The Ruiterwag

The Broederbond has a fully-fledged junior secret organisation for Afrikaner Nationalists under 35. Although autonomous and functioning as a separate organisation the Ruiterwag is directly under tight Bond control. Broeders are seconded to key positions on the national executive and in the cells of the Ruiterwag. The organising secretary, a paid official, is on the Broederbond staff and attends UR meetings.

The Ruiterwag is thus not a front organisation, but a subsidiary of the Broederbond. In organisation it is largely a replica of the AB, although different names are used in its organisational structure.

Its members are organised in cells called "guard posts" *(wagposte")*. Each cell has a "post council" *("posraad")* and consists of the "Riders" *("Ruiters")* and one "Chief guard" *("hoofwag")* who is a Broeder.

Its annual conference is called a Guard Council *(Wagraad)* and the national executive – the equivalent of the UR – is called the President's Council *(Presidentsraad)*. It consists of five ruiters, one of whom is President, and two chief guards, who are seconded Broeders.

It also has the system of outside membership for ruiters not attached to a specific cell.

The affairs of the Ruiterwag thus run virtually parallel to those of the Bond. Until the age of 35 a person may be both a Ruiter and a Broeder, although very young people prefer to belong only to the Ruiterwag.

From a small beginning in 1958, when it was founded, the Ruiterwag today has more than 4 000 members. At the beginning of 1963 it had only 414, but this jumped rapidly to 1 200 in early 1966.

The average age of a ruiter is between 27 and 28.

An analysis of its membership shows its strong position in the teaching and church professions. In 1966, for example, of the 1 200 members 240 were teachers (20 per cent); 172 were clerks in government and the private sector; 141 students; 73 professors and academics; and 58 ministers of religion.

C. Aims and Philosophy

The aims of the Broederbond can be summarised as follows:

Firstly, to maintain a separate white Afrikaans volk, seemingly at all costs.

Secondly, the establishment of Afrikaner domination and rule in South Africa. Thirdly, as part of this process, the subtle Afrikanerisation of the English section. Finally, the maintenance of a White South African nation built on the rock of the Afrikaner volk with the Broederbond the hard core of that volk.

This ambitious philosophy is based on two concepts: the first is Christian Nationalism; the second is Brotherhood, in an almost mystic sense.

Since the controversial Van Rooy circular of 1934 the Broederbond has been on the move, and throughout its actions runs a golden thread: the faith that the Afrikaner volk has a God-given right to a separate existence and identity – though, ironically, it is the product of the mixing of Germans, Dutch and others and has existed for little more than 200 years. Furthermore, that it has a Christian, God-sanctioned mission to fulfil in southern Africa. This is clearly spelled out in a document called "The Basis and Aims *(Grondslag en oogmerke)* of our Aspirations."

The very first paragraphs state this: "The Afrikaans volk is called into being by God in the southern corner of Africa with its own Christian calling *(roeping)* to honour His Name.

"The separate calling of the Afrikaner as a volk with a consciousness of its own and a unique nature and character, is founded in the Protestant Christian conviction that God disposes fully at all times over its fortunes *(lotgevalle)*."

In a 1968 document entitled "The Task of the AB and the Future" the basis of Christian Nationalism is set out briefly.

It is important to note that in Afrikaans "Christelike-Nasionalisme" is spelled with a hyphen, making it a separate concept, apart from its two components, Christianity and Nationalism.

In the late Sixties there was a debate over the hyphenation issue. The so-called verligtes – among them Piet Cillie and Schalk Pienaar – clashed with the conservatives, the overwhelming majority claiming that it should be spelt with a hyphen. This clash involved deep and subtle philosophical differences. In practice today the term is accepted with the hyphen, and is a religious, political and philosophical concept of special significance.

Dealing with this concept, the 1968 document stated that the "Christian National philosophy of life *(lewensbeskouing)* is the only source from which we derive our way of life and is the foundation on which every expression of life must be based." Christian means "the Calvinistic Protestant religion . . . We therefore believe that we have been called by God to responsible Afrikaner nationhood." National meant that "each volk possesses its own identity or psychic structure which distinguishes it from every other volk."

The existence and growth of the Afrikaans language was in the first place the expression of such a separate identity. The second proof was the political and constitutional growth of a distinctive volk towards a republican form of government. Indissolubly bound to this was Afrikaner loyalty and patriotism, which rejected and detested racial mongrelisation *(verbastering)* in every sphere of life and particularly loathed miscegenation.

An annexure entitled "Our Code" was attached to circular 2/68/69. Ten features which characterised the relationship between Broeders individually and Broeders and the Bond were set out.

Firstly, "We must regard each other as kindred souls"; secondly, in his relationship with other Broeders, a member must be loving *(liefdevol)*, sympathetic and tolerant; thirdly, "have appreciation for a Broeder in your association with him"; fourthly, "truly *(waaragtig)* trust your Broeders"; fifthly, always "realise that Brotherhood means to serve"; sixthly, "always be prepared to take the initiative in the battle of the volk"; seventhly, "apply self discipline"; eightly, "be really interested in each other" – congratulate each other on birthdays, and sympathise with setbacks; ninethly, "know, appreciate and respect each other's abilities, however weak"; and, finally, "keep the faith in the guidance of destiny by an Almighty Father and in the justice of the Afrikaner cause."

In numerous Bond documents, speeches and study papers there are lengthy expositions of its Christian National philosophy. It basically provides a rationale for the support of the NP and explains why Afrikaners who are not Nationalists – many of whom nonetheless believe in the rights of an Afrikaner volk – are not part of the true volk. Some even question whether they are good Afrikaners at all.

The speeches and papers of Piet Meyer during his 12 years as Broederbond chief provide important revelations of Broederbond thinking. While in recent years there has been a tendency by verligte, or perhaps more pragmatic Broeders, to play down Meyer, the fact remains that his views have never been challenged or rejected by anybody in the AB.

Moreover, his views represent the hard core of Broederbond philosophy and thinking, providing the intellectual justification for NP policy and behaviour.

One issue to which Broeder leaders have constantly given attention is the question of what role the Bond can play in existing political, cultural and other Afrikaans organisations. Meyer dealt with this in his chairman's speech to the 1965 Bondsraad. He said that national life was organised in three main spheres: the State, the church, and the volk; and he stressed the "intimate bond between these spheres, particularly from a Christian Protestant viewpoint."

The volk had its own destiny and function "which can only be realised and exercised by a people's – organisation" – obviously the Broederbond. On page two of his speech Meyer said that the "AB has been placed in the favourable position of being able to merge all the forces of these spheres into one unity, by constantly bringing together in itself all the real leaders of all our people's activities.

"In this manner the respective functions of our church, State and volk can be exercised in an Afrikaans context . . ." The Bond had to give leadership to the volk. Stressing this, Meyer urged Broeders to influence their neighbourhoods through their good example "from the morning to the evening, every day, throughout the year . . ."

The speech which Meyer gave at the Bondsraad of October 1966, a few weeks after Verwoerd's assassination, can be regarded as a blueprint of Afrikaner supremacy and domination. (See Annexure J).

I discussed this speech in *Die Verkrampte Aanslag* from page 232 onwards. In my analysis I made the fundamental error of concluding that it was in direct conflict with the declared policy of Verwoerd, followed by Vorster, of Afrikaans-English co-operation and unity.

I also interpreted it as a verkrampte move against the NP leadership. I was wrong; that speech represents the basic views of so-called verkramptes like Treurnicht and Dr Koot Vorster, but also those of so-called verligtes like Wimpie de Klerk and "lang Dawid" de Villiers.

Afrikaner supremacy and domination has always been the aim of the Broederbond and the Broeders in the NP leadership are simply implementing this long-term policy in instalments.

In blunt terms ("Tonight we must be honest with ourselves") Meyer stated as the Broederbond ideal the "complete political nationalising and ultimate cultural Afrikanerisation of our English-speaking compatriots." He warned against the dangers of Afrikaans-English co-operation which could lead to integration and the Anglicising of Afrikaners. Here, as in speeches by other Broeders and in other study documents, the point was made that a policy of Afrikaner-English equality would in practice benefit the English, leading to a mixed language or the dominance of the English. The English culture was also rejected because it carried "a clear modern liberalistic stamp *(stempel)."*

The Afrikaans philosophy of life could not be integrated with the English humanistic philosophy. This meant that there could only be "either the purposeful Afrikanerisation of the English-speaker, or the tacit acceptance of a non-conscious but increasing Anglicisation of the Afrikaner."

Pleading for drastic action he said that "the next step . . . is a planned confidential economic action . . ." This was a subtle reference to the investigations of Professor P.W. Hoek, at the request of Verwoerd, into the economic ramifications of Anglo American.

On page seven of his speech Meyer stated that the "Afrikanerisation of the English-speakers is in essence an educational task – it must start in the schools." He advocated the total Afrikanerisation of English-speakers in all spheres of life until English was mostly an international language, with Afrikaans the predominant language in everyday life.

Afrikaners should not become divided on the question of Afrikaner-English co-operation and integration. And "the most important divisive force at the moment is the liberalism of our time, which is particularly strongly represented by our English-speaking compatriots and their Press." In misleading terms this liberalism was increasingly being accepted and propagated by a constantly growing number of Afrikaners.

Meyer warned against "unnecessary association with organisations which not only do not contribute in any way to the Afrikanerisation of the English-speakers, but usually end in the Anglicisation of the Afrikaner youth in particular."

He gave a vital analysis of the role of the Broederbond which was apparently conveyed to Verwoerd – for his approval – when the UR threw a birthday function on his behalf. Meyer compared the AB to a pyramid.

The Broederbond had helped to build up "all four sides *(sic)* of this Afrikaner pyramid. The four sectors of the pyramid are the political, the cultural, the economic and the educational sides, with our own Afrikaans Christian National philosophy of life and the world *(lewens en wêreldbeskouing)* as the base."

In the middle Sixties a very significant remark was made in a Broederbond paper delivered at a AB gathering dealing with the "practical influencing of Afrikaner youth." Calling for the ultimate "total political nationalising and eventual cultural Afrikanerisation" of the English, it stated that at this stage this intention could not be divulged to the outside.

There can be no doubt that the Afrikaner's political Broeder leaders over the years concealed from the English their real aim – not only of Afrikaner domination, but also of Afrikaner imperialism designed to weaken and crush English culture and influence. Afrikaner Nationalists, inspired by the Broederbond, had embarked on a reversal of the policy of Lord Milner, who after the Anglo-Boer War set out to systematically Anglicise all the Afrikaners.

Two statements perhaps epitomise the aspirations of the Bond. At its fiftieth anniversary celebrations on the farm Tweefontein near Bapsfontein, Henning Klopper, one of the founders, spelled out the importance of the Broederbond in an emotional speech. Next, the Speaker of the House of Assembly triumphantly proclaimed: "Do you realise the power assembled here between these four walls? Show me a greater power on the whole continent of Africa! Show me a greater power anywhere in the world, even in the so-called civilised countries!

"We assist our State, we assist our church, we assist every big organisation that has been born out of the volk, and we make our own contribution unseen . . . we have brought our volk to where it is today.

"We have given the volk the necessary leaders. Each time a leader was available to be elected from the ranks of the Afrikaner Broederbond. When we lost Dr Malan we had Advocate Strijdom. When he died we had Dr Verwoerd. When he was taken in a tragic manner from our midst, in a second, God had another man ready for us . . . It is our duty to support him; our duty to supply his successor when he is no longer there. If he is no longer there another man must step in. Thus our work never ends."

The Afrikaner was involved in a never-ending struggle, aided by the Bond. This was the crux of the deathbed message of Dr A.M. Moll, one of the founders, read at the 1934 Bondsraad, and which was again quoted by Treurnich when he addressed the Bondsraad in 1968 on the topic "The AB Today."

Moll had said: "Broeders, I do not envy you life, but only the privilege still to be able to fight for our nationhood. In the world struggle there is no turning point. We are all still Voortrekkers on the road of our beloved South Africa. It is too early to dismount.

"Everything will come right if we strive for right and justice."

144

PART VI

The Broederbond in Action

It is safe to say that there is nothing that occurs in Afrikaner Nationalist ranks in whatever sphere or at whatever level, high or low, which is not secretly discussed by the Broederbond and in which it is not involved – sometimes directly, indirectly at other times.

Sometimes the Bond initiates action, usually through the FAK when the issue is cultural – in its widest sense – or educational. At other times it discusses the matter via the UR with "friends" in responsible government positions in order to get clarity, raise doubts, or present proposals.

And at the dagbestuur level in each area, town or village, when local Broeder leaders secretly become involved in some local issue involving the public, it is never known that the Broederbond is in control where ostensibly the voice of the local church council or school committee is speaking.

One thing should be clear. The Broederbond does not dictate as such to the various bodies in government, church, cultural affairs, etc. There is, rather, direct interaction between the Bond and these bodies.

After all, the AB is the reinforced scaffolding of the fortress of Afrikaner nationalism. It can, therefore, not dictate to itself. The key people with whom the Broderbond discusses matters of the day are all Broeders anyway.

The Broederbond never talks officially to outsiders. In its capacity as the custodian of the soul of Afrikaner nationalism, it sees its duty as being to talk to, influence and "persuade" those in high places who, in fact, are all Broeders. This interaction leads to an exchange of ideas where it is often difficult to establish who is responsible for a particular decision – the Bond, or the other body.

Moreover, it must also be remembered that all the Bond study papers are without exception drafted by Broeders either directly involved in government or with the subject concerned.

So the man who can influence decision-making on any particular topic is placed in a strong position to do precisely that.

Perhaps the philosophy of Holism of General Smuts is applicable to the Broederbond. The organisation represents the leaders of every component of the Afrikaner Nationalist movement, and it can thus be said that the Broederbond as such is larger than all its manifold parts. It is in this fully Holistic concept that the real power and influence of the Broederbond lies.

It is impossible to discuss everything the Broederbond has done or is still engaged in doing. Several books would be needed. I intend to analyse specifically, though briefly, the involvement of the Broederbond in certain fields – government, education and religion. And finally I will give a number of snippets of Broederbond activities, to give some indication of its variety of concerns and its omnipresence.

Much of what I will discuss comes from documents of the Sixties and Seventies. And other issues have been partly revealed by some newspapers.

It should be noted that evidence of the very substantial involvement of the AB in public life is frequently not to be found in Bond documents – circulars, study papers or UR minutes – but is sometimes only mentioned in a cursory sentence. What then appears in print – never of course intended for the prying eyes of outsiders – is often only the tip of the iceberg. And icebergs can be very dangerous.

A.   The State

Siezing and maintaining power for the Afrikaner has shaped the Bond's history since 1918. The supreme example of the close, indissoluble connection between the Broederbond and the Government was the investigation into the Broederbond, the Freemasons and the Sons of England in 1964. Broeder Verwoerd, as Prime Minister, had the closest consultations with Broeder leaders prior to the appointment of a Commission of Inquiry.

Also highly significant are the remarks in a circular of the time in which Broeders were told not to be concerned by the inquiry because Verwoerd would not allow anything to damage the Broederbond.

The Verwoerd incident focusses attention on another factor: the close relationship between the Broederbond leadership, as embodied in the UR, and the Prime Minister. How this relationship developed from the days of Verwoerd to Vorster, along with its changing character, has been discussed. But the fact remains that the UR is to this day in the position where it holds constant, confidential discussions with Vorster. The Prime Minister briefs it on matters of vital public importance – Rhodesia, Namibia, the Soweto riots. And he gives the UR confidential background information which does not appear in the Press, and which is often only given to the Cabinet, while Parliament is uniformed.

Vorster knows that these private briefings will lead to the "correct" comment in the next Bond circular, aimed at keeping 12 000 opinion-makers throughout South Africa, Namibia and Rhodesia informed about crucial developments; and thus encourage them to give their support to whatever publicly unpopular moves he may contemplate.

The turning point in the Broederbond-State relationship came in 1963 when 17 task groups and committees were appointed, with over 200 members, to act as a shadow government, keeping an eye on every important public body and sector of public life from the Cabinet downwards.

It is important to note that these watchdog committees were not in opposition to or in conflict with existing bodies. Without exception they included men, in particular senior government officials, directly involved in the body under surveillance. The effect of this system, manned by the AB's intellectual elite, was to exercise a powerful and significant influence on the decisions of the Government and its relationship with the bodies involved.

I will now give the full list of members and the committees concerned. Although there have been changes since then, committees later scrapped and new ones formed, nothing better tells the story more effectively of the Broederbond – Government inter-relationship than this list.

Many of the Broeders are still active in various capacities; some have died; others have new jobs; yet others have left for the HNP. I will give the position they held in 1963 if their present position is not known.

"Non-White" Affairs

Chairman: Professor J.P. Bruwer, (former Commissioner-General of the Indigenous Peoples of SWA); M.C. Botha (then Minister of Bantu Administration); Dr W.W.M.

Eiselen (Homeland Commissioner General); J.P. Dodds (senior Bantu Administration official); Prof E.F. Potgieter (Homeland Commissioner-General); I.P. van Onselen (senior Bantu Administration official); Dr H.J. van Zyl (then Secretary of Bantu Education); Ds C.W.H. Boshoff (Professor in Theology and now chairman of SABRA); Dr P.G.J. Koornhof (former Broederbond secretary, now a Cabinet Minister); Prof G.V.N. Viljoen (Rector of RAU and present Broederbond chairman); M.T. de Waal (Johannesburg industrialist); F.S. Steyn (then an MP, now a judge); J.H.T. Mills (then Secretary of the Transkei Civil Service, now Secretary for Coloured Affairs); S.F. Kingsley (then Director of Bantu Affairs, Pretoria Municipality); P.J. Riekert (top government official); Prof P.F.D. Weiss (then Director of the government-sponsored Africa Institute and later a HNP candidate).

Associate Members:

J.H. van Dyk (Department of Bantu Administration and Development); Prof H. du Plessis; Prof P.J. Coertze (former anthropology department dean at Pretoria and a member of the HNP); W.J. Grobbelaar; P.W. Botha (at the time Deputy Minister of Coloured Affairs and now Prime Minister); J.L. Boshoff (Rector, Turfloop); Dr A.A. Odendaal; Dr F.C. Albertyn.

Coloured Group:

Convener: F.D. Conradie (MEC for the Cape and former UR member); Kobus Louw (then Secretary for Coloured Affairs); A.C. van Wyk (now an MP).

Indian Group:

Convener: Prof S.P. Olivier (Rector, Indian University College); Ds R.J.J. van Vuuren.

Technical and Natural Science Matters:

Chairman: Dr E.J. Marais (Rector, University of Port Elizabeth); Dr H.O. Mönnig (member of the Prime Minister's Scientific Council); Dr S.J. du Plessis; Tom Meyer (MP); Dr A.J.A. Roux (head of the Atomic Board); Dr S.J. du Toit; Dr S.M. Naudé (scientific advisor to the Prime Minister); Prof L.J. le Roux.

Associate Members:

Dr C.M. Kruger (manager, Iscor); Dr B.C. Jansen (head of the Onderstepoort Veterinary Research Station); Dr A.W. Lategan; Dr S.J. du Toit; Dr O.R. van Eeden; Prof Dr P.W. Groenewoud; Prof H.L. de Waal (former chairman SA Akademie vir Wetenskap en Kuns); Dr D.M. de Waal; Prof P.S. Zeeman; Prof R. Truter; Prof J.M. le Roux; Dr L.A. Prinsloo; Prof C.A. du Toit; Prof A.P. Malan; Dr J.M. de Wet; Dr S.J. du Plessis; Prof P.J.G. de Vos; Dr C.C. Kritzinger; J.G.H. Loubser (general manager of the SA Railways).

Youth Affairs:

Chairman: Ds J.S. Gericke (former Moderator of the NG Kerk); Ds C.L. van den Berg (Youth Minister for Ned Hervormde Kerk); Dr S.C.W. Duvenage (professor at Potchefstroom University); Prof J.E. Pieterse (a founder of the Ruiterwag – he also headed the national investigation into youth affairs at the University of Pretoria); Dr M. Swart (head of the Rapportryers); J.F.P. Badenhorst (head of the Voortrekker youth movement);

147

W.S.J. Grobler (then FAK secretary, ex-MP); H.J. Moolman; C. de P. Kuun (senior Broederbond official); Dr J.C. Otto (MP and former headmaster); R.W.J. Opperman (head of the Olympics Committee and a senior Perskor official); Dr A.P. Treurnicht (former Broederbond chief and MP – then editor of *Kerkbode*); Ds J.E. Potgieter (then an NG Kerk student minister and a founder of the Ruiterwag); Dr D.J. Coetzee.

Planning:

Chairman: Dr P.S. Rautenbach (today head of the public service); Dr H.O. Mönnig; Dr F.J. Marais; Dr P.J. Riekert; J.F.W. Haak (then Minister of Economic Affairs); Dr P.M. Robbertse (head of Council of Social Sciences); Prof S. Pauw (former Rector of Unisa); Prof L.J. le Roux; Prof S.A. Hulme; P.Z.J. van Vuuren (then an MEC); W.W.S. Haveman (Administrator of Natal); Dr F.J. Potgieter; M.A. du Plessis; J.J. Marais; P.J.V.E. Pistorius; Dr H. Steyn; A.J. du Toit; J.H. Niemand (Secretary of Community Development).

Press Matters:

Chairman: J.F. Marais (then a judge – now a leading PFP MP); P.A. Weber (managing director, Nasionale Pers); P.J. Cillie (editor *Die Burger*); M.V. Jooste (managing director, Perskor); H.P. Marnitz (former editor *Die Vaderland*); J.J. van Rooyen (former editor *Die Transvaler*); C.D. Fuchs (SABC); J.H. Steyl (Transvaal Secretary National Party, and a Senator); Steve de Villiers (SABC).

Associate Members:

H.H. Dreyer (Nasionale Pers); D.J. van Zyl (Nasionale Pers); T.J.A. Gerdener (former Minister of the Interior and Administrator of Natal).

Economic Affairs:

Chairman: Dr A.J. Visser (a Senator); J.F.W. Haak (then a Cabinet Minister); Dr M.S. Louw; Prof C.G.W. Schumann; Prof W.J. Pretorius; C.H.J. van Aswegen (SANTAM); C.J.F. Human (FVB); H. de G. Laurie (Perskor); Dr P.E. Rousseau (head of the South Africa Foundation); Dr J.G. van der Merwe; Dr F.P. Jacobz; Dr M.D. Marais; J.A. Hurter (head of Volkskas); T.F. Muller (General Mining and Iscor); W. Pauw; P.K. Hoogendyk; D.v.d. M. Benade; R.P. Botha.

Associate Members:

Dr T.W. de Jongh (Governor Reserve Bank); Dr A.D. Wassenaar (Sanlam); S.J. Naudé; Dr H.L.F. Snyman; P.J.F. Scholtz; P.J.C. van Zyl; G.J.J. Visser; H.D. Wessels; J.N. Swanepoel; D.M. Hoogenhout; F.J. Marais; Dr E.L. Grové; A.J. Marais; J.P. van Heerden; L.G. van Tonder; E. Cuyler (a former Senator); G.J. van Zyl; P.G. Carstens; J.J. Venter; J.G.H. Loubser (Railway's general manager); B.P. Marais; Prof H.J. Samuels (former head of the Armanents Board).

Agriculture:

Chairman: S.P. Botha (Minister of Water Affairs and of Forestry): A.J. du Toit; G.J. Joubert; J.F. de V. Loubser; W.A.A. Hepburn; P.W. van Rooyen; H.E. Martins (then an

MP and Deputy Minister of Transport); P.S. Toerien; C.C. Claassens; Dr. J.C. Neethling (senior official in the Department of Agriculture); Dr P.D. Henning (senior official of the Water Affairs Department).

Associate Members:
J.M.C. Smit; Dr B.C. Jansen; Dr C.M. van Wyk; S.J. Brandt; Dr J.G. van der Wath; De la H. de Villiers; S. Reineke; D. Grewar; N.J. Deacon; A.M. Lubbe; Adv P.R. de Villiers; L.C.R. Bührmann; S.P. Malan; P.J.H. Maree; G. Radloff; W.v.d. Merwe; Prof S.A. Hulme; J.P. Hamman; C.D.C. Human; S.J.J. van Rensburg; P.J. Kruger.

Africa:
Chairman: Prof P.F.D. Weiss (then director of the Africa Institute); W.C. du Plessis (a former Administrator of South West Africa); Dr T.E.W. Schumann; Prof A.J.H. van der Walt; Prof J.H. Coetzee (Univesity of Potchefstroom); P.J. Cillie (editor *Die Burger*); B.J. van der Walt (then an MP and ex-Administrator of SWA): Dr C.P.C. de Wet; D.B.R. Badenhorst; M.A. du Plessis.

Education:
Chairman: Prof H.J.J. Bingle (ex-Rector of Potchefstroom University); Prof S. Pauw (ex-Rector Unisa); Dr G.J. Jordaan (chairman National Educational Advisory Council); Dr P.M. Robbertse (head of Council for Social Research); A.J. Koen (then Director of Education in Transvaal); S. Theron; E.E. van Kerken (then Director of Education, Free State); A.G.S. Meiring (then Director of Education, Cape); M.C. Erasmus (Secretary for Education); Ds P.M. Smith (senior leader of the Hervormde Kerk).

Associate Members:
Dr W.K.H. du Plessis; Prof G.J.J. Smit; A.J. van Rooyen; Dr P.A. Conradie; S.C.M. Naudé.

Religious "Weerbaarheid" ("Ability to Defend")
Chairman: Ds P.M. Smith; Ds J. du P. Malan (NGK Minister); Prof B.J. Engelbrecht (NHK); Prof S.P. van der Walt (Gereformeerde Kerk); Prof T.N. Hanekom (Stellenbosch University); Ds S.J. Gericke (NGK Moderator – member of the UR); Prof F.J.M. Potgieter (Stellenbosch University); Ds D.P.M. Beukes (NGK- member of the UR); Prof S. du Toit (Gereformeerde Kerk); Prof E.P. Groenewald (Pretoria); Dr A.P. Treurnicht; Prof H. du Plessis; Prof F.J. van Zyl (Hervormde Kerk); Prof P.S. Dreyer (Hervormde Kerk).

Africa and World Committee:
Chairman: Dr P.J. Meyer; Dr P.E. Rousseau; S.P. Botha; J.A. Marais (former MP); J.A. Hurter; M.A. du Plessis; Col H. van den Bergh (former security and Boss chief); Dr. P. Koornhof; Dr E.J. Marais.

English Relations:
Chairman: Prof S. Pauw; Dr P.J. Meyer; Prof H.J. Bingle; F.D. Conradie; S.A. Hofmeyer.

Jewish Problem Committee:
Dr G.F.C. Troskie (headed committee).

Trade Unions:

Chairman: Ds D.P.M. Beukes (Moderator of the NGK); S.J. Botha (secretary of Albert Hertzog's financial interests in Pretoria); A.E. Grundlingh (former Mine Workers' Union boss); C.V. de Villiers (Railway Commission); D.G. Malan; R.H. Botha; W.C. Massyn; J.F. Kloppers; R.S.J. du Toit; R.C. Malherbe; I.D. Oelofse; C.F. Vosloo; J.H. Swart; G.H. Beetge; B. Auret; Dr E.L. Grove.

Sport:

This was headed for a long time by Prof A.N. Pelzer. Others on it were Johan Claassen, former Springbok rugby captain; Kobus Louw; and R.J. Opperman.

The *Immigration Committee* was headed by Dr Piet Koornhof. A task force to combat Communism, liberalism and other enemies such as Freemasonry was headed by Prof F.J. van Zyl.

This massive Broederbond involvement and the Broeders concerned merely re-emphasised that the Broederbond and the State were one.

In the report of the chief secretary for the period August to December 1963 there is further evidence of these inseparable ties. On page one an item shows that BOSS, the controversial Schlebusch Committee and the subsequent Piscom (the parliamentary committee on security) emanated from Broederbond discussions. The report noted that the Africa and World Committee had submitted "the following matters for consideration and enactment: (a) The stablishment of a national security service. (b) The establishment of a select committee to investigate anti-South African activities."

A few years later both became reality. The Bureau for State Security was formed in the late Sixties as a super-security body, and the investigations into organisations such as the Christian Institute and the Institute of Race Relations for alleged subversive and anti-South African acitivities started in the early Seventies, leading to bannings and other prohibitions on people and organisations. Piscom now waits in the wings.

The chief secretary noted that the scientific task group would influence high schools to urge pupils to study science. But page four strikes a more sinister note: the UR would "negotiate with the Minister concerned" to make an arrangement whereby the Minister would then see to it "that such scientists are in advance taken into the hands of the right people to ensure that they return to South Africa."

The report noted, on the same page, that the Africa task group would confine itself to southern Africa and the Portuguese territories. It was decided that a full memorandum on the broad political situation would be made available to the Department of Foreign Affairs. The study document on the three High Commission territories however, would be printed and widely distributed – with the aid of the Department of Information, thus using up tax-payers' money to disseminate Broederbond propaganda.

Other *ad hoc* committees were appointed subsequently. The committee dealing with the affairs of young members of the SA Police consisted of S.W. de Beer (chairman), G.J. van Wyk, F. de M. Cilliers, C. de P. Kunn, M.J. Prins, J. Muller, F.P. Retief, J.J. van Heerden, and H.J.P. van Zyl. Its purpose was to counter the influence of the Freemasons among policemen.

The Broederbond had found that the Freemasons had infiltrated the SAP in large numbers and that in the late Sixties there were at least 15 Freemasons for every Broeder in the force.

Alarm was expressed that Freemasons were occupying key positions in the SA Police Training College in Pretoria. A document in the late Sixties, drawn up by the police committee, found that because of the full programme of students at the college they were not directly exposed to Broederbond attempts at brainwashing.

The committee recommended that "friends" (i.e. Broeders) who were members of the police should get together in certain centres to give attention to the protection of young policemen against Freemasons and other "influences alien to the volk" ("volksvreemdes"). They should also make "concerted efforts" to see that those holding key positions in training centres were not members of "alien" organisations.

Among sensitive areas in which the task force committees involved themselves were race relations and "non-White" affairs. The Broederbond had a sub-committee dealing with the Black Homelands, headed by Professor P.F.D. Weiss, director of the Africa Institute. And in the Sixties it established a special sub-section to give assistance to the Basutoland National Party (BNP) of Chief Leabua Jonathan, before and after the 1965 general elections in Lesotho. The Weiss committee, or a subsidiary was also involved in supporting pro-Government groups in the Coloured elections, and in certain Homelands.

When Koornhof was still Broederbond chief secretary, he was also first secretary of the Weiss committee, which was financed by the Christiaan de Wet Fund. Other founding members, in 1963, were J. Mills and S.P. Botha.

The minutes of the UR meeting of August 22 and 23, 1963, noted (page four) under the heading "Basutoland election": "Broeder chief secretary (Koornhof) tabled reports of liaison with well-disposed Bantu. The UR also discussed the necessity of action regarding the coming to independence of Bantu Homelands in general . . ."

An initial sum of R10 000 was made available by the Christiaan de Wet Fund, and tens of thousands of rand given later. The phrase "Homeland action" became used to describe the Broederbond's support for pro-Government "non-White" groups in general.

On page four of the minutes of the UR dagbestuur of November 7, 1968, it was noted that R1 000 had been spent in the Transkei (obviously in support of Chief Kaizer Matanzima) and R14 852,21 in Lesotho. Louis van der Walt, at the time a Broederbond official, later employed by certain security services, was the link with Lesotho; he actively trained BNP officials in election techniques and strategy.

Chief Leabua Jonathan, leader of the BNP and Lesotho's Prime Minister, was completely in the dark at the time. He did not have the faintest inkling that the South African support he was receiving was not from private individuals, as he had been told.

The Bond's involvement in Coloured politics was even more spectacular. Its special committee, again supervised by Louis van der Walt, then employed by the Republikeinse Intelligensie Diens (RID), the "ghost squad" of the Special Branch, actively assisted the pro-Government Federal Party, then led by the late Tom Schwartz. (I wrote about this in the *Sunday Times* in 1973).

Pretoria-staged elections for the Coloured people were due in 1968. Because of anti-Government sentiment among Coloured voters, the four white parliamentary representatives – mostly pro-Progressive Party – were to be abolished. Preparations were far advanced to introduce the so-called Improper Interference Act, which would preclude Whites from becoming involved in "non-White" politics – either directly as a representative, or financially.

The legislation was due to go through in October 1966, shortly after Verwoerd's death. The intention was obvious: with the other parties out of the way, the Broederbond could

151

secretly support the pro-apartheid Federal Party (today the Freedom Party) and thus ensure victory for it.

However, at the last moment, Koornhof and S.P. (Fanie) Botha – then MPs, but still involved with these "non-Whites" Broederbond political actions – realised that the legislation would also affect and jeopardise the Bond; Koornhof was immediately asked by the UR to convey an urgent message to Vorster and the Cabinet. In fact, even before Verwoerd's death, Koornhof and Fanie Botha urgently asked to leave a UR meeting in Cape Town because they wanted to hold discussions in Parliament aimed at preventing the Bill from going through.

The upshot was that the Government postponed the legislation until 1968. This enabled Van der Walt to continue with his efforts to build up the Federal Party machine – an effort which, as it turned out, failed.

The minutes of a special UR meeting on October 3, 1966, held in Bloemfontein on the eve of the Bondsraad, recorded (page one): "Broeder P.G.J. Koornhof gave a brief outline of the circumstances that led to the draft legislation involving improper (political) interference being referred to a select committee."

The Broederbond thus had breathing space to continue with its secret political activities.

In October 1968 the UR issued a special circular dealing with the Coloured elections. Discussing the political parties, it said: "For the sake of clarity it is indicated that if Coloureds, or their leaders, seek advice or information, it should be recommended to them that they support the Federal Party."

This advice was in direct conflict with the provisions of the non-Interference Bill. It was clearly intended that Broeders should wherever possible "persuade" and "influence" Coloureds to vote for the pro-Government party.

The circular continued: "During the last few years a political consciousness has started among the Coloureds. In terms of our principle of guardianship it is necessary that there should be guidance from the White man to ensure development in the right channels. The law on improper interference restricts active influencing."

This last sentence was obviously intended as a smoke-screen to conceal – even from its own members – the active involvement of the AB. It is significant that these discussions about and references to the activities of the Weiss committee, found in UR minutes of the time, were never reflected in the monthly circulars.

The Broederbond's Coloured initiative involved senior officials of the Department of Coloured Affairs, including P.W. Botha and Marais Viljoen (then respectively the former and present Minister of Coloured Affairs); F.L. Gaum (secretary of the Department at the time); and H.L. Greyling, chairman of the Coloured Development Corporation.

Another feature of the Weiss and Homeland action committees was the fact that none of their reports were in writing, not even those to the UR. All were given orally. UR minutes simply recorded, for example, that a report had been given by the Weiss committee, or whatever sub-committee was involved, with no reference to its content.

Nor were any of these activities reported in any of the chief secretary's annual reports.

Thus only a handful of top Broeders were in a position to really know what was going on. Some Broeders claim that even Verwoerd was not aware at the time of the involvement of the Weiss committee in the Lesotho elections, though it would be most surprising if this were the case.

A brief glance at the study papers of the Broederbond during the Sixties and early Seventies shows that they involved the entire spectrum of government decision-making. Mostly

152

they kept Broeders informed about aspects of government policy and implementation, but sometimes they were used as sounding boards to prepare the way for contentious legislation. The papers are attached to the circulars and discussed at monthly cell meetings.

Sometimes they were delivered at Bondsraad meetings, or joint gatherings of a number of cells. These are some of the topics covered: aspects of the urban Bantu: the official term, until recently, for Africans. It has always been resented by Africans, since it implies ethnicity and subordination in South African politics; the policy for Coloureds (several papers over the years); the effect of immigration on the relative composition of population; internal security; how to establish a civil defence unit; emergency planning and a national plan of survival; the economic position of South African farmers; Afrikaans as a second language for the Bantu; how and when to greet the Bantu by hand; how immigrants can become drawn into the community; white entrepeneurs in Bantu Homelands; The Stock Exchange; our defences in our relationship to "non-Whites"; labour integration in South Africa; adaptations regarding Bantu labour in agriculture; the sports policy; agricultural matters; Indian removals in Johannesburg; and many others.

Sport was the major issue on which Vorster, in 1970, used the Bond to effect change. International pressure forced him to make ever more concessions to prevent total international sports isolation. Vorster, in fact, knew that he had to move towards integrated sport, although this was something he furiously and vehemently denied. He was not, however, prepared to risk yet another split in his own ranks. So he employed the strategy of putting the ball in the Broederbond's court, placing the onus on it to draft a new policy which would be "multi-national" – in theory, at least, something different to fully-fledged multi-racial sport.

At the end of 1970 a UR report stated that "a fruitful two-day discussion between a large number of friends from different sports controlling bodies from all over the country" had been held. As a result a committee formed out of the "friends" had "submitted a number of fundamental formulations for consideration to the UR." One member of this committee was Treurnicht, known for his strong verkrampte views on sports integration. Others included R.W.J. Opperman, then chairman of the South African Olympic Committee; J.J. Claassen, former Springbok rugby captain; J.F. Louw, then a vice chairman of the SA Rugby Board; and Professor Pelzer.

These "fundamental formulations" were circulated to all cells in April 1971, shortly before Vorster made his sports policy announcement in the House that month. The document was entitled "Sports Policy," and was accompanied by another document entitled "Sport and the present onslaught against SA."

It is important to note that when Vorster made his announcement in Parliament, his exposition was identical to the Broederbond's "fundamental formulations." He even used some identical phrases and paragraphs in his speech. This was clearly not a case of the Broederbond having made representations to the Government; but of the Broederbond actually drafting a policy. The UR stated in the introductory paragraph of the policy document: "This policy formulation has been considered by the UR and has been submitted to friends in responsible circles, and it is expected that it will in the next days and weeks be reflected in official government statements."

This paragraph makes it clear that Vorster and the UR had agreed in advance on what official government policy would be – precisely what had been drafted by the Broederbond. One thing went wrong, however. Vorster made his statement in Parliament before all the cells had had time to study it properly. So here was a strong negative reaction from a number of them, and Treurnicht and Koornhof had to address a number of cells to pacify angry Broeders.

Another achievement of the Broederbond in the sphere of sports politics was the establishment of a national centralised sports council. This emanated from discussions and planning at that time. Professor Hannes Botha and R.W.J. Opperman were particularly actively involved, although Botha has since then clashed with the Government (in 1977) on the issue of sports integration.

A 1970 circular spelt out to Broeders how urgent it was for Afrikaners to play a far greater role in the administration of sport; the main reason was that sport was becoming a great political issue. The circular said: "In our case sport has important implications regarding our national and international relations . . . Divisions and individual friends are therefore requested to give special attention to the sports clubs in their areas."

The circular claimed that the reason for "embarrassing" statements made by certain sports administrators was that many of them were not Afrikaners. It warned that sports teachers played an important role in moulding young minds. Sports teaching was still largely in the hands of English-speaking people, and the situation had to be redressed. Broeders were told about the "beautiful progress" made by Afrikaners to win control of rugby, athletics and gymnastic bodies. This "did not come by itself. It was achieved by Afrikaners who exerted themselves in junior positions and who joined forces on a national basis."

Of particular importance was the special circular of October 1971, which dealt with the comments sent in by the cells in response to the study documents on sport sent out in April that year. Stressing the importance of the administration of sport being in the hands of people who supported Nationalist policy and rejected multi-racial sport (though the Bond was later forced to abandon this hardline stance), the October 1971 circular stated: "The UR believes that this can best be achieved by the establishment of our own active sports council, on which nominated people with a good background can keep watch over the implementation of the policy. The UR is paying special attention to this matter."

This documentary evidence clearly exposed the grand design to capture complete control of South African sport. Aided and abetted by the Government, the Bond worked behind the scenes to implement a carefully prepared blueprint.

In the years following, moves in sporting circles towards establishing a national umbrella sports council – in particular, proposals of men such as Hannes Botha, Opperman and Professor Charles Niewoudt – reflected this strategy. In fact, all the aspects of the Government's unfolding sports policy – including the building of a massive international sports complex in the Seventies – were touched upon in earlier Broederbond documents.

The Rhodesian crisis was another issue on which Vorster deployed the Bond as an instrument to counter negative reaction to unpopular policies. His special visit to Pretoria in August 1974, when he stated that South Africa and Rhodesia were "in the same boat", and that S.A. would stand by Rhodesia, has already been mentioned.

But that was not enough. Verkrampte circles openly questioned his détente moves, which led to a meeting between Smith and Black nationalist leaders in late 1974, and the release of many of the latter from jail because of South African pressure.

To counter any adverse Broeder reaction, a special top secret document, written by General Hendrik van den Bergh was circulated to all cells in February 1975. As the hero of the internal war against "Communism and terrorism" nobody could accuse Van den Bergh of selling out white interests in S.A. In his circular he made it clear that South

Africa had to abandon its traditional attitude towards Rhodesia; that it must accept the inevitability of Black majority rule in Zimbabwe within the next few years; and that SA had to accept some form of local "integration."

The communication was regarded as so confidential that copies were apparently not handed out to members. After the circular had been read aloud to the cells it was immediately returned to head office in Johannesburg – either by special post or by courier. This was treatment only accorded to very special and top secret documents.

Van den Bergh informed the Broeders that South Africa would experience the "everlasting hate" of Black Africa if it did not accept a Black majority government in Rhodesia – something the South African Government was not stating publicly at that time.

To secure overall peace in southern Africa it was important that there should be peace in Rhodesia; but it was even more important that there should be peace in South Africa. General Van Den Bergh stressed that the common enemy of southern Africa was Communism and that it was important to co-operate with Black Africa to fight this ideology; so a Rhodesian settlement was essential.

Van den Bergh also made it clear that to reach a better understanding with Black Africa, South Africans would have to accept that "certain forms of integration" were inevitable.

Nationalists regarded it as significant that he used the virtually taboo word "integration." Official party propaganda had always denied that the Government was moving towards "integration," as alleged by verkrampte critics. Van den Bergh was also seen as clearing the way for the abolition of certain discriminatory measures.

The document came at a time when Ian Smith and the White Rhodesians were collaborating closely with key Afrikaner verkramptes and rightwing Broeders – including Dr J.D. Vorster, brother of the Prime Minister, and Treurnicht – in an attempt to whip up conservative support in SA to prevent Vorster from "selling out" the Rhodesians. So Van den Bergh's document was proof of the joint Broederbond-Government strategy to counter any such backlash.

Over the past two years the Bond has also been closely involved with the Government on important policy decisions concerning the Coloureds, the new constitutional proposals, sport, Namibia and Rhodesia. Chairman Gerrit Viljoen has been the intellectual driving force.

The constitutional proposals concerning Coloureds and Indians have been extensively discussed. That the UR was consulted before the report of the Erika Theron Commission was tabled in Parliament, is made clear by the July 1976 circular, which informed members: "The UR had special discussions with the relevant responsible friend" (i.e. the Minister) before the release of the report. The provisional comment of the Government on the report represents "the outcome of these talks."

When the plan was announced, the UR said in a 1977 circular: "We have noted with pleasures that the contents of our memorandum are in many respects reflected in the new dispensation for Coloureds and Indians.

"Our friends in the Government will undoubtedly handle the matter to the best of their ability."

And the circular of September 1, 1977, No 7/77/78, stated: "The UR is pleased to say that friends in responsible circles took part in our 'brainstorming' sessions (on the position of the Coloureds and a new master plan for survival) and that there was a healthy exchange of ideas."

In response to questions from members the circular affirmed that the UR was indeed a

155

party to the discussions that preceded the new dispensation. The Broederbond's view had been put to "responsible friends long before the plans were announced."

Circular 8/77/78 of the following month again stressed that "the contents of our memorandum on the political future of the Coloureds is reflected in many respects in the new dispensation for Coloureds and Indians."

And, on the situation in southern Africa, the UR on several occasions gave advice or assurances to members. In a 1977 circular discussing the negotiations on Namibia and Rhodesia the UR stated: "The UR can give you the assurance that responsible friends (in the negotiations) are using the interests of South Africa as their yardstick. They will continue to do nothing which could harm South Africa's interests."

The UR was clearly well-informed at the time of the Angola invasion, and of the ensuing events, while the rest of South Africa – including Parliament, rank-and-file National Party members and the families of soldiers – were kept in uncertainty and suspense.

A circular of the time had this to say: "The UR wants to assure divisions that it is keeping itself well up to date (on Angola) through discussions with responsible friends (Cabinet Ministers); through references that such friends make at meetings; and in certain cases through the personal involvement of UR members." It stressed that in "a situation like the one in which our country currently finds itself, it is absolutely unthinkable that detailed information of a confidential nature can be extended to our general membership."

Then, in circular No 4/76/77 of June 1976, Viljoen had a go at Rhodesia and its leaders, accusing them of duplicity, double talk and a lack of integrity in the negotiations for a settlement. The circular was written after discussions with South African Cabinet Ministers, and at a time when Rhodesia-South Africa relations were at a low eb and when Rhodesia had been charged by SA of stalling the negotiations; it came only three months before the September 1976 Kissinger visit. Viljoen said that Rhodesia was propagating one policy to the outside world, while privately subscribing to another one altogether. South Africa, said Viljoen, would only involve itself in Rhodesia's problem if this was in its own interests. It would not back Rhodesia in all circumstances.

This is another example of how Vorster used the Broederbond to cover his back. With the mass of White South Africans emotionally pro-Rhodesia, it was vital that the 12 000 influential Broeders be convinced of the necessity of countering a possible verkrampte backlash against his Rhodesia policy.

After the Soweto riots of June 1976 the UR held lengthy discussions with Vorster. Circular No 10/76/77 gave the details, informing members that Vorster had told them of certain conclusions that had been reached during a period of "reflection and self examination" after the turmoil.

Vorster had come to the conclusion that separate development remained the only way to handle the race problem, and urged the AB to back this policy fully.

Of importance is the Bond's "master plan" to ensure the survival of whites in South Africa, drawn up shortly after the riots. It was set out in several study papers and dispatched with the usual monthly circulars.

The third paper was on the theme of "The Master Plan for the White Land," and dealt with strategy. This involved the development of the Bantu Homelands, while the rest of South Africa would be kept under White control. The plan reflects the thinking of key men in government circles – all Broeders – who were present when these issues are discussed, and helped effect their implementations.

Some aspects of the plan have already been pushed into being.

There are two crucial components. Firstly, the harnessing of the entire economy, both private and public sectors, to resettle Africans on a massive scale in the Bantustans. Secondly, the indoctrination of the entire population – roping in the English, Coloureds, Indians and Blacks – to accept the Christian National viewpoint and to swallow the concept of ethnic identities as the cornerstone of a political solution. SABRA – the South African Bureau of Racial Affairs – had to co-ordinate and supervise the mobilisation of the entire South African population behind the barriers of separate development.

It is important to note that in recent years SABRA has played an increasingly important role in influencing government thinking. The conservative professor of theology C.W.H. Boshoff, is SABRA's chairman, and as a senior Broeder has been working closely with Gerrit Viljoen, himself a former SABRA chief.

In terms of the plan, a number of organisations must be drawn into an umbrella movement to implement details. They include a number who are directly Broederbond-controlled, and others who have been infiltrated: the SABC, both White and Black services; all teachers' organisations and educational institutions which can indoctrinate young people ("for at least one generation") into accepting the need for the protection of group identities; all the Afrikaans churches; the FAK; the South African Agricultural Union; the Afrikaanse Handelsinstituut; the Federated Chamber of Industries; various labour organisations and municipal associations; Akademiese Aksie (the organisation of 1 200 Nationalist academics established in 1973 to counter the verlige rebellion); women's organisations; and youth bodies such as the Voortrekkers and the Rapportryers.

The plan specifically called for a wide propaganda onslaught on English-speakers. Only a year later a major feature of the November 30, 1977, election campaign was the drive directed at wooing English voters.

Some of the features of the plan had already been accepted by the Government. In calling for the removal of racial discrimination as far as possible, it insisted that this should be linked to "Homeland citizenship." Africans would thus be given an incentive to take out Bantustan citizenship to escape the burdens of discrimination.

The plan also called for the drastic revision of all legislation covering Black rights, such as permanent residence and home ownership in "White" areas. And, in fact, when one compares these aims with the steps actually implemented by Dr Connie Mulder, Minister of Plural Relations (formerly Bantu Administration) early in 1978, it is evident that the abolition of race discrimination is indeed coupled with "Homeland" citizenship and the refusal to allow true home-ownership for Blacks in urban areas.

This alone shows the efficacy of Viljoen's "think tank" approach. With 12 000 opinion-makers primed to support a certain line of thinking, Viljoen and Vorster can rest assured that it will slowly permeate throughout society as a whole.

A problematic area of the Broederbond's relationship to the Government is how it influences particular decisions or appointments. Sensitive decisions are never recorded in documents. However, a close analysis of the governmental structure shows that virtually every top job is occupied by a Broeder.

Here are a few examples of the Bond-Government inter-relationship.

The secretarial report for the period 1963 to 1965, signed by Piet Meyer and Naudé Botha, thanked the Broeders (page 11) for their response to a March 1963 circular calling on them to make themselves available as police reservists, or to co-operate with other voluntary organisation on internal security. "Broeders in responsible circles testified that the action of the AB in this regard undoubtedly contributed to achieving rest and peace in our country."

The minutes of the UR meeting of December 1, 1965, noted (page 13) that the UR had discussed "the problems that are raised from time to time regarding State administration, and considered the possibility of holding talks with Broeders in responsible circles" on the issue. Meyer, P.E. Rousseau, J.A. Hurter (of Volkskas), and H.J.J. Bingle were appointed as a committee to collect the relevant facts, and it was decided to make moneys available for such an investigation.

In 1966 a problem arose over a prospective investigation into the effects of flat schemes on the size of white families. This could apparently not be done through "friends" in government and, according to the minutes of the UR of August 30, 1966 (page five), it was decided "that Broeders at universities who dealt with sociological problems must be requested to carry out such an investigation."

At the UR meeting of March 21, 1968, the question of "objections to the manner in which appointments are made in government councils" was discussed. This referred to the appointment of candidates not approved by the Broederbond.

According to a report submitted to the UR meeting of June 26 and 27, 1968, the Voortrekker cell in Pretoria had expressed doubts on the extent to which white capital was being employed to develop Bantu Education. The cell was advised by the UR to invite Broeder H.J. van Zyl – then Director of Bantu Education – to address them on the matter. Another example of Broeder-Government co-operation.

The UR of June 26, 1968, again discussed the matter of government appointments. The question was raised whether "Broeders in responsible positions are unable to contact local cells, central committees and regional councils to obtain recommendations about possible appointments . . ." the UR apparently took no official decision, indicating that the Bond was not satisfied with the operation of an official "old boys" Broeder network.

Circular No 7/69170 of October 7, 1969, also dealt with the issue of "official appointments." It stated: "Friends point out that it is expected from civil servants such as magistrates to make recommendations for certain appointments. Where the attitudes of the civil servants are not correct, wrong recommendations are often sent through and ill-disposed people are appointed. We should be wary of this.

"Such officials can also influence their subordinates not to accept membership of the Rapportryers and other specific Afrikaner organisations. Where such cases rear their heads suitable action should be taken to neutralise the negative influence."

Another issue in which the AB has played a major role has been that of the constitutional position of the State President. Throughout the Sixties the question of the status of the President frequently came up for discussion at UR and cell meetings. The feeling was always strong that at the opportune time the Republic's constitution should be changed to create an executive President, and to have a new national flag without the Union Jack forming part of it.

In 1968 Meyer wrote in a report: "A week before Broeder H.F. Verwoerd was violently killed in the House of Assembly he gave permission to me, as chairman of the UR, for the AB to start a campaign for a new republican flag, and for changing the existing form of the State Presidency to bring it more in accordance with the position and basic content of the Transvaal and Free State Republics – of course with the necessary changes to conform with present-day demands and circumstances.

"As far as the latter is concerned our Broederbond will give the necessary attention to it when the time is ripe and convenient." He thanked Broeder John Vorster for holding out the prospect "of a new flag to symbolise and bind our republican era."

In 1968 the UR asked Professor Charles Niewoudt of the University of Pretoria to investigate the question of an executive President. So the present moves towards a fresh constitutional arrangement for Whites, Coloureds and Indians with a strong executive President represent the fulfilment of a long-cherished Broederbond dream.

B. Education

No field in South Africa is more completely dominated by the Broederbond than education. The history of the AB has always been closely interwoven with the Afrikaner's fight to assert his control over education – first, his own; then that of all other race and language groups.

After the 1948 election victory the Bond was not directly active in the educational field. Matters were left largely in the hands of the Government or, rather, the Broeders in education. The essential aim was control of all education in South Africa under one single controlling body – so that education would be completely in Broeder hands.

At the end of 1959 the AB appointed its committee for educational matters under the chairmanship of H.J.J. Bingle, Rector of Potchefstroom University. During 1962 the task force committee was broadened to the point that its membership reads like a who's who of South Africa's top educationists (see previous chapter). It included the Rector of Unisa, the chairman of the National Educational Advisory Council, the head of the Council for Social Research, all four provincial Directors of Education, and the Secretary of Education.

In a report completed in 1963 the group demanded that the spirit and direction of education for Afrikaans-speaking children must accord with the teachings of the Afrikaans churches and conform with the history and culture of the Afrikaner nation. Following this the UR accepted a policy for a national education system. A committee was appointed comprising H.J.J. Bingle, J.S. Gericke (then Moderator of the NG Kerk), J.H. Stander (Natal director of Education), and A.P. Treurnicht. It submitted a memo on such a system to government Broeders.

The question of a national education system was debated at the 1964 and 1965 Bondsraad meetings. The main issue was to what extent the provinces, which traditionally controlled their own education, should retain some authority. A study paper entitled "The Task of our Education" stated bluntly: "The question is whether education is so completely involved with vested interests, personal empires and political implications that only the use of a central power will achieve any movement. Is the Afrikaner Broederbond not that central power?"

Another study paper said: "We won the first battle with the establishment of the National Educational Advisory Council. Now we must follow, and strike quickly before the work and enthusiasm slacken."

At the October 1966 Bondsraad, in Bloemfontein, Bingle reported on fresh proposed educational legislation. According to page 14 of the minutes he said: "Draft legislation has been prepared and submitted to the Minister concerned, and it is expected that it will be introduced during the next session of Parliament." The legislation would support a "national educational pattern."

So Broederbond educational experts – who all occupied key government education jobs

– actually prepared the new legislation. Speaking after Bingle at the Bondsraad, chairman Meyer reported that "enormous progress" had been made. He said that "a central policy can only be of value if it is implemented, and therefore central control is essential. A formula must be found to see to it that the central policy is implemented."

In a special memo submitted at the UR meeting of September 6, 1968, dealing with educational matters, Bingle reported on behalf of the educational committee on the new legislation regarding White teaching training. He referred to the two principles accepted at the 1958 Bondsraad: namely that there should be a national educational policy, and that it should have a Christian National character.

Bingle assured the UR that both these principles were incorporated in the new law on teacher training. Had the sysem been in conflict with these principles, it would have been unacceptable to the Broederbond.

Dealing with new salary scales for teachers, Bingle reported that "The UR was kept informed about . . . these proposals through Broeders serving on the National Educational Advisory Council." And a month later, at the 50th anniversary Bondsraad, Meyer said: "It is our Brotherhood, which with unstinting labour at Bondsraad study committees and by-means of consultation with educational heads at provincial and national levels – who were and are Broeders – which has been able to formulate the ideal of a national education policy for our volk and our country. We have carried it through to its present stage and will continue to do so in the years that lie ahead."

At the same meeting Treurnicht said it was "epoch-making" that the government had passed a law on Christian National education the previous year.

By the early Seventies the Broederbond dream of a single national educational policy under central control was finally fulfilled. Present policy is the policy of the Broederbond, and implemented by Broeders with the AB keeping a careful watch over matters.

The Bond takes no chances that it will lose its absolute grip on education. In 1977 the Transvaal Education Department created a new, key post at every school. This was "Head of Department – Educational Guidance" to deal with vocational guidance. The post involves responsibility for religious education; youth preparedness; educational programmes in hostels; training cadets; enlightenment programmes; and visits to veld schools. It is thus an ideal post for brainwashing young shoolchildren with the doctrines of Christian Nationalism. The precariousness of the Afrikaner identity is constantly drummed into the pupils.

It is therefore not surprising that a 1977 Bond circular stated: "It is of the greatest importance that these positions, as well as other positions as heads of departments, are filled by teachers with the correct attitude and motivation . . . Friends are asked to offer their services for these key positions."

Various examples over the years reveal to what an extent education has been used as a tool for indoctrination of the youth.

In circular No. 5/64/65 of August 3, 1964, members were urged to pay special attention to teachers when recruiting new Bond members: "When one considers the important role education continues to play in the formation of our volk, the recruitment of suitable teachers cannot be over-emphasised."

Education has also been used subtly, and not so subtly, as an instrument to influence English-speaking children. According to item 21 of the minutes of the UR meeting of December 1, 1965, the position of the English-speaking section was discussed. Meyer raised the possibility of English participation in national festivals. In a discussion Treurnicht warned that the political support of the Englsish did not mean they had become Afri-kaners. There were still the questions of language, church and "philosophy of life".

The following decision was noted: "The UR decides that a committee must be appointed to investigate the possibility of Afrikanerising English-speakers . . . Special note should be taken of the role that the teaching of history at schools can play." Bingle and Pelzer were proposed for the committee. Item 23 of the minutes, which dealt with "cultural mat-ters," noted (page nine) that the UR had decided "that Broeders in the various educational institutions should be consulted about the positive influencing of students."

According to item 8 of the minutes of the UR meeting of August 29 and 30, 1966, in Cape Town, Bingle spoke of "the necessity of approaching right-minded officials in executive positions." What could be more clear? The Bond was actively scheming to have Broeders appointed to senior positions in education.

Dealing with the problems of a proposed committee on university financing, Bingle sug-gested that negotiations should take place "at a personal level with friends in the highest responsible circles." The UR also decided "that there should be liaison with Broeders at the various Afrikaans universities and colleges regarding the holding of youth leaders' courses and the expansion of the Ruiterwag. And there should, as far as possible, be liaison between the various universities and colleges regarding the influencing of students." Public funds were thus used to promote secret Broederbond aims.

Item 19 of the minutes of the UR meeting of October 16, 1967, noted: "The UR decided to recommend that Broeder G.J. Jordaan be appointed as full-time chairman of the Natio-nal Educational Advisory Council." And Jordaan was indeed appointed.

In the Sixties UR discussions laid much stress on the establishment of parents' and teachers' associations. It can be accepted that all these bodies at Afrikaans schools are Bond-controlled and manipulated. The UR decided that the Rapportryers should be used to build up these associations and that all cells be informed this was a "special task".

The AB was even used as a market research organisation for the SABC, of which Broeder Meyer has been chief since the end of the Fifties. Circular No. 3/63/64 of August 7, 1963, contained a questionnaire on the schools radio service. It inquired about the use of the system and members were asked to obtain the information from schools in their areas through "tactful inquiries with headmasters."

The total control that the Broederbond exercises over South African education is re-flected by its membership. Educationists comprise the largest single group – 2 424 (20,36 per cent) of the total membership of 11 910 in 1977. This includes not only educationists in-volved in Afrikaans schools, but also in the education of other language and race groups.

Broeder Koornhof (No. 6844) is the Minister of National Education; his predecessor, Johan van der Spuy, was Broederbond secretary as well. Broeder Treurnicht (No. 4240) is a Deputy Minister in the Department of Education and Training (formerly Bantu Educa-tion). Chairman Gerrit Viljoen (No. 6157) is Rector of the Rand Afrikaans University.

Educationists serving on the last UR included Professor E. Marais (No. 4955), Gabriel Krog (director of Indian Education), Prof Charles Fensham of the University of Stellen-bosch, and Prof B. Kok, former Rector of the University of the Orange Free State.

The Rectors of all the Afrikaans Universities are Broeders – E.M. Hamman (Pretoria), Tjaart van der Walt (Potchefstroom), J.N. de Villiers (Stellenbosch) and W.L. Mouton (Bloemfontein).

The Broeder Chancellors of the Afrikaans Universities are: N. Diederichs (No. 560 RAU); John Vorster (No. 3737, Stellenbosch); Hilgard Muller (No. 3380, Pretoria); Jan de

Klerk (No. 2490, Potchefstroom); Anton Rupert (No. 3088, University of Port Elizabeth); and Professor B. Kok (University of the Free State).

The chairman of the university councils are Piet Meyer (RAU chairman); Dr R.L. Straszacker (vice-chairman RAU): Ds J.S. Gericke (No. 1999, Stellenbosch); A.D. Wassenaar (No. 3947, Port Elizabeth); Dr S.J. Naudé (No. 788, Bloemfontein).

The heads of all the Black universities are Broeders. They include Professor S.P. Olivier (No. 6991, Rector of the University of Durban Westville, for Indians); Prof J.A. Maré (No. 5340, former Rector of the University of Zululand; Prof J.M. de Wet, Rector of Fort Hare; Prof J.L. Boshoff, former Rector of the University of the North; and C.J. Kriel, former Rector of the University of the Western Cape (for Coloureds).

All the Directors of Education in the four provinces and South West Africa, the Secretary of Education, and all senior and other officials in key positions in education departments are Broeders.

The reaction of Dawid van der Merwe Brink – the MEC in direct control of education in the Transvaal Provincial Administration and leader of the National Party in the Provincial Council – to reports in the *Sunday Times* in January 1978, stating that there were Broeders among educationists, was somewhat amusing.

He claimed that he did not know whether there were Broeders among educationists in the province – curious coming from a man who himself is Broeder No. 4798.

C.   The Church

The three Afrikaans churches are completely in the hands of the Broederbond. Almost 1 000 ministers of religion belong to it or the Ruiterwag.

Given the reverence in which a minister is held in Afrikaans society, these religious Broeders occupy far more important positions than even the teachers.

As the spiritual leader of his congregation such a man is in a unique position to steer affairs in the direction laid down by the Broederbond. Together with this is the fact that, almost wihout exception, the church councils are dominated by Broeders, although they seldom number more than 10 or 15 per cent of the 70 or 80 council members.

The leaders of the elders (the council consists of elders and deacons – the younger men) are almost invariably the AB leaders in the local area or suburb. And the leadership of all three Afrikaans churches is Broederbond-controlled, with Broeders occupying all the key positions on the Moderature, as paid officials, or as editors of church magazines, etc.

Since its inception the fate of the Broederbond and the Afrikaans churches has been interwoven. The church gave the Bond its religious basis and philosophy of Christian Nationalism. Simply, this meant the Broeder church leadership supplied Christian justification for everything done in the name of Afrikaner Nationalism – including its race policies.

Dr William Nicol – the influential Transvaal Moderator of the N G Church in the Forties – was a founder member, and Ds J.F. Naudé its first president. N G Church leaders have served on the UR – Ds J.S. Gericke, the general Moderator was one; and Ds D.P.M. Beukes, the present Moderator, continued to occupy his position in the Seventies. The Afrikaans churches have been an inseparable part of the Afrikaner Nationalist political structure, and are partners in everything done by the National Party Government.

The inseparable link between the church, Broederbond and N P provides the basis for the irrefutable claim that the NG Church and its two sister churches are "volkskerke" and that they constitute the National Party at prayer. The involvement of almost half of all Afrikaans ministers has given the Broederbond respectability among Afrikaner Nationalists who might otherwise reject such an organisation.

Religious matters as such are not often discussed at Broederbond or UR meetings – their interests are well looked after by the Broeder ministers.

Over the years the issue of the Broederbond and the church has been half-heartedly raised by brave and courageous individual ministers – but they never got far. The majority of elders attending Synods are Broeders, which meant the dice was loaded against them from the beginning.

In 1946 a NG Synod – after an "investigation" in which the committee was packed with Broeders – found that the Bond and membership of it was not in conflict with the scriptures and loyalty to Christian principles. The matter, however, would come into the open with a vengeance for the first and last time in the early Sixties. This was after the Cottesloe Conference drama when some NG Church leaders associated themselves with highly critical resolutions on aspects of government policy.

For the first time, Afrikaans theologians, ministers and church members went through the agonising process of questioning the very moral basis of apartheid and whether it was compatible with the demands of the scriptures and Christian justice. This, of course, brought them into direct conflict with the Broederbond as the custodian and guardian of Afrikaner Nationalist interests, and with its Broeder church members who presented the policy in "acceptable" theological terms. The conflict was to provide historic evidence of the AB's workings.

During 1963-1964, when the Broederbond issue was publicly raised in NG Church circles, I was approached by a rebel theologian, who knew of my involvement in the *Sunday Times'* exposés. Would I be prepared to show some of the documents in my possession to a leading NG Church theologian who was looking for arguments against the Bond? I was, and in due course this man contacted me. But he was obviously panic-stricken that somebody would discover he was making investigations into the Broederbond. I had to meet him late at night in Linden, where he parked his car under a tree, away from street lights.

I picked him up and took him to my Blairgowrie home. There I had to drive into the garage and close the doors before he would get out to enter my house through the kitchen.

When he left, after reading all the documents, he was shocked and angry and even more totally committed than before to oppose the Broederbond, absolutely convinced that its secret membership and character were incompatible with Christianity and churchgoing.

Today this man is a well-known NG Church leader, and a senior member of one of the NG Regional Synods. When I bumped into him at the 1974 General Synod in Cape Town – which toned down all resolutions which could lead to a softening of apartheid – he, of course, did not blink an eye.

Today he seems totally committed to defending his church's policy of justifying apartheid, though with a modern coating. He appears to enjoy his powerful position in the NG hierarchy. What happened to his resolution, his sincerity, his conviction that the Broederbond had to be combatted at all costs? Was it the subtle warning, issued to several dissident NG theologians, that they would wreck their future in the church if they campaigned against the Bond? Or was it the argument that if they wanted to liberalise the church's attitude on race, their only hope was to abandon oppostion to the Broederbond? Many of the young ministers who were non-Broeders fell for this gimmick, only to find themselves in

1978 in a racial *cul de sac*. The "change from within" call did not even dent their church's stance.

Another important incident occurred some years later in the early Seventies. I was in contact with a NG Church minister who was furious at Deputy Minister Treurnicht's refusal to allow church halls to be used by Blacks for church services. He was a Broeder, although we never discussed it. This man, too, met me on occasion in quiet plaes, scared of being seen. Then I received a written message from him through a go-between in which he stated that his contacts with me had become known – obviously because of telephone tapping – and that he was in trouble. He did not specify with whom.

Since then he too has been rather silent on controversial political and racial issues.

In early 1978 I had a discussion with an Afrikaans theologian, also a Broeder. He detested the Broederbond, he despised himself, but could not break with it.

Lack of courage? Perhaps. But he and other trusting, pious young ministers, once they leave the theological faculty, soon find themselves subtly pushed by the key elders on their congregation's church council towards becoming a Broeder.

To resist is very difficult, though some are opposed to it on Christian principles. My contact mentioned a number of examples of young ministers who had resisted the pressure of elders, and of the hell they went through as a consequence.

Others do not think membership wrong initially, because all the highly respected church leaders and most theological professors are Broeders. But later, I was told, the agonising hours of soul-searching and inner conflicts begin, with growing doubts about whether a Christian should belong to a secret organisation which is a bulwark of a government and policies seemingly increasingly in conflict with the scriptures.

These three incidents made one over-riding impression on me: the factor of fear weighed heavily with those who questioned the validity of the Broederbond. However strongly they felt, they were helpless; once this organisation declares you an enemy of the volk, and starts its whispering campaign – kept out of circulars – you are a marked man.

Very few are tough enough or in a position to resist the reprisals. And even if you can resist them physically and economically, the price of total ostracism is too high for most to pay.

The year 1963 was a momentous one in the annuals of the AB, full of shocks for the organisation. On March 24 the *Sunday Times* published disclosures made in a report by a group of prominent Afrikaner businessmen, intellectuals and farmers, who had investigated the Broederbond and Ruiterwag. It disclosed the control these organisations had over the Afrikaans churches; that the violent campaign against Freemasonry and "new deal" thinking on colour issues was inspired by the Bond; and that prominent Afrikaners – including Nationalists – who did not belong to the secret societies, or opposed their ideas, were discriminated against in public life. (See Annexure K).

The Broederbond was struck two further blows when their candidates were defeated by verligte theologians in March and April 1963, for the positions of Moderators of the Northern and Southern Transvaal. Dr F.E. O'Brien Geldenhuys, who had just resigned from the Broederbond, beat Broeder A.M. Meiring; and Beyers Naudé, who though still a member was wrestling with his conscience and had already started *Pro Veritate,* beat Broeder H.J.C. Snijders.

Then on April 9, 1963, the Southern Transvaal Synod debated the issue of Broederbond membership at length. This followed the unexpected recommendation of a 21-member synodal commission, headed by Dr A.C. Barnard, that the AB should submit to investigation. The recommendation was, however, rejected by a three to two majority, though only after an historic debate.

The committee called for a "thorough investigation" on the grounds that "rightly or wrongly there are doubts in many hearts in the church" about the secret society. It also expressed the hope that the Bond "will not only welcome such an investigation but will facilitate it."

Introducing the proposal, Dr Barnard said: "If the Broederbond has nothing to hide, let it welcome an investigation – and so assure the church that it really is what it stands for . . .

"I fully realise how sensitive this matter is, for quite a number of ministers here belong to the Broederbond. I realise, too, that in asking for an enquiry I might expose myself to criticism. Yet I feel, in all honesty, that we must examine the Broederbond in the light of God's Word."

Barnard was supported by Dr J.D.W. Kritzinger who stated that the Bond was dividing believers into two groups. If its cause was good and just, an investigation ought not to be feared.

Ds D.P.M. Beukes – whose membership of the UR at the time was not publically known – led the counter-attack. He submitted a special statement given to him by a former Broederbond secretary – Lombard – and asked for endorsement of the 1951 finding by the Council of NG Churches that there was nothing wrong with the Broederbond, and that it was "a sound and wholesome" body. The statement presented the Broederbond in the most innocent light, and claimed that secrecy was necessary for the fulfilment of its aim – the preservation of the Afrikaner volk. Furthermore, the most outstanding figures of Afrikanerdom belonged to the Bond, but to divulge their names might offend other loyal Afrikaners who had been by-passed. The body's secrecy was simply a practical way of achieving its aims, and not a matter of principle. "In itself secrecy is neither good nor evil. Prominent Afrikaners are often overlooked for purely incidental factors of a practical and fleeting nature." The Broederbond was a "democratic" body and any improper conduct within its ranks would be censured at the annual congress.

Beukes said that a new investigation would only cause friction, and in the light of the AB's disclosures about itself was unnecessary. "Such an investigation will only sow suspicion and uncertainty at a time when we cannot afford to divide Afrikaner forces." No investigation would satisfy everybody, least of all the enemies of the church.

On June 30, 1963, I reported on a new pamphlet written by Professor A. van Selms of the N H Church, one of the foremost Afrikaans theologians of his day. The 15-page document was entitled "The Church and Secret Organisations, with reference to the Freemasons and the Broederbond."

Van Selms made a scathing attack on the Bond, warning against the dangers which this secret organisation held for the church, and comparing its systems of infiltration into other organisations with that of the Communists. He contended that the Broederbond members of the church were hypocrites. At meetings they prayed for divine guidance, but were compelled to vote or go along with the Broederbond.

"I declare openly that I regard the continuance of membership of the Broederbond by somebody who calls himself a Christian as a lack of moral judgment." (See Annexure L for the full text of the *Sunday Times* report on Van Selms pamphlet).

On August 25, 1963, the *Sunday Times* reported that the White River Church Council of the NH Church had expressed "grave anxiety" about the grip the Broederbond had gained on the Afrikaans churches. In a letter to the General Church Assembly it wanted to know what the attitude of the N H Church was to the Bond. Referring to the reports in the *Sunday Times* the Council wrote: "Following certain exposures about the Broederbond which were made in the Press, we must demand a firm statement regarding the attitude of the church towards the Broederbond. Certain facts contained in the exposures are, from the church's point of view, definitely most alarming."

The Council, most of whom were Nationalists, analysed the information revealed in the reports. The letter, signed by Ds J.P.B. Viljoen and J.H. Brits, the secretary, went on: "It appears from the Press exposés that the Broederbond has thrown its octopus-like grip around the Afrikaner's churches, and that it is most probably busy winding itself like a python around our church to strangle our dearly bought Christian freedom and to squeeze all spontaneous life from it until we will in the church, as in our culture, become a spiritually impoverished instrument of a power group."

This ferment in the N H Church came after the de-frocking of Professor Albert Geyser in 1961, later set aside by a Supreme Court decision. Geyser and a small group of liberal theologians had criticised the N H Church's support for apartheid, and advocated the removal of clause 3 of the church's constitution which specifically precluded "non-Whites" from becoming members. Geyser and others also attacked the Broederbond for its role in his de-frocking. All his "accusers" and "judges" in the Church Tribunal had been Broeders.

On September 8, 1963, I reported that another "devastating" attack had been launched on the Broederbond – this time by members of the Gereformeerde Church (the Doppers) in a five-page petition dealing with the activities of secret societies in the church. It was to be submitted to the Synod in January 1964 and stated: "The Afrikaner Broederbond is contrary to the nature of the church. Membership of the Broederbond is contrary to the scriptures. There is uneasiness and uncertainty in our church whether decisions, taken at lower or higher levels, are exclusively and only based on God's Word through the guidance of the Holy Spirit."

The petition stated that two decisions of the 1936 Synod were contradictory – one condemned the Freemasons; yet the other said it was not necessary to investigate the Broederbond.

The petitioners referred to St John 3: 19 – 21. "As far as the Afrikaner Broederbond is concerned, we want to underline the 21st verse. 'But he that doeth truth cometh to the light, that his deeds may be made manifest, that they are wrought in God.'

"A member of the Broederbond does not come to the light with his activities . . . These are surrounded by a wall of secrecy, so that it cannot be evident in public that these works are wrought in God."

The question was then posed that "if the aims of the Broederbond are exclusively in the cultural field, why must secrecy be guaranteed? A person's activities should be controllable by fellow-Christians . . . One can do much in the so-called cultural field which cannot endure the test of the scriptures." And, finally, serious doubts were expressed whether the Holy Spirit and God's Word were the only guiding factors in decisions at various church meetings.

"The formula of the affirmation of elders and deacons states that all forms of tyranny and domination must be excluded from the congregation of God. It is known that a small minority, which is well prepared, can easily get a certain resolution adopted at meetings without the others present knowing that they have already taken that specific decision among themselves.

"It has become known from the Press that 'Broeders' received instructions on how the Afrikaner Broederbond wanted the Southern Transvaal Synod of the Nederduits Gereformeerde Church to decide. And even if this news cannot be accepted as evidence, then the possibility is still there . . . In this way you get tyranny and domination in the church. It is possible that members of the Broederbond are bound beforehand to accept a certain point of view and to act accordingly, before they go to Synod regional meetings or church council meetings.

"Not only is mutual deliberation then senseless, but the meetings start with prayers to ask God to lead the thoughts and discussions which are then profane if certain Broeders, by mutual deliberation, have already decided on a point of view.

"For specific decisions it is necessary to make a thorough study of the scriptures – for example on the colour policy, or the compatability of the membership of the Afrikaner Broederbond with membership of the church. What sense is there in these studies of the scriptures if the result has already been decided? Thus the Spirit is sorrowed and extinguished." (See Annexure M for extracts of the petition dealing with theological arguments).

On November 3, 1963, I reported yet another attack on the AB by a churchman, Ds J.A. Swanepoel of the Witpoortjie congregation of the N H Church. He claimed that the Bond was influencing church decisions and appointments. At the General Assembly of the church in Pretoria in 1961 he was told by two different people that at a meeting of "an organisation" which "controlled" the Assembly the previous evening it had been decided that if a "certain person" withdrew what he had written and said, he would be "left in peace."

When the elders at the General Assembly came to be chosen, a letter was circulated advising members not to vote for this man because he belonged to a particular political party.

Secret instructions on what attitude church members should adopt were sent out when a Christian newspaper – *Pro Veritate* – was published which promoted ideas conflicting with those of the Broederbond.

Ds Swanepoel concluded: "The church's witness is determined and formed by what the Broederbond's views are, even if they are possibly in conflict with the Gospels. Things are not called by their names in circulars issued by the Broederbond, but it is always made quite clear what the intention is."

Swanepoel urged the church to pay attention to a movement which was "inducing the church to deny God and which is damaging the Gospel of Christ." He also urged every member and minister of the church – who would one day have to answer to God – to take note of the significant warnings contained in Professor Van Selms' pamphlet.

Then, on November 24, 1963, Professor Albert Geyser joined in the attack, accusing the Bond of making use of the church for political purposes. This came in a Press release in which he admitted that he had given Broederbond documents handed to him by Ds Beyers Naudé- a former regional chairman of the Broederbond in Johannesburg – to a reporter.

"Among the documents which were given to me to read were pieces that showed unmistakenly that they were aimed at making use of the church for political aims," he said. "There were pieces that contained interpretations of the scriptures and their application that served the ideology of the Broederbond, but which rendered unrecognisable the demands of the Bible for neighbourly love, justice and humanity.

"These people are making the church, which is the Bride of Christ, a handmaiden of politics. And, above all, I observed in the documents the kind of quasi-Biblical argument that I

167

encountered during my heresy trial. I was aware that at my heresy trial three-quarters of my clerical judges were Broederbonders," he stated.

This statement followed the public revelation that Naudé was involved in the Broederbond document issue, and after Naudé and Meyer had issued public statements.

On the same day as Geyser spoke out, Professor B. Keet, one of the leading Afrikaans theologians of his day, and the highly revered former head of the Stellenbosch Theological Seminary, told the *Sunday Times* that after Naude's disclosures the Afrikaans churches would have to face the Broederbond issue squarely. Keet said that the issue had become a public one which could no longer be hushed up. "The facts in Ds Naudé's disclosures have not been contradicted. On the contrary they appear true. They will have to be faced by the churches.

"A secret society which works in an underhand manner cannot always remain secret. The Broederbond bubble has burst, and the public can now see what is going on."

Professor Keet, who was one of the staunchest supporters of the Christian Institute, said that attempts would probably be made to "dishonour Ds Naudé." His revelations about the Broederbond might well be used against him in the controversy over his status in the church. There were a vast number of clergymen in the Afrikaans churches who were members of the Broederbond, and they could well bring pressure against Ds Naudé. But Naudé had come out of the controversy with honour. He had done what his Christian conscience demanded; he felt the power of the Broederbond over the church and acted accordingly.

Professor Keet said he was disturbed by the role the police had played in the matter of the Broederbond documents. As Prof Geyser had noted, what had the Security Branch to do with the matter? Prof Keet said he was fully aware that many members of the D R C wanted the Broederbond question brought under full public scrutiny, and this would have to be done when the Synod met again. He understood that some ministers would in fact raise the issue.

Keet pointed out that Naudé had been faced with a severe test: he had felt his honour was at stake and as a Christian was unhappy about the secret workings of the AB.

Now that he had acted, his reservations had gone. "He is now a happy man, and can go ahead with his work as a Christian," Professor Keet said. Furthermore, it would be extremely difficult for members of the Broederbond within the church to attempt to suppress what had been brought to light. No matter what influence they brought to bear, the issue would be resolved in public. And this was how it should be.

The struggle within the church over the status of clergymen associated with the Christian Institute would continue, as before. It was being fought out in the Press and behind the scenes and would "continue because the conscience of the church is involved."

The NG Church hit back when the Cape Synod – all Broeders – published a letter on December 4, 1963. It had this to say of Naudé: "We wish to declare, for the reassurance of our members, that this malicious attempt to sow suspicion against our church is groundless and void of all truth." The church was not controlled from outside. Its decisions, "taking into account the difference of opinion which sometimes occurred within its own ranks, were the outcome of the opinions and honest convictions of every delegate . . ."

The letter ended: "Any attempt from whatever body, to hamper the autonomous judgment of the church from outside by means of political or moral pressures, would have elicited immediate and relentless opposition from our side. The absence of such opposition can therefore only demonstrate that no cause for it exists."

Professor Ben Engelbrecht, then minister of the Johannesburg East NG congregation, warned in *Pro Veritate* on December 12, 1963, that the church should "wrest itself loose from the bonds which absolute nationalism is tying around it." He attacked the manner in which certain church leaders had, either directly or by suggestion been labelled the "tools of liberalism and Communism."

"National politics, which has fallen prey to the absolutism of nationalism, knows and recognises only one principle of selection – the exclusive, that which belongs to the nation," he wrote.

"The only yardsticks which apply here are those which are in line with the history, the past and the future of the nation."

At the end of November 1963 there was a sharp clash between pro- and anti-Broeders at the Eastern Transvaal Synod of the Gereformeerde Church, when the Broederbond was sharply attacked for interfering in church matters. A Bond-sponsored motion to halt the discussion was defeated and, with a substantial majority, the matter was referred to the General Synod which met at the end of that month in Potchefstroom.

The resolution discussed at this meeting came from one of the church councils on the Reef. Doubt was expressed whether membership of the Broederbond was compatible with being a theological professor, a minister or a member of the Gereformeerde Church. It alleged that because of the Press reports of recent months, the church had become implicated, and that suspicions were undermining true, public brotherhood in Christ.

This criticism led to a violent counter-attack by Professor S.P. van der Walt of the Theological Faculty at Potchefstroom. Giving every indication of having lost his temper, he bitterly attacked those – especially the English Press – who criticised the Broederbond. He compared the body with a military council whose meetings and decisions were also secret and pointed out the various achievements of the Broederbond in the economic and cultural spheres.

Van der Walt's tirade had a polarising affect. For some it confirmed their suspicions of the Bond. But bitter attacks were made on the English Press – Ds J. Visser of Primrose, for example, saying that it came from the devil.

All this fighting talk was of no avail. The beginning of February 1964 saw the Gereformeerde Church Synod in Potchefstroom unanimously rejecting a petition by four members calling on the church to express itself against all secret societies, including the Broederbond. The Synod decided the Broederbond was not a secret society in the same mould as the Freemasons, which conflicted with the spiritual nature of the church. It rejected the petition because its arguments against secret organisations were not convincing. The Synod's resolution, however, said that membership of secret organisations should in no way interfere with the discipline of the church or the actions of parish councils. "In no circumstances may such an organisation make its weight felt in the church. An Afrikaner brotherhood, and the promotion of national interests, no matter how praiseworthy, must never be emphasised at the expense of the brotherhood in Christ or in any way overshadow it."

In a letter to *Die Kerkbode,* mouthpiece of the NG Church, Dr J.D.W. Kritzinger returned to the attack on February 1, 1964. He urged the Southern Transvaal Synod to review its decision of April 9, 1963, not to investigate the Broederbond. The ban on church members belonging to the Freemasons should be extended to all secret organisations. When believers became divided into groups, there was mistrust and suspicion instead of mutual trust and unanimity.

169

"He who enters an exclusive brotherhood creates an alien presence within the body of Christ and damages the functioning of the body . . ." The infiltration of a relatively small number of people into key positions meant that the government of Christ could be supplanted by the control of a secret organisation. "So it can happen that a whole church can be influenced and . . . take decisions which are not inspired by the Spirit of Christ, but by the specific movement . . .

"Because the church cannot call the secret organisations to account, there remains only one alternative, namely that members of the church should belong to no secret organisation."

Three young NG theologians also attacked the AB in an article entitled "The Christian and Secret Organisations," published in *Die Kerkbode* on July 13, 1964. They were Dr A.C. Barnard, now on the Natal Moderature; Dr W.D. Jonker, now a Professor at Stellenbosch; and Dr A.J. Venter. They stated that the Broederbond had the influence and channels to brand anyone asking for inquiry into the organisation as a liberal, a Communist, a frustrated deviationist, or an enemy of the Afrikaner.

Secret organisations should expect to be mistrusted, they said, because their tactics are similar to those of Communists: a small group of people in key positions achieved their preconceived plans through indoctrination, infiltration and various front organisations. They pointed out that while the church had investigated two secret organisations, condemning one (the Freemasons) and exonerating the other (the Broederbond), many clergyment and elders were in fact members of the Bond and had helped to "judge" their own organisation.

This article virtually marked the end of the anti-Broederbond revolt in the Afrikaner churches.

The NH Church appointed a special one-man investigator, J.C. Oelofse, to look into the AB. He was an attorney, and an elder. At the time he was also a member of the secret Afrikaner Orde (a fact not known then) and he became a Broeder in 1968. His finding was that the Broederbond in no way influenced the church. Geyser and other Broederbond critics boycotted his investigation because they said that a panel of inquiry should have included an eminent theologian, and could not have been completed within three months, as Oelofse managed.

Broeder church leaders stifled all discussion in church circles about the AB in the turbulent early Sixties.

The Bond's major intervention in church affairs came directly after the December 1960 Cottesloe conference. On January 9, 1961, after weeks of public debate and after Verwoerd had specially mentioned the issue in his New Year's message to the nation, a circular was sent out on January 9, 1961. It assured all cells that the UR was watching the situation closely.

It stated: "After the publication of the decisions of the conference of member churches of the World Council of Churches in Johannesburg, many AB members expressed their deep concern about their nature and purpose . . . and about their possible affects on national life. At a special meeting in Pretoria the UR gave its serious consideration to the whole affair and obtained the necessary information about it. To prevent any serious harmful outcome for our volk which might follow from this conference, the UR would like to report as follows to divisions . . ."

Setting out the factual position it subtly hinted that the matter would be thrashed out at the Synods. Of course, these were now under Broederbond control and the elders (mostly Broeders and staunchly pro-NP) would see to it that the younger liberal ministers did not get out of hand. "It is self-evident that our organisation dare not, and will not, intrude in the affairs of the church . . . The UR draws attention to the fact that the three Afrikaans member churches of the World Council of Churches will deliberate over the whole affair at the forthcoming Synods and will then decide as individual churches on the recommendations of the conference." The circular noted that the Bond differed from the recommendations of Cottesloe on the issues of Coloureds in Parliament, and rights for Africans in "White" areas.

It went on: "The UR would like to call upon our members to be careful in all that they say and do in connection with the conference recommendations and not to play into the hands of the enemy English Press, which is moving heaven and earth to sow discord between Afrikaner and Afrikaner in church matters."

In his speech to the Bondsraad on May 21, 1963, Meyer dealt at length with the wave of public criticism in church circles. From his remarks it is clear he did not expect the demands of the Southern Transvaal Synod for the investigation into the Bond to gain much support. He said: "Although the UR has taken into account the publicity that in some church councils resolutions will be submitted arising from the decision of the General Synod of the N.G. Church about the Freemasons, asking that the affairs of our organization too should be investigated, we nonetheless thought that the regional synods would not again consider such a proposal in view of the previous findings of the Council of Churches.

"However when we heard that the Commission of Current Affairs (Aktuele Sake) of the Southern Transvaal Synod had appointed a commission of investigation into the affairs of our organisation without reference to the previous finding of the Council of Churches, we decided after careful consideration and after consultation with leading minister members to take the Synod in our confidence, thus to persuade the Synod to drop the matter.

"After all our organization had remained exactly the same since the previous investigation, and if certain members of the Synod was convinced that the previous investigation by a commission of the Council of Churches was one sided and incomplete, why should they then accept another commissions report?

"The UR was convinced that the appointment of a similar commission at this stage would lead to a campaign to drive a wedge between the Afrikaner and his church and should therefore be opposed.

"A short official document in which the basis and structure of our organisation was explained was given to Ds D.P.M. Beukes to submit to the Synod. After Ds Beukes had explained the matter, the Synod decided to drop it." There would certainly be no submission to an intensive investigation.

The secretarial report of Meyer and Naudé Botha for the period March 1963 to February 1965 also dealt with the matter. Page six reiterated what Meyer had told the Bondsraad: that the UR had decided not to agree to an investigation and that Beukes would be provided with the necessary information to submit to the Synod.

The report contained these significant remarks: *"Through mutual consultation with Broeders in the leadership of the various churches the UR continued to do everything in its power* to prevent . . . a split in the volk.

"The UR regarded it as necessary to call on Broeders who are taking the lead in the various churches, and on each Broeder, to control the spread of liberalistic ideas through our church.

"For the positive action of Broeders on the editorial staff of church newspapers, syno-

171

dal commissions, Moderatures, superior church bodies, etc., in maintaining the unity of the Afrikaner in the sphere of the church _ the UR has only the highest appreciation."

In these years the phrase "liberalistic tendencies" was continually used to refer to those ministers who dared to question or criticise aspects of the government's race policy and church support for it. They were presented as being disloyal to the Afrikaner volk.

Attacks from within the churches caused considerable consternation in Broeder circles. This was reflected in the minutes of the UR meeting of August 22 and 23, 1963.

According to page two of the minutes, Ds Beukes, a member of the UR, "suggested that a reassuring statement should be circulated to all divisions regarding the membership of Christians to secret organisations." And Broeder P.M. Smith, then a member of the moderature of the NH church, warned that an attack on the Bond via the churches was imminent.

Ds H.J.C. Snijders, Moderator of the Southern Transvaal Synod, had been invited to attend this meeting. According to item 33 of the minutes the following was noted: "The UR held a discussion on certain church affairs, particularly in view of the latest reports about the possible discussion of the Broederbond at Synods. The following viewpoints were presented:

"A. The attack on the Broederbond with the three Afrikaans Churches take place in a co-ordinated manner. B. The Church is damaged as a result of the unrest sowed by it; C. The Christian Institute will try to promote Church integration, D. The liason between Church leaders and volksvreemdes (strangers to the volk) must be investigated, E. The Afrikaans Church is the biggest fortress (vesting) of the Afrikaner against foreign influences and therefore it must be broken, F. The Broeders in leading church positions must act against foreign influences in the church, G. A reassuring declaration of the Church as a whole is necessary."

The UR decided that the task group entrusted with religious matters should look into how best the Afrikaans churches could co-operate in countering liberal influences.

"A committee consisting of Broeder D.P.M. Beukes; P.M. Smith; J.S. Gericke; H.J.J. Bingle; and A.P. Treurnicht must be appointed to draft a communique for the circular on the question of whether membership of a secret organisation can be reconciled with membership of a Christian church."

Only Bingle was not a church leader. Gericke, Beukes and Treurnicht (as editor of *Die Kerkbode)* occupied key positions in the NG Church; and P.M. Smith was a force in the NH Church.

The management committee of November 7, 1963, decided to request the Afrikaans newspapers to give no publicity to the activities of the Christian Institute. And at the special UR meeting of November 12, 1963, it was decided, according to page two of the minutes, "that any reference to church affairs in our documents must be very carefully handled." In other words there should be as little evidence as possible of the closeness of the link between Broederbond and church.

In the period 1962 – 1964 the Broederbond was used to counter any criticism of government policy.

The special circular of August 1, 1962, dealt with "onslaughts against our existence as an independent, Christian National Western country in South Africa." It said the most dangerous threat" is certainly the growing, organised attempt to tell us that our separate nationhood is something un-Christian – that the maintenance of it, through preventing mixing in all spheres of life, is unbiblical . . ."

172

The claim – even by some in the Bond – that apartheid was un-Christian would hasten the process of Communistic domination in South Africa. The UR therefore "makes an urgent call on our church leaders to expose and combat in a clear and determined manner the liberalistic onslaught on our Christian – Protestant religious life and on the Christian National philosophy of life . . .

"Church leaders should ask themselves if this present cry of liberalism and humanism is in accordance with the calling of the church to preach Jesus Christ as the saviour of sinners, or whether He is the champion of all sorts of social advantages."

The circular stressed that "one of the most important and urgent tasks with which our organisation should assist is the implementation of our apartheid policy."

Thus we find the Broederbond – State – Party – Church alliance, bolstered by religio-philosophical arguments, justifying the existence of the Bond and the membership of Christians.

Another study document circulated in 1962 stated that everyone was aware of groups in the church who were not only disloyal, but were setting up their own organisations. The church had no objections to "well-meaning" criticism; but the right and proper channels – obviously all Broederbond-controlled – had to be employed.

Circular 5/62/63 of December 1, 1962, gave an interesting indication of Bond strategy in church affairs. It contained an instruction to Broeders on church councils how to act when the Broederbond was discussed. "In order to raise the least sensation and suspicion, friends are advised not to try and prevent such demands for discussions but to let them run their natural course and then suggest that the matter be referred to the various Synods."

The UR meeting of December 1, 1965, discussed how the church could be used in the fight against the Freemasons. It was decided, according to item 22 of the minutes, "to leave it to the Afrikaans churches to give judgment on the religious aspects of Freemasonry and to inform the public."

Item 22 of the same minutes noted that "the Broeders in Church circles will be requested to deliberate about the role of the Church in the promotion of our cultural aspirations."

UR members who were church ministers, such as Gericke, Treurnicht and Beukes, were directly involved in political and other national issues. In this way the Afrikaans churches became full partners in the political decisions affecting Afrikaner Nationalism. Indeed, Broeder churchmen became constitutional experts!

After the middle Sixties the controversy surrounding the Broederbond in the Afrikaans churches died out. All opposition was ruthlessly crushed, and Beyers Naudé lost his status as minister when he became Director of the Christian Institute.

Some churchmen felt it would be strategically better to abandon the fight against the Broederbond in exchange for possible support on the liberalisation of race attitudes. This proved to be wishful thinking, however. People like Dr Willie Jonker, who had criticised the Broederbond and refused to become a Broeder, became marked men. Their influence is minimal and weak in the Broeder-controlled church establishment. In 1978 the NG Church is still as conservative in racial matters as ever.

Another minister who was crushed for his opposition was Murray Janson, the popular Pretoria academic. Once Broeder 7131, he resigned a few years ago. For questioning race policies and for his uneasiness about the role of the Broederbond he had to pay a price. Against all expectations he was unsuccessful in obtaining a professorship at the University of Pretoria in the NG Church Department of Theology, and he failed to be elected to the Northern Transvaal Synod.

He is now a lecturer in the Department of Theology at the University of South Africa. In fact, this department, which is not controlled by the NG Church, as are those at the Universities of Stellenbosch and Pretoria, has become a bastion of those theologians rejected and discarded by the Broeder NG establishment. Theologically and academically, it is the strongest in the country.

Non-Broeders like Professor David Bosch and Prof Ian Eybers are among the most outstanding NG Church theologians; but they are barred from the NG's theological faculties because of their critical attitude to the church's race policies.

Twice Bosch – who is internationally acclaimed as a theologian – has felt the might of the Bond. In 1966 he was by-passed, after being promised the position of professor in missionary studies at the University of Pretoria; Broeder C.W.H. Boshoff, son-in-law of Dr Verwoerd, was appointed. A few years ago, against strong Broeder objections, the NG Church theological committee chose him for the professorship at the University of Stellenbosch. But in an unprecedented step the Broeder-controlled board of the seminary of the Stellenbosch theological faculty decided to abolish the professorship, regrading the post to that of senior lecturer. This meant a large drop in both seniority and salary.

It is important to note that in all investigations into the Bond by the church the final advisers were the church Broeders themselves, who thoroughly blocked any objective non-Broeder evaluation. Those who criticised Naudé for forming the Christian Institute proved to be ineffective within the church, and over the years the Afrikaans churches have remained the foremost bastion of Afrikaner Nationalism, with the Broederbond entrenched in the inner temple of the tabernacle.

D. Broeder Snippets

In this section I will briefly deal with a number of random issues to give a further insight into Broederbond thought and action.

Perhaps only the enemies of the Broederbond – or rather those bodies, people and organisations regarded by the Broederbond as its enemies – tell its real story, so often glossed over in minutes and circulars.

Enemy number one, of course, is the Freemason movement. A semi-secret organisation, it is regarded by the absolutely secret Bond as its biggest opponent. One major reason is that the Freemasons are said to be much larger numerically and that at least 60 per cent of all Freemasons in South Africa are Afrikaans-speaking.

AB documents are full of warnings and exhortations to fellow Broeders to prevent young Afrikaners falling into the clutches of Freemasonry and its "denationalising" influence.

Other public enemies include the following: the International Junior Chamber of Commerce; the Rotarians; Lions International; the Round Table; the American Field Service (AFS) scheme; and Moral Rearmament. As far as the Broederbond is concerned they all have one feature in common: they are international bodies, not tied by bonds of language, ethnicity or race. They must be opposed because they breathe "internationalism."

In Bond philosophy the spirit of "internationalism" with its accompanying "liberalism" ranks as a bigger threat than Communism. Additionally, these service organisations are all regarded as fronts of the Freemasons. Hence the tremendous efforts to build up the Rapportryers movement as the effective counter.

Broeders are expressly forbidden to become members of any of these highly respectable organisations, which are described as *"volksvreemde"* ("foreign to the volk"). Only the UR can grant permisson for exemptions. Afrikaans schools have been warned to avoid as far as possible any awards or financial assistance from any of these bodies. Thus the secretarial report for the period 1968 – 1970, signed by Meyer and Naudé Botha, urged schoolmasters to "tactfully" reject any such donations.

The fight against the Freemasons was strengthened when church Broeders condemned the organisation on religious grounds; it forbade its members to belong to it and Freemasons were forced off church councils.

Professor B. Booyens of Stellenbosch was asked by the UR at its meeting of March 21, 1968, to investigate the AFS. He was to submit a report why Afrikaans children should not be encouraged to go on one-year exchange programmes to the United States of America.

This reflects the AB's fear that a too close contact with this and similar organisations could dilute the nationalism of Afrikaners. The Broederbond is the hard inner core of the Afrikaner volk, and Afrikaner Nationalists form the rock on which the South African nation is built. Hence the fear.

The South African nation comprises Afrikaner Nationalists – and others. Yet while Broeder leaders talk about broad South Africanism and English-Afrikaner unity, the Broederbond continues to embody Afrikaner imperialism. English voters are welcome in Parliament and even in the Cabinet – but there is an absolute line beyond which they cannot proceed, however loyal they might be to the NP's race policy.

Another body which attracted the Bond's wrath was the SA Foundation, which came under fire from some cells during the Sixties. However, Etienne Rousseau, a Foundation leader well known for his highly verkrampte views, managed, as a UR member, to persuade the Broederbond that the Foundation was doing useful work overseas to counter anti-government propaganda.

* * * * *

The Jews are regarded by the Broederbond, as by the Nazis, as a "problem." At the UR meeting of March 21, 1968 – not 1938 – the UR discussed the "Jewish problem." The minutes noted that the following decision was taken: "Arising out of requests from different divisions, the UR decides that a committee will be appointed consisting of Broeders G.F.C. Troskie, P.W. Hoek and G.H. Beetge to deliberate about the Jewish influence on the economy of South Africa."

Troskie was then the national chairman of the Medical Association of South Africa, and a UR member. Hoek was a well known Pretoria acountant, later director of Iscor. Beetge was then a Broederbond organiser, and today is an executive member of the HNP and a close confidante of Albert Hertzog.

The same UR meeting discussed immigration policy, and in particular the question of Jewish immigrants.

Item 24 of the minutes states: "Broeder J.A. Hurter draws attention to the possible implications of the admission of Jewish immigrants, especially in the light of the predominant role which this population group already plays in the South African economy.

"Broeder Koornhof explains that the department concerned was very careful to admit immigrants of that population group. He mentioned some aspects of the work of the department and stressed that it was vital that right-thinking officials be appointed. This matter must be discussed at a high level with the government . . ."

The meeting decided to appoint a committee on immigration affairs – *inter alia* to keep a watch on the Jewish "problem" – which included P.G. Koornhof, A.B. v. Niekerk Herbst

175

(the chief administrative officer of the NH Church), J. van der Sand, and J.H. Hatting – the latter a salaried official for an immigration organisation.

There are some interesting features to this "Jewish investigation." Not one word of it was breathed to the outside, and it was never mentioned in government circles concerned with immigration that Jews were being particularly watched. Moreover, the decision to investigate was not taken by a few cranks or eccentrics. It was taken with the concurrence of the following UR members: chairman Piet Meyer, head of the SABC; vice chairman J.S. Gericke, then general Moderator of the NG Church; H.J.J. Bingle, then Rector of Potchefstroom University; F.D. Conradie, still a Cape MEC and leader of the National Party in the Cape Province; J.A. Hurter, the managing director of Volkskas, known as the official Broederbond bank; P.G.J. Koornhof, then MP, now a Cabinet Minister; A.J.G. Oosthuizen, then head of the NH Church; Professor A.N.P. Pelzer, then vice-Rector of the University of Pretoria; A.P. Treurnicht, then editor of *Die Kerkbode*; G.F.C. Troskie; and J.H. Stander, Director of Education in Natal.

Other officials present were chief secretary Naudé Botha; F.J. Beyleveldt; M.J. Kruger and I.A. Meyer (under-secretaries); F.P. Retief and J.H. Swart (liaison secretaries); and G.H. Beetge.

Absent with apologies were S.P. Botha (now a Minister), E.J. Marais (Rector of the University of Port Elizabeth), and P.E. Rousseau (industrialist and later SA Foundation president).

In other words, this secret investigation was sanctioned by top leadership, people occupying key positions in public life.

The investigation into the "Jewish problem" had two ironic features: 1. Rousseau in his capacity as president of the SA Foundation was later to receive strong financial and other support from Jewish businessmen and companies. The Foundation, in its doomed struggle to improve South Africa's image abroad, has never objected to financial support from South African businessmen, whatever their language, religion or culture.

2. Koornhof, who secretly helped draft the Bond's "Jewish" policy, when he was head of its committee on immigration, later became Minister of Immigration replacing Senator A.E. Trollip, who was of English descent.

It is no secret that Afrikaners are generally alarmed that they control only 20 per cent of the economy, the rest of it apparently in the hands of the English, including the Jews. So an investigation into the reasons why 80 per cent of the economy is in non-Afrikaner hands might perhaps have validity. What is strange, however, is that this investigation was confined only to the Jewish section and not to the English as a whole. The latter probably have the largest share of that 80 per cent.

Clear evidence of the Broederbond's obsession with the Jews.

What happened to this Jewish investigation and whether a report was ever submitted to the UR is not clear.

* * * * *

Closely connected to the Jewish investigation was that into Harry Oppenheimer's Anglo American empire by Broeders Hoek and H.J. van den Bergh in the late Sixties. That this investigation actually took place first came to light in August 1970 when the ultra-right-winger Ras Beyers revealed the existence of the Hoek report into Anglo American at a meeting in the Northern Transvaal.

176

A week later the *Sunday Times* and myself were interdicted (at midnight in the Pretoria Supreme Court on a Friday) from publishing the contents of the report.

The interdict was applied for after I had phoned Ras Beyers and arranged to obtain the secret Hoek report from him.

The contents were a bombshell. It called for the total break-up of Anglo American – which directly or indirectly then controlled 950 companies – and the nationalisation of some subsidiaries. The theme of the report was that Anglo could not be tolerated since it had market control of many strategic minerals, and was politically opposed to the government.

There was much speculation on the origin of the report; who had inspired it; why it was never published; and why publication was prevented by a court interdict.

There was a direct link between the Broederbond and the Hoek report and there are important references to this fact in Broederbond documents. On October 18, 1967, the UR held a meeting with Vorster, in his capacity as Prime Minister. Two days prior to this a memo was drawn up to be submitted to the P M. In part it stated: "The matter which at the moment is causing our organisation greatest concern is that our national policy of separate development can be wrecked through economic integration under the leadership of the powerful Oppenheimer group . . . The issue is also directly linked with the slow progress shown by the Afrikaner in the economic field."

The memo went on: "We will sincerely appreciate it if you give us permission, and assure the co-operation of the Ministers concerned (all members of our organisation), to determine ways and means by which Oppenheimer's grip on our national economy can be shaken off in a judicious manner. We will gladly in due course submit a plan of action to you . . ."

Vorster's reply is not known. But he apparently gave the green light.

In later years I discovered the full background to the Hoek report. A Broederbond delegation went to Verwoerd to ask him to have Anglo American investigated. Verwoerd had wanted to investigate the corporation at the time when calls were made for an inquiry into the Broederbond in January 1964 – but he later abandoned the idea because he felt that he might be forced to investigate other sensitive matters as well. Nonetheless he backed a private Broederbond investigation, which brought P.W. Hoek and Joggie Vermooten – a Pretoria accountant – onto the scene.

A group of Afrikaner Orde members in Pretoria also became involved, apparently through Gert Beetge. In 1968 Hoek, when the report was completed, gave it to Vorster and Van den Bergh, who roneod it. About a dozen copies became available in very select circles.

However, after further discussion in 1968 and 1969, Vorster apparently changed his mind abruptly to drop the drastic proposal of breaking up Anglo American.

This about-face by Vorster – as it was seen by conservative Nationalists – led to one of the frustrated few who had a copy to send it to Ras Beyers, who in turn brought into the open the Broederbond's grand ambition of curtailing the Oppenheimer empire.

The Hoek affair was a clear example of Vorster aborting a Broederbond venture which he realised would embarass him at a time when he needed the co-operation of the Oppenheimer group to withstand foreign pressures.

* * * * *

The Broederbond, by its very nature, has never taken Afrikaner-English co-operation seriously. Thus, at a meeting of the UR on August 21, 1967, it was decided that "consideration cannot be given to the establishment of an organisation that included both Afrikaans and English-speakers."

* * * * *

Another old enemy has been the Catholics, though this church has never been regarded as serious or dangerous as the Lions, Rotarians and others mentioned earlier.

A circular of September 1, 1962, urged Broeder doctors (item seven) not to send their patients to Roman Catholic hospitals. This request apparently did not have the desired effect, since circular 6/63/64 of November 1, 1963, repeated the call. And the secretarial report submitted to the UR meeting of June 27, 1968, mentioned that "interesting reports" were being received from cells about the purchase of agricultural land by Roman Catholic bodies. The UR was requested to ask Broeder S.P. Botha (then M P and now a Minister) to give his attention to the matter, the idea obviously being to stop the purchases – for reasons not known.

* * * * *

Two MP's in the present South African Parliament are former Broeders – one a Nationalist; the other a member of the Progressive Federal Party (PFP), now the official opposition.

They are respectively Dr J.S. Marais (former No. 8029), one-time boss of Trust Bank; and ex-Judge J.F. "Kowie" Marais, who once headed the Broederbond task force on Press Matters.

The membership of Dr Marais was terminated – after the matter was discussed at a number of UR meetings in the Sixties – because he attended meetings irregularly. Kowie Marais, interestingly enough, only resigned from the Broederbond after he became a PFP MP in November 1977.

Jan Marais was apparently strongly opposed to the Broederbond, though he had been a member for a brief spell. A fact not generally known is that the end of 1974, when the Broederbond was much in the news, he sent a circular to all his top Trust Bank officials advising them not to belong to any secret organisation – whether the Broederbond or the Freemasons.

An ex-PFP MP, N.J. Olivier, is also a former Broeder – No. 4085. His membership was terminated in the late Sixties together with that of J.S. Marais, at a time when he became an outspoken critic of the government.

B.P. Marais of Johannesburg (No. 3803) was another prominent Afrikaans businessman whose membership was terminated in the late Sixties together with that of Jan Marais, also for non-attendance of meetings.

Anton Rupert, the Afrikaner industrialist, was No. 3088. It is believed that he might have resigned at the end of 1974 when members were given the choice of resigning at the height of the HNP crisis.

The expulsion and resignation of three top Afrikaans businessmen would seem to suggest that the AB no longer exercises the same influence as in the past among businessmen, and no longer holds the same attractions for them.

This is somewhat ironic. In the late Thirties and early Forties the Broederbond played a crucial role in building up new Afrikaner business concerns. In fact, it should get most, if not all, the credit for the Afrikaner business revival of the Forties, when FVB and other companies were launched and the Handelsinstituut formed.

* * * * *

In 1968 there was a considerable stir when the Transvaal Women's Agricultural Union – a predominantly Afrikaans organisation – invited a prominent woman from India – an international leader of a women's movement – to visit South Africa and to address branches. The invitation was later withdrawn and the trip cancelled and it now appears that the Bond played an essential behind-the-scenes role in stopping the visit.

For example, a secretarial report submitted to a UR meeting recommended that the executive "use its influence to prevent the visit from taking place."

* * * * *

The sensitivity of the Broederbond about references of whatever kind to itself in public is illustrated by an event in October 1976. The censors – that is, members of the Publications Board, which is Broederbond-controlled and orientated – ordered that all references to the AB and Rapportryers be removed from a new Afrikaans film, *"Beeld vir Jeanie."*

The official reason for the cuts was that the ordinary man, who knows little of the organisations, could gain the impression that Broederbonders and Rapportryers used the guise of nationalism and religion for personal purposes!

* * * * *

This again raises the question of the absolute secrecy of the Broederbond and its obsession with it. At big rallies, especially at farms and halls, members are urged that "non-White" employees should not be permitted in the vicinity. Ludicrously, a major problem over the years has been whether the houswife would come in to serve tea while a cell meeting was in progress. This has been strongly rejected because it could cause "embarrassment." (See Annexure R for the latest secrecy instructions).

The obsession is such that there should "not even be a whisper" about the Bond in public places; nor should its name be mentioned in telephone discussions. An incident in the Forties illustrates this. Professor Willem Kleynhans, then an extra-mural student at the University of Pretoria, was loudly discussing the Broederbond with friends at a table in a Pretoria restaurant, "Die Koffiehuis." Soon afterwards Dr Jan Pienaar, a leading Pretoria Broeder, passed by the table, leaned over and whispered in his ear: "Willem, about the Broederbond – *Sjuut!* (hush)."

In the early Sixties there were constant warnings about the maintenance of secrecy. A melodramatic aura accordingly shrouds all AB activities – whether of the cells, the UR, the Bondsraad or at covert attendance of conferences of other bodies.

For example, circular 1/62/63 lectured: "Be cautious towards anyone who publicises his membership by using the greeting or referring to certain friends." This followed a "leak" scare in the society as a consequence of which it cancelled a Bondsraad. Broeders were also warned against discussing issues on the telephone since this could cause "serious embarassment to our high-placed friends."

Circular 3/62/63 warned: "Because of the extraordinary interest and curiosity about our organisation which a section of the Press is showing, the UR considers it necessary that every member and branch should realise the importance and urgency of preserving the confidential character of our organisation. Be careful where and how you talk . . . and ensure that every possible measure is taken to guarantee the secrecy of your branch meeting.

"For example, avoid a conglomeration of motor cars at a meeting-place; do not discuss matters over the telephone; and when you write to friends in other branches about our affairs use discreet wording and make sure the address is correct.

"Friends who attend congresses are cordially requested not to discuss our organisation or gatherings . . . Whispered voices are also audible to others.

179

"Friends who are officials or officers of the organisation holding the congress are often seriously embarassed by the injudicious talk of friends."

* * * * *

In 1968 disciplinary steps were instituted against three senior members of Nasionale Pers following complaints by verkrampte Pretoria Broeders. They were P.A. Weber, the managing director of Nasionale Pers; Piet Cillie, editor of *Die Burger;* and Schalk Pienaar, editor of the Sunday paper called *Die Beeld.*

However, nothing came of the action. Still, feelings against the "verligte" Nasionale Pers were at one stage apparently running high in the Bond. At the UR meeting of December 1, 1965, it was reported that the nomination of P.A. Weber as a co-opted UR member had been withdrawn and replaced by that of F.D. Conradie, the Cape MEC. Nasionale Pers at the time threatened to retaliate and expose the Broederbond.

* * * * *

The SABC is, of course, one of the sternest bastions of the Broederbond. When Meyer took over as chief at the end of the Fifties, the corporation underwent drastic changes. Programmes such as "Current Affairs" were introduced; and in what it now broadcasts or shows on TV, the SABC reflects the dogma and philosophy of conservative isolationist Afrikanerdom. The line is blatantly to induce all South Africans to accept Broederbond doctrine and thinking, and the absolutism of race separation and ethnic differences.

According to item 28 of the minutes of the UR meeting of December 1, 1965, which dealt with "relations with non-whites," it was decided "that a letter should be sent to Broeder S.M. de Villiers in which he is thanked for the work done by Radio Bantu." De Villiers was then chief of Radio Bantu.

By 1977 there were 49 Broeders in the SABC radio and television services. They include ex-chairman Meyer (No. 787); Steve de Villiers, now director of the Afrikaans and English radio services; Dr J.H.T. Schutte, director general (programmes); T. van Heerden, director of Bantu and exteral services – of the Oorwinning (Victory) cell; B.J. Steyn, head of the SABC in the Free State – a former member of the President Swart cell in Randburg; L.S. Seegars, director of the schools radio service – of the Roodepoort cell; J.J. Olivier, Afrikaans and English programmes organiser in Port Elizabeth; Gert Yssel, deputy director-general of the H.F. Verwoerd cell in Randburg; E. van H.E. Mischke, head of stores and supplies – of the Christo Beyers cell in Johannesburg.

Broeders on the SABC board of control: W.A. Maree (No. 3669), a former Cabinet Minister, and Professor S.J. Terreblanche. Meyer heads the SABC's Bantu programme control board; Broeder E.F. Potgieter, a Bantu Homeland Commissioner General, is one of the board members.

This means that all decisions concerning radio and TV programmes, SABC policy and strategy are decided by Broeders. So South Africa today resembles Nazi Germany where a propaganda radio machine under Goebbels brainwashed an entire nation. Those Broeders who studied German propaganda techniques in the late Thirties learnt their lesson well.

* * * * *

How Broeders in the government and other bodies played a role in obtaining bursaries for students was revealed in circular 4/62/63 of November 1, 1962. Item 10 stated: "Divisions are requested to provide us as soon as possible with the names and addresses of promising Afrikaner students with mathematics for matric, who want to study engineering or are

180

already studying and who need a bursary or loan. Friends who are involved with the granting of State and other bursary loans will be pleased to obtain the information." It speaks for itself.

* * * * *

Circular No. 6/62/63 of February 1, 1963, revealed how the AB was interfering in sports bodies, plotting for control. This was especially true of the national sport-cum-obsession, rugby. As usual it was couched in seemingly innocent language.

Item 10, entitled "Rugby Affairs," stated: "As there will be many activities in the field of rugby this year, all divisions are requested to use their influence to ensure that the management of local rugby clubs is entrusted to reliable and competent persons, and that representatives in the rugby unions and representatives to the SA Council can be judiciously selected."

* * * * *

The question of racial mixing and contraventions of the Immorality Act, which prevents sexual intercourse between whites and members of other race groups, has caused the Broederbond considerable concern. The management committee of the UR. of March 6, 1967, discussed the sensitive issue. According to item 16(b) it was decided "that the management committee be requested to appoint an expert Broeder to investigate the influence of non-White nurses on White children."

This came at a time when there was a great deal of unscientific speculation that the increase in Immorality Act contraventions was due to the fact that White children was getting used to Blacks as nannies, servants, *et al.* This apparently broke down racial barriers and weakened a healthy "revulsion" for Black races.

The UR meeting of June 26, 1968, reported that the question of a socio-psychological study into the Immorality Act had been discussed with a "Broeder in the National Bureau for Educational and Social Research" – a government body. Alas, no bursaries were available at the time for "a promising post-graduate" student to do the necessary research.

Ironically, by 1978 – when the burning necessity for changes in racial attitudes was plain to all – the lot fell upon chairman Gerrit Viljoen to publically inform the Broeders that a rethink on the "immorality" issue was needed.

* * * * *

Circular No. 7/69/70 of October 7, 1969, again revealed the Bond's animosity to anything in education and cultural life that was not Broederbond/Afrikaans-controlled, especially if it involved activities where Afrikaans and English children mixed.

The enemy this time was no less than the dreaded Drakensberg Boys' Choir, the S.A. equivalent of the Vienna Boys' Choir. It is highly regarded in genuine musical and cultural circles. Nonetheless, item 14 of the circular stated of the Drakensberg Boys' School: "As far as can be ascertained, this school enjoys considerable support by Afrikaners from other provinces than Natal.

"Although the disposition of the school towards Afrikaners is good . . . the medium of instruction is English and the school has an un-Afrikaans spirit."

The message was clear: keep your children away lest they be contaminated by English children.

* * * * *

The minutes of the UR meeting of December 1, 1965, noted (item seven) that the objection of Broeder S.P. Botha (at present a Minister and then a UR member) against the possible membership of W.P. Niekerk of Tzaneen would be considered. It was not stated what Broeder Botha's objection was.

Item 8(g) of the minutes of the same meeting noted that: "The request of Broeder J.T. Jordaan of Vryheid regarding communications with his wife cannot be complied with and the secretariat must be requested to negotiate further with him."

Broeder Jordaan is a leading minister of the NG Church and a member of the Moderature of Natal. He had obviously asked the UR for permission to discuss Broederbond matters with his wife. The rejection demonstrates that in the Bond's eyes, its own affairs take priority over the deepest intimacy between man and wife.

* * * * *

Like father, like son. At any rate, that is the case of Broeder I.A. Meyer (No. 8410), the son of ex-chairman Piet Meyer. In the late Sixties and early Seventies he was a full-time official and paid organiser of the Bond with special responsibilities to the Ruiterwag. In fact, in 1972 he was chairman of the Ruiterwag.

His first name is Izan. The elder Meyer has strongly denied that it is an anagram of Nazi. Izan was born during the war against Hitler.

* * * * *

A classic example of the AB's *modus operandi* is its relationship with SABRA (the S.A. Bureau for Racial Affairs) which was established in 1948 as a direct result of the organisation's initiative.

Broederbond circulars and private correspondence provide abundant evidence that SABRA is basically a puppet front organisation.

Broederbond cells were asked to form study circles which were then asked to affiliate to SABRA. In the final analysis SABRA is little more than a Bond/NP rubber stamp.

The official Broederbond circular further instructed Broeders as follows: "A short report is included with this circular. It will be especially appreciated if your members would encourage organisations such as city councils, cultural bodies and others to affiliate to SABRA.

"The affiliation fee is R20 per year. This enables an affiliated body to send two representatives to the general members' meetings – the highest body of authority which elects the council . . . Also encourage other well-disposed Afrikaners to become ordinary or life members of SABRA.

"Friend Dr C.J. Jooste is at present director of the Bureau. It should, however, not be assumed that other staff members or representatives of SABRA are fellow members (i.e. Broeders) until inquiries have been made at our head office."

A clear warning to Broeders who belong to SABRA to be careful of non-Broeder members. They were also warned not to reveal their Broeder identity to non-Broeder Afrikaners.

* * * * *

The possibility of establishing a separate women's organisation was discussed on a number of occasions by the UR. Time and again it was turned down, the AB being a citadel of male chauvanism. Nonetheless it was decided that attention should be given to encouraging "right-minded" existing women's organisations. The Broeders apparently decided that secret meetings, signs, initiation ceremonies, code numbers, etc., are not for women. Who knows what they might hatch out in secrecy?

* * * * *

An interesting phenomenon is that of the *"dubbeldore"* (literally translated it means a double-yolked egg). The phrase refers to Broeders who also belong to the Freemasons, the AB's bitter enemy.

Although the Bond decided in the Forties that Broeders could not belong to the Freemasons, there have been a number of well-known "dubbeldore." D.T.E. Dönges, the later Minister of Finance and erstwhile UR member was one; so was Tom Naudé, former Speaker and Cabinet Minister and it is claimed that Diederichs became a Freemason in his later years.

* * * * *

Dr J.D. Vorster, Moderator of the NG Church and brother of the Prime Minister, and General J.M. Keevy, former Commissioner of Police, are two prominent Afrikaner Nationalists who had great difficulty becoming members of the Broederbond.

The problem facing the somewhat conservative Dr Vorster was that the Cape Town area where he lived was controlled by "verligte" Broeders. Although a prominent figure in the church and in Afrikaans cultural organisations, he was kept out until 1966, despite earlier attempts to enlist the aid of influential Broeders and politicians on his behalf.

General Keevy is said to be the man who had to wait longer than any other aspirant Broederbond member. His "sin" was that he was a Freemason. Though he resigned from that organisation in order to become more eligible for the Broederbond, it was held against him for a long time and, before he was eventually admitted, his name was circulated and turned down on more occasions than that of anyone else.

I wrote on this in the *Sunday Times* of September 24, 1972. Within days General Keevy promptly replied. There were not "a word of truth" in the *Sunday Times* report. But Broeder Keevy did not clarify what he was denying; of his Broederbond membership there was no doubt. He was Broeder No. 8125 of the Pretoria (Elandspoort) cell at the time of his acceptance.

* * * * *

Since 1940 until the early Seventies the AB maintained a system to ensure that certain jobs fell only into Broederbond hands. It was called "Help Mekaar" ("Help one another").

Through a network of about 800 cells throughout the country, information about vacancies in almost every field was sent to the head office in Johannesburg. These ranged from vacancies on public bodies and in the professions to openings for tailors and shoemakers.

The chief secretary circulated the information in his monthly circulars, and at monthly meetings the 15-odd members of each cell took cognizance of any jobs on the go.

The "Help Mekaar" column listed: The job or vacancy to be filled. The name and address of the Broeder who would give further details about the position, and who had to be contacted by interested persons. The method of writing to, or communicating with, the appropriate Broeder.

Thus the circular of September 1, 1962, noted the following: Two senior vacancies existed in the Springs Municipality – assistant electro-technical engineer and assistant city treasurer.

For information about these vacancies Broeders had to "consult" H.B. Lloyd, P.O. Box 465, Springs. Envelopes had to be marked "personal."

Another example of the "Help Mekaar" system concerned two vacancies in the Town Council of Vryheid. From the circular of December 1, 1962, it appears that the position of electro-technical engineer and town clerk became vacant. Broeders were advised to get further particulars from C.D.D. van Reenen, P.O. Box 244, Vryheid. Van Reenen was a town councillor.

The name of Professor S.P.E. Boshoff also appears on this list as one of the "friends" to be approached for information on the vacancy for a medical practitioner in Caroline.

'A further example concerns the position of secretary of the Eastern Province Rugby Union, which became vacant towards the end of 1962. Broeders had to communicate with W.H. Delport – better known as Willem Delport, the Springbok hooker on the 1951-52 rugby tour of Britain – at 12 Hallack Avenue, Port Elizabeth. This information was circulated in the circular of November 1, 1962.

From a circular issued in August 1962 it transpired that the Broeders of Bloemhof had a unique problem – there was no White shoemaker in the town! How was this burning need to be met?

The circular said: "Because there is no local White shoemaker, friends have undertaken to supply the necessary equipment to enable a White man to start such a business. Consult M.W. Strauss, P.O. Box 101, Bloemhof."

* * * * *

Dr Diederichs defeated Ben Schoeman for the Presidency in 1974. Schoeman had for some time been regarded as the favourite; but the caucus decision should have come as no surprise.

As a former Broeder chairman the election of Diederichs (No. 560) was a major achievement for the Broederbond, which had strived for a Republic for so long. Curiously enough, it has been said that Diederichs is now a Freemason too. That would make him the biggest "dubbeldoor" in the land.

* * * * *

A central fact about the Bond is its die-hard conservatism. Until at least 1977 it lagged way behind any of the cautious liberal changes implemented and planned by the government in the field of race relations – except of course on the few occasions when it was used by Broeder Vorster to obtain conservative support for changes.

As an organisation it has never initiated verligte changes or moves. It stands for the *status quo* and all its moves must be seen in that context. Take the sports policy. As late as 1976 the Bond was reassuring members that the new policy did not mean mixing at club level; yet the government had already tacitly given the green light.

Behind these ox-wagon attitudes lie the church and educational establishments – the most conservative segments of the Afrikaner Nationalist movement.

In 1974 the University of Pretoria completed a secret sociological survey into Afrikaner attitudes. Thousands of people were interviewed at the request of the National Party.

The survey showed that the most verkrampte section of the Afrikaans population was aged between 16 and 22. This is contrary to youth attitudes in all other societies, where this age group is invariably the most rebellious when it comes to questioning traditional norms. This group of Afrikaners was *more* opposed than any other to changes in sport policy and the removal of "unnecessary" racial discrimination.

184

A leading Afrikaner academic explained this to me. He said it was because of the impact church and Christian National education was having on youthful thinking. This age group was particularly susceptible. It is only after they have been out of school for a few years, and more in a wider society, that they begin to discard some of the narrow conservative dogmas with which they had been spoon-fed. Then, perhaps, for the first time they become receptive to new ideas.

* * * * *

In 1964 the Broederbond involved itself in the elections of the South African Nursing Council. Item 12 of circular 6/64/65 of September 2, 1964, stated that the FAK was trying to obtain the co-operation of various women's organisations "to exert a positive influence in the coming elections." Friends in "the bigger centres who are able to exert influence among nurses" were requested to contact the secretary of the FAK, Broeder W.S.J. Grobler.

* * * * *

One of the main characteristics of any Broeder is his fear. Few ever resign, and rebellion against the organisation is unthinkable because of this. There is fear of victimisation; of ostracism; of not obtaining promotion or a new appointment; of losing business contracts; of being branded a traitor; and of being accused of betraying and stabbing the Afrikaner volk in the back.

So while tens of thousands of non-Broeder Afrikaner Nationalists resent the organisation, there are few who dare to speak out against it. That would single them out for subtle punishment.

Ministers of religion, faced by Broederbond-infiltrated church councils, are in an even more difficult position. They suffer in silence, fearful of speaking out.

Here is one example of the Broederbond grip. In 1957 Dr Theo Wassenaar, then leader of the National Party in the Transvaal Provincial Council, rebelled against his party leadership and formed a new party to foster Afrikaans-English co-operation. He drew crowds of thousands, including Nationalist Afrikaner rank and file. But his glory was short-lived; he was a Broeder and pressure was applied upon him not to split Afrikanerdom. The result was that this well-respected public figure withdrew completely from politics and faded into oblivion.

* * * * *

On two occasions Joel Mervis, former *Sunday Times,* editor, was confronted by National Party leaders about Broederbond stories by myself which he published in 1972. Dr Piet Koornhof, at a public banquet for the sportsman of the year in 1972, had a lengthy argument with Mervis, who was seated next to him. He was at pains to assure the editor that the Bond was not anti-Semitic.

And, according to Mervis, he had a long discussion with Vorster in 1973. Afterwards he told me that the Prime Minister had said I was exaggerating in my articles, and that the Broederbond was not as influential an organisation as I had made it out to be. Wishful thinking on Vorster's part? He himself in his time has taken the Bond seriously enough – and help mould it to his own purposes.

* * * * *

It frequently occurs that a person, because of his status in Afrikaner society, is often erroneously believed to be a member by other Broeders. The upshot is that in their dealings with such a person, Broeders become evermore open and even discuss Broeder affairs with him, so revealing certain AB activities.

The UR compiles the names of those who are commonly mistaken for AB members and from time to time the UR includes a list of their names in one of the monthly circulars with the specific warning that they are not Broeders and that actual Broeders should be careful in their dealings with them.

Here follows some of the names which have been thus blacklisted in a number of circulars. A 1962 circular listed the following non-members: J.B. Roode; PK Tolwe; P. Schabort MPC, Frankfort; J.H. (Kalfie) Steenkamp ex-MP Groblersdal; Dr J. van Tromp, Strand; C. van Gass, a Klerksdorp attorney. The circular of February 1, 1962, listed the following: W.J. Steyn, Director of Civil Service Training, Pretoria; Frans P.R. van Wyk of Fraserburg; J.L. (Koos) Wentzel, Bloemhof; P. van Wyk, Magistrate Ventersburg; Dr C.E. Prinsloo, National Bureau for Social and Educational Research, Pretoria; and Dr Z.J. Rabie, director of export promotion, Pretoria.

Ironically, in the circulars of November 1, 1963, and December 1, 1964, Broeders were warned that a number of FAK organisers were not Broeders. They were J.G. du Plessis; F.H. Pretorius; H.S. van der Walt; J. Taljaard; C. Young; W. Mc Donald and C.S. Smit.

The circular of March 1, 1963, listed the following: J.H.L. Serfontein, Bethal; A. Crause, Pretoria; Dr T.S. van Rooyen, senior lecturer in history, Pretoria University; J.D. van Graan, school inspector, Springbok; Ds V.E. D'Assonville, Johannesburg; Ds J.C. Kruger, Kempton Park; Dr C.H. Badenhorst, Department of Education, Pretoria; K. du Plessis, school inspector, Kroonstad.

Those members whose membership is terminated, either by resignation or expulsion, and are thus officially "eliminated," are also listed from time to time.

In a 1962 circular three men were eliminated: Dr F.E. O'B Geldenhuys, Pretoria; P.C. Grobler, a farmer of Balfour; C.H.S. Coetzee, teacher, Van Rheynsdorp.

The circular of April 9, 1964 listed G.C. Rossouw, attorney, Adelaide; A.D.J. van der Gryp, Duiwelskloof; S.A. Walters, Vredenburg; Dr P.J. van Zyl Pietermaritzburg; D.J. Brand, a missionary, Dordrecht.

In the circular of June 2, 1964: J.D. Fick, Heidelberg; Cape; C.H. Vermeulen, Cape Town; F.L.F. Vos, Johannesburg. August 1, 1967: F.J. v.J. Wiese, Alberton; J.H. Kruger, ex-teacher from Durban and East London; P.R. Nell, Lady Grey; J.W. van Eeden, farmer, Swellendam; A.H.H. Brink, auditor, Johannesburg; W.A. Moolman, Vanwyksvlei; J.H.P. Schutte, Coligny; Dr G.P. Kellerman.

The circular of April 13, 1965 listed the following members who resigned voluntarily as a result of the Special Circular of March 10, 1964, which gave them the option of resigning after the exposés during the Beyers Naudé crisis: J.J. Muller, professor, Stellenbosch; J.W. Hanekom, minister, Darling; Dr O.W. van Niekerk, Mafeking; W.A. de Klerk, writer, Paarl; A.M. van Wyk, Hermanus; T. Botha, minister, Johannesburg; J. Maarskalk, teacher, Pretoria; D.J. Brand, missionary, Dordrecht.

The same circular listed the following members who were eliminated for other reasons in the period October 1963 to February 28, 1965 : M.D.C. Steenkamp, Welkom; A.M. Gericke, Standard Bank Manager, Krugersdorp; W.F. Boshoff, missionary, Bloemfontein; J.D. Fick, Heidelberg, Cape; G.C. Rossouw, attorney, Adelaide; J.S.C. Marais, Pretoria; F.P.P. Myburgh, minister, De Aar; B.L. Muller, attorney, Rustenburg; H.J. Marnewick, accountant, Johannesburg; C.H. Vermeulen, librarian, Cape Town; Dr P.J. van Zyl; N. Dumas, Grabouw; C.J. Myburgh, Springs; J.L. Strydom, lecturer, Umtata.

* * * * *

The UR keeps close watch on the number of meetings attended by each of its 12 000 members. Members and cells are constantly urged to meet regularity; and there are generally some 10 or 11 gatherings per year.

In 1969 the UR circulated a blacklist of members who had not attended meetings regularly between 1964 and 1968. It included the following Cabinet Ministers of the time: J.F.W. Haak (No. 2916); J. de Klerk (2490); A. Hertzog (456); H.E. Martins (4425); B.J. Vorster (3737); and Marais Viljoen, now Acting State President (3226).

Other politicians blacklisted at the time were P.S. Marais MP (7022); H.S. Swanevelder MP (1936); P.H. Meyer MP (6273); P.Z.J. van Vuuren MP (6210); Dr C.V. van der Merwe MP (4079): H.C.A. Keyter MP (1699); H.S. Schoeman, MP and now a Minister (6844) S.W. van der Merwe, MP, and now a Minister (6571); H.J. Botha, MP (5085); Dr Paul van der Merwe, ex Namibian MP (7494); W.H. Delport, MP (4572); T.Langley, MP (7755); Adv Jimmy Kruger, MP and Minister (8048); J.J. Loots, now the Speaker (3079); J.C.B. Schoeman, MP (3087); and J.M. Henning, MP (6382).

There was some commentary on the defaulting members. F.E. Bellingan (7456), a business manager of the Kruitberg cell, Bloemfontein, had "a lack of interest." The same was said of Dr R.S. Venter (5627) of the same cell. However, J.Z. (Jannie) le Roux (6703), Chairman of the Transvaal Rugby Union of the Christiaan Beyers cell, Johannesburg, was excused because he had been overseas twice.

P.J. Naudé (5326), a programme manager of the same cell was "indifferent," and the same applied to D.H. Bezuidenhout (5546), a cattle inspector of Kingwilliamstown. Gé Korsten (6747), the well-known SA singer of the Brandwag cell Pretoria, received the same chiding – too many other engagements?

Several prominent businessmen also appeared. Among them were Dr Anton Rupert (3088) of the Helderberg cell, Stellenbosch, who averaged two meetings a year; P.J.F. Scholtz (7052) of Sanlam, of the Leeuwenberg cell, Cape Town; J.C. Marais (1869), the general manager of Sanlam, of the Wynberg cell, Cape Town; and Mike Pieterse (7245) of the Eersterivier cell, Stellenbosch.

Two wellknown businessmen, Dr J.S. Marais (8029) of Cape Town and B.P. Marais (3803) of the Danie Theron cell, Johannesburg, whose membership was later terminated, were also on the list.

Part VII

The Broederbond and the Future

I will deal briefly with these questions: has the Broederbond still any role to play? Has its power and influence waned? Is it only a question of time before it disbands or comes out into the open? Can it become an instrument for so-called verligte change? The first answer is that any organisation as powerful as the Broederbond, by its very nature, composition and structure, will continue to exercise clandestine power in public life.

It is an irrelevant question whether its power and influence are less than a decade ago. Even if this was the case, one is in the field of relativity whether one describes the Bond as powerful, or less powerful. It is powerful.

There is no evidence that the Broederbond has lost its influence, regardless of changes in its relationship with the political leadership of the NP. Whatever tinkerings have been made to its structure, it is still the secret wing of Afrikaner Nationalism, co-operating with the politicians to ensure a common aim – the maintenance of Afrikaner power and survival at all costs.

And it should not be forgotten that the AB's power cannot be measured only in terms of its role at the highest national levels. Its most significant influence is perhaps exerted on other levels: In town and village councils; schools and parent committees; agricultural bodies and church councils; hospital boards and NP committees. Here its influence is decisive. The views of the relatively small number of Broederbonders generally prevails. When it comes to appointments in the civil service, universities and schools Broederbond membership is the silver spoon in the mouth of the elite.

This power and influence will never change. The Bond is not an informal loose old boys' network which meets in anything like an Afrikaner equivalent of the Rand Club. Firstly, it is institutionalised, with a written constitution, rules, regulations and recorded membership. Secondly, its membership and activities are secret, giving it a power and dimension no other informal establishment can boast. And it differs radically from other semi-secret organisations like the Freemasons in that it is restricted not only to one language group, but to members of one political party.

So it remains to this day the inner chamber of Nationalist Afrikanerdom, where the leaders of all sections meet to consult and co-ordinate decisions affecting Afrikaner interests in every sphere of life.

Although some Afrikaner voices have proclaimed that the Bond should come into the open since its original reason for secrecy no longer exists, it is highly unlikely that this will ever happen. The organisation's very effectiveness, its strength and influence, is largely due to the fact that it is secret. Without this it would not have played the ruthless historical role it has done; and it would be unique if such a power machine, with its own momentum, decided to alter the very basis that gives it influence. These who believe that the Broederbond will become an instrument advocating bold new liberal or radical political reforms in South Africa, live in a dream world.

The leaders at the top may make verligte liberal noises – they can even indulge in chats with men like Dr Ntatho Motlana of the (banned) Soweto Committee of Ten – but there is no chance whatsoever that the Broederbond will do anything contrary to fundamental Nationalist thinking.

Over the years the Broederbond had, with one exception, never initiated any liberal changes. The exception was in 1971 when the Bond leadership, in conjunction with the Cabinet, decided to prepare the blueprint of the government's new sports policy. This was, in fact, not a Broederbond initiative at all, but a case of the government manipulating the organisation for NP purposes. None of the verligte initiatives of the past few years, strictly within the broad framework of Nationalist policy, have emanated from the AB – although leading verligte Broeders were frequently involved.

Gerrit Viljoen, the present Broederbond chief, continued to push the concept of a Coloured homeland in the early Seventies when other verligte Broeders were advocating a closer political relationship with the Coloured people.

In the debate about opening amenities in "white areas" to all races, the Broederbond again did not take the lead, but played a role in moulding public opinion. They waited until it was clear that the government was moving in that direction. There was no verligte Broederbond pressure on the party hierarchy.

Then again, in the debate on the Mixed Marriages and Immorality Acts, the Broederbond leadership was either silent or antagonistic to change, though some individual Broeders were involved in the debate. And even though Viljoen in mid-1978 made some interesting noises on the subject, thus causing great excitement in the press (Afrikaans and English alike) and in diplomatic circles overseas, all he actually said was that these two acts had to be re-examined. He did not commit himself to their dismantlement. In 1974, when the Potchefstoom intellectuals and other verligtes openly questioned these policies, for the first time, precipitating storm and consternation in party circles, Viljoen was not heard.

It is important to examine the views expressed by Professor Viljoen in a press interview published on August 1, 1978 (See Annexure Q). Viljoen is a pragmatic conservative, and a number of verligte Nationalists are to the left of him. In his utterances there is no indication whatsoever of a radical departure from government policy.

Viljoen expresses a pragmatic view of how to adopt basic Nationalist thinking and practice to modern and complicated circumstances; essentially there is no dilution of the concept of retaining Afrikaner power and exclusive identity. While he pleads for the abolition of most discriminatory laws, the cornerstones of apartheid – the Immorality Act, the Mixed Marriages Act, the population register and the Group Areas Act – are sacred cows not to be prodded.

The biggest sacred cow of all is that the Whites will never share power with "non-Whites". Although the new constitutional plans give the impression that there will be powersharing between Coloureds, Indians and Whites, this is clearly not the case. There will be 10 "independent" Bantustans for Africans while the non- Africans – Coloureds Indians and Whites – will be catered for in one political constellation – apparently.

But in fact there will be no powersharing, no joint Parliament. There will be three Parliaments for each group, with a super Cabinet and an electoral college to elect an executive President. And these bodies are composed in such a way that it is not merely the Whites who will retain power: Nationalist Afrikaner rule is entrenched for all time.

Only the majority parties in each ethnic parliament will be represented in the electoral college. So any chance of the White opposition leaders joining forces with the Indians and

189

Coloureds – who are violently anti-apartheid and anti-government – to choose a non-Nationalist President, or even a "non-White" one, is excluded.

Thus the new constitutional deal is aimed purely at entrenching Afrikaner Nationalist power, though in a sophisticated manner.

Beyond this, the grand plan is then for the non-african political group, together with the Bantustans and representatives of the urban Africans, to form a constitutional umbrella body – which is sometimes grandly compared with the European Parliament or European Economic Commission.

However, this body will merely be for consultation purposes; and as decisions can only be reached by consensus, de facto nothing can ultimately be changed without the consent of the White Parliament. So the status quo will be retained – with peripheral changes.

This was precisely the plan the National Party originally submitted to the Turnhalle constitutional conference in Namibia; a very impressive looking constitutional structure would be created but power would effectively remain in Afrikaner Nationalist hands. Thus any Broederbond initiative in this sphere can only be part and parcel of governments strategy.

It is in this context that the talks which began in August 1978 between leading Broeders – Professor Viljoen, Wimpie de Klerk and others – and urban black leaders like Dr Motlana and Dr S. Nyembezi must be evaluated. The mere fact of the talks appeared to signal a major breakthrough. For the Broederbond leadership to become involved in a dialogue with bitter opponents of apartheid, (Dr Motlana was detained without trial for six months) would seem to constitute a notable volte face in the tough no-nonsense attitudes of Afrikaner Nationalism over the past 30 years.

It certainly reflected the anxiety of the many thinking Nationalists that the Bantustan concept could never provide a political answer to the demands of millions of urban Blacks who had revealed their emotions in the near-apocalyptic disturbances associated with June 16, 1976.

These Afrikaners feel that Africans in the cities should be included in the new constitutional framework.

But what does the Motlana – Viljoen contact really add up to? Viljoen, as a pragmatic conservative is a devoted adherent of Nationalist philosophy. Black and White must be politically separated to eternity, and all he called for – according to the news interview – was for urban Blacks to have representation in the umbrella consultative body. This reflects the view of key Cabinet Ministers – and was a concept floated by Prime Minister Vorster in public statements in 1971. It is highly unlikely that the August 1978, Broederbond-inspired talks with Blacks will produce concrete results. Viljoen and his Broeders are bound by Nationalist race ideology.

Apart from this, the major obstacle to the Broederbond actually propagating a verligte line – assuming it ever wanted to – is the question of Afrikaner unity. If the Bond moved in a verligte direction towards genuine powersharing, even on a group basis, both it and Nationalist Afrikanerdom would split from top to bottom. The majority is conservative. And in the final instance the unity of Afrikanerdom is more important than anything else in the minds of the frightened leadership.

This was blatantly apparent when the NP discussed their original plans for the non-African political framework. The right-wing of the Party, under the leadership of Dr Andries Treurnicht, was prepared to come out in open revolt at the far-reaching verligte implications of genuine power-sharing, as some wanted.

The HNP split had been traumatic, for both the Broederbond and Vorster. A further split, however small, had to be avoided at all costs. The NP believes – perhaps justly – that rancour in Afrikaner ranks enables the Afrikaner's political enemies – the Progressive Federal Party, the English Press and Blacks – to exploit any division with the aim of forcing through a non-racial policy of political integration.

In the November 1977 general election the NP drew for the first time at least one third of the English vote. Superficially, this could be taken to mean that the character of the National Party must slowly change. Championing the rights of all whites, the NP is indeed bound to lose, reluctantly, its exclusive Afrikaner character. But this is yet one more reason why the Broederbond will not disappear from the scene. Where for more than three decades the interests of the NP and the Bond were virtually synonymous, the Broederbond will now have to act more diligently than ever as the real watchdog of Afrikaner Nationalist interest.

It will examine closely whether the emergence of a broader white South African nationalism will be detrimental to Afrikaner interests diluting the power of Afrikaner politicians and the shining ideal of Afrikaner domination.

Fundamentally, the Broederbond's thinking remains what it has always been: White political unity can only be built on the foundation of Afrikaner Nationalism. Afrikaner Nationalism is the only truly indigenous white nationalism with its roots in the soil of Africa. And ultimately that foundation is based on the rock of the Broederbond.

Those who always cannot understand why Afrikaner Nationalists cannot change, why the Afrikaners – 90 per cent of whom support the NP – avert their eyes from the coming conflagration, must look to the Bond for their answer.

A study of Afrikaner politics in the Twenties and Thirties revealed far greater fluidity, flexibility and openness than at the present time. The Afrikaner cohesiveness, the rigidity, the intolerance of present-day nationalism was not there then.

I know there are many factors contributing to this development: but there is no doubt that the biggest single factor contributing to the present state of affairs is the existence of the Broederbond. It ensures that while dissension, debate, disagreement and differences are all possible, they are only so within the strict framework of loyalty to the NP. Once an Afrikaner rejects that concept he is hounded out of the flock of the faithful. There are numerous instances when the views of leading Nationalists expressed in private have been absolutely contrary to the basis of Nationalist ideology. But because fear of the repercussions of being a "traitor" to Afrikanerdom prevails, few dare to break openly with the establishment.

And if you are a Broeder your chances of revolt are nil – even though you may decide to resign for moral reasons.

With the Afrikaans churches intimately involved in the whole Bond structure, it is difficult for any Christian Afrikaner to challenge its secrecy, its modus operandi and its very existence. The churches provide the necessary moral-religious justification for all that.

The Afrikaner Broederbond has played a crucial role in the upliftment of the Afrikaner people since 1918; its establishment and initial secrecy may be justified, given the English recalcitrance, double talk, hypocricy and attitude of superiority prevailing then.

In the Thirties it laid the secret foundations, and prepared the way for, the ultimate Nationalist victory of 1948, leading three decades of Afrikaner domination and creating the massive structure of apartheid.

But in the process it has produced an unfree people; the Afrikaner nation is in bondage, fettered by chains of fear and insecurity. This unfreedom, this insecurity, may yet lead to the downfall of Afrikanerdom itself. In its sincere anxiety to preserve and protect Afrikanerdom at all costs, the Broederbond is probably steering the Afrikaner towards inevitable downfall and destruction.

With its distorted faith in a Messianic mission, claiming a Biblical destiny and a God-given right to exist, the Bond has fostered a Masada mentality, a death wish.

It refuses to accept the realities of Africa, the legitimate aspirations and demands of the Black majority. But with its very determination to retain and entrench forever Afrikaner domination – now camouflaged by quasi modern concepts – the Afrikaner Broederbond is actually actively treading those very steps that will lead to the destruction of the very identity it so passionately wishes to preserve.

Explanatory Notes

Volk. In English the phrase "nation" is used to describe a cultural and a geographical unit. Volk, however, refers to the Afrikaner people, as distinct from the South African nation comprising many cultural or ethnic entities. In Afrikaans volk has a powerful emotional connotation – for the true the Afrikaner, his volk takes precedence over the South African nation.

Verlig. This Afrikaans phrase has been used since the mid-Sixties to describe the views of liberal members of the National Party. They are the verligtes, and verlig basically means enlightened.

Verkrampte. This means the opposite of verlig; the views of conservative Nationalist are verkramp, and he is called a verkrampte.

Volkskongres. A national congress of the volk. Whenever the Afrikaner comes up against a crisis in the national or even local spheres, a volkskongres is called to discuss it. Representatives are elected on a countrywide basis.

Broedertwis. Fraternal strife. The phrase is often used when Afrikaners quarrel among each other.

Annexure A

Our Bondslied

Words and Melody by
Dr. Jan H. Pienaar
Original Words: **I.M. Lombard**

Composition: by
Stephen H. Eyssen

Ceremonious
1.   Come, sing the joyous Bondslied
     There's work for you and me
     Come strive with might and main
     And do it brave and free.

     In word and will and soul and bone
     Be strong and never fear
     Because he is a Brother alone
     Whose fight is brave and clear.

Refrain:

    Because he is a Brother alone
    Whose fight is brave and clear
    For God and Tongue and Volk and Bond
    In this southern land so dear.
    Come, thankful hearts,
    Let Him be adored
    Pay Him homage,
    God, the Lord.

2.   Give me your strong brother's hand
    Your word as pledge forever
    That wherever I wander in the land
    Your trust will fail me never;
    Together we will strive
    Strengthened by God's Hand
    For God and Tongue and Volk and Bond
    In this dear southern land.

Refrain:

    Because he is a Brother alone
    Whose fight is brave and clear
    For God and Tongue and Volk and Bond
    In this southern land so dear
    Come, thankful hearts,
    Let Him be adored
    Pay Him homage,
    God, the Lord.

3.   Your blessing, Lord, we humbly ask,
    To seal our hearts and task,
    Guide our steps for evermore!
    Labour with your money's crown
    Will ran all blessings down!
    Come, thankful hearts, let Him be adored,
    Our homage, God, the Lord!

Refrain:

    Because he is a Brother alone
    Whose fight is brave and clear
    For God and Tongue and Volk and Bond
    In this southern land so dear
    Come, thankful hearts,
    Let Him be adored
    Pay Him homage,
    God, the Lord.

Annexure B

GENERAL J.B.M. HERTZOG'S SMITHFIELD ADDRESS, NOVEMBER 7, 1935, EXPOSING THE AFRIKANER BROEDERBOND

In asnwering the question, who is responsible for the present discord among our people?, you must permit me to go back briefly to 1913-14 when the old Nationalist Party was formed; for the first time, the Afrikaans-speaking portion of our population was torn into two. As you will all still remember, leading men in the Church and the congregation pleaded strongly with us against the breaking away and the separation. Congresses were even held to try and persuade us against breaking away from the South African Party, and to go back.

The answer will also still be fresh in the memory of all of you, namely, that as soon as we had realized the three great ideals which we had gone out to strive for: namely, national freedom, language equality, and acknowledgement of the motto, South Africa First, we would again take the hand of those whom we had left behind and would again work with them in a spirit of national unity.

We went from platform to platform in all the Provinces – Natal no less than the Free State – and everywhere we invited and encouraged the population – English-speaking no less than the Dutch-speaking – to come and help us to realize our ideals, and each time we also gave them the assurance that when we had succeeded in gaining our ideals, we would see to the resortation of the unity of the Afrikaner nation, English-speaking as well as Dutch-speaking.

Our struggle was extraordinarily successful. By November, 1926, we had already achieved our three fixed ideals to such an extent that Dr Malan, in a press interview with the *Volksblad* of November 24, 1926, when speaking about the Declaration of our Freedom by the Imperial Conference, had to exclaim with passionate enthusiasm:

I look upon this as the most important step which has ever yet been taken in the actual and enduring conciliation of the two races. . . . By this the walls of division between English- and Dutch-speaking Afrikaners will fall away completely, and any feeling of grievance against England which might still exist, would disappear, and on the foundation of a general S.A. patriotism, a great united South African nation will be built up.

That this was not just an emotional outburst of a timely nature by Dr Malan, but actually his decided conviction, appears from his opening speech of October 7, 1927, before the Nationalist Party Congress at Robertson which, as reported in the Minutes of the Congress, reads as follows:

Continuing, Dr Malan pointed out that in the past there had been striven for the restoration of the unity of our people but that the reconciliation movement . . . had failed because the Nationalist Party strove for unity with independence. The last-mentioned has now been obtained, and it is therefore clear that the restoration of the national unity is today an obvious matter.

Even in February of last year (1934) the following report of a press interview by Dr Malan with the *Vaderland,* was approved by him when in the proof.

Dr Malan declared himself enthusiastically in favour of a united Afrikanerdom by which was meant an Afrikanerdom of English-speaking as well as Afrikaans-speaking people,

194

on the foundation of South African nationality. It would be a happening of tremendous significance to the Afrikanerdom of the future and to our country, if we could unite all national feeling Afrikaners in united strength, on the forward path, and so eradicate the unfortunate division and quarrelling which has during the past twenty-two years existed between Afrikaner and Afrikaner.

Quite a number of other extracts from speeches by Dr Malan since November, 1926, could be made which would show to what extent Dr Malan was convinced that with the obtaining of our national freedom the time had also arrived for a united Afrikanerdom of English- as well as Afrikaans-speaking people: but after what I have already quoted it will be unnecessary for you to be still further convinced of Dr Malan's feelings during that period about the necessity of bringing into being a south African national unity, in which all Afrikaners, English-speaking as well as Dutch-speaking, would be included.

Without four months, however, after his enthusiastic declaration of February 27, just quoted by me, pleading for national unity between all Afrikaners as something which would be of tremendously great significance for our country, we find Dr Malan at a Conference of the Nationalist Party in Pretoria, where, in co-operation with Dr N.J. v.d. Merwe, exerting all his strength to destroy national unity at that Conference, we see him call his followers together to separate themselves and establish a separate party of 'purified Nationalists'. Instead of continuing with his pleading for a united Afrikanerdom, Dr Malan suddenly swerved and became the champion of division and quarrelling among the Afrikaner people.

A sudden swinging round of this kind, such as carried out by Dr Malan tearing the Afrikaner people right to the depths, must have had a very serious reason as its prime cause. I will come back later to the answer as to what that reason might be. Meanwhile, I must remind you how that, have since Coalition, I constantly requested Dr Malan as well as Dr van der Merwe, with their Cape and Free State schismatic followers, to tell all 'What was the object and what did they think to gain by division and quarrelling, which could not equally well have been obtained by national unity and co-operation?' To this question they have constantly failed to give a satisfactory answer.

It was clear to me from the beginning that they could not give an honest satisfactory answer; and just because I was convinced of it, that they were busy driving after something, by means of national disunity, of such a nature that they did not dare to make it public. It was clear to me that racial feeling, ill-feeling toward the English section of the Afrikaans population was influencing their conduct. I had also, on various occasions, persisted that Dr Malan and other purified Nationalist leaders did not want to work with the United Party, mainly for the reason that they were cherishing a strong racial feeling against the English-speaking people amongst us, and because they wanted to domineer over them and to accept no equality in co-operation with them.

This was strongly censured as a gross insult by Dr Malan and his purified Nationalist fellow leaders that I should have laid such a thing as a charge against them.

I do not wish to deal Dr Malan any injustice and therefore, when I this evening repeat the statement that he was led by racial feeling and the desire to rule and to domineer over the English-speaking portion of our fellow Afrikaners, it is a statement which I am now prepared to prove out of documents about the genuineness of which there is no doubt whatsoever.

Before I start to give you the proof of what I have just said, you must allow me to make a disclosure to you of a discovery which fell to my lot recently. It concerns a secret society called 'The Afrikaner Broederbond' and the relation in which Dr Malan and other prominent leaders of the purified Nationalist Party stand to it.

The Afrikaner Broederbond is a secret society founded in 1918. According to its original destiny and object it was entrusted with the praise-worthy object of caring for and watching over the cultural needs of the Dutch-speaking Afrikanerdom, with a clear stipulation in its Constitution: party politics are excluded from the Bond. There can therefore be no objection made to the Broederbond's membership being confined to the Dutch-speaking people, and, as a purely cultural association, I will accept it that the Bond also did good work.

As far as the Bond was of a purely cultural nature with purely cultural objects, no particular objection could either be made to its having come into being as a secret society, except that out of the nature of the case with secret societies they may be misused for other ends than those destined for them and also cause great danger.

Unfortunately this is exactly what happened also with the Bond. Party politics could not for always be kept out of it; and according to the measure that the influence and political views of a certain section in our public life increased in the Bond, the Bond recreated from a cultural to a party-political association, as will appear from what I am further going to tell you.

Already in August 1932 this Broederbond had advanced so far on the road of a political association that the Chairman of the Executive Council, which is the highest authority of the Bond, could declare as Chairman of the Bond Congress, with the general approval of the Congress:

> We, the Afrikaner Broederbond, may not withdraw its hand from the cultural work because so many wide-awake maintainers have come to the front. But yet, for the time being, provision has been made in that first actually national need.

> In accordance with this new situation we find that the AB is slowly handing over the cultural work itself to our so much bigger son, the FAK, and I think that we shall be wise to follow the same course also with this Bond Council.

> I consider the national culture and the welfare of the nation will not be able to flourish to the fullest extent if the people of South Africa do not politically break all foreign bonds.

> After the cultural and economic needs, the AB will have to dedicate its attention to the political needs of our people. And with this the aim must be a completely independent real Afrikaans Government for South Africa. A Government which by its embodiment in our own personal Head of the State, bone of our bone, and flesh of our flesh, who will inspire us and bind us together to irresistible unity and power *(sic)*.

Yet the Bond had quickly to go much further on the party-political road. On January 16, 1934, a circular letter was sent out by the highest executive authority of the Bond, namely the Executive Council, signed by the Chairman, Professor J.C. van Rooy, and the Chief Secretary, Mr I.M. Lombard. This letter, which was addressed to all members of the AB, read as follows:

> Our test of Brotherhood and Afrikanerhood is not a party-political direction but . . . persons who strive for the ideal of the everlasting existence of a separate Afrikaans nation with its own culture. Above all at the former Bond Council it was clearly expressed that one expected from such persons that they would have as their object Afrikanizing of South Africa in all its pheres of life. Brothers, your Executive Council cannot say to you:

196

'Further party-political Fusion or Union or Reunion; or fight against it . . . but we can however make a call on every Brother to choose in the sphere of party politics what, according to his fixed conviction, is the most profitable for the object of the Bond and the Bond's ideal, as recorded above and as known to all of us. Let us keep the eye fixed on this that the main object is . . . that the Afrikanerdom shall reach its ultimate destiny of domination in South Africa.' . . . Brothers, our solution for South Africa's troubles is not that this or that party shall gain the upper hand, but that the Afrikaner Broederbond shall rule South Africa.

In order to realize the real tendency and the meaning of the words just quoted by me from the Chairman's speech of Professor du Plessis and the Circular from the Executive Committee of the Bond, one must take note here that to become a member of the Broederbond a person must comply with the following demands:

1. He must be Afrikaans-speaking.
2. His home language must be Afrikaans.
3. He must strive after the ideal of the everlasting existence of a separate Afrikaans nation with its own culture.

As has been declared on certain occasions by Mr du Plessis, Professor van Rooy, and others, in the Broederbond circles, under the designation Afrikaner only the Dutch Afrikanerdom is understood, which also is made abundantly clear in the Constitution and other articles by the Bond.

When one considers now that when the two Potchefstroom teachers use the words Afrikaner and Afrikanerdom, they mean only the Dutch-speaking Afrikaner and Dutch-speaking Afrikanerdom, and when one further takes into consideration, that the membership of the Afrikaner Broederbond is strictly limited to the Dutch-speaking persons, the words of Mr du Plessis as little as those of Professor van Rooy, leave any doubt as to what is meant here.

The high ideal and the striving of the Afrikaner Broederbond is, according to what they communicate to us, to let the Dutch-speaking Afrikanerdom gain domination in South Africa, and to bring about that the Dutch-speaking Broederbond shall rule South Africa!

Very nice, is it not? Flattering to the soul of the Dutch-speaking Afrikaner, like you and I! Only it suffers from a great defect – the defect that must necessarily lead to the downfall of Dutch-speaking Afrikanerdom itself, if there is any continuation of perseverance in this kind of Afrikaner-jingo self-glorification; it is being forgotten, for instance, that there are also English-speaking Afrikaners in South Africa, who also are entiled to a place in the South African sun. When will this mad, fatal idea cease to exist with some people of thinking that they are the chosen of the gods to rule over others? The English-speaking tried it and did not manage it over the Afrikaans-speaking. The Afrikaans-speaking also tried it and did not succeed over the English-speaking people. Neither the one nor the other will ever succeed in dominating the other; and when Potchefstroom fanaticism is out once more to try and incite Dutch-speaking Afrikanerdom to a repetition of the past, then I would ask the Dutch-speaking Afrikanerdom – my nation – has South Africa not yet suffered enough in the past from Afrikaner quarrelling and disagreement? Is our language, our freedom, of so little value to us and so little significance, that we must once again gamble with it all purely on account of racialism and fanaticism?

When I called out a little while ago, 'Very nice, is it not? Flattering to the soul of the Dutch-speaking Afrikaner like you and I!' I unfortunately forgot one thing. Out of the dic-

197

tates and stipulations of the Broederbond, even as from the Circular letter of the Executive Committee and Professor van Rooy, it appears quite clear, unfortunately, that when there is any talk by them about the Afrikaner or the Afrikanerdom which must dominate South Africa, you and I, not being Brothers, are not included in it? You and I will just have to comfort ourselves, that we shall never have the privilege of sharing in the Broederbond domination in South Africa! We are not Afrikaners!

Yet, what is more, even all the Broers do not count as Afrikaners, or are accounted worthy of having a share in that privilege of domination! According to the test put forward by the Executive Council and Professor van Rooy, as to the true Afrikanerhood, it is only people who have as their aim the Afrikanizing of South Africa, in all its spheres of life. Since this means an Afrikanizing with the exclusion of the English language and the English Afrikaner, so also a fusion brother, like you and I, and everyone who is a supporter of national unity, is immediately excepted from the privileged circle of real Afrikaners, predestined by Professor van Rooy and his Executive Council to domination in South Africa!

With the opening speech of Mr du Plessis quoted by me, and the Circular letter of the Executive Council, signed by Professor van Rooy, the Afrikaner Broederbond is deprived of its cultural mask, and has entered the political arena with no undecided call to arms! As will appear much more clearly just now: the Broederbond has been translated into a secret purified Nationalist Party which busies itself with secret propaganda work for the advantage of the interests of the purified Broeders and of the purified Nationalist Party.

As can be expected, since 1932, the Bond has been placed more and more at the disposal of the purified Nationalist Party, and its doors have been set wide open for everyone who can go through as leaders and prominent members of the purified Nationalists. The wider the doors are opened to the purified Party, the tighter they are closed to the United Party, so that while, since that time, not a single foremost political person, active in the politics and belonging to the United-minded or the United Party, has been admitted to the Bond, the Broederbond's membership list has been added to by nearly all the prominent bearers of arms and propagandists of the purified Nationalist Party.

The Broederbond has also, since that time, fallen almost exclusively into the hands of the purified Nationalists, with the pushing aside as far as possible of all Brothers who do not belong to the purified Party. It is also to the Purified Nationalist Brothers that we must impute the fact that the Bond, since that time, has been misused for the purposes and objects for which it was never intended, and which so badly shocked the feeling of right and honesty among the Brothers who did not belong to the purified Nationalist Party, and that some of them were obliged to take refuge in actual protest.

I have just said that since 1932 the Bond has been more and more placed at the disposal of the purified Nationalist Party and its purposes. To the question how that this can be possible without the knowledge of the Fusion-Brothers in the Bond, the answer is quite simple. The nonpurified, who are known as unsympathetic with the purified politics, or as active Fusionists, are simply ignored and avoided as apostate Brothers, and are left as far as possible in the dark with regard to what is going on. As regards matters of interest to the purified Nationalist Party, they are not consulted, and thus remain in ignorance of what is being done.

How easy it is for a section to intrigue to their hears' content, as pointed out here, is understandable when I say that it is an order to every member of the Bond that every member must be well acquainted with every other member of his division. Everyone knows therefore, for instance, who is a Fusionist or not and who must be avoided as an apostate.

Whatever therefore may have been the cultural aim and striving of the Afrikaner Broederbond in the past, in the light of what has been laid before me, there can be no doubt that we have today in the Broederbond to deal with a secret political association accessible only to and consisting only of Afrikaans-speaking members, the leading political spirits of whom are determined to rule South Africa over the heads of the English-speaking among us; and who are striving to raise Dutch-speaking Afrikanerdom to domination in South Africa, with the neglect of the rights and claims of the English-speaking portion of our population.

This is the declared striving of the Bond as a secret political association, as we have now heard, as well out of the words of the Potchefstroom professor, du Plessis, speaking as the Chairman of the Broederbond Congress, and also out of the Circular of the Executive Council itself, specially circulated for information to all members of the Bond.

Of this secret Broederbond, which places as its ideal, dissension and disunity among the Afrikaner nation by the exclusion of the English portion from the government of the country, Dr Malan, since Coalition, has become a member.

It is quite clear at present to everyone why Dr Malan changed so suddenly from a supporter to an opponent of Afrikaner national unity. His joining of this secret anti-English Afrikaner movement must have obliged him inevitably to discard the policy of national unity with the inclusion of the English-speaking Afrikaner; and he was also further obliged by his connection with the Broederbond to enter the road of national disunity and disagreement.

Out of what has been communicated by me three perfectly clear theorems follow:

1. That membership of this secret association is completely incompatible with co-operation for the realization of a united Afrikanerdom of English- and Afrikaans-speaking.
2. That Dr Malan, by becoming a member of this secret association, necessarily had to become untrue to his former doctrine of a united nation and necessarily had to refuse co-operation with the United Party as was done by him.
3. That when Dr Malan denies that, with his refusal to work together with the United Party for national unity, he was influenced and is still being influenced by racial feeling and the desire to domineer over the English portion of our population, he is making himself guilty of falsehood.

The question with which I began my speech to you this evening has been answered now. We know now quite definitely who and what is responsible for the national division and disagreement amongst us. What a miserable figure is cut by Dr Malan in this pitiful episode of our national history.

Yet what I have said here this evening about Dr Malan concerns to no lesser degree his chief lieutenants, Dr van der Merwe, Adv. Swart, Dr C. W. du Toit, Adv. J.G. Strydom, Messrs Werth, Haywood, Martins, etc., all of them members of the Broederbond, and thus all of them, together with Dr Malan, obliged not to support any national unity in co-operation with the English portion of our fellow-citizens.

Even as Dr Malan, they have taken an oath secretly to permit no co-operation from the English side with an eye to national unity, and in this way they stand in direct racial conflict with our English fellow-Afrikaners, striving by means of an Afrikaans-speaking domination to place the foot on the neck of English-speaking South Africa.

We also see now in what a close relation the Afrikaner Broederbond stands to the purified Nationalist Party. The leaders and the leading spirits of the one are the leaders and leading spirits of the other. If we take the Transvaal we find: Adv. Strydom, Mr L. J. du Plessis, and others as members of both. If we take the Cape, we find: Dr Malan, Rev. C.W. du Toit, Mr Stephen le Roux, and others. When we come to the Free State, we have: Dr van der Merwe, Adv. Swart, Messrs Werth, Haywood, Hiemstra, Dr van Rhyn, etc. There is no doubt that the secret Broederbond is nothing else but the purified Nationalist Party, secretly busy underground, and that the purified Nationalist Party is, as the secret Afrikaner Broederbond, carrying on its activities above ground. Between the two the unity of Afrikanerdom is exchanged for a Republican-Calvinistic Bond!

By leaving the territory of pure national culture and mixing itself with politics, the Afrikaner Broederbond abandoned its youthful innocence, and suddenly became a most threatening danger, as well to the rest and peace of our citizen society, as to the pure irreproachableness of our public life and of our civil administration – even when it moves in the economic-cultural sphere.

To realize the nature and extent of the danger with which we are being threatened at present by the secret interference and activities of the Broederbond, it is necessary for me to communicate to you something from the secret documents of the Bond about its organization, members, and various other particulars.

How densely secret the Bond is in all its goings out and comings in, becomes evident immediately from the extremely small number of persons outside its ranks which even knows about its existence, although it has been in existence for seventeen years already, and there are but a few towns or villages in the Free State in which it has not got its organization doing active work.

The members of the Bond are not many – at the utmost about 2 000. The strength of the Bond does not lie in its membership, but in its secret organization, which, for instance, is spread over the whole of the Free State like a network, destined for active propaganda, where through each cell or nest, any kind of information useful to the purified Nationalist Party, whether true or false, can be gathered up and spread still further. The kind of propaganda which goes out from these nests is of the same nature as what is found again daily in *Die Volksblad* or *Die Burger*. Here, in this network of secret propaganda, the strength and influence of the Bond mainly lies. Yet not only here. The Broederbond stands in secrecy in the closest relationship with a whole number of other institutions, which are being exploited by interested politicians and semipoliticians, who intentionally use them secretly as instruments for the furtherance of secret aims. The FAK, the Handhawersbond, the Helpmekaar, the Voortrekkers, the Republican Bond, the Calvinistic Bond, however useful and necessary some of them might also be for the Dutch-speaking Afrikaner nation and their interests, are all being systematically used and misused by means of the Bond. Under a very solemn promise every member is bound to the most stringent secrecy. Nothing concerning the Bond, its existence, its members, its activities or organization dare to be made known.

The Bond is organized in local divisions or branches of at least five members, each with its own directorate and its own by-laws. For the rest, each division stands by itself and does what its directorate pleases as a separate independent unit, if need be without knowledge of the rest – a secret circle or little circle within a secret organization. At the head of the Bond stands the Executive Council of nine members, chosen annually at the Bond Council or Congress, and embued with unlimited powers of control over the affairs of the Bond.

To become a member the person concerned has to go through a very severe and secret test, on the mould of the Freemasons. First the person must be proposed by two members, and even without his knowledge; and before this proposal can take place, proof must first be given that he satisfies certain stringent qualifications. Then, secondly, he must, again without his knowledge, be approved of, and this must be done by the members of all the divisions. Three adverse votes can reject him. Thirdly, he must be approached in a careful manner to find out whether he would like to be a member, and fourthly, if he agrees, he must be introduced, under oath, by the laying down of the most solemn promise of silence, fidelity, etc. Up to the very end the Executive Council retains the right to reject him as a member. The Broederbond is thus a closed circle of Brothers bound together by oath, compelled to keep the uttermost measure of secrecy.

In the secret Manual, printed for the use of the members of the Bond, it is laid down that Brothers must try to support the interests of Brothers, and that Brothers must, as far as possible, support each other's undertakings. This spirit of giving preference by a Brother to a Brother and his interests, appears throughout the rule of the Bond, and controls the relations between Brother and Brother. So much is this the case that in the Domestic Regulations of certain Divisions of the Bond, which have received the approbation of the Executive Council of the Bond, among others the following is definitely stipulated: 'Furtherance of each other's interests in social life . . . will be the duty of the Bond . . . Brothers will, where possible, support each other's business with word and deed, and be intercessor one for the other when the opportunity offers.'

Even if the Broederbond had never deviated into a political organization and had continued to go forward as a purely cultural association, there would still, necessarily, have been gross injustice happening on various occasions, along a secret way, to further the interests of a fellow-Brother to the disadvantage of a non-Brother, who had an equally great or greater right of address. Since the Bond was a secret body, with the most stringent obligation on every member to the uttermost secrecy about everything that took place, and that it was therefore quite impossible what was happening behind the curtain, there was also no protection for this non-Brother against the secret supporters of the Brother; and there was nothing in general for the Bond to be misused as an instrument or organized injustice against non-Brothers, yes, even to organized action in conflict with the best interests of the state and the civil service.

As a sample of how the Broederbond misuses its power as in a secret political association, I must remind you what happened a while ago when the so-called Le Roux motion came before Parliament. While the discussion on this was proceeding, the Broederbond set to work secretly, and secretly, in an organized manner, propaganda was made by the Brothers in the country districts in support of the motion. The Brothers, encouraged by purified Nationalists in Parliament, succeeded in managing to have numbers of telegrams sent to practically every Member of Parliament from the country districts, with the object of bringing pressure to bear on them to force them to vote for the motion. By its secret actions the Bond wanted to give the impression that the Members had to do with a spontaneous expression of feeling by the people in the district concerned.

The Bond here deliberately took part in a game of deceit, in which it hoped to influence the free vote of members of Parliament in favour of the purified Nationalists in Parliament. The Broederbond, a secret association, made use deliberately of its secret character to mislead the representatives of the people of the Union in the fulfilling of their national task!

Another sample of secret interference and secret misuse of the Broederbond is found in the following: The purified Brothers in Parliament some time ago in Cape Town, found themselves inconvenienced by the want of co-operation among the Brothers who, according to their wish, should have voted against the Government. To improve this condition of affairs, the purified Brothers without the knowledge of other Brothers, agreed to make use of the secret existence of the Bond with its secret authority and influence. Suddenly one fine day, the Brothers in Parliament received a notice that a certain gentleman from Potchefstroom had been appointed, or was going to be appointed, as Political Commissioner of the Bond at the Parliament, and that the task would be laid upon him to be present at all meetings of Parliament, from somewhere in the Gallery, with power from time to time, from his exalted seat, to issue orders to the Parliamentary Brothers, ordering them how they were to vote, etc.

This was a little too much for the Brothers in Parliament, who were not ready to be placed under a Bond dictator as voting cattle. Mutiny and rebellion were the result from the side of the Fusion Brothers, and the Broederbond had to put its Political Commissioner back into its pocket and get away.

The Fusion Brothers in Parliament deserve our compliments! But I cannot help warning them that he who eats with the Devil needs to provide himself with a long spoon!

Once again it appears from this to what extent the Bond and the purified Nationalist Party are one and the same body, functioning in two different compartments – the one above, the other under the ground.

What is there to prevent the Brothers seeking to further each other's interests in appointments and promotions in the civil service to the detriment of non-Brothers better entitled to it? Has it not already happened more than once without its even having been known?

I am putting the question to you tonight! What protection have you and I and our children, who are not members of the Broederbond, against the misuse of secret influences by Brothers by which we shall be prevented from enjoying what rightly belongs to us?

Well do I know that responsible officials of the state, members of the Broederbond, have requests made to them by fellow-Brothers on the acknowledgement of preference of the interests of Brothers above those of non-Brothers. If I understand it well, the request is sometimes extended to such an extent as to state that Brothers in the service should allow the orders of the Broederbond to supersede even the lawful regulations of the civil service.

Fortunately these efforts fail, and for the reason of the opposition which such presumptuous demands immediately experience from the officials concerned.

If the orders of the secret Manual to which I have referred, or of the Domestic Regulations of the Division quoted by me, had to be strictly followed, then, where a Brother had a shop, his fellow-Brothers would have to buy from him for that would be Bond duty, as expressed by the rule quoted. Where there is an opening in the service, whether for appointment or for promotion, then a Brother would have to exert himself to see a fellow-Brother competitor appointed or promoted to that post, for in terms of the regulation that would be Bond duty. As far as the Broederbond and the Brothers are concerned, it would matter very little what our claims might be for the support of our shops; or what claim you or I might have to an appointment or a promotion. We are not Brothers and therefore we simply do not count.

Meanwhile we are denied the opportunity of acting in an honourable, open way for the protection of our threatened interests. Everything against us happens in a secret way underground, where you and I cannot possibly know what is being done, or what secret methods are being employed there to deprive us of what belongs to us.

In connection with the Broederbond, I have this evening to direct a very serious word to the teaching class. When I was at Oudtshoorn lately, at a Circle Conference of the United Party, and the Conference had gone in to Committee, there were unexpected complaints by a number of persons about the excessive participation of teachers in politics, and finally a very serious appeal was made to me by a prominent woman delegate.

These were her words: 'In God's name, General, we mothers make a call on you to do everything in your power to prevent our children in school being so put up against their parents. You have no idea how bad it is.'

This charge of improper influence exercised by teachers on children on the school benches, had already come to my ears more than once here in the Free State. What was the truth about it? If it were true I could not picture to myself a grosser and more serious misuse of position and office.

I do not know if it is true. Yet what I really know is that the number of teachers in the Broederbond form more than one-third of the Bond's membership. I know also that there are few towns and villages in the Free State where the Bond has not made a little nest for itself of five or more Brothers, which must serve as a centre for Bond propaganda; and I know that there is pretty well not a single one of these nests where one or more teachers are not sitting hatching. When it is accepted that there are on an average at least two teachers in the Free State for each of these hatching nests – indeed a too low estimate – then one can form a fair idea of what the underground activities and interferences carried out by teachers behind the curtains of the school benches must be. When to the number of these underground purified teacher Nationalists is added, as ought to be done, the above ground purified teacher Nationalists, then I can well see that the parents of children from nonpurified houses have something to complain about.

Is this a state of affairs which should be permitted by the state?

We have seen that the Broederbond is a secret political association, which has placed before itself as an aim, the dominance of the Dutch-speaking portion of the population over the English-speaking portion, by which the nation is being torn asunder to dissension and bitter disagreements.

Should it be allowed that teachers, who are being paid by the state to educate the children of the nation, should misuse the opportunity given them of coming into contact with the children, for the peace-political propaganda? Is it right that it should be permitted to teachers through membership of the Broederbond, to declare inimical frame of mind to the English-speaking section of the parents of the children which they have under their care, and who, equally with the Afrikaans-speaking parents, pay their salaries?

The common participation in public by some teachers in ordinary party politics, has already been for the parent and for the educated public in general such a tremendous clashing against what was considered becoming and proper, that opposition had to be registered against it, which led to a certain measure of control. Now, seeing that the impression had arisen by the parent of a secret devotion to the ignoble task of bringing the youthful childish mind secretly in rebellion against that of the parent, it might well lead to very sad damage to what still remains cherished by the public of respect and goodwill to the teachers as a class.

203

Membership of a secret association must necessarily bring the person concerned under suspicion by his fellow-men, and let him decline in the same proportion in the trust if not in the respect of his environment. When this suspicion manifests itself in the direction of parental fear of the corruption of the youthful minds of their children, that suspicion will not neglect, no matter in what degree, to cause a feeling to arise of hatred and contempt.

The great misfortune of contempt or hatred of this kind is that it does not confine itself to the guilty individual, but spreads itself and very soon embraces the whole of the class to which that individual belongs. That this is going to be the result for teachers as a class, which will arise through the relationship of some of them to the Broederbond, is to be expected. The teacher where he sits in secrecy today, must come out into the open. There is nothing which needs the bright daylight more to remain sound than does our education.

The teacher class has never received anything from me but the greatest and most upright affection and respect, and as long as they are faithful to the charge of the welfare and education of the youth of South Africa, they will enjoy that respect and good feeling from me. But as has again been shown by what I have just said this evening, it cannot be expected from me that I shall remain silent about individual pedagogic misuses and evil deeds on account of my kindly feeling toward teachers as a class.

That on various occasions, when I have drawn attention to misuses and misdeeds, carried out by individual teachers, a cry has arisen, such as happened recently again at the Free State Teachers' Congress, cannot frighten me from doing my duty toward my people. Whether I was justified in speaking as I did at the Congress at Bloemfontein two months ago, and this evening repeated and did again here, I am willing to leave to the judgment of men and women who still possess a feeling of what is honourable and fitting. I only wish this evening to offer a little communication to the Executive of the Orange Free State Teachers' Association, which I think will interest them!

In August last year they were good enough to send me, unasked for, through their Secretary, the assurance that they:

> As a Teachers' Association, have never taken any part in party politics, and that they [we] do not approve of this active participating by teachers in public, and further that [we] are not aware that an active part has been taken by teachers in the Orange Free State,

an assurance which was accepted by me. Now, however, I have come into possession of better information, and I want to communicate to them that they would not have given me that assurance had they not been deceived and kept in the dark by their fellow teachers, who are members of the Broederbond!

The Executive Committee will forgive me if I tell them that I have just had in my hands the minutes of a Broederbond Congress with an agenda no less comprehensive of all possible political and party political points for discussion than that of any other party political congress and that this Congress was attended by not less than twenty-one teachers among the more or less 100 delegates, among them six teachers from the Free State.

What I have laid down before you this evening displays a state of affairs which might well cause the question to arise of 'Whither are we going?' by everyone who loves South Africa and has a feeling of responsibility.

Has the Afrikaner nation sunk to such a hopeless degree that it must seek for its salvation in a secret conspiracy for the advancement of racial hatred, of national dissension and of fraternal dissension? Is there for the Afrikaner son and daughter no higher striving, no nobler duty assigned than that of racial hatred and division? Does there remain no higher ideal for our children to reach than that of racial domination and of racial domineering?

Annexure C

In reply to Smuts' attacks on the Afrikaner Broederbond, Professor J.C. van Rooy, Broederbond Chairman, and Mr I.M. Lombard, Secretary, issued a series of five articles explaining the aims and objects of their organization. This was made public December, 14, 21, 28, 1944, and January 4, 1945. Below are summaries of these reports printed in the English-language newspaper, *The Friend,* published in Bloemfontein. The complete texts may be found in Afrikaans in *Die Transvaler.*

December 14, 1944

'The Afrikaner Broederbond was born out of the deep conviction that the Afrikaner nation was planted in this country by the hand of God and is destined to continue to exist as a nation with its own character and own calling,' says a statement issued by Professor J.C. van Rooy and Mr I. Lombard, Chairman and Secretary, respectively, of the Broederbond.

'The aim of the Broederbond, taken literally from the constitution,' the statement continues, is:

(a) 'The establishment of a healthy and progressive unanimity among all Afrikaners who strive for the welfare of the Afrikaner nation.

(b) 'The awakening of national self-assurance among Afrikaners and the inspiration of love for the language, religion, traditions, country and people.

(c) 'The promotion of all the interests of the Afrikaner people.

'The language of the Bond is Afrikaans. Party politics is excluded from the Bond. Only those can be members who are Afrikaans-speaking, of Protestant belief, of clean character, who are firm in the principle of maintaining their Afrikanerhood and who accept South Africa as their only fatherland. From every member it is expected that he will live and act in the firm belief that the destiny of nations is guided by the hand of God and that he at all times by his behaviour will hold high the honour, dignity, and good name of the Afrikaner Broederbond.

'Hitherto the Afrikaner Broederbond has never defended itself in public against the frequent absurd, uninformed, and also shamelessly false accusations. Its members have become members with the definite understanding that they will get absolutely nothing for themselves from their membership – not even fame or honour for service that may be rendered to the Afrikaner nation.

'Their powers and talents must be dedicated entirely and unselfishly to the interests of their nation in accordance with the demands of a Christian conscience and an unimpeachable character.

'Now that the Prime Minister, General J.C. Smuts, in his ignorance or driven by those of his followers imbued with a spirit of persecution, has found himself called upon, together with them, to try to stone the Bond, the interests of the Afrikaner nation demand that the history, objects, nature, aims, methods, and activities of this servant of Afrikanerdom be so revealed to the latter that it will cling with both hands to that weapon to help itself in its national struggle and will not allow an injustice to be done to its (the Broederbond's) members or injury to be done to the value and extent of its work.

'The Afrikaner Broederbond is giving its evidence in full belief in the God of its fathers before the court of its people in whose judgment and in whose conscience it has the fullest confidence.

'The Bond appeals to the people to judge whether its life and work deserve abuse and suppression instead of appreciation, and whether those who have faithfully served their fatherland in a legal way and in observance of all the obligations to which an honourable person and a professed Christian is subject, deserve martyrdom in any form.

'The people have the power not only to judge what is right, but to demand that the Government let justice prevail, and if this does not happen, then to throw in its forces in the struggle which in such an event must necessarily follow.

'Since this official statement and appeal to the people as the highest court of justice in the land, as well as the series of statements the Secretary has been instructed to prepare, give the facts for which the hostile press and persons apparently have been yearning, we challenge them to publish this and the other statements fully. Then their readers and audiences, too, can judge what is probable and correct.

'If this demand – because after all the slander against the Bond it has, like a victim whom they already want to lead to the gallows, a right to a final demand – is not fulfilled, but the revelation of facts and the defence are again concealed from Government supporters, as happened when a member of the Bond replied to Mr H.G. Lawrence conclusively, then we declare now that such assailants, who only stab in the back and run away, are hypocritical cowards. They have chosen to spread the basest accusations and the most flagrant untruths about the Bond; they are now in duty bound to publish the other side in the form in which the defenders are compelled to defend themselves.

'While it is not possible, within the scope of this statement to give many details, a promise is made here to do full justice to the various other matters of interest, one by one, in further statements. But we wish to take this opportunity to emphasise the following matters most strongly:

(1) 'It is not true that the Broederbond is a subversive organization which incites sabotage or will tolerate it from members in any form. It is absolutely untrue that the Bond has ever encouraged the giving away by its members of state secrets or tolerated it. On the contrary, the Bond takes the attitude that complete loyalty to their duties and official oath is a necessary guarantee that members will comply with the desired high religious and moral demands in their lawful work for the benefit of Afrikanerdom in the challenge the Government, or the Public Service Commission, or any other legal body or any person to prove the contrary.

(2) 'It is not true, as General Smuts alleges, that members consist "mostly of teachers and civil servants", and that "the rest are mostly party-political persons". Of the total membership of 2,672, at the most 8.4 per cent are civil servants and at the outside 33.3 per cent teachers. These figures include civil servants and teachers who have already retired on pension or who, after joining the Bond, have left the service and are now carrying on other callings. The rest are mostly farmers.

'No more true is General Smuts' allegation that membership is limited to influential persons in key positions. In point of fact the standard used is the zeal and readiness of persons to work for popular causes, and to make sacrifices regularly, monetary or otherwise, without any expectation of reward, and the tendency is rather to give preference to zealous young men so that they may have the opportunity to learn to perform useful national service. Older persons in key positions already have that opportunity.

206

(3) 'It is not true that the Broederbond is undemocratic or Fascist. On the contrary the Broederbond is pre-eminently organized on democratic lines. Every executive is elected by its members annually. The highest Executive Council and the Chairman are elected every two years by secret ballot by chosen delegates to a congress. Even in the admittance of new members these democratic principles apply, because every member has the fullest say on the question of who is to be admitted. In contrast with the allegation that members may not know one another, actually any member may have the fullest information about every other member.

'Further, it is an indisputable fact that the Bond accepts a system of democracy in accordance with the traditions of the Afrikaner people as carried out by its model republics. It is absolutely denied here in public that the Bond at any time declared itself in favour of a National-Socialist system for South Africa or that it has ever had, or sought, any connection with the Nazi rulers of Germany.

'The Bond denies as a barefaced lie the allegation made in the *Sunday Times* that the Zeesen broadcaster Holm is a member, or ever was a member of the Bond, as well as the other efforts made in this connection to throw suspicion of traitorous deeds or alliances on the Broederbond.

'Space does not allow any further details. Therefore, they will be supplied later. Also in the coming session of Parliament its members are free to put the Broederbond's case. In all fairness, however, now that this evidence has been laid before the people it can be expected that no rash or hasty action will be taken by the Government.

'No self-respecting person and no body with a sense of honour can submit to injustice and oppression. The Afrikaner people have had to endure much during this war. To begin with, no ordinary citizen was trusted with the possession of a firearm for his own protection. Then followed attacks on Afrikaans schools, the Church and almost all Afrikaans organizations, even *volkspele* [folk dances] and *jukskei*. It has now come to this that an association with high ideals, whose only sin was not to advertise its work for the benefit of its people, must suffer under venomous misrepresentations and be threatened with further demonstrations of hate, as well as persecution, by the authorities.

'If it is conceded that the Government, through ignorance perhaps, fears that the Broederbond is taking measures similar to those which it (the Government) possibly knows friendly disposed secret associations such as Freemasons, the Sons of England and the Jewish patriotic association take, or might take, against the interest of nationalist-inclined Afrikanerdom, then it (the Government) should realize now that it has to deal with an organization concerning whose work and aims it is entirely misinformed.

'While, thus, it is expected that the Government will not obstinately anticipate the verdict of the people, the members of the Bond, too, will take up a waiting attitude.'

December 21, 1944

The Broederbond, in the first of the series of promised statements on its activities, deals with two matters – the secrecy maintained in regard to deliberations, and the rule that no member of the Broederbond may disclose the membership of any other person.

A statement issued by the Secretary of the Broederbond and published in *Die Transvaler* says: 'The fact that the Broederbond is confidential in nature has led to the basest accusations of deceit, subversion, and so on. Yet there is nothing strange about this – that is to say, nothing that is not in accordance with what is happening throughout society.

'By this I do not mean that in the case of the Broederbond one is dealing with the mysterious secrecy of the Freemasons. It has nothing to do with the secret promotion of the interests of a group, as in the case of Jewish societies.

'Here one is not dealing with secret intrigue, as is sometimes found in connection with the deliberations of money magnates and even in the political sphere.

'One is not dealing here with the secret promotion in South Africa of the interests of a foreign country or the quiet pushing ahead in state appointments of one section of the people, as the Sons of England does.

'No. The confidential character of the Broederbond is comparable with what one finds at a Cabinet meeting, at a meeting of directors of a decent business undertaking, or at an executive meeting of a church or cultural organization before it comes to a decision which can be conveyed to its members.

'When the Smuts Cabinet deliberates on matters of policy – not only in connection with the prosecution of the war – it does not broadcast everything immediately! More especially does it not do so when it has not yet reached clarity or agreement in regard to policy of methods of action. Does such a procedure make a Cabinet a crafty machine that wants to undermine the interests of the people? Of course not.

'Why, then, must the Broederbond be so banded while it is only a deliberation body, where members discuss privately what they consider to be best for the Afrikaner people?

'When members have thus arrived at a conclusion on any matter, for instance in regard to economic, social, or cultural life, their attitude has always been submitted fully and publicly to the judgment of the people.

'On a subsequent occasion I shall develop this thought further, when I show how the Bond works, and I shall give examples of how the results of members' deliberations have always been laid openly before the people.'

Dealing with the question of secrecy in regard to who are members of the Bond, the statement says it is a strict demand which applies even to those who resign, that members undertake not to reveal one another's membership.

'The reason for this is obvious,' the statement says. 'Those who regard the progress of Afrikanerdom with the greatest jealousy, and who try to prevent it in every way, do so in very cunning ways. If here is someone in their employ who, they know, devotes his talents and spare time in an entirely lawful way to the Afrikaner people, then they withhold promotion or make his life intolerable in other ways.

'During a century of injustice the Afrikaner has learnt that his greatest sin in the eyes of his enemies is that he wants to be loyal to his nation.

'Therefore the crafty fighting methods employed by those who want to deny Afrikanerdom its place under the sun are the reason why those who can be persecuted in this way have the right to conceal the fact that they, as sons of the fatherland, are doing good but always lawful work for their people.

'The present presecution shows how a measure which was found necessary in the earlier days of the Bond, and which meanwhile had been largely tradition, is really justified today.'

December 28, 1944

The membership of the Broederbond and the size of groups to discuss various plans were dealt with in a second statement issued by Mr I.M. Lombard, Secretary of the Broederbond, last night.

208

The Bond, he said, had been built up by ordinary people who wanted to consider how the national life of the Afrikaner could be enriched. They had organized themselves into small groups and each member was free to take part in discussions.

Not only was it necessary to make groups small, but they had also to be representative of the various professions. If a number of doctors, or teachers, or mineworkers or highly placed officials only formed such a group they could only talk and think about things which concerned their limited sphere of work, and they would not know how the lives of other sections of the people were affected.

The view was adopted that every group must contain a small number of members who could easily meet to discuss various matters and who were representative of as many different sections of the people as possible. If there were one or two teachers in a section, no more teachers would be appointed to it, even though there were other outstanding teachers in the vicinity.

The exclusion of many good Afrikaners from the Bond had resulted from this attempt to keep groups small from the point of view of efficiency and from the attempt to obtain representatives from different sections of the Afrikaner people.

The statement said that every member of the Bond had the right to propose new members and to vote on their acceptance. If members of a local division considered that a person could not co-operate with them in their small discussion circle they had the right not to accept him. The Prime Minister had the right not to accept certain members of his Party in his Cabinet.

Every association had its own rules and customs, and those of the Bond were certainly less objectionable *(aanstootlik)* than those of the exclusive clubs of which the Britisher was so proud.

The Bond did not ask for the right to prescribe how the Toc H, the BESL or the SOE should choose their members. They, in turn, had no authority over the Broederbond's enrolments.

It was absolutely untrue to say that all sorts of good Afrikaners were excluded from the Bond because there were objections to their work or characters.

December 30, 1944

Mr I.M. Lombard, Secretary of the Broederbond, in the third of his series of statements about the activities of the Bond, describes the procedure adopted in connection with research by the Broederbond into various problems affecting Afrikaners.

He gives two examples – the language and culture of Afrikaners and their economic status – and describes how, after the fullest investigation into the matter, the FAK (Federation of Afrikaans Cultural Associations) and the *Volkskas* were established.

Mr Lombard states that he hopes that these two examples will help to show the Broederbond, through intensive study and serious deliberation, has often been able to help in the establishment of institutions and organizations of great value to Afrikaners, which function openly and which are public property.

The Broederbond also made certain monetary demands on its members to raise funds for good Afrikaans causes. The Broederbond contributed £1,000 toward the repatriation of the Argentine Broers, £500 towards the Daisyfield Orphanage School in Rhodesia, £3,000 for study loans for students at he Afrikaans Medical Faculty at the Pretoria University, and

£3,000 for study loans for students at the Afrikaans Engineering Faculty at the Stellenbosch University.

'All the work of the Broederbond can be measured by these examples,' Mr Lombard says. 'Dare anyone with an honest conscience say that it is not noble, unselfish work and born out of love of the nation?'

January 4, 1945

In the fourth of his series of statements on the activities of the Broederbond, Mr I.M. Lombard, Secretary of the Bond, deals with whether or not the Broederbond is a political or a subversive organization.

'In our first statement, Article 6 of the constitution was quoted that party politics is debarred from the Broederbond,' the statement says. 'I wish, however, to quote more fully what the rules and regulations have to say on this subject. They read as follows: "In connection with the activities of general district meetings, the meetings may discuss any national problem or historic point with a view to ascertaining, in an impartial manner, what is the best for the moral, intellectual, social, and political progress of our nation.

' "No speaker may, however, act as a propagandist for any existing political party or for party politics as such.

' "On the other hand, the Bond desires that all brothers should strive for the following seven ideals in their political activities:

' "(1) The removal of everything that is in conflict with the full international independence of South Africa; (2) putting an end to the inferiority of the Afrikaans-speaking section and their language in state organizations; (3) the separation of the Coloured races in South Africa, while allowing them independent development under the guardianship of the European; (4) putting a stop to the exploitation of the resources and population of South Africa by foreigners, including more intensified industrial development; (5) the rehabilitation of the farming community and the guarantee of a civilized existence by employment for all European citizens; (6) the nationalization of finance *(geldhandel)*, and the systematic coordination of political economy; (7) the Afrikanerizing of public life and our education and teaching in the Christian-National sense, leaving free the internal development of all sections of the community who do not constitute a danger to the state."

'I quote this part of the constitution fully purposely, because it has already been misrepresented by the Government press.

'It is unthinkable that in any country the Government should expect that there should be people who have no opinion about fundamental principles. Even the public servant in Britain is not forbidden to take a personal or philosophical view of national problems.

'The English Church in South Africa, for example, adopts a policy in regard to the treatment of natives, politically. In connection with such political questions as participation in and membership of the British Empire it makes itself heard. Anyone who reads the newspapers knows to what extent the English Church intervenes in political questions. Yet the Government never dreams of banning membership of the English Church to public servants.

'The Government, as such, even encourages public servants to be active propagandists and collectors for participation in the war – something which is in the midst of the political conflict in South Africa.

'The Government does not object to membership of the Sons of England. This body has,

210

however, repeatedly interfered in the active political struggle and has openly clashed with the Government of the day – the flag question, to quote one example.

'While the Broederbond may not believe in an independent South African as a principle without being judged, Sons of England members may make one of their aims the strengthening of the British connection and even the watering down of the constitution and the constitutional freedom laid down in the Statute of Westminster.'

The statement says that while the Broederbond is branded as a political organization to which public servants may not belong, membership of the Unity Truth Legion – a secret organization in the true sense of the word and one which spies on fellow citizens – is encouraged.

Annexure D

Press Statement by Prof. Albert Geyser published on November 21, 1963 in Rand Daily Mail explaining his role in the expose of Broederbond documents. It appeared under the headlines "Geyser is the third man. He photographed secret papers to expose Bond."

The report stated:

PROFESSOR ALBERT GEYSER, central figure in the heresy trial, revealed last night that he was the man who had photographed Broederbond documents lent to him by the Rev. C.F. Beyers Naude and had handed the reproductions to a journalist.

Professor Geyser, a minister of the Nederduitsch Hervormde Kerk and now Professor of Divinity at the University of the Witwatersrand, said Mr. Naude was in no way responsible for the publication of the documents.

In a statement issued last night, he disclosed:

• That he had decided to make the documents public because he wanted to frustrate the aims of the Broederbond.

• That two police officers, one a member of the Security Branch, had visited him on November 11, just after they had interrogated Mr. Naude.

• That he had asked the officers why it was necessary for a member of the Security Branch to investigate an allegation of theft.

• That the documents he examined proved unmistakably that the Broederbond was harnessing the power of the Church to further its political aims.

In state of concern

Professor Geyser said he had issued a statement as a result of the reaction of the Executive Council of the Broederbond to the statement made by Mr. Naude, and also because of rumours that Mr. Naude had handed the documents over for publication.

Professor Geyser's statement, in full, reads: "About seven months ago Mr. Naude visited me. He was in a state of extreme concern. He felt himself bound to his oath of secrecy as a member of the Broederbond, but at the same time he was undergoing an intense struggle with his conscience over the menace which the Broederbond constituted, particularly in respect of the Christian Church in South Africa.

"His emotional struggle was aggravated by the knowledge that he would soon have to take part in a discussion about the Broederbond and its influence on the Church at a meeting of the Synod.

"He was unable to face this task, burdened by a double membership (the Church and the Bond) and a double loyalty.

"I was not surprised when he came to me with his problem, for in the previous two years, while I was being tried on counts of heresy, I often went to him in my need.

"He gave me a number of documents issued by the organisation so that I could draw my judgment from them and assist him in his struggle.

"At that time I was very busy preparing for my court action against the General Commission of the Nederduitsch Hervormde Kerk and I asked for time to read the documents at my leisure.

Other sources

"In previous years if often happened that I received, from other sources, Broederbond documents for perusal. What I read in these documents convinced me in an increasing measure that a man could not belong to the Broederbond and the Church.

"Among those that I read were pieces that showed unmistakably that they were aimed at making use of the Church for political aims.

"There were pieces that contained interpretations of the Scriptures and their application that served the ideology of the Broederbond, but which rendered unrecognisable the demands of the Bible for neighbourly love, justice and humanity.

"My immediate observation was that these people were making the Church, which is the Bride of Christ, a handmaiden of politics. And above all, I observed in these documents the kind of quasi-Biblical arguments that I encountered during my trial.

"For this reason I decided that the only way to frustrate these aims and views would be to make them public.

"There was a second reason for my decision: I was aware that three-quarters of the clerical judges at my heresy trial were Broederbonders.

"I was also aware that the heresy charges, brought against me came remarkably soon after I had published a condemnation of secret organisations, including the Broederbond. I also realised that extracts from the Bond documents in my possession would assis me greatly in my defence.

"I photographed the documents and gave the negatives to a person whose good faith I did not doubt. This person had for a long time been collecting Broederbond documents. We had an agreement to exchange facts that we had gathered about the organisation. I knew that he was a journalist.

Pleasant

"Two officers, one from the Security Branch, paid me a visit on November 11, shortly after they had been to see Mr. Naude. Our conversation was pleasant and to the point. I answered all their questions, and in my turn asked them whether they were members of the Broederbond, which they denied.

"Then I asked them how it was that a member of the Security Branch had been entrusted with the investigation of a charge of theft and house-breaking, where, in the first place, there was no question of theft and house-breaking, and secondly, when the safety of the State was not involved.

"I asked them this because I was wondering whether the publication of Broederbond documents was tantamount to undermining the safety of the State, and whether the security machinery of the State was being used to keep a secret society secret.

Smuts

"On the other hand, if it is an offence to force the Broederbond to the surface without contravening any law, then I am guilty of the same offence as General Hertzog and General Smuts.

"If the Broederbond has nothing to hide, let them make all their documents public."

Annexure E

Two editorials by Lawrence Gandar in the Rand Daily Mail.

November 22, 1963: "Root Out This Evil Thing."

Has it struck you as odd that the S.A.B.C. should interrupt its regular programmes on both services to broadcast a summary of the Rev. Beyers Naude's statement about Broederbond documents followed by the furious reply of the Broederbond's executive committee?

Do you not think it remarkable that the chief of the Security Police should be investigating in person an allegation by the Broederbond of theft in connection with these documents?

Here is a clandestine political organisation, with no offices and no address, a completely faceless body except for piecemeal exposures in the Press, summoning the assistance of the Police Force at the highest level because some of its circulars have been photographed and published. Here is a secret society apparently able to command time – at the shortest notice – on the national broadcasting network.

Security matter?

Are we to assume that the security of the Broederbond is equated with the safety of the State? Are its internal concerns so vital that publication of its private documents is treated as a security matter? Are the police required to help preserve the secrecy of a secret organisation? Is an embarassment for the Broederbond so important that radio programmes must be disrupted for it to reply – not, mark you, in the name of any recognised person but as the disembodied organisation that it is?

It all seems utterly mad and God knows what the members of the diplomatic and consular corps must be thinking. Yet this week's events have a desperate reality.

They constitute one of those rare moments when the public catches a fleeting but frightening glimpse of the Broederbond in action. It is a moment of insight into the extraordinary, subterranean structure of power in South Africa. Down the years the Broederbond has been a shadowy form appearing fitfully on the national scene and vanishing again except for sporadic reports in the newspapers. Indeed, many have come to regard it as a creation of the "English Press," a bogey to scare voters with at election time or, at worst, as a small inconsequential group of political cranks.

Yet for 15 years the Broederbond has run South Africa – not in day-to-day administration but in laying down the principles of government, the philosophical guidelines along which the country is steered. Dr. Malan and Mr. Strijdom were Broederbonders but not leading members as Dr. Verwoerd is. Almost all the members of the Cabinet are Broeders and so are three-quarters of the National Party parliamentary caucus.

Highest levels

The Broederbond has penetrated to the highest levels of the Civil Service, the Police and Defence Forces, the Railways, the schools and the Afrikaans universities. Its 8,000 members organised in 350 cells control most of the main branches of our national life. Over 40 per cent of the ministers of the three Afrikaans Churches are Broederbonders and there is a direct link between Broederbond policy and Church decisions. The notorious Geyser heresy trial was the work of the Broederbond.

Education is a special target. Teachers form a large element of Broederbond membership. The Broederbond organised the recent move to oust Rhodes University from Port Elizabeth. It is leading the drive to establish an Afrikaans university in Johannesburg. Only yesterday the name of the new Rector of Potchefstroom University was announced. He is a Broederbonder, of course.

And the S.A.B.C.? Here is the most powerful single weapon of mass communication in the country and the Broederbond has captured it. Its chairman is Dr. Piet Meyer who is chairman also of the Broederbond. He forced out Mr. Gideon Roos as Director-General and brought in Mr. J. J. Kruger, former editor of "Die Transvaler" as "cultural adviser." Now the S.A.B.C. is busy disseminating the Right-wing propaganda which it claims is part of the national outlook. Dr. Meyer himself is the author of a book in which democracy is decried as "foreign ideology" and he has given addresses in which he attacked "unscientific" ideas of equality among peoples and races.

'Bond must rule'

There is no mystery about the aims of the Broederbond. These were enunciated in an early circular; "For Afrikanerdom to reach its ultimate goal of dominance in South Africa . . . the Broederbond must rule." Nor have these aims changed. A special circular, of August 1, 1962, said: "The main task remains the separate existence of the Afrikaner nation, with its own language and culture . . . We must do everything in our power to persuade English-speaking people to co-operate with us on the basis of the principles of the National Party . . . We should constantly be on guard that this does not result in the Afrikaner becoming more Anglicised as the English-speaking person is Afrikanerised . . . It is not they who must assimilate us in their circles, but we who must assimilate them in our circles."

These are not unsubstantiated charges against the Broederbond. They can be documented every inch of the way. Recently a leading Afrikaner, Professor A. van Selms, described the Broederbond's system of infiltration into other organisations and spheres as similar to that of the Communists. And now the Beyers Naude episode has come to reveal, once again the hidden power of the Broederbond and its ruthless determination to crush all non-conformity of thinking in our country.

The Broederbond has become a cancerous growth in the living body of South Africa. It is an arrogant, self-chosen elite, operating by stealth and intrigue, its early cultural aspirations swamped by neo-Fascist ideas on race and colour. By refusing to face the facts of the 20th century, it is driving this country to its destruction. It is an evil that must be rooted out before it is too late.

–The Editor

November 29, 1963: "Speak Up, Dr Verwoerd!"

Why has the Prime Minister, Dr. Verwoerd, remained silent about the Broederbond? Why has the chairman of the S.A.B.C., Dr. Meyer, who is also chairman of the Broederbond, said nothing about the extraordinary broadcast of an anonymous Broederbond statement on both services of the S.A.B.C. last week?

In any normal society, revelations such as those of the past 10 days about the grip this secret society has on the national life of the country would have forced any Prime Minister and any head of a public utility so directly implicated into issuing public statements?

Make no mistake, this latest partial unmasking of the Broederbond – when news broke in the "Rand Daily Mail" that the chief of the Security Police had personally interrogated the Rev. Beyers Naude about a leakage of Broederbond documents – is an issue of the utmost political significance.

Deeply stirred

Dr. Verwoerd's own newspaper, "Dagbreek," said in a leading article on Sunday: "It is a long time since minds were so deeply stirred as has been the case during the past week with the disclosure about Broederbond documents. The reports in the daily papers were but the smallest perceptible reflection of the underlying disturbances and emotional storms that have raged in the minds of most people."

Clearly this is no trifling matter. Yet the two men most involved – they have been openly named as the top men in the Broederbond – have kept silent. Is their oath of secrecy to the Broederbond more important to them than their duty to the public? It would seem so.

In news reports, special surveys and leading articles in the past ten days, the "Rand Daily Mail" has amply demonstrated the excessive power and baleful influence of the Broederbond. Its members constitute almost the entire Cabinet. Other Broeders have penetrated to the highest levels of the Civil Service, the police and defence forces, the railways, schools and universities. These men belong to a secret organisation. To whom do they owe their first allegiance: To the Broederbond or to the State?

Faceless clique

The question is of vital importance to us all. Are we a normal democracy or are we ruled by a faceless clique responsible to no one but themselves? Who take the decisions? Who give the orders? Let us illustrate this point by referring again to the S.A.B.C.'s Broederbond broadcast. Who wrote the statement? Where did it come from? Who bears the responsibility for it? No one knows. That is the trouble with the Broederbond. It cannot be called to account. It controls the country but nobody controls the Broederbond except its secret members.

Do not be persuaded that all this is merely a scare in "die Engelse Pers." Two of our

215

greatest Prime Ministers, General Hertzog and General Smuts, saw the Broederbond as such a menace that they fought it tooth and nail.

As General Hertzog put it: "The Broederbond is nothing other than the National Party working secretly underground, and the National Party is nothing else but the secret Broederbond pursuing its activities above ground." He saw clearly that the Broederbond could be "misused as an instrument for organised action in conflict with the best interests of the State and the Civil Service."

Puppet strings

Since then, the Broederbond has trebled its membership and today it is in command of the Government. The National Party is its "front organisation" going through the motions of normal political activity. Underground, pulling the strings of the puppet, is the Broederbond, taking its decisions in secret conclave. Is it any wonder that the history of South Africa these past fifteen years is shot through with authoritarianism?

What happens now? For a moment last week the Broederbond panicked and showed its hand. Now it has submerged again. No doubt its top members are hoping desperately that President Kennedy's assassination has pushed its own activities into the background of the public mind.

Nationalist newspapers are putting up big McCarthy-style smokescreens. A sudden proposal for a "volkskongres" on the threat of Communism is being energetically promoted as a means of rallying the shaken ranks of Nationalist Afrikanerdom. Communism apparently, is a threat only to the Afrikaner volk who must be coerced into accepting that any form of independent or critical thought is instigated from the Kremlin.

We do not intend to let the Broederbond slip away into the darkness so easily. It must be held fast in the daylight. Accordingly we challenge the Prime Minister to come into the open on this issue. Let us hear what he has to say about all these carefully documented reports of behind-the-scenes control of the organs of government by a secret society.

Or is the Prime Minister unable to make any appropriate statement on this matter of wide public concern? Is he, in fact, wholly under the control of the Broederbond?

SPEAK UP, DR. VERWOERD, WE CANNOT HEAR YOU!

–The Editor

Annexure F

Editorial by Joel Mervis in the Sunday Times of November 24, 1963:
"The Great Broederbond Burglary of 1963."

"As a result of Broederbond pressure, the Special Branch police are becoming the Gestapo of South Africa."
This crisp assessment comes from Mr. Japie Basson, M.P. for Bezuidenhout; and we believe it is shared by many people who have watched the activities of the police in connection with the SUNDAY TIMES disclosures of secret Broederbond documents. If the Special Branch are now shocked to learn that they are looked upon as another Gestapo, they have only themselves to blame.

There are certainly some curious features about the investigation, and quite a number of questions need to be answered. For example, what do the Broederbond, the Police and the Special Branch have to say now about the so-called "burglary" of Broederbond documents? It was this "burglary," we were told, which led to the investigation. Is there a Broeder, somewhere, suffering from hallucinations, who imagined or invented the "burglary"? That it was pure imagination is obvious from the evidence of the Rev. Beyers Naude and Professor Geyser. They prove beyond doubt that no "burglary" ever took place.

Phantom Burglary

Yet it was on the strength of this phantom burglary, this figment of a fevered Broeder's imagination, that investigations on a vast scale were carried out.

Naturally, if a complaint of theft is made to the police, they are bound to investigate it. But the police are not fools; nor do they lack energy: It seems to us, therefore, that they might well have directed their talents and energy, in the first place, to discovering whether a burglary had in fact been committed. After all, the burglary must have taken place somewhere. Where was it done? And what was broken into? From the disclosures made by Mr. Naude and Professor Geyser it is plain that the police could not have obtained a shred of evidence to prove that any burglary had been committed at all.

Senior Officers

Quite plainly, there was no burglary; and the police should have discovered that at the beginning. Instead, they mis-directed and misapplied their energies in trying to solve a crime that had never been committed. The public may well wish to ponder over the fact that on the strength of a non-existent, imagined, highly-fictional "crime", four senior police officers ostentatiously raided the offices of the Editor of the SUNDAY TIMES; and a senior officer from the Security Police interrogated Mr. Naude and Professor Geyser.

The police must feel discomfited now to discover, after all the drama and excitement, that there was not any burglary at all and that, in effect, they were simply being used by the Broederbond to find out how the SUNDAY TIMES obtained the secret documents, and at the same time to discredit Mr. Naude. That, at any rate, is how Mr. Japie Basson and others see it, and their judgment appears to be sound.

Main Issue

The success of the police in tracking down the "leak" to Mr. Naude and Professor Geyser, dramatic though it may be, should not be allowed to divert public attention from the main issue, which is just as real and important now as it was before. The publication of the secret Broederbond documents has emphasised the objectionable feature of the Broederbond, namely, its secrecy. As long as this organisation continues to operate in secret, it will continue to be feared and disliked – feared because it is powerful, disliked because it is secret. But whether it is feared, hated, or loved, its activities will remain a matter of profound public interest.

When the SUNDAY TIMES began its systematic exposures of the Broederbond ten months ago it knew it was coming up against the most powerful organisation in the country. And even though the SUNDAY TIMES knew that it stood alone, and would have to carry

217

on the fight alone, we were not deterred from doing our duty to the people of South Africa. We think we can claim, in all modesty, to have been faithful to the highest traditions of responsible newspaper practice and that, in the process, we have torn the mask from the Broederbond as has never been done before. After our ten-month campaign, standing alone, to expose the Broederbond, we find it sufficient and adequate reward to see this week, at last, vigorous denunciations of the Broederbond not only from prominent men in public life but also from many sections of the Press.

Not the end

The drama of this week's events, however, has not brought the Broederbond story to an end. If anything, it emphasises the dangerous character of the secret Broederbond. The SUNDAY TIMES, even if it has to continue its fight alone, will not cease to expose the Broederbond where it can.

Annexure G

Last speech by Dr Piet Meyer as Broederbond Chairman to the Bondsraad on April 6, 1972.

Our Task in the Political Sphere

I. The Religious, Cultural and Political Spheres

1. We must always distinguish sharply between the religious, the broad cultural and the political spheres as independent, autonomous spheres, each with its own nature, function and destiny.

2. The area of activity of our organisation is the cultural functions and issues of the Afrikaner nation with its own distinctive identity, based on a historically separate, Christian-Protestant, linguistic and cultural community with its own God-given Christianising mission in Africa. The broad cultural sphere includes not only Afrikaans linguistic and artistic resuppression, but also Afrikaans scientific activity, teaching and education, economic self-development, social interaction, legal system and constitutional system.

3. Our independent cultural sphere of activity which is not subordinate to the sphere of the church or state, nevertheless is intimately associated with the particular functions and activity of our Christian-Protestant churches and of our Afrikaans-national political action.

4. The determination of our ruling that our organisation stands outside party politics, is a recognition and endorsement of the autonomy of the political sphere. It includes, among other factors, the fact that our organisation as such may never interfere in the domestic affairs of the Afrikaner's national-political organisation. We also do not have the right to demand that the relevant political party and its leaders should be responsible to our organisation in their activities. It also includes the fact that our organisation is also not responsible for Afrikaans-national political action – that is not our affair.

5.	The fact that our organisation stands outside organised party politics does not mean, as a result of the intertwining of every Afrikaner's calling duty and task in all the various spheres of activity, that our organisation has no task and duty with respect to the organized performance of tasks in other spheres of life. Our members are and always should be active members of their own Afrikaans churches and of their own national-political party and should always receive guidance from our organisation in this respect – this is also valid for our church and party with regard to the cultural sphere. It is and always should be the case that cultural leaders are simultaneously church and political leaders, that political leaders are simultaneously cultural and church leaders and that church leaders are simultaneously cultural and political leaders.

6.	Although our organisation stands outside organised party politics, nothing prevents it from working with any political party, even a governing non-national party, to promote our Afrikaans cultural aims, this includes, in particular, our organisation remaining in the closest contact with our own national-political organisation and intimately co-operating with them when they form the government, thus ensuring that the Afrikaner's cultural striving is also realised by political means.

7.	Because a nation's constitution also forms an inherent part of his culture, it is self-evident that a cultural organisation will also concern itself directly with this issue. Thus it has been an important aim of our organisation, from its inception, to exert itself for our own Republican constitution in our country. We continually strive for a greater Afrikaans-historical content for such a constitution.

## II.	Short Historical Survey

1.	Since its inception our organisation has continuously been involved in the political sphere.

2.	The general duty of our organisation in the political sphere is that our members should constantly strive to combat Afrikaner-divisions in this sphere and to promote the greatest possible national-political unity of action.

3.	In the years of coalition when a serious political division came into being among nationalist Afrikaners, we proceeded to recruit and enlist leading national politicians as members of our organisation, namely the late Dr. D.F. Malan, J.G. Strijdom, Dr. N.J. van der Merwe, C.R. Swart, H.F. Verwoerd, and others. In these years our organisation strongly and clearly propagated the Republican ideal as the most important means to Afrikaner unity in the political sphere.

4.	This, among other factors, led Gen. Hertzog as head of the Coalition Government to regard our organisation as an undesirable organisation and to reveal details about it. The Executive Council then negotiated with him and came to an agreement with him to prevent him from taking further action against us.

5.	With the take-over of the government by Gen. Smuts in 1939 a secret investigation into the activities of our organisation was carried out. On the basis of this report, which was full of lies and childishly inaccurate data, the Smuts government instructed all state officials who were members of our organisation, to resign. No co-operation with the Smuts government was possible.

6. In 1948 with the change of government to the National Party under the leadership of Dr. D.F. Malan, an intimate association between the A.B. and the brother-leaders of the Party came into being. This co-operation had already existed in the war years with the support which our organisation gave to the attempts to overcome the serious divisions among nationalist Afrikaners. The large re-unifying gathering at Monument-koppie was organised by the A.B. Our organisation also called into being the Unity-Committee. The U.R. also arranged a Policy-Committee which drew up a Republican Constitution for our country. Our political leaders were also represented in this group.

7. During the first premiership of Adv. J.G. Strijdom we worked with the National Party in order to expand South Africa into a Republic as soon as possible.

   At a special Annual Conference at which Adv. Strijdom also appeared, the basis and form of the coming Republic was thoroughly set out.

8. It was, however, Dr. H.F. Verwoerd, who was a member of the U.R. for a long time, who called upon the active co-operation of our organisation when he decided as Prime Minister to hold a Referendum about our becoming a Republic. We did not only use our funds to enlist public support for the Republic but also harnessed the energies of our own members and of outside supporters in this cause.

   Because of hostile reactions which were aroused against our organisation especially by the Freemasons, among the members of the National Party we also co-operated with Dr. Verwoerd to institute a judicial enquiry into the activities of secret organisations. In the report of the judge concerned our organisation was cleared of any form of incorrect behaviour and action, particularly with regard to interference in party political affairs.

9. Our close and intimate co-operation with our national-political leaders was continued when Adv. John Vorster became our new Prime Minister. We did everything in our power to prevent a group of nationalists from founding their own party in opposition to the National Party which was under the leadership of memers of our organisation. And where some of our own newspapers conducted their own campaign in this connection, we tried to keep the split as small as possible.

   Our organisation, as in the case of our previous Prime Ministers, was in close contact with Adv. Vorster in all matters which are of great importance to the Afrikaner and which directly affect our nation as a linguistic and cultural community. Not only his door, but the doors of all the members of his Cabinet were always open to us in this regard. The calls for support in various causes never fell on deaf ears.

III. Co-Operation with regard to National Political Affairs Affairs that affect the Afrikaner directly.

During all the abovementioned premierships our organisation experienced the closest co-operation and sympathetic support regarding issues affecting the future of our people. We mention only the most significant of these:

1. The Afrikaner's responsibility, role and place in the Public Service and semi-Government bodies; with the help of our own political leaders it was possible to open up possibilities for the promotion of culturally aware Afrikaners in these services, especially

220

after the weakening of the public Government-machinery during the war years. For capable and hard-working Afrikaners there was no longer any obstacle to prevent him from occupying the highest posts in the Government and semi-Government service.

2. With the sympathetic understanding of our political leaders the Afrikaans businessman could also move forward with greater confidence, as a result of complete equality of rights, towards which our organisation had stimulated him. The results of this was the greater participation of the Afrikaner in the private business world of our country. Although his backward state is still a cause for concern today.

3. Perhaps the most important fruit of mutual consultation and co-operation is our progress in the educational sphere in the interest of the children of our nation. Afrikaans mother-tongue schools which came into their own under our National Government, are truly the foundation and basis of our survival as a separate linguistic-cultural national community. Mutual co-operation also led to the expansion of a complete national educational system for our country – probably one of the greatest national-political achievements of our time.

4. Our organisation also consistently made its energies available to our political leaders for the 'thorough' application of our policy of separate development. It is not possible, in the framework of this short exposition, to reflect our contribution in this connection completely. This concerns not only theoretical contributions but also practical action which is not yet fully calculable. I mention only two contributions here: the contribution of SABRA and of Radio Bantu in which our members play a large role. Recently we made a particular contribution, with regard to our multi-national sports policy, to organise this important matter in the interests of our country and all its peoples, on the basis of our policy of separate development.

5. An issue that also constantly claims the closest co-operation of our organisation and our national-political action, is the necessity of continued immigrant contributions to the complete expansion of our national economy. Without a powerful unfolding of our national economy our independent survival, as well as the application of our policy of separate development, will be seriously threatened. On the other hand we must also firmly ensure that our own national composition, nature and character are not permanently harmed by immigration. Our organisation has already acted strongly and decidedly on this issue. We also enjoy the constant support of our political friends in this connection. The naturalisation of immigrants in our own community is also of the greatest importance to our organisation.

6. Many other national-political issues, with which we occupy ourselves, are regularly summarised in our annual reports.

IV. Present situation and urgent future action

1. Our present task in the political sphere is mainly determined by the fact that many Afrikaner nationalists have recently either lost their enthusiasm for linguistic-cultural and our national-political action or become so involved in small personal grievances that they have lost sight of the great Afrikaner cause. According to a very accurate calculation 70 000 Afrikaner Nationalists from the Transvaal did not vote for National

candidates in 1970. Of those 33 000 voted for the HNP, 15 000 for the U.P. and 22 000 did not vote at all. Add to this the fact that about 7-10% of urban Afrikaners and 15%-20% of rural Afrikaners in the Transvaal still vote for the U.P.

2. It is not the task of our organisation, and we are also not in a position to analyse this situation correctly and fully – what *is* our task is to arouse the enthusiasm of culturally aware Afrikaners for our national-political unity movement in the interests of our people's own separate survival and to overcome political boredom in our own ranks.

3. It is self-evident that any effective co-operation that we can achieve in this connection, can and must be with the leaders of the governing National Party. Not only are the members of the present Cabinet, with a few exceptions, members of our organisation, but they are also the people who continue our close mutual co-operation in the national-political sphere since 1948.

4. As regards the HNP, since the founding of this party, which took place under the leadership of some of our members, the UR has clearly stated that our organisation does not deny any member the right to follow his own opinion in party politics or to join a political party of his own choice as long as he does not, as a result, behave in a way contrary to our Bond's constitution, spirit, policy and aims. And where the UR takes disciplinary action against a member, it does not do so on the basis of his membership of a particular party of group, but because of his own individual action as it conflicts with his personal undertakings in our organisation.

5. Recently our task in the political sphere was also to try and prevent a second national-political party from coming into being. We did not succeed in this. Afterwards we did everything in our power to keep the division as small as possible. It was our particular task to prevent this division from being carried over into our organisation. In this we were largely successful.

6. Against the background of the sketched present situation it is clear that we as Afrikaners, especially as members of our organisation, must again fill our own people with enthusiasm for our extremely important national-political action and in this way simultaneously demonstrate, to the internal and overseas saboteurs and enemies, the greatest possible political unity. We must not only begin to work for the next election in a positive way, but also carry it through to a great National victory under the banner of our unified Afrikanerhood.

7. In order to work in the closest co-operation with our political leaders, our organisation's specific task must include the following:

   (a) We must systematically stimulate the national-political responsibility and duty of every member and of every Afrikaner, especially of our young Afrikaners, to achieve a great victory in the next election, on the basis of united Afrikaner strength.

   (b) We must inspire the national Afrikaner to see for himself a positive national task for the future, and to stop hair-splitting investigations into the reasons for the existence of the present situation. Our political leaders know better than us which possible shortcomings must be removed in the sphere of organised national-political forward activity.

(c)   As a cultural organisation it is our special task to begin planning and organising all-embracing and inspiring cultural functions on a grand national scale, functions such as the Ossewatrek, the Monumentbyeenkomste, the Taalfeeste (Wonder van Afrikaans) and others of the past. In 1974 it will be fifty years since our first National Government came to power with its policy of South Africa First – a government which was of the greatest significance for Afrikanerdom, not only politically and economically, but also culturally. It could, for example, offer a good opportunity for great national festivals before the next election.

(d)   We must cease all old wives' tales and gossip about one another and sly criticism of our own leaders in all spheres of life, and wipe it out completely. To speak directly to one another is to understand one another and to gather together our strength for the future.

(e)   We must harness all our communications media in a positive way in order to gather up the Afrikaner's national-political energy for the struggle for survival into the future, and not divide those energies. Our members must play a leading role in this.

8.   While we are doing all these things, we must never forget that our organisation's own duties are in the cultural sphere. Another speaker will discuss this. And everything that we tackle in our own sphere, everything that we undertake in co-operation with our national political leaders, must always happen in the closest touch with our religious-clerical leaders in the light of God's Word. A thorough discussion of this matter is also on our agenda.

Annexure H

Die Vaderland, whose editor, Mr Dirk Richard is a non-Broeder, twice interviewed Dr Andries Treurnicht on the Broederbond issue. This was at the time of the *Sunday Times* expose's. The translated and edited question and answer articles are reproduced here.

The glib replies, the hair-splitting arguments, presenting the Broederbond as a harmless, even somewhat powerless organisation, represent the standard Broederbond tactic when it comes to defending the organisation.

Die Vaderland, September 18, 1972.

Question: The following allegation has been made. Many members of the government and Cabinet are prominent members of the Broederbond. This means that the very people making proposals to the government do the deciding. What method is used to make submissions to the government, and what is your comment on the accusations?

Answer: On the method I would rather say nothing. For the rest my answer is that the government and the Cabinet stand in the firing line. Any decision which it takes . . . it must account for to the Opposition and the public.

Because most government members are members of the Afrikaans churches, so the same accusation can also be made in that case. There are also farmers in the government. Government members do not live in ivory towers without any relation to practical life.

223

Question: But it is argued that the Broederbond is a secret organisation whereas these other organisations are not.

Answer: The church and other organisations often make confidential representations to government. But the cabinet must be able to account for, satisfy and defend its decisions in the face of the entire public and country.

Any organisation can make representations to the government, including the Freemasons – and I almost went to say the Black Sash. If you break down that principle, you undermine democracy.

The *Rand Daily Mail* and other sources must realise that this what they are advocating is undemocratic. These are the actions of people who want to dictate to others from their own liberal viewpoint to which organisation they may or may not belong. In this way they become the most intolerant people of all.

Question: In view of the apparent leakages from the Bond and the manner in which the exposés are used for political purposes, can it still function as a secret organisation?

Answer: The basic task of the AB is not just to remain secret. It does not use its hands to cover its face, but to work in the interests of the Afrikaner.

It will not abandon its secrecy, and it will make no difference to its task of protecting and promoting the cultural interests of the Afrikaner. It will continue to do so.

It is sad that certain members are breaking confidentiality. But this makes no difference to the task of the organisations. It just embarasses certain individuals.

Question: Why must secrecy be maintained?

Answer: Because we must give people the opportunity to work for the interests of the Afrikaner.

Question: Will the present divisions in the AB ranks not paralyse the organisation? And in view of the unpleasant politicking which goes with it, does it not do more damage than good to the cause of the Afrikaner, the National Party and the AB itself?

Answer: It is an organisation which concentrates on the interests of the Afrikaner. If your fellow Afrikaner is quarrelling and attempting to sow suspicion, then it is a reflection on those people . . . Strife between people who share the same culture does not make a good impression (on the outside).

The HNP is busy dying. These attempts to sow dissension in the ranks of a confidential cultural organisation show its last agonies. My viewpoint is that these people have no alternative for the NP policy. As such they have no right to exist as a political party.

But to say that I deny or reject them as Afrikaners will be wrong. We would like to bring all Afrikaners together as Afrikaners in one culture.

Die Vaderland, October 17, 1972

Question: The constitution of the AB lays down that party politics are excluded from the Bond. But by excluding the Hertzogites from the Bond, the NP has chosen sides with the NP. Thereby it had landed in party politics.

Answer: One cannot take this stipulation too literally. Now the dissenters (the HNP) want cultural organisations to suspend their moral support for the NP. They must remain totally neutral.

This means that they want the cultural organisation to sanction the political division. In this manner Afrikaner culture will become powerless; It will play into the hands of the enemy.

Question: According to reports, Ministers serve on the executive of the AB. Most of the National MPs are believed to be members of the Bond. If that is so, does it not give the impression that the Bond is excessively integrated with the NP?
Answer: Most members of the government are also members of the Dutch Reformed Church. The same argument can then be used when the church makes representations to the government. Nothing prevents a Minister from being an elder and a member if the Moderature of the church. There can and should be no objection.

Question: Why can the AB not reveal its membership lists?
Answers: A member can in certain circumstances obtain permission to reveal his membership. But members undertake not to reveal the membership of each other. The reason is obvious. Those who view the progress of Afrikanerdom with the greatest envy and who want to obstruct it acts in a very cunning manner. They discriminate against somebody in their service who, according to their knowledge, is completely legitimately making available his talents and free time for the Boere volk. They make life unbearable for him.

Question: The allegation is been made that the Broederbond creates jobs for pals. In other words it pushes its own people in important positions.
Answers: The AB promotes the interests of the Afrikaner as such. Its membership is limited, but representative of all circles and professions in Afrikaner society. It strives definitely for the promotion of the Afrikaner. But not only for its own members. It strives especially for the promotion of Afrikaners outside the Bond.

Question: It is said that the AB abuses its secrecy and influence to strangle, to dictate and to dominate spheres such as the political, the church, and the civil service.
Answer: The AB in fact seeks to know the viewpoint and leadership of these spheres. Its membership is also, as was said, representative of all levels of the Afrikaner society.

The confidential nature of the AB is comparable to that of meetings of a board of directors, the Cabinet or management bodies in general. Discussions are not trumpeted forth in public, especially when unanimity has not yet been reached.

The AB is in the first place a body of discussion. A matter is discussed by all the divisions and also by the executive council. Therafter the confidential nature of the AB ceases to exist. The final plan is then submitted to the volk.

But it is not submitted by or through the AB. The Bond is a service organisation which does not seek recognition for itself. If, for example, it is a matter concerning education, then it is submitted through its members who are in education, to the public educational authorities. The Bond does not claim credit for itself.

An important reason for the confidential nature of the Bond is precisely because its members must serve their volk without expecting something in return.

Annexure I

The initiation formula as published in an appendix to the UR Agenda of March 21, 1968.

Appendix to U.R. Agenda 21.3.1968.

Blue-print

Confidential

Initiation formula for Brothers

1. **As preparation**

   Song: (Optional)

   As soon as the Aspirant-Brother(s) is ready for initiation, a suitable song, e.g. Ps. 146:1 or 130:3 can be sung.

   Proposer:

   In these moments of deep solemnity every Brother remembers his own initiation and by way of renewal he makes the initiation vows applicable to himself.

   Prayer:

   The proposer or another Brother who has previously been requested to do so.

   Bible-reading:

   The proposer reads out a short, suitable text from the Scriptures.

   N.B.:

   The sequence of the Bible-reading and prayer can be reversed.

2. *Proposer:*

   Reads out the full name of the Asp. – Br.(s) and says:

   After careful consideration it has been decided to invite you to become a member of the Afrikaner – Broederbond. Therefore you were called to come and discover tonight what the Afrikaner-Broederbond is and what will be expected of you as a Brother.
      If you thereafter decide to join our Brotherhood, you will have to make a ceremonious and binding oath of loyalty.
      Before we can go over to that, it is necessary for you to delcare on your honour that:
      You are not a member of any secret or half-secret international organisation nor are you connected with any such organisation by co-operation and that you therefore ceremoniously and unconditionally promise, if you are not admitted to the Broederbond tonight, to reveal nothing of what you discover tonight about the Broederbond and its members to anyone outside this meeting.

Proposer:

Announces the full name of the Asp. – Br.(s) and says:

What is your answer?

Asp. – Br.(s) answer : Yes.

3. *Proposer:*

Now that you have bound yourself to strict secrecy, the following can be revealed to you:

The Afrikaner Broederbond was born of the deep conviction that the Afrikaner nation with its own nature and task was called into being in this country by God's hand and is destined, for as long as it pleases God, to remain in existence. The members of the Afrikaner-Broederbond are mission-conscious Afrikaners who strive to represent and serve the best that is in our nation. Nobody has any claim to privileges because he is a Brother, as the Afrikaner-Broederbond is a service – organisation, not a benefit-organisation. Whoever joins, does so in order to give, not in order to receive; in order to serve, not to be served or to reap any personal advantages.

On the basis of our faith in God, the Afrikaner Broederbond sets itself the aim, in the service and honour of God, to join its members with a strong bond of mutual trust and patriotism, to bind with love and work altruistically, in the midst of possible differences, for the realisation of a healthy and progressive unanimity among all Afrikaners who strive for the welfare and advancement of all interests of the Afrikaner nation.

As membership of the Afrikaner-Broederbond brings great responsibilities with it, it is therefore necessary that you carefully consider what is expected of you.

4. *Alternate Speakers.*

First Br.: It is expected of you to live and behave in the firm belief that the fates of nations are determined by an Almighty Godly hand, and to cling to the Christian-national tradition which is the heritage of our Afrikaner people, as founded in the Word of God.

Second Br.: It is expected of you to remain true to yourself and your conscience, but also to respect the otherness of your fellow-Brothers, bearing in mind that we are single in heart, in mind, and in striving, but are not the same and do not wish to be the same.

First Br. It is expected of you to do everything in your power to realize and to support unanimity among all purposeful Afrikaners, and to promote the building and independence of the Afrikaner people in the cultural, economic, and every other sphere of life.

Second Br. It is expected of you to strive for the realisation of the Bond's ideals not only by co-operation in an organised effort, but also by individual action in your own work – will and sphere of influence, inspired and supported by your fellow-Brothers and guided by the Bond's ideals.

First Br. It is expected of you to hold high in your behaviour the honour, dignity and good name of the Afrikaner-Broederbond.

Second Br. It is expected of you to attend faithfully the monthly branch-meetings and to co-operate continually in a spirit of true unanimity and honest brotherhood with your fellow-Brothers.

5. *Proposer:*

Announces the full name of the Asp. – Br.(s) and asks:

Do you understand the aim we have in mind and the spirit that inspires the Broederbond? and

Do you subscribe as a purposeful Afrikaner to the foundation and aim of our activities as they have been presented to you?

Asp. – Br.(s) answer: Yes

Are you now prepared to accept the conditions for membership and to enter into an unbreakable bond?

Proposer:

Announces the full name of the Asp. – Br. and says:

What is your answer?

Asp. – Br.(s) answer: Yes.

6. *Proposer:* In the hearing of the gathered Brothers which you have call as witness, I request you to answer to the following:

Do you undertake:

(1) To serve the Afrikaner people through the Afrikaner Broederbond in everything for which it stands, loyally and honestly.
(2) Not to reveal anything which you find out about the Afrikaner Broederbond and its members to any outsider, unless you have received prior permission from the Executive Council of the Afrikaner Broederbond.
(3) Not to reveal your own membership except in really urgent circumstances, but never that of a fellow-Brother.
(4) Not to become a member of any secret or half-secret international organisation without the permission of the Executive Council of the Afrikaner Broederbond or to associate yourself with it by co-operation.
(5) To fulfil the requirements which the Bond management may impose upon you according to the regulations and to submit reasonably to the brotherly discipline and connection which the Bond management must apply according to the regulations.

(6) To submit yourself to immediate dismissal as a Brother if you break your vow in any respect
and
(7) To regard all your vows as binding until death even if your membership is forfeited – to regard all your vows as binding until death.

Before your answer is expected, you are now given a few minutes to meditate.

A moment of silence . . .

Proposer:

Announces the full name of the Asp. Br.(s) and says:

What is your answer?

Aspirant – Br.(s): Yes.

Proposer:

On behalf of the Afrikaner Broederbond I accept your oath of loyalty. In the words of our motto I sincerely wish you strength.

Be strong in the practice of your Brothership. Be strong in your faith when the struggle is hard.

Be strong in love of your nation.

Be strong in service of your nation.

Proposer:

Comes forward and says:

With this handclasp I declare you a Brother. I now also request the other Brothers who have here stood witness to the unbreakable bond you have entered into to confirm with a sincere handclasp that we accept you from now on as a fellow-Brother.

Afterwards you will be led out to confirm in writing the declaration which you have here made orally.

ANNEXURE J

Speech by Dr Piet Meyer Chairman of the Broederbond at the Bondsraad Bloemfontein October 3, 1966 in which he spelt out the Broederbond blueprint for Afrikaner Domination and Imperialism.

The Survival of the Afrikanervolk

I. Introduction

1. What I have to say tonight, on behalf of the U.R. and our organisation, about the survival of the Afrikanervolk, I wish to say against the background of the cruel murder of Dr.Verwoerd, the brother who undoubtedly did more than any other brother recently in carying out an international struggle to ensure the survival of our country and its people, including the Afrikaner nation. He sealed this struggle with his blood in Parliament, on the terrain where he mainly conducted this struggle, namely the political terrain.

2. As you will recall from the special circular about Dr. Verwoerd, he was fond of comparing the national structure, the national establishment which must continually be built up and fortified for this struggle, with a pyramid. At a birthday celebration which the U.R. organised for him at Libertas, I told him on our behalf that our organisation would help to build up all four sides of this pyramid, as far as it concerns the Afrikaner nation, and that this would be based on his own historic foundation. The four sides of the pyramid are the political, cultural, the economic and the educational sides, with our own Afrikaans Christian-national world-view as a basis.

   He, Dr Verwoerd, was a leader, a keystone, who not only embodied all these sides of the white pyramid – he was always statesman, man of culture, businessman and educationist at the same time – but he also continually expanded our pyramid, our own Afrikaans pyramid, within the larger white pyramid, on its own Crhistian-national foundation.

3. My task tonight is to describe briefly to you, with all its aspects and aims, our Afrikaans-Christian-national establishment, which is being built up and maintained in the present national and international situation by our leaders, with the A.B. as the central source of energy. I shall do this as clearly and honestly as possible, without misleading you, without blinding myself to weaknesses, without being diplomatic but also without parading before you the spectris and ghosts of a guilty conscience.

4. At the next S.A.B.R.A. conference I shall be dealing with the question of the survival of the white community in South Africa. In order to avoid unnecessary repetition, that paper will afterwards be sent to all our branches. You should however take note that the S.A.B.R.A. paper deals with the future of the Afrikaans/English cultural community as a branch of the Western world. Tonight we are mainly concerned with the survival of the Afrikaans cultural community as the bearer of the white community of our country and simultaneously as the guarantee of a peaceful co-existence of whites and non-whites in our country.

   Tonight we must reach clarity as an organisation about the process of Afrikaans/English integration which has already advanced rather far, especially in the social, political and economic spheres. We must then determine how we must control this process so that it does not bring about the downfall or weakening of the white political community and eventually affect adversely the non-white population groups of our country.

We must thus deal frankly with one another tonight – about something which, if we were to make it public at this stage, could do more harm than good. Once we know clearly where we are heading and how we are going to get there, we can perhaps achieve our greatest task thus sofar in the interests of our country and all its people, but especially of our own people, by communal but discreet activity in the public sphere.

II. Basic Propositions

In order to know where we want to go and how to get there, our starting point must be clear and we must know precisely where we stand. I shall sum it up in a few propositions:

1. The future of the white Afrikaans/English community and the future of the non-white national groups of our country are in the first place closely bound up with the survival of the Afrikaner nation as an indigenous, separate and independent Western cultural community in Africa. Thus, the more purely, strongly, and self-consciously the Afrikaner nation behaves in all spheres of life in South Africa, the better the prospects for all groups of people in our country, the safer will be their future. I say this without any chauvinistic over-estimation of our nation and its value.

2. The fact that Afrikaans and English-speakers in our country today move side by side and together on the road of the South African Republic – thus not as before opposed and even hostile to each other – has allowed the process of Afrikaans/English integration to work in favour of the English world-view, English culture, English life-styles and English behaviour patterns more than ever before. No Afrikaner who thinks penetratingly about affairs has ever said that the future of the Afrikaner lies in isolation – then we might just as well say that our future lies in a vacuum! Afrikaans/English integration has already caused almost 200 000 Afrikaners to anglicize completely, including their home language. And this tendency is increasing, not decreasing. How many English-speakers were totally afrikanerised after the 2nd World War I do not know – I do not often come across them. What I do know, is that the English-speakers who have completely afrikanerised are mainly English plattelanders and impoverished English city-dwellers. The Afrikaners who have been totally anglicised, however, came predominantly from our highest and middle income groups.

    The integration of Afrikaans and English-speakers has been deliberately announced and promoted by our politicians since the establishment of the Republic, and it has been based on the principles of the National Party. The result of this is that Afrikaners have carried over this desirable and necessary politicial Afrikaans/English co-operation into other spheres of life without formulating for themselves a clearly defined basis and goal. This leads inevitably to the growing anglicisation of the Afrikaner rather than to the afrikanerisation of the English-speaking South African.

3. The Afrikaner/English integration now takes place in different ways and to different degrees in the various spheres of life.

(a) In the political sphere the English contribution to an integrated white community is our present parliamentary system with the emphasis on state citizenship as a collectivity of all state subjects, irrespective of differences of origin or culture, everyone potentially equal. The specifically Afrikaans contribution in the political sphere, namely our Republicanism, has not yet achieved full development and completion in our political life. The most important Afrikaans political contribution so far is the regulation of the relationship between white and non-white races on the basis of the principle of the homelands and separate development within the same comprehensive political allegiance.

(b) In our country's administration of justice the Afrikaans Roman-Dutch legal tradition has largely been maintained with the addition of elements of English Common Law, the English system of evidence and English law formation by means of precedents.

(c) The Afrikaans/English integration in the social sphere, i.e. regarding forms of intercourse, behaviour patterns and life-style, is predominantly and almost exclusively shaped by the English community. Our eating habits, our ways of dressing, visiting and reception, our social etiquette, our forms of relaxation, etc., are almost exclusively cast in a typically English mould.

(d) In the economic sphere the Afrikaans/English integration has led to predominantly English industrial, commercial and financial forms, whereas the more specifically Afrikaans economic contribution has remained confined to the sphere of agriculture.

(e) In the educational sphere the Afrikaans/English integration has progressed so far that it is difficult today to distinguish what is of Afrikaans and what of English origin. The most important Afrikaans contribution is apparently the practical maintenance of the close connection between education and religion. The principle of bilingualism within a neutral educational system means, however, that the Afrikaner is more exposed to anglicisation than the English-speaker to afrikanerisation, especially on the secondary and tertiary educational levels.

4. The final outcome of this process of integration will thus be a completely integrated Afrikaans/English cultural entity with predominantly English context and forms but still expressed, I should add, perhaps only provisionally, in two languages, namely English and Afrikaans. Whether the one final spoken and cultural language will be English or a bastardized English/Afrikaans, if we leave this process to itself, the future will reveal. You notice that I do not ever mention pure Afrikaans as a possibility if the present integration process goes on unhindered. One need only mention two facts to support this proposition: the superior power of English newspapers, magazines, books, textbooks, etc., by which the English/Afrikaans spirit and community are fed and formed; and the fact that the majority of the Afrikaner nation is taken up in an English business world.

5. The fourth basic proposition with regard to the present Afrikaans/English situation affects our youth, our schools and our universities.

One of the most important findings of the scientific investigation into the affairs of youth which was piloted by our organisation, (this was provisionally mentioned to me), is that Afrikaner youth stands for and desires complete Afrikaner/English integration, and do this without any clarity about what it implies and where it is logically leading.

We should have expected this finding if we had reflected what a difficult struggle nationally aware Afrikaans teachers in our schools, and Afrikaans lecturers at our institutions of higher educatiotion, have to inculcate the Afrikaans world-view, cultural context and life-style into Afrikaner youth, and encourage them to maintain and enrich these attitudes, within a neutral and divided educational system.

Since the war years our organisation has been campaigning, by means of intensive study, at Bond Annual Congress and public conferences, for a national educational policy founded on our Christian-national world-view which, with central control but provincial execution, would soon put an end to divided education at the secondary school level and to an untenable educational neutrality. The conceptual legislation for this is ready and we have been given the promise that it will be tabled next year. Our time to prepare our youth for their particular task within the process of Afrikaans/English integration is running out.

6. Another basic factor is related to this issue, namely that the growing immigration supplement to our white population is a strengthening of the English-speaking community in all areas of life, including the English world-view. It is all very well to keep the controlled framework of immigration under surveillance, but the fact is that immigration is not an advantage to the Afrikaner in order to extend his language, culture and world-view to the non-Afrikaans community, but just the opposite, a strengthening of the language and culture of the English-speaking people in our country.

We know only too well that we must try to mesh the immigrant into our group, but we know equally well that it would have to happen against all the laws of natural interpersonal intercourse and thus can only succeed in a few individual cases. Mother-tongue education in our country also leads to the children of immigrants, with a few exceptions, attending English schools.

7. We must also bear in mind that the English world-view and life-style in South Africa is favoured by currents and events in the Western world, especially in North America. English culture in South Africa bears an obvious modern liberalistic stamp and is directly and intimately connected with the present Western world in content and form, by the English language, which is the most widespread Western language.

Where Afrikaans culture finds itself next to, and opposed to, English culture in South Africa, it thus simultaneously comes into direct and intimate contact with Western culture as such, and thus with all its contemporary, especially American, expressions. The continual strengthening of English cultural life in South Africa by means of the English language, stemming from the whole Western world, therefore means that the Afrikaans/English integration process in our country is actually the integration of an indigenous Afrikaans culture with the Western world-culture, carried and fed by the English language.

8. The sixth and perhaps most important proposition with regard to our survival as Afrikanervolk, touches a standpoint which could swing the process of Afrikaner/English integration and everything connected with it directly and strongly in our favour rather than in the favour of the English-speakers. This circumstance is fourfold.

233

(a) The Afrikaans Calvinistic world-view is in essence impossible to integrate with the English deistic-humanistic world-view;

(b) Afrikaans is an African language, rooted in Africa, flows from the African soil and African history, and is thus not easily uprooted in Africa by a Western non-African language;

(c) The Afrikaner's history of the bitter and the sweet, of defeats and triumphs, of revilement and rebellion – even of murder of man, woman and child – and this often stemming from the English-speaker in South Africa, is not easily eradicated from the system of our nation. Just like its language, its history is and remains the life-blood and creative source of a nation's independent existence;

(d) Furthermore – the healthy and happy relationship between the white community and the non-white communities in South Africa and in Africa, is a relationship borne by the Afrikaner, is a part of our Afrikaans world-view and life-style. The more apartheid as a political policy is accepted by the English-speakers of our country, the better our chances of drawing them closer to us, rather than the other way about.

We must take all these basic propositions into account, if we are serious about the survival of the Afrikaners.

III. Conditions and Requirements for the Survival of the Afrikaner Nation.

1. We have stated that the survival of the white community in South Africa and the happiness and well-being of the non-white peoples of South Africa depend on the survival of the Afrikaner nation with its own language, culture, character and life-style, growing out of our Christian-national world-view. If the Afrikaner were completely anglicized, the white community of our country would increasingly accept the English world-view as an integral part of the present liberalistic world-view of the Western world, and then, as in the U.S.A., would move in the direction of white and non-white integration. That would lead not only to the end of the white community in South Africa but also, as a further consequence, to non-white South Africa, like the rest of Africa, falling into a state of chaos and poverty and finally being overcome by communist China.

2. If it is thus desirable and necessary from the point-of-view of the whites and non-whites of our country that the Afrikaner nation should survive with its own language, culture and character, we must know precisely what this implies and how the essence of the Afrikaans language, culture, world-view and character can be maintained and extended in the process of Afrikaans/English integration.

3. It comes down to the fact that our organisation should outline a clear purpose for ourselves in this connection and that we should carry this purpose over to the outside world in such a way that it is accepted and lived out not only by the Afrikaner, but eventually also by our English fellow-citizens and all the non-white peoples of our country.

4. This purpose can be nothing less than, to formulate it for our organisation, the complete political nationalisation and eventual afrikanerisation of our English compatriots – if this can still be done. We shall in any case not be able to stop the eventual complete

234

cultural integration of Afrikaners and English-speakers in our country while our control of this process is of a very limited kind.

If we should leave this integration process to itself, it would undoubtedly lead to the predominant anglicisation of the Afrikaner and that would mean the end of his own distinctive cultural life. We speak too readily of an Afrikaans and an English culture in South Africa which can and should be maintained as such by each language group. As I have indicated this is already largely a fiction. And to suppose that our Afrikaans/English co-operation, and thus integration, can be limited to the political sphere, is superficial wishful thinking.

Therefore our purpose can only be: either the deliberate afrikanerisation of the English speaker or the silent acceptance of the unconscious but certainly growing anglicisation of the Afrikaner. That the communal language of this completely culturally-integrated white community of South Africa would finally be English or bastardised English/Afrikaans or English and bastardised Afrikaans, would then make little difference.

5. If our stated purpose must be the complete political nationalisation and the growing cultural afrikanerisation of the English-speaker in our country in the interests of the whole white and non-white population, we must indicate precisely what this includes or can include and how it can be realised.

The political nationalisation of the English-speaker includes mainly his open support of our country's policy of separate development and of South Africa first. It also implies the permanent Afrikaans acceptance of the British Parliamentary system. But it should also mean that the present system of a Head of State, which is the continuation of the old Governor-generalship under the name of "State Presient", and a separate Head of Government should be changed by the combination of these two functions in a way which would be based on our Republican tradition but at the same time keep pace with our constitutional development thus far. The possibility of a "sapperige" [S.A.P-supporting] Afrikaner with English support regularly being appointed as State President instead of a national Afrikaner should be removed.

6. The aim to nationalise the English-speaker politically will only be of permanent value in ensuring the survival of the Afrikaner nation, if it goes hand-in-hand with the predominant afrikanerisation of our country's economy. Political nationalisation of the English-speaker which does not simultaneously lead to a fair Afrikaans share in our economy, including the press, the film and entertainment-industry of our country, will simply not be of a permanent nature. And there is not much time left to achieve this.

It will no longer be possible to develop the Afrikaans share of the economy, in relation to our numerical strength for the genuine survival of our people and its language, culture and world-view, along the slow path of founding our own institutions and expanding our existing undertakings. The next step is not another economic national congress, but well-planned confidential economic action which is possible and practicable.

In this process our country's industrial, commercial and financial undertakings will still bear a predominantly English stamp, but without taking up the Afrikaner mainly as an employee. If the Afrikaans influence in our economic life grows by means of increasing entrepeneurship and leadership, the anglicising influence will decrease.

A very important factor in this connection is that the Afrikaner still practises and control our agriculture. The farming community is still the strongest single national force in the life of the nation. The stronger and healthier we keep our farming community, the more powerfully Afrikaans nationalism will pervade our country.

7. The successful political nationalisation of the English-speakers, combined with Afrikaans control of our country's economy, including the mass media and the entertainment industry, will not on its own ensure the growing afrikanerisation of our English fellow-citizens until the independent survival of the Afrikaner nation is assured. These are mainly external factors which will only lead to the desired result if the inner energies and ideals which determine the white man's creative, interpretative and scientific work in our country are deeply and genuinely rooted in the Afrikaans spirit and traditions of our country. This will only happen if nationally aware Afrikaners will be and remain our country's great artists, philosophers, scientists and educationists and if the leadership and inspiration will go out from them to the whites and non-whites of our country. And this will only happen on the basis of thorough study, hard work and perpetual effort.

    In this connection we must not forget that the sources of study in our country are predominantly English and that precisely in this sphere the powers that anglicise the Afrikaner are much stronger than those which afrikanerise the English-speaker. And the Afrikaner is led into the contemporary so-called world culture by means of English – i.e. as regards his art, philosophy, science and education. Without our own Afrikaans scientific and expert works and textbooks which must then be translated into English for our schools and universities, the process of predominant anglisation cannot even be checked, not to mention the conversion of the process into one of afrikanerisation.

8. The afrikanerisation of the English-speaker is in its essence an educational task – it must begin in our schools. And it is just here that our basic problem lies. At our Afrikaans schools the Afrikaans child is led into Afrikaans cultural life not by a national educational system, but by a nationally aware corps of teachers through the medium of Afrikaans. In our English-medium schools the children of our English-speaking compatriots and of the great majority of immigrants are led by means of English onto English and contemporary Western cultural life – something which our neutral educational system promotes. Fortunately for us the Afrikaans community provides a growing number of Afrikaans teachers for the English-medium schools.

    The fact remains, however, that our schools contribute very little to the afrikanerisation of the English-speaking community. Here, too, the problem is a lack of suitable textbooks. We shall have to think rationally in order to ensure the survival of the Afrikaner nation in the sphere of education, the central area for everybody, by allowing the Afrikaner's language, culture, life-style and world-view to come into its own in the education of our youth, and by simultaneously ensuring that our language and culture develops a power of attraction for English-speaking youth. How this can be brought about, must be determined by a thorough investigation.

9. This brings us to the most important condition and prerequisite for the survival of the Afrikaner people, a condition, which we can provide without waiting upon others and without involving the English-speaker, and that is the consistent embodiment of our

236

own Christian-national world-view, the pure maintenance of our mother-tongue, Afrikaans, and the honouring of our own history and traditions. These are not three different prerequisites but three aspects of the same prerequisite.

Our Christian-national life- and world-view can shortly be summarised as follows:

The Afrikaans world-view is rooted in the Protestant Christian belief that the Holy Trinity of the Holy Scripture reigns over the whole of reality, created by Him, with man who, created in His image, but fallen into sin and redeemed by Christ, is his fellow-worker on earth. Man can never remove the boundary between God and His creation.

The Afrikaans world-view is an acceptance of the prescriptions, the norms, the truths, the claims of the Bible as the Word of God, for man's activities in all the spheres of life, prescriptions, norms and truths which are regularly announced by our Afrikaans churches and consistently held up to us. Our world-view includes the belief that the life and work of a Christian and of a community which in their ideas, actions and feelings accept the Christian prescriptions as norms, are not only directed by human urges, motives and ideals, but by a calling from God Himself.

The Afrikaans world-view is a conscious acceptance of its own and separate Godly christianising mission in Africa and in the world, for the welfare of our fellow man and to the honour of God.

This world-view had a formative influence on Afrikaans national life which grew mainly out of Dutch national life. Our world-view as well as the new circumstances in which it developed, brought about a change from Dutch urban citizenship, cold practicality and formality to Afrikaans free citizenship, to controlled warmth and simplicity; the Dutch un-heroic was replaced by the Afrikaans individual heroism.

This basic faith and his new life circumstances also caused the Afrikaner to reveal the qualities of submissive – persevering, dependent-independent, self-contained-outgoing, impassive – over-sensitive, reserved-exhibitionistic, stubborn-indulgent, in various nuances and combinations. He falls readily into a condition of apathetic and ill-humoured inertia and of aimless indecisiveness when the integrity of his character weakens.

The Afrikaner follows and supports a national leader of firm principles through thick and thin and shows him the greatest respect and service. But when he is powerless against the circumstances of his life and mistrustful of his fellow-man because he feels himself unjustly treated, his willingness to serve degenerates into guile, into outsmarting-politics, into complaints and reproach and the sowing of suspicion.

The Afrikaner likes to plan ahead as a man of principle, likes describing the road ahead in the smallest detail, enjoys drawing up constitutions – and keeps punctiliously to it even if circumstances later change radically. He is the planner who easily becomes the slave of his plans. He always formulates the principle of a matter beforehand and tries to adopt his experience to it. This often degenerates into a concern for principles which turns every method into a principle. He has no sense of compromise.

10. In order to embody the Afrikaans Christian-national world-view as purely as possible in the Afrikaans national life, it must be clearly distinguished from that of our English-speaking fellow-citizen.

The English world-view is in essence an attitude which is based on, and stems from, the Englishman's practical experience and encounter with reality as he observes it through his senses. Reality as it is precipitated in his world-view consists of energies, facts and things which he as a human being can control and can use to serve him.

His religious attitude is rooted in his practical experience of the good, the beautiful, the just, the efficient and the reasonable. For him the Christian faith is a confirmation of this experience. His guilt and redemption are not an essential component of this Christian belief. God is, logically speaking, a verifiable Power who set this world going according to his own rules, but does not interfere directly in its proceedings. A sharp line is drawn between faith and ideas, between revelation and experience – faith is a private affair.

English national life is essentially the expression of a strong-willed character which is concentrated on self-control, on the practical, the useful and the efficacious. This is concretely expressed in the English ideal of the ''gentleman'' as the knightly, self-controlled, active man of will who exercises and extends his endurance through competitions and trials of strength in the field of sport, at school, in economic life, in national and international politics.

This strong-willed being is, however, as in no other Western community, bound by traditions, conventions, and unwritten laws which characterise English national life, however much the Englishman may feel himself to be an individual. This sense of community leads to a special sense of responsibility towards one another which is expressed in, among others, the typical ''charity''-organisations. English nationalism has so far been the strongest Western nationalism which could spread itself over a large part of the earth without undergoing essential alterations anywhere. It could create a ''Commonwealth'' of the most disparate ingredients without sacrificing any of its own being and culture in the process.

From all this it is clear that the Englishman does not concern himself with the future, that he does not plan ahead. He does what has to be done now and leaves the future to take care of itself. He can simply not understand that other communities might not want to take over his views and institutions, with great thoughtfulness and appreciation, to their own advantage.

11. The afrikanerisation of the English-speakers of our country thus means in essence that the English-speaker has to make the Afrikaans world-view his own; that he will integrate his ideals and life-style with those of the Afrikaner; that he will adopt Afrikaans history as his own; that he will accept Afrikaans as his national language, alongside English as the international community language, of the white population of South Africa, i.e. that the integrating Afrikaans/English cultural life of our country will be embodied more and more in Afrikaans, and that English will increasingly become, in translation and usage, our community's international language, while both will remain the official languages of our country. We shall then be able to speak of Afrikaans – and English-speaking Afrikaners.

12. It is obvious that we are concerned here with a process of generations, a process which will, however, only succeed if our organisation *now* agrees on the proposed plan, and thoroughly plans a rational execution of it. If we cannot agree on what our

aim should be and if we leave the present Afrikaans/English integration process to itself we know, as I have previously indicated, what the outcome will be.

Our organisation now stands, after almost fifty years, before its greatest and most important task. Whether we can still achieve much in this connection to ensure the survival of the Afrikaner nation as an independent cultural community with its own un-bastardised language and a genuine Christian-national world-view, I do not know. What I do know, is that we can and may not avoid this responsibility, especially not by making ourselves guilty of spiritual laziness, of an unscientific and sentimental approach to the question, and of unrealistic wishful thinking.

13. The essential pre-condition to ensure that the English-speaker will claim for himself, and for our enrichment, the Afrikaans world-view; integrate himself more and more with Afrikaans national life; gradually honour and accept Afrikaans as his national Africa-language and accept Afrikaans history as his history, is that the Afrikaner himself should do all this in the first place. An Afrikaner who rejects the Christian-national world-view of his people, who does not use his mother-tongue purely in all circumstances and everywhere, who sacrifices his own national character and who conceals or forgets his own national heritage, is directly contributing to the anglicising of his people and the final integration of whites and non-whites in South Africa. Such an Afrikaner himself puts an end to the survival of the Afrikaner nation.

IV   Our Unity and Outward Policy

1. Even if we should agree on all the conditions and requirements for the survival of our country, even if we should agree on what the factual position is now and what short- and long-term aims should be set up and achieved, and we nevertheless permit our Afrikaner nation to be internally devided in the process of Afrikaans/English co-operation and integration, we have already lost the struggle.

2. And the most important diversive power at the moment is the liberalism of our time which is especially strongly represented by our English-speaking compatriots and their press, and is accepted and propagated by a steadily increasing number of Afrikaners, mostly in cautious and misleading forms.

3. The liberalism of our time – which is the philosophy of the person who has detached himself from his family, his parents, his people; who has detached himself from dogmas, norms and criteria which keep him and reality on a steady course; who subjects himself, like the communist, to a so-called historical urge towards progress and renewal – is the philosophy of the Westerner of our time whose community structure has undergone a revolutionary charge. Like the Western world's community structure in the previous century as a result of the industrial revolution, characterised by an almost unbridgeable class division in the secondary economic sector. This revolution in our time has been followed by a radical development in the tertiary sector; i.e. the services sector, a revolution which has fundamentally altered the structure of our community life.

This revolution in Western community life boils down to the fact that approximately only 10% to 15% of the country's economically active population will make a living in agriculture, only 20% in the factory system and thus almost two-thirds eventually in the service activities, i.e. trade, civil service, the professions, etc. In our country, as far as the whites are concerned, these percentage are already, respectively, 10%, 34% and 56%.

Whereas the class-divisions of the previous century gave rise to communism as a life philosophy, the economic development of our time, in the tertiary sector, which has led to a community structure based only on degrees of difference, is expressed in the philosophy of liberalism which accepts no essential differences between man and man and which proposes no opposition, but only transitions and nuances, between truth and falsehood, good and evil, beauty and ugliness, justice and injustice.

This alteration of structure includes a greater mobility within the community; there are only degrees of difference between the various income groups and everyone can move from one to another; employees become more and more impersonal participants and the leaders of the service activities; just like the most minor officials, are employees; the service-officials' future security is guaranteed by pension funds; all these degrees of difference are only differences in status which go together with positions and external tokens. This is the essence of our liberalistic world.

The liberalism of our time is thus not a philosophy thought out by scientist's which we can accept or reject, but is the philosophy in which the revolution of the contemporary Western world is expressed. You thus realize how difficult it is to combat and overcome this philosophy which is becoming an extension of communism in terms of our time's alterations of structure, especially if we take into consideration the fact that the Afrikaner not only works all the time in close and intimate contact with the English-speaking South African in the tertiary sector and thus ensure their future together, but simultaneously, by means of this community structure, are closely involved with the Western world which, by means of inter-communications media, grows steadily smaller and intertwined and everywhere reveals the same nature and characteristics.

3. The liberalism of our time has led to a horizontal duration of people, namely the line from right to left. This is the line from the so-called conservative point through a middle position, a theoretical-liberalistic position, until the communistic position. This dividing line affects the Afrikaner and English-speaker, as the white community of our country, to the same degree and causes not only the linguistic and cultural differences between the Afrikaner and the English-speakers but all differences between the white community and the non-white communities to be thinned out into only differences of degree.

   Cultural integration which happens on a liberalistic basis has no determining aims but results in arbitrary equality. This line-division of the community thus means the absorption of the Afrikaans/English community into an egalitarian entity on a liberalistic basis and finally, together with the non-whites, into an equal, bastardised, South African community with no specific colour and with no generally accepted norms.

4. This liberalistic line-division is accompanied by definite so-called good and bad associations, namely, they wish the conservative point "bad" descriptions like the traditional – antiquated; the immature-extremistic; the emotionally unliberated view; the fear-ridden dogmatic; and with the moderate point, the liberalistic point and even, for

the communist, with his own position, the "good" associations like the progressive-renewing; balanced adulthood; free intellectual thought; the sensitive and manly voice of the conscience.

Our age has already begun to adopt these associations unconsciously although every thinking man knows that all of these qualities can occur at any point on the line; alongside ignorant liberalists we find scientifically enlightened conservatives; alongside immature moderates we find adult conservatives; alongside an antiquated communist civilisation we can find a renewing conservatism, etc. etc.

But now comes the worst stupidity by which our nation is divided, namely the claim that we must be afraid not only of the dangers of the left but also of the danger from the right! The danger from the right is naturally the "danger" of too definite norms, too high standards, too strict dogmas, too difficult requirements, which are sometimes applied in ways which do not take account of "special" circumstances. To call this a "danger" is certainly to place our future in danger.

The dangers of the left are naturally the dangers of vague norms, or none, of gradual or unlimited equalisation, even of brutalisation and the abyss. The dangers of the left we have always thoroughly perceived and we will continue to combat and struggle against them.

The dangers which we do not, however, sufficiently distinguish and perceive, are: The liberalistic moderate danger which places degrees and nuances between right and left; the danger of compromises between truth and falsehood, right and wrong, good and evil; the danger of shifting standards and norms; the danger of diplomatic and popular manoeuvres for the sake of short-term successes; the danger of a bundling together of conservatives and liberalists in order to avoid the logical consequences of a conflict and thus to obtain a majority vote.

And how all of this ties up with a certain McCarthy in America, with his good or weak insights and methods with regard to his country's problems, I do not know. We are in any case adult enough to handle our own problems in our own particular circumstances without any need of overseas "associations".

A last comment in this connection – and this concerns a fundamental association; if I am always seen non-disapprovingly in the company of a crowd of drunkards, even if I do not drink with them, I am guilty of an association which condones the wrong, the sinful. If the liberalist constantly associates himself with the things which the communist also says and does, he is guilty by association. Let we not try to talk ourselves out of this fundamental guilt by association.

5. This brings us to less dangerous but nevertheless unnecessary association with organisations which not only do not contribute to the afrikanerisation of the English-speakers, but rather can and mostly do tend towards the anglicising and liberalising of especially Afrikaner youth. These associations make claims on our time and energy, which is scarcely being harnessed for our own cause. Can we ever justify this?

6. Our organisation must obviously tackle its task of ensuring the survival of the Afrikaner nation in the interests of the white and all the non-white nations of our country by means of, or together with friendly and congenial outside organisations; organisations which we should help to expand.

241

(a) We think in the first place of our own public arm, the F.A.K. which must be organised and harnessed for this purpose. There are also all the national and local cultural bodies which are under the leadership of brothers. Especially the strong and important "Afrikaanse Handelsinstituut en Sakekamers" and the wide-spread Rapportryers movement can help to carry our task outward into the world.

(b) A second group of friendly bodies with whom we must work closely in this matter, is the S.A. "Akademie vir Wetenskap en Kuns" and all other scientific institutions and bodies, including S.A.B.R.A.

(c) The National Party and its leaders play the decisive role in the process of the political nationalisation of the English-speakers of our country. We shall continually have to consult with the brothers at the head of this important organisation in order to ensure that this process of political nationalisation goes steadily hand in hand with the strengthening of the Afrikaner's economic position, and to ensure that it does not unnoticeably lead to the anglicising of the Afrikaner as far as his own Christian-national world-view, the maintenance of his own language and cultural content and the honouring of his own history are concerned.

In order to ensure the support of our National political leaders we shall have to be given the assurance that no suspicion is sown against the A.B. at any branches of the Party or by certain Parliamentary members or officials – in order to prevent this the A.B. has always permitted a judicial enquiry into it's affairs. From its own side the A.B. will never interfere in the domestic affairs of the National Party and will always instruct its members to give their maximum and faithful support to the National Party and its leaders.

7. To conclude; man can plant and water but without the Godly energy of growth nothing will come into being and nothing can be achieved by man. For our survival the first and last condition and requirement is that we shall plant and water in such a way that God's blessing will rest on us. He will allow our people to survive, as long as His work is done and it glorifies Him. May our Afrikaans churches never desert our people as a people in our striving after our own survival in realisation of our God-given calling and may every Afrikaner and every Afrikaner family always be found in our one "Boerekerk" where the Word of God will be proclaimed until the end. If God is for us, who will be against us?

Let us then as Brothers, without ever tiring, build our Afrikaans national pyramid firmly and strongly on its own Christian-national foundation to the honour of God and the security of the independent survival of the Afrikaner nation with its own genuine Calvinistic world-view and mission, its own language and culture, as our permanent tribute to the late Br. Hendrik Verwoerd.

Sunday Times report on March 24, 1963 on the Broederbond grip on the church.

It was headlined:

Broeders tighten hold on D.R.C.
Afrikaners join fight against "unhealthy grip"

The report stated:

Well over 40 per cent of the Ministers of the three Afrikaans churches are members of the Broederbond or its youth wing, the Ruiterwag.

This disclosure is made in a report of the findings of a group of prominent Afrikaner business men, intellectuals and farmers who recently investigated two secret societies.

Furthermore, the findings of the investigators indicate that the D.R.C. today is more firmly in the grip of the secret societies than ever in the past.

Other points emerging from the inquiry are:

- Broeders fill all key posts, from editorships of church magazines to executive positions;

- The violent campaigns against Freemasonry and "new deal" thinking on colour issues, were inspired by the Broederbond and Ruiterwag.

- Prominent Afrikaners who do not belong to the secret societies – or abuse their ideas – are discriminated against in public life.

The report was drawn up against the background of growing hostility to the Broederbond's "unhealthy grip" on Afrikaner life.

This hostility flared up recently in the Free State over a court case, and in Middelburg, Transvaal, where the secret society squeezed three members out of the Management Commitee.

Within the N.G. Kerk itself, there is mounting concern over the Broederbond's influence in purely religious matters. Two rings – Ventersdorp and Brakpan – have asked the Southern Transvaal Synod for a probe into the Broederbond's church activities.

Resistance expected

When the issue is discussed early next month, Broeders and Ruiters are expected to fight any attempt to expose their activities.

The last Dutch Reformed Church committee which investigated the Broederbond found that it was a harmless cultural organisation. Of the 5 committee members, however, 4 were Broeders.

The latest anti-Broederbond report says: "It is a tragedy that relatively so few Afrikaners realise what damage these exclusive secret societies are doing to our national life. Some even doubt the very existence of these societies.

"Fortunately, it is slowly becoming evident that these self-appointed groups of 'super de luxe' Afrikaners seek domination not only over the so-called enemy, but over their fellow-Afrikaners, too.

"A great deal of suspicion is growing among good Nationalists who do not belong to these secret societies. They are painfully discovering that Broeders and Ruiters discriminate against them, as well as against the so-called enemies of the people."

This had become blatantly obvious in the way Broeders were apparently given preference in promotions in the Civil Service, at universities and in business.

"Most of the men who, during the last three or four years, have made spectacular rises in public life by way of appointment, are Broeders or Ruiters. Some of them have been catapulted from virtually nowhere into high positions – simply because the Broederbond wants its yes-men in key posts.

"On the other hand, non-conformist Afrikaners are denied promotion or frozen out of prominent positions. Very few men who do not belong to one of these secret societies have any hope today of reaching the top.

"The independent thinker who speaks out openly is treated as a public enemy. He will be harassed at every opportunity and in every possible way by devious, secret means.

"Whispering campaigns will be used to discredit him, without his ever having an opportunity to defend himself or face his adversary. Or he will be smeared in the Afrikaans Press as a liberator enemy of the people.

"One D.R.C. Professor is being secretly labelled on the platteland as a Communist, although he is known throughout South Africa as one of the most outspoken effective and informed voices against Communist ideology.

"In this way, he is being discredited in the eyes of church members."

The report says that the secret societies are a "social disease" because they exploit the fear psychosis of Afrikaners and pervert Afrikaner idealism.

Students controlled

"Many students at Afrikaans universities are unaware of the Ruiterwag's activities, even though it virtually controlls student life in some centres.

"But those student leaders or junior staff members who think for themselves are either secretly smeared as liberals or quietly excluded from senior positions."

While many had joined the secret societies for the highest motives, they were guilty for not speaking out against injustices committed by these organisations.

Annexure L

Sunday Times report of June 30, 1963 on the booklet by Prof A. van Selms in which he condemned the Broederbond on Theological grounds. It appear under the headline: "**Van Selms Attacks the Broederbond. 'Broeder' church members are hipocrites.**"

The report stated:
Professor A. van Selms, Professor of Semitic Languages at the University of Pretoria, has launched a scathing attack on the Broederbond. He especially warns against the dangers which this secret organisation holds for the church.

Professor Van Selms compares the Broederbond's system of infiltration into other organisations with that of Communists.

He contends that Broederbond members of the church are hypocrites. At meetings they pray for divine guidance; but they are compelled to ignore the arguments of their colleagues because they are committed to vote or argue the way the Broederbond has ordered them to do.

The professor says: "I declare openly that I regard the continuance of membership of the Broederbond by somebody who calls himself a Christian as a lack of moral judgment."

Professor Van Selms makes this attack in a 15-page pamphlet, which was published yesterday. It is titled "Church and Secret Organisation, with reference to the Freemasons and the Broederbond."

Professor Van Selms, a Doctor of Divinity, spent several days in the witness box at the Geyser trial, where he gave expert evidence on behalf of Professor Geyser.

This is the first time Professor Van Selms has openly attacked the Broederbond.

He says in the pamphlet that "it is obvious that the church is public and acts publicly." After quoting many texts, Professor Van Selms explains, on theological grounds, why it is so.

"The church knows no secret doctrine. The doctrine of the church is, in its whole, a public doctrine. There are no doctrines which the church hides from the public and discloses only to a small privileged group."

He rejects as a fallacy the allegation made by people – "we will not call them learned men" – that there are no religious objections against secret societies, because the church in the first centuries of its existence was allegedly a secret body.

Even during all the persecutions "the church never made a secret of its doctrine, aims and methods."

Discussing secret discussions in the church, which are allowed under certain circumstances, the Professor says:

"Absolutely unthinkable in the church is the existence of groups, colleges, organisations or any other institutions, of which the members are not known by name.

"The existence of such bodies would be in absolute conflict with the public character of the church.

Dangers

"The church takes no decisions which are not brought to the public notice. It takes no actions to which other people may not be witness."

He points out the dangers of secret organisations to the church and compares the system of Communistic infiltration with that of secret societies.

"It is known that a minority of only 10 per cent, which comes well organised and thoroughly prepared to a meeting, usually succeeds in turning the meeting its way and obtains control of the key positions by filling them with its supporters.

"The Communists in the past played this game with great fervency and competency in several countries. Today, however, it is not only the Communists who are doing this. They find good imitators in opposite camps.

"Should these tricks be known to the other members of the meeting they could resist them; but the other members do not know that a secret scheme is, in fact, being operated."

Professor Von Selms continues: "They think that it is spontaneous support, which the one gives to another, and have no suspicion that everything has been pre-arranged.

"In innocence, they come to the meeting: and, as honest people, they come to it with open minds.

"So it happens that the honest become the victims of the secretly organised group, often without realising anything about it.

"The secret group does not reveal itself; its power lies in its hypocrisy."

Professor van Selms further points out that the danger for the church lies in the fact that the members of such a secret body are party to a previous decision taken in secret.

"There is no point in arguing or deliberating with them at the meeting. At the meeting they cannot talk and act in accordance with their own insight and conscience. They are bound before they come to the meeting."

In a final chapter, Professor Van Selms poses the question: "With all this, do I have the Broederbond in mind?"

He replies: "Yes, most definitely, and especially the Broederbond . . . Of course, it is also applicable to other secret organisations."

Referring to the Freemasons, he says that "the danger of the Freemasons for the church is not nearly as great at this time and in this country, as that which is threatening from the Broederbond. I am no member of the Broederbond, and I am also not a Freemason . . .

"But the secrecy in which the Broederbond is shrouded, is far greater than that which surrounds the Freemasons.

"It has often happened in my life that people have told me that they were members of the Freemasons; it has never happened to me that someone has told me that he was a member of the Broederbond.

Freemasons

"Of the Freemasons there is an extensive literature, both by members and opponents. Anybody who wants to, can take note of the aims and methods of Freemasonry. Books and pamphlets by the Freemason organisation itself are often published.

"But, as far as I know, the Broederbond has never put out a document in which it makes itself known in public. One can search through all the libraries in this country without ever finding a history of the Broederbond.

"As nobody has ever told me: 'I am a Broederbonder; I was never in a position to warn such a person personally against the road on which he finds himself."

Annexure M

Theological motivation for objections to the existence of the Broederbond by members of the Gereformeerde Kerk (Reformed Church – Doppers) submitted to church bodies in 1963.

Published in a report in the Sunday Times of September 8, 1963, with headlines:

"Why did Synod not probe activities of secret Broederbond?"

The report said:

At the 1936 Synod two resolutions concerning secret societies were discussed, says the petition from members of the Gereformeerde Kerk. Article No. 84 dealt with Freemasons, and the Synod reaffirmed its 1897 decision as quoted above – and referred the matter to a commission for further investigation.

Regarding the resolution which asked the church "to express itself on other secret societies and organisations such as the Broederbond," a report of a commission was accepted (article No. 85) that "on the information available, the Synod has no desire to investigate the case of the Afrikaner Broederbond, and thus leaves the matter alone."

A Ds. S.J. van der Walt asked that his vote be recorded against the decision.

In attacking the contradictory decisions of the Synods of 1936 and 1958, the petitioners now say:

"It is undoubtedly clear that the Synodal decision of 1897, Section 155, refers to all secret societies without exception. The Freemasons are only quoted as an example. It is said of all secret societies that anybody who is a member of such a society cannot be a member of the Gereformeerde Kerk, and if that is the case, then he is the subject of mutual admonition and official discipline.

"It is further clear that the Afrikaner Broederbond, in fact, is a secret society, as appears from Section 73 of its constitution; as the decisions of the Synod of 1936, Section 85, and the Synod of 1958, Sections 305 and 306, imply; as it also appears from the statements by Ds. D. P. M. Beukes, at the Synod of the Nederduits Gereformeerde Kerk of the Southern Transvaal in April, 1963, and as it appears from publications in the Press."

The petitioners further express their amazement that the 1936 Synod did not want to investigate the Broederbond and that the 1958 Synod decided to uphold the decisions of 1936 and 1897.

"The Synod argues these contradictory decisions on: 'By reason of available information' (1936) and because at the Synod of 1936 'the documents were tabled' (1958). But these documents and information are not referred to in the Decisions (Handelinge) as if the members of the 'church may not know on which grounds the honourable Synod took these contradictory decisions and, after their attention was drawn to it, yet still upholds it'."

Closed doors

Their second objection is that the Broederbond is contradictory to the nature of the church.

"According to the Scriptures and Confessions, the true believer knows only one brotherhood, that is in Jesus Christ, in whom they are united with heart and will as members of one

247

body. This brotherhood, this family membership, excludes every other brotherhood (Matthew 12:48)."

"This brotherhood is public . . ."

They point out that the Broederbond is a closed society because only special people are invited to it. As evidence of this the report of Ds. D. P. M. Beukes to the Nederduits Gereformeerde Southern Transvaal Synod is again quoted.

"The brotherhood of Christ works in public . . . whereas the Broederbond works in secret, behind closed doors (Section 73 of the Broederbond Constitution).

"The brotherhood in Christ has no secrets, and especially not secret doctrine . . . The Constitution, aims and functions of the Broederbond are secret, and discussions are held behind closed doors. Only seldom, and then because of pressure from outside, is information given to non-Broeders, information which is considered not to be damaging to the Broederbond.

Secret signs

"The membership of the Church, the brotherhood in Christ, should be known to everybody and may never be hidden (Mark 8: 38). On the other hand the membership of the Broederbond is secret; with secret signs the Broeders identify each other; only in a few cases may a person admit that he is a 'member', but in general it should be concealed."

As far as this aspect is concerned they say that "the membership of the brotherhood in Christ excludes membership of the other brotherhood. "Nobody can serve two masters." (St. Luke 16: 3).

"Supervision by the church cannot be exercised over somebody who has made promises of secrecy. A Christian who places himself under the supervision of the Church Council (Kerkraad) withdraws a part of his life from that supervision because he is bound by a promise of secrecy to the Afrikaner Broederbond.

"He can also not bring to the notice of the Church Council concerned sins which he sees in the faith or life of a fellow Broeder in the organisation."

Annexure N

Sunday Times report of January 27, 1978 on the question of secrecy. It was entitled:

The bond of silence –

The report stated:

The most remarkable characteristic of the Afrikaner Broederbond is the tight discipline and total secrecy it has been able to enforce on members from the early Twenties.

True, there have been leaks, but they have been relatively few considering there are now more than 11 000 members and the organisation is 60 years old.

Broederbond operations are more secret than those of the security police or even the Bureau for State Security (BOSS), whose activities can sometimes be glimpsed in court, and whose telephone numbers are in the directory.

With the Broederbond everything is secret: Membership, office-bearers, activities.

Members are, of course, sworn to secrecy on induction. Secrecy is emphasised at almost every meeting and in every document. Loose talk, even between father and son, or husband and wife, is strictly forbidden.

A good example of the obsession with secrecy is newsletter 3/76/77 which informed members of the Broederbond's move from the Christiaan de Wet Building to Auckland Park:

Phone personally

"Our office now is in the new building, Die eike, 1 Cedar Avenue, Auckland Park, Johannesburg. Our telephone number is 31-4161. (This was changed to 726-4345 on August 6, 1977, when the new automatic exchange at Auckland Park came into operation).

"This must not be supplied to non-members, and friends (members) are requested to phone personally and not to use the number through their private secretary or secretaries.

"Although we can be reached through the FAK's (Federasie van Afrikaanse Kultuurvereniging) number, it must rather be avoided, because the lady on that switchboard has not been informed about our affairs.

"Our office is on the first floor and is marked as Uniediensburo (Edms) Bpk. Visiting friends (members) can use the stairs or lift to the first floor and, at the office, ask for the official they want to see.

"It is definitely not necessary to make inquiries on the ground floor, which is occupied by the FAK and Rapportryers. Although the male personnel of the FAK are friends (members), the females are not all married to members. Unnecessary inquiries, therefore create embarrassment.

"Also remember that our second floor is occupied by our youth organisation, Junior Rapportryers, Jeugraad and ASB (Afrikaanse Studentebond). The ASB organiser is not a member."

The newsletter warned, too, that casual visitors, friends of Broederbond members or other people may be in the building at any time, and that membrs must never assume that anyone they encounter in the building is a Broederbond member.

A few months later (July 1, 1976), members were again reminded about the need to inquire only on the correct floor, because some members had made indiscreet inquiries on the ground or second floor.

To complete the security arrangements at the building, the Broederbond appointed Mr J.J. Schoeman, a retired member from Vereeniging, as caretaker. He lives in a flat on the top of the building.

The Bond has a number of postboxes which it uses, and it has set out strict instructions on how memers should communicate by post. This involves the use of phoney names of individuals or "businesses".

These procedures, postbox numbers and names are changed regularly.

The last time was in April, 1977. When members were told: "An extraordinary circular regarding the addressing of postal matter is included . . . This replaces the existing instructions in your possession, which must be destroyed."

Every year the officie closes between Christmas and New Year, as it did recently from December 23 to January 3, and members are told not to post letter or make telephone calls in this period.

Secretaries and treasurers who go on leave during December must arrange for the safe-

249

keeping of all Broederbond documents where circulars should be sent in their absence to obviate the security risk of unclaimed letters.

Broederbond documents must not be copied without the permission of the Executive Council. Where such permission is obtained, a careful check must be kept of all copies made, as members were reminded in a circular dated March 26, 1976.

One Broeder found himself in hot water when it was discovered he had a tape recorder at a meeting. He appeared before the Executive Council and only his "good attitude" (goeie gesindheid) saved him from expulsion (April, 1, 1976).

The Executive Council also recently forbade blacks and coloureds to be employed at braais.

"Sometimes they are within hearing distance of the meeting place," a circular warned (May 3, 1976). It ordered members to report breaches of this rule "so that steps can be considered".

Termination of membership in the Broederbond is announced in circulars, which also instruct members not to discuss Bond affairs with these former members.

Sometimes the office has to warn against people who are mistakenly regarded as members. The October, 1977, circular stated: "Your attention is drawn to the fact that Professor Dawid de Villiers, of Stellenbosch (also known as Heilige Dawid), is not a member It appears he is accepted as one and has already been given information about our organisation and the Ruiterwag."

Every security risk is reported, such as when two Broederbonders were heard discussing Bond affairs in a restaurant.

"Discussions in public places like restaurants, hotels lounges, etc, must be avoided at all costs," the executive instructed (October, 5, 1976).

The next month, members were warned against dubious methods of identification, such as using certain phrases to establish membership.

One such phrase is: "Do you also eat grapes?"

All members were asked urgently not to use this method because it could lead to great embarassment.

"It happened recently that a non-member was invited to a meeting." (November 22, 1976).

The safekeeping of secret Broeder documents is emphasised regularly. The office must know at all times which documents branches have.

"Missing documents must be traced," the executive said (February 2, 1977).

"Old documents must be destroyed. Divisional committees must delegate somebody to go through the documents with the secretary and to burn the old ones. A list of destroyed documents must be attached to form R."

The Ruiterwag serves as a kind of junior Broederbond. The organisations have basically the same aims, but in situations where a father belongs to the Broederbond, and his son to the Ruiterwag, they must not discuss the fact. (August 1, 1977).

Strict security

"Open discussion of the two organisations' activities (between father and son) is strongly condemned and must not be allowed under any circumstances.

"It is a violation of confidentiality which the Executive Council will view in a serious light."

Members attending annual meetings are not allowed to arrange their own accommodation at hotels, or with relatives who are not members.

"If they arrange their own accommodation with members, they must supply us with the addresses." (April 1, 1976).

The meetings are held in the strictest security, members sometimes not knowing where they will take place until shortly before the time.

Members guard the doors and nobody is allowed in without proper proof of membership. An identity ticket must be shown every time the hall is entered (April 1, 1977).

Annexure O

The Broederbond octopus in 1944 when in opposition. The diagram was drawn by Dr. E.G. Malherbe then head of Military Intelligence.

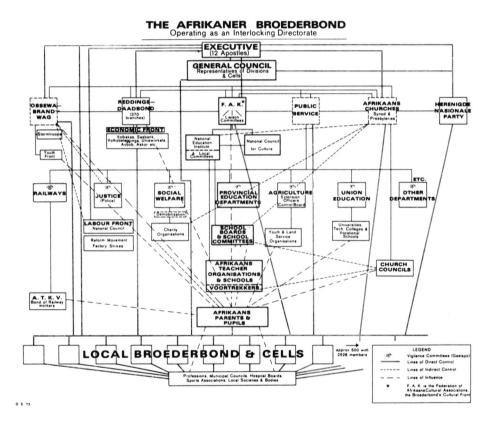

Annexure P

On the opposite page the author illustrates graphically how the Broederbond Octopus tentacles have extended in the South African society.

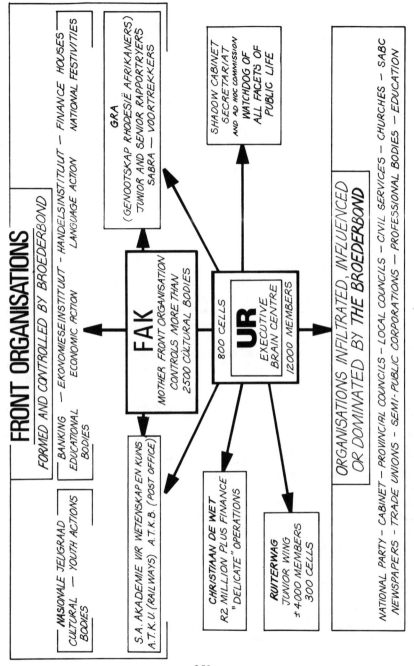

FRONT ORGANISATIONS

FORMED AND CONTROLLED BY BROEDERBOND

BANKING — EKONOMIESEINSTITUUT — HANDELSINSTITUUT — FINANCE HOUSES
EDUCATIONAL   ECONOMIC ACTION   LANGUAGE ACTION   NATIONAL FESTIVITIES
BODIES

GRA
(GENOOTSKAP RHODESIË AFRIKANERS)
JUNIOR AND SENIOR RAPPORTRYERS
SABRA — VOORTREKKERS

SHADOW CABINET
SECRETARIAT
AND AD HOC COMMISSION
WATCHDOG OF
ALL FACETS OF
PUBLIC LIFE

FAK
MOTHER FRONT ORGANISATION
CONTROLS MORE THAN
2500 CULTURAL BODIES

UR
EXECUTIVE
BRAIN CENTRE
12000 MEMBERS

800 CELLS

NASIONALE JEUGRAAD
CULTURAL — YOUTH ACTIONS
BODIES

S.A. AKADEMIE VIR WETENSKAP EN KUNS
A.T.K.U. (RAILWAYS) A.T.K.B. (POST OFFICE)

CHRISTIAAN DE WET
R2 MILLION PLUS FINANCE
"DELICATE" OPERATIONS

RUITERWAG
JUNIOR WING
± 4000 MEMBERS
300 CELLS

ORGANISATIONS INFILTRATED, INFLUENCED
OR DOMINATED BY *THE BROEDERBOND*

NATIONAL PARTY — CABINET — PROVINCIAL COUNCILS — LOCAL COUNCILS — CIVIL SERVICES — CHURCHES — SABC
NEWSPAPERS — TRADE UNIONS — SEMI-PUBLIC CORPORATIONS — PROFESSIONAL BODIES — EDUCATION

Annexure Q

Interview by Prof. Gerrit Viljoen in Rand Daily Mail on August 1, 1978. In it he tries to present NP policy in most favourable light. The headline was: **"Viljoen: verligte on a narrow ledge."**

The report stated:

OF all the millions of South Africans who agree that the original apartheid structure is unworkable, Professor Gerrit Viljoen Rector of the Rand Afrikaans University, occupies a unique position.

As a verligte Afrikaner and one of the National Party's top brains, he is at the forefront of the planning for change. Through his direct contact with the Government's decision-makers, he has access and insight into the direction in which South Africa is being steered. As chief of the Broederbond, he holds the most important position in the secret cell system that is being geared to prepare conservative Afrikaners for change.

In an interview with HELEN ZILLE, Prof Viljoen spelt out what he regards as South Africa's major problems and outlined the alternatives verligte Nationalists believe could provide solutions.

Prof Gerrit Viljoen describes the "realities of the South African situation" like this: Inside South Africa, the majority of blacks reject apartheid. Internationally, racism has become the number-one crime that attracts world hostility. The spirit of the liberation movements has swept over the white-ruled South and there is the growing threat of internal tensions being exploited by super-power rivalry.

"Clearly apartheid's original formula cannot cope with this situation," he says. The solution: "We must learn from our past mistakes and build on the present system to cancel them out."

Prof Viljoen believes that one of the National Party's greatest mistakes was to impose on blacks a policy worked out by whites without consultation. The result has been an overwhelming rejection by blacks of a system regarded as a white formula for the purpose of domination, he says.

He makes it clear that the holding of an all-race national convention to "cancel out" this historical mistake is impossible within the context of National Party politics. It would mean acknowledging the necessity for power sharing between the races, something which Afrikaners have always been promised will never happen.

So the verligte looks for another way out – a way of introducing the principles of negotiation and consultation so that they will appear to have been inherent in the party's basic policy from the start.

At the same time, the verligte attempts to convince blacks that the changes – introduced unilaterally – are genuinely aimed at giving them a joint stake in the future.

It is a narrow and slippery ledge and the verligte has to find issues that can be argued both ways simultaneously. The first step has been taken on the subject of discrimination.

Here the major problem is convincing Afrikaners to give up measures they have always been told were essential to ensure their survival and identity. The way out of this is a reassessment of the concept of identity.

Prof Viljoen believes it is possible to sort out those measures that are essential to maintaining Afrikaner identity and those which under the guise of "identity measures" were only designed to protect the Afrikaner against a black majority as he battled to come to his own under an English imperialist minority.

254

Now these measures only serve to entrench discrimination and must be scrapped, he says. A key example is job reservation.

But he insists there are three vital "identity components" which will have to remain:

• Separate school education.
• Separate living areas.
• A way of regulating a family structure so that the basis of group politics is not destroyed.

"Even if the Mixed Marriages Act must go, we should take the strongest exception to marriage across the colour line," he says.

This statement hits right at the heart of the verligte philosophy and defines the limits within which he is prepared to accept change. The basic premise remains group politics: whites, coloureds, Indians and 10 black ethnic groups.

Prof Viljoen says he accepts that a large number of urbanised blacks have no affiliation with an ethnic group and regard their blackness, not their ethnicity, as the root of their "identity".

He also accepts that he has no right to define for another person what his identity should be.

But he believes it is possible to accommodate this group by "working on the present structure".

In the immediate future, work on the present structure will continue in two main areas.

To start with, he says, there will be negotiation and consultation on the new constitutional proposals until the Coloureds and Indians accept them. "I don't want to believe that they won't accept them," he says. The present format, he explains, was the only way of granting equal rights to coloureds and Indians in a way that would be acceptable to Nationalists.

They had always been promised there would be no joint parliament and no power sharing, so three parliaments were created, the real power passed on to a joint Cabinet Council and the system described as sharing responsibility rather than sharing power.

If this system can be launched, the next step will be to create an "interstate consultative body", to bring together the representatives of the homeland governments with South Africa's mixed Cabinet Council. Urban blacks would have representation drawn from the community councils in this body that would take decisions on inter-state affairs and the problems affecting urban blacks.

The goal, therefore, is a working confederation, in which South Africa and independent homelands retain maximum powers, but meet to discuss and decide on matters of common interest.

Of course, this system can only work if enough blacks go along with it: if urban blacks serve on community councils and homeland leaders take independence.

Chief Gatsha Buthelezi is regarded as one of the major obstacles, because as leader of the largest group, he rejects anything to do with the homelands concept. The verligte Nationalist is searching for ways of making concessions so that Chief Buthelezi will accept independence.

But assuming that enough blacks accept this plan and work within it where do things go from here?

"The policy is entirely open-ended," says Prof Viljoen.

One opinion, of course, is that the groups decide they like this working confederation, where each leader retains maximum power in his own independent territory.

255

But there is another possibility: "In time we may find that the things we have in common outweigh our differences. Then we can opt for closer co-operation until eventually we could decide to become a federation in which all South Africans, black and white, have equal rights within a single system."

The means to this end would be a merger between the South African constitutional arrangement and the inter-state consultative body.

The outstanding irony of this all-race federation option is that it is the one the Progressive Federal Party constantly stresses is the only feasible one.

Prof Viljoen points out that there are two key differences between the federation plans. For Nationalists, a federation can only be built on the basis of group politics. The PFP seeks a federation where divisions are worked out on a nonracial geographic basis rather than a group basis.

The second key difference lies in the methods by which the two parties propose to get there.

The PFP calls for a national convention as soon as possible to work out a new constitution with black leaders. National Party verligtes say it has to go their way – via adaptation and development of the homelands policy.

The interview with Prof Viljoen makes it clear that, in persuading the white right, the most important verligte tactic is to keep the choice open. There must always be a way back and out if things don't work according to plan. Convincing blacks involves entirely different problems: the verligte has to hold out a goal while persuading them to accept his method of getting there.

Prof Viljoen accepts that this method has huge problems, one of the biggest being that each group believes it is being conned in favour of the other.

On the right this could lead to a split in Afrikanerdom – the thing they wish to avoid at all costs.

On the left is the growing black consciousness movement, that accepts that whites have a place in South Africa if they are prepared to fit into an African system. In other words, the black nationalists, like the white nationalists, want to dictate the terms, justifying their claim not on their right to survive, but on their right as a majority group.

While the verligtes are using tactics of semantics and logical argument on the right, they have resorted to police action on the left. They stress, however, that this is necessary only while they make the changes they hope will convince enough blacks of their sincerity and the viability of sharing power their way.

The obvious question arises: are the goal and the method not mutually exclusive?

This could be so – but it is a chance the verligte Nationalist takes because it is the only chance he believes he has.

There is a clear perception that things may not work out this way: time, the world and the majority of South Africans are against them. That is why, in the very top echelons of the Party, a new debate is beginning. As Prof Viljoen describes it: How do we maintain our identity and survive if we lose power?

Annexure R

List of some 1 800 Broederbond members extracted from various documents over a period of time. It is possible that some of those mentioned may have died already, or are no longer members.

ADENDORFF C.H., Manager, Senekal
AUCAMP W.A.S., Regional Manager (Sanlam),
Bloemfontein (De Bloem)
ALBERTS J.L.M., Teacher, Windhoek-Wes
ACKERMAN P.J.P., Pretoria (Olifantsfontein)
7778
ARCHER W.E.C., Farmer, Trompsburg
AGENBAG J.A., SAR, Tiervlei
ARENDT F.W., Post Office, Germiston
ARNOLD A.C., Town Clerk, Windhoek
AGENBACH H.P.M., Wallekraal
ALLEN J.L., W.G.A., Port Elizabeth
AUCAMP I.J., Pretoria, 7786
AUCAMP P.v.Z., Bothaville
ADENDORF I., Bantu Investment Corp., Pretoria
ALBERTSE C.E., Tradesman, Bloemfontein, 4877
ACKERMAN P.C., Farmer, Parys, 2048
ALBERTS B.C., Mine Engineer, Pretoria, 4381
ALBERTYN C.F., Editor/Farmer, Porterville,
1759

BEKKER G.v.G., Farmer, Steynberg, 1310
BOOTHA L.J.C., Farmer/ex MP, Thabazimbi
1785
BOTHA P.B.F., ex Teacher, Thabazimbi, 4846
BONNET P.J.G., Miller, Volksrust, 1805
BROECKMAN C.W., Pensioner, Witrivier, 493
BOSHOFF H.J., Pensioner, Zululand, 4417
BEYERS A.S., Farmer, Lichtenburg, 3686
BOTES N.S., School Principal, Pretoria, 2667
BRINK D.S.v.d.M., Attorney/MEC.,
Rustenburg, 4798
BASSON A.J., Farmer, Picketberg, 4075
BEKKER M.J., Senator, Calitzdorp, 2012
BESTER P.A., Med. Doctor, Bellville, 3648
BLOM J.C.J., Manager Golf Club, Bethal,
5213
BRITZ B.A., Townclerk, Bethlehem, 3356
BOSHOFF J.R., Townclerk, Bloemfontein, 6563
BELLINGAN F.E., Business Manager,
Bloemfontein, 7456
BURGER P.duT., Hosp. Supt., Carletonville,
5352
BOTHA R.P., Businessman, Durban, 631
BÜHRMANN I.C.R., Farmer, Ermelo, 5758
BRINK, A.J., (Prof), Durbanville, 7419
BOTHA F.J., Farmer, Ermelo, 5758
BOTHA A.C., Pensioner, George, 1968
BEZUIDENHOUDT D.H., Stock-Inspector, King-
williamstown, 5546
BOTHA H.J., M.P., Kokstad, 5085

BODEMER H.C., Secr. Social Welfare, Pretoria,
1068
BOSMAN P.E., Secr. Social/Welfare, Pretoria,
1068
BEKKER O.J., Scribe, Senekal, 3668
BREYTENBACH H.P., Farmer, Utrecht, 2704
BRINK C.H., Director, Cape Town, 3304
BEUKES M.J., Farmer Warden
BONTHUYS H.J., SAR, Bloemfontein (Sannaspos)
BEZUIDENHOUT A.P., Farmer, Delmas
BOOYSEN W.H., Advocate, Durban (Port Natal)
BOSMAN H.L.B., Med. Doctor, Eshowe,
BRITZ I., Accountant, Germiston (Sonhoogte)
BRESLER H.A., SAR, Krugersdorp (Republiek)
BADENHORST M.J., Police, Paarl (Drakenstein)
BOSMAN W.A., School Principal, Pongola
BEYERS P.J., Farmer, Riviersonderend
BOTHA T.J., Manager, Boksburg (Genl. Alberts)
BOUWER J.J., Farmer, Griekwastad
BUYS L.J., Minister (Religion), Middelburg (Tvl)
BUYS M.E.L., Civil Service, Somerset-Wes
Hottentotholland)
BUCKLE J.P., Funeral Undertaker, Boksburg-North
BOTHA H.P., Navy, Durban (Dirkie Uys)
BINGLE H.J.J., Professor, Potchefstroom, 1663
BOTHA S.J.J., Director of Companies, Pretoria
Hartebeespruit 7728
BADENHORST C.H., Professor, Wellington
(Groenberg) 1710
BOTHA D., Doctor Specialist, Pretoria (Harte-
beesspruit)
BOSHOFF H.J., Shipping, Kempton Park-Noord
BASSON A.L., Town Councillor, Stellenbosch,
(Simonsberg)
BASSON S.P., Farmer, Devon
BOTHA A., Teacher, Harrismith
BLIGNAUT J.B., Chemist, Benoni
BOTHA P.J., Asst. Magistrate, Witbank (Dirk
Mostert)
BEUKES J.W., Grabouw 7723
BEYERS J.A., Venterspos 7725
BOTHA B.C., Brakpan-Wes, 7724
BASSON L.J., Rouxville, 7783
BOTHA M.C., Manager (Store), Vryheid East
BEKKER C.J., Heidelberg South, 7797
BOTHA G.S.M., Cape Town, 7798
BADENHORST J.J.L., Nigel, 7796
BOOYSEN D.J., Carletonville, 7818
BADENHORST, J.U., Dewetsdorp, 7807
BARNARD A.T., Secretary (Santam), Bellville
(Loevenstein)

BOSHOFF L.F., Manager (Coca-Cola) Brakpan
BOTHA M.F., Secretary (Divisional Council),
  Hofmeyer
BENEKE M.J., Manager (Citrus Coop) Komati
BOTHA C.D., Farmer, Verkeerdevlei
BURGER H.A.J., Principal, Aberdeen
BOTHA L.R., Captain (Police), Benoni-North
BEZUIDENHOUT P.R., Farmer, Christiana
BURGER H.L., Minister (Religion), Kroonstad
BOTHA H.P., Med. Doctor, Pretoria
BUYS S.P.B., Minister (Religion), Barkly-East
BOOYSEN J.J.H., Teacher, Bloemfontein-East
BINGLE P.W., Teacher, Naboomspruit
BURGER P.J., Manager Northern Canners,
  Duiwelskloof
BRINK N.J., Farmer, Viljoenskroon
BASSON M., Dept. Agriculture, Middelburg (Tvl)
BRUWER J.M., Municipality, Swartruggens
BOSHOFF H.C., Teacher, Port Elizabeth
BOTHA A.J., Farmer, Warmbad
BOTMA M.C., Building Contractor, ex-MP
  Walvis Baai
BUYS J., Teacher, Benoni
BADENHORST A.A., Teacher, Louis Trichardt
BOTHA J.F., Farmer, Vaalhartz
BRINK C.T., Teacher, Warmbad
BRINK A., Petrus Steyn
BRITZ A.W., Durban
BOTHA T.S., Boshof
BOTHA S.D.P., Coligny
BOTHA M.J., Jozini
BARTLEMAN T.W., Marquard
BARRY R.v.R., Robertson
BOTHA A.P.J., Volmoed
BOTHA F.J., Devon
BOTMA A.J., Makwassie
BURGER J.J.B., Niekerkshoop
BARNARD W., Klerksdorp
BARNARD H.J., Pretoria
BEUKES C.J., Oudtshoorn
BRANDT R.B., Randburg
BREEDT A., Pretoria
BOSMAN W.J.J., Parys
BOTHA P.J., Potchefstroom
BUYS P.W., Minister (Religion), Potchefstroom
BIERMAN D.F., Pk. Uitval
BESSELEN J.E., Potchefstroom
BERGH G.J., Hartenbos
BERGH M.M., Bothaville
BEZUIDENHOUT N.J.D., Kareedouw
BOSHOFF S.P.E., Pretoria
BURGER H.L., Minister (Religion), Bloemfontein
BEUKES D.P.M. Minister (Religion), Moderator
  NGK, Johannesburg, 2735
BOTHA S.P., Cabinet Minister, 4418
BOTHA T.J.N., Chief Secretary AB, Alberton 6159
BEYLEVELDT F., Under secretary AB, 5749

BOOYSENS B., Professor, Stellenbosch
BOTHA R., Architect, Pretoria
BOSHOFF Prof. C.W.H., Chairman SABRA
  Pretoria
BOTHA R.H., Johannesburg
BADENHORST J.F.B.
BADENHORST W.H.
BARNARD J.P., Pensioner, Benoni, 516
BESTER C.J., Farmer, Bredasdorp, 5065
BARNARD S.J., Pensioner Teacher, Calitzdorp,
  2168
BOTHA J.J., Pensioner, Durban, 1011
BRUWER D.J., Attorney, Edenville, 1473
BUHRMAN H.T., Farmer, Ermelo, 713
BOTHA P.W., Prime Minister, George, 4487
BADENHORST F.H., Farmer, Harrismith 1563
BADENHORST W.A., Farmer, Harrismith, 2266
BOSMAN L.D., Inspector of Educ., Heilbron, 916
BESTER W.J., Pensioner Farmer, Hermanus, 3457
BARNARD H.F.P., ex Teacher, Knysna, 2125
BADENHORST C.G., Farmer, Koffiefontein, 2589
BRUMMER B.J., ex Veterinary, Kroonstad, 2097
BRITS J.J., Inspec. of Schools, Kroonstad, 1704
BRINK M.L., Pensioner/School Principal,
  Krugersdorp, 44
BADENHORST H.W., Farmer, Marquard, 1822
BADENHORST C.H., Farmer, Messina, 3261
BRINK G.E., Director, Montagu, 3060
BARNARD Dr. D.J., Emeritus Minister (Religion)
  Parys, 2404
BIERMAN D.F., Teacher/Farmer, Potchefstroom,
  2294
BOSHOFF S.P.E., ex College Principal, Pretoria,
  3077
BUYTENDAG Col. B.M.G., Security Prime
  Minister, Pretoria, 7266
BOTES P.W., Lecturer, Pretoria, 4887
BOTHA M.C., ex Minister, Roodepoort, 2073
BENADE J.M., Minister (Religion), Rustenburg,
  1732
BOSHOFF W.H., Civil Servant, Salisbury, 6430
BOSHOFF F.P., Director G.R.A., Salisbury, 6837
BRINK H.E., ex Professor, Stellenbosch, 4525

COETZEE P.W., Farmer, Burgersdorp
CONRADIE J.F., Farmer, Montagu
CRONJE H.J., Farmer, Edenburg
COETZEE J.H., Minister Religion, Elandsfontein
CONRADIE J.F.T., Civil Service, Pretoria
  (Wesmoot)
COETZEE S., Carpenter, East London
CARSTENS J.E., Secr. (Rembrandt), Paarl
  (Di Patriot)
CALITZ J., Accountant, Port Elizabeth
COETZEE J.P., Director, Pretoria (Breukelen)
CILLIE C.D., Farmer, Paul Roux

CONRADIE R.P., Adm. Officer (University) (Stellenbosch) (Eerste rivier)
CELLIERS J.G., Messenger of the Court, Glencoe
COETZER W.C., Vryheid, 7769
COETZEE, A.G., Knapdaer, 7760
COETZEE J.C.v.Z, Alberton, 7726
CROUSE P.L., Port Elizabeth West, 7722
COETZER F.W.C., Lichtenburg, 7787
COETZEE L.C., Pretoria (J.J. Bosman), 7876
CONRADIE J.G.J., Accountant, Durbanville
COETZEE J.L., (Minister (Religion), Johannesburg
COETZEE J.N., SAR, Germiston
COETZEE W.C., Scientist, Witbank
COMBRINK P., Minister (Religion), Upington
CRAFFORD J.E., Farmer, Chipinga
COMBRINK L.W., Dentist, Worcester
CRONJE J.M., Missionary, Carletonville
COOKE B., Farmer, Barrydale
CHURCH S.J., Businessman, Bothaville
COERTZE J.H., SAR, Residensia
CONRADIE T.A., Sasol, Sasolburg
COETSEE F.P., Teacher, Christiana
CRONJE P.J., SAR, Ontdekkers
CLAASSEN J.D., Minister (Religion), Port Elizabeth
COETZEE N.J.A., Teacher, Johannesburg
CLAASSEN N., Scientist Onderstepoort, Pretoria
CILLIERS A.v.Z, Knysna
COETZEE N.C., De Wildt
COETZER C.R.F., Pretoria
CLOETE F.S.M., Ermelo
COETZEE J. Chr., Professor, Potchefstroom
COETZEE A.G., Teacher, Potchefstroom
CELLLIERS D.J., Potchefstroom
COETZEE J.H., Professor, Potchefstroom
CLAASSEN D.J., Potchefstroom
CRONJE H.L., Volkskas, Ladybrand
CILLIERS J.L., Hermanus
COETZEE L.C., Pretoria
CONRADIE F.D., MEC Cape Town, 4765
CLAASSEN J.T., Potchefstroom
CILLIE P.J., Former editor Die Burger
CUYLER EBEN, Former Senator, Johannesburg
COETZEE P.S.Z., Minister (Religion), Bloemfontein, 561
CROUS T.J.H., Farmer, Brandfort, 1941
CLOETE C.A., Attorney, Harrismith, 696
CILLIERS J.L., Magistrate, Humansdorp, 5176
COETZEE P., Pensioner, Krugersdorp, 1568
COMBRINK G.F.M., Manager Co-op, Potgietersrust 2590
CLOETE J.M.J., Pensioner, Pretoria, 1800
CLOETE O.A., Minister (Religion), Richmond, 2154
CRONJE P.J.J., Farmer, Theunissen, 2692
CLOETE J., Pensioner, White River, 1646
CONRADIE P.J., SAR, Bloemfontein, 2973
COETZEE J.W., Minister (Religion) Ceres, 3565

COETZEE C.P., Bodyguard State President, Pretoria, 6347
CRONJE G., Professor, Pretoria, 1409
CLAASSEN S.P., Farmer, Wepener, 2778

DE LA HARPE M.M., Med. Doctor, Pretoria (D.F. Malan)
DE JAGER D.F., Farmer, Cornelia
DUVENHAGE J.P.M., Magistrate, Hertzogville
DREYER H.M.E., Minister (Religion), Klerksdorp North
DE VILLIERS J.F., School Principal, Lady Grey
DE WET D., Teacher, Pretoria (Boerefort)
DE VILLIERS J.A., Teacher, Chrissiesmeer
DE JAGER J.J., Farmer, Douglas
DE JONGH J.V., Farmer, Graafwater
DE KOCK D.J., Manager (Co-op), Venterstad
DE KLERK W.A., Inspector (Dept. Lands), Vryburg
DIPPENAAR D.J., Teacher, Alberton
DEKKER L.W., Accountant, Bloemfontein (D.F. Malherbe)
DE KOCK J.N., Dentist, Henneman
DU PLESSIS G.F., AB Auditor, Johannesburg (Emmarentia)
DE BEER T.L., Auditor, Johannesburg Klipriviersberg)
DE VILLIERS S.M., SABC, Johannesburg (Oorwinning)
DU TOIT J.J.F., Teacher, Johannesburg (Joon van Rooy), 4224
DELPORT W.H. Attorney, Port Elizabeth West, 4572
DREYER A.G., Dentist, Johannesburg (Danie Theron)
DE WET J.H. v. H., Med. Doctor, Malmesbury (Swartland)
DU PLESSIS J.P., Teacher, Fochville
DU PLESSIS E., Med. Doctor, Vredefort
DE WET L.J., Agent (W.G.A.), Cradock
DU TOIT A., Minister (Religion), Duiwelskloof
DE BRUIN J.G., Agent (K.O.P.), Paul Roux
DE BEER S.J., Attorney, Adelaide
DE WET W. De V., Farmer, Robertson
DE BEER Z.H., Advertisement Agent, Johannesburg (Linden-Noord)
DREYER P.J., Asst. Magistrate, Tzaneen
DU TOIT P.E.J., Miner, Swartruggens
DU PREEZ A.J.J., Snr. Clerk (Co-op), Lichtenburg
DELPORT H.P.J., Manager (Volkskas), Witbank
DE BEER Z.A.J., Mafeking, 7727
DE WET P.W., Pietersburg (Piet Joubert), 7728
DU PLESSIS M.A., Pretoria (Voorslag), 7756
DU PLESSIS A.S., Vanderbijlpark (Overvaal), 7800
DE BEER P.J. van Z., Bloemfontein (Berg en Dal), 7813
DE VILLIERS L.C.J., Pretoria (J.J. Bosman) 7820
DE WET A.J.P., Johannesburg (A Kriel), 7891

259

DE VILLIERS I.L., Minister (Religion),
Otjiwarongo
DE REUCK F., Asst. Manager, Caledon
DE SWARDT J.J., Senior Lecturer (Univ.), Pretoria,
8287
DU TOIT P.E.J., Miner, Swartruggens
DU PREEZ A.J.J., Clerk (Co-op), Lichtenburg
DE VILLIERS J.H., Farmer, Barrydale
DE GRAAF H., Dentist, Durban
DE LA REY J.H., Lecturer (Teachers Training),
Heidelberg
DREYER N., Teacher, Pretoria
DE VILLIERS E.E., Elec. Engineer, Carletonville
DE KLERK F.W., Minister (Parliament),
Vereeniging
DE WAAL J.A., Sasol, Sasolburg
DU BOIS N.W., Teacher, Moorreesburg-
Koringberg
DE JAGER G.F., SAR, Pretoria
DU PREEZ A.J.J., Teacher, Benoni
DU PLESSIS A.S., Iscor, Vanderbijlpark
DU PLESSIS G.F.C. Iscor, Vanderbijlpark
DU PLESSIS D.P., Farmer, Brandfort
DE LA BAT R.S., K.W.V. (Market Research)
Paarl
DE KOCK S.D., Municipality (Engineer), Randburg
DURANDT L.C., Attorney, Vrede
DU TOIT H., Med. Doctor, Welkom
DU PLESSIS G.F., Agric. Instit., Stutterheim
DURANDT J.A., Minister (Religion), Esselenpark
DU PLESSIS G.N., Prisons Dept., Pretoria
DE KOCK C.J.J., Hertzogville
DE WIT W.A., Umtali
DELPORT J.P., Hertzogville
DELPORT P.W.J., Johannesburg
DE JAGER J.T.H., Salisbury
DU TOIT P.J., Worcester
DE KONING L.W., Brakpan
DE SWARDT D.M.S., Cornelia
DU PLESSIS F.R. de V., Reivilo
DE WET P. le R., Wolseley
DU TOIT B.A., Minister (Religion), Germiston
DE VOS E., Man. Director, Florida
DE BRUIN J.R., Kuilsrivier
DU TOIT D., Pk. Golela
DU TOIT F.P., Pearston
DU PLESSIS L.J., Potchefstroom
DE WET J.M., Potchefstroom
DU PREEZ D.C.S., Potchefstroom
DU TOIT S., Potchefstroom
DU TOIT S., Professor, Potchefstroom
DU PLESSIS J.S., Potchefstroom
DUVENAGE S.C.W., Prof., Potchefstroom
DUVENAGE J.P., Potchefstroom
DU PLESSIS P.J., Potchefstroom
DEKKER G., Professor (Publication Board),
Potchefstroom 209

DU TOIT J.H., Potchefstroom
DREYER J.G.M., Potchefstroom
DIPPENAAR M., Potchefstroom
DE KLERK A.J., Cornelia
DU TOIT, Minister (Religion), Estcourt
DE JAGER L., Postmasburg
DU PREEZ H.P., George
DU PREEZ M., Pretoria
DE VILLIERS Tol., Gansbaai
DU PREEZ P.J., Breyten
DU PREEZ P.J., Kestell
DE WIT J.M.A., Ermelo
DU TOIT S.J., Riviersonderend, 7850
DE KOK J.S.B., Stellenbosch, 7874
DE KLERK P.F., Graaff-Reinet
DU PLESSIS H.J.C., Middelburg C.P.
DE BEER J.J., Minister (Religion), Pretoria
DREYER D.C.L., Johannesburg
DU TOIT R.S.J.
DE BRUIN P.H.
DE LANGE J.P., Professor RAU, Johannesburg
DE VILLIERS C.V.
DE JAGER A.J., Farmer, Aberdeen, 4905
DE BEER J.H., Pensioner, Benoni, 3250
DU TOIT P.J.N., Businessman, Bloemfontein, 2358
DU TOIT J.A., Farmer, Bredasdorp, 4519
DAVEL J.S., Farmer, Calvinia, 541
DU BUYS A.J., Farmer, Bloemfontein, 5379
DE VILLIERS I.J., Farmer, Coligny, 4725
DE VILLIERS I.S., Farmer, Coligny,3585
DEVILLIERS de la H., Chairman SAAU, Ficksburg
DE JAGER M.P., Farmer, Kestell, 979
DU TOIT D.S., ex-Farmer, Kirkwood, 2483
DE VILLIERS B.M., Farmer/Dir. of Comp.,
Malelane, 3751
DU TOIT F.P., Farmer, Malmesbury, 5487
DU TOIT M.M., ex-Farmer, Mooreesburg-
Koringberg, 2613
DE VILLIERS J.W., ex-Teacher, Odendaalsrus,
2116
DE WIT H.L., Attorney, Petrus Steyn, 1583
DUNN P.J., ex-Postmaster, Philipstown, 2864
DE WITT J.J., Farmer/ex-Police, Porterville, 5297
DU PLESSIS Dr. P.J., Vice-Principal, Potchef-
stroom, 3001
DIPPENAAR M.H., Farmer/Owner Drive Inn,
Potchefstroom, 3989
DE KOCK N.E., Emeritus Minister (Religion),
Pretoria, 2340
DU PLESSIS P.J.C., SAR, Pretoria, 3143
DELPORT P.C., Asst. Secr. Agriculture, Pretoria,
6047
DE LANGE J.T. Manager Co-op, Pretoria, 1588
DIEDERICHS Dr. N., ex-State President, Pretoria,
560
DE KLERK W.A.C., Teacher/Farmer, Schweizer
Reneke, 215

DREYER J.F., Farmer, Sterkstroom, 5529
DE VILLIERS A.H., Strand, 2536
DU PLESSIS W., Farmer, Tarkastad, 4975
DE BRUYN P.W.J., Teacher, Vryburg, 1013
DU TOIT E.J., College Principal, Wellington, 1039
DU PLESSIS Sand, ex Administrator,
  Bloemfontein, 3910
DU TOIT J.H., Businessman, Calvinia, 2229
DE VILLIERS D.J., Farmer, Ficksburg, 3735
DE JAGER P.R., Senator, Johannesburg, 5992
DE KLERK J. ex-Minister, Krugersdorp, 2490
DEACON N.J., Manager Meatboard, Pretoria, 5682
DU PLESSIS D.F.H.F., Businessman, Pretoria,
  9080
DREYER T.F.J., Senator, Pretoria, 271
DU TOIT J., Med. Doctor., Pretoria, 271
DE JAGER C.I., Farmer, Pretoria, 4644
DE WET J.M., Farmer, Standerton, 943
DE VRIES H., Farmer, Strand, 2536
DU PLESSIS H.R., M.P., Vryburg, 4302
DU PISANIE F.J., MPC, Vereeniging,
DU TOIT J.F., Minister (Religion), Pretoria, 1883
DE BRUYN G.C.J., Businessman, Pretoria, 3589
DU PLESSIS W.C., ex-Administrator, Windhoek,
  2600

ESTERHUYSEN D.J., Auditor, Vasco
  (Ruyterwacht)
ERASMUS J.A., Clerk Forestry Dept., Eshowe
EBERSOHN P.C., Inspector, Springs, (Geduld)
ENGELBRECHT G.C., Inspector Bantu Education,
  Bloemfontein (Bergen Dal)
ESTERHUIZEN H.C., Farmer, Victoria-Wes
ENGELBRECHT J.J., Germiston (Sonhoogte), 7729
ERASMUS D.F., Johannesburg (Rand Sentraal)
  7757
ENSLIN J.S., Dept. Customs, Port Elizabeth
ELLIS A.P., Dept. Justice, Pretoria
ELS A.L., Farmer, Heilbron
ERASMUS J.M., Schoolboard Secretary,
  Ladysmith
EYSSEN J.C.B., Dept. Information, Pretoria
ELS J.C., Volkskas, Wesselsbron
ESPOST V.A., Teacher, Vasco
ENGELBRECHT C.J., Teacher, Humansdorp
ERASMUS A.M., Teacher, Kakamas
ERASMUS P.J.E., Farmer, Pretoria (Kaalfontein)
ERASMUS L.J.B., Farmer, Koppies
ERASMUS D.F., Minister (Religion), Heilbron
ELS C.J., Farmer, Cathcart
ESTERHUIZEN W.C., Keetmanshoop
ENGELBRECHT G.P., Vrÿzee
ELS N.J., Benoni
ENGELBRECHT P.J.B., Minister
  (Religion), Luipaardsvlei
EISELEN G.T.S., Potchefstroom

ENGELBRECHT G.J.C., Farmer, Adelaide, 3190
EBERSOHN P.H., Stationer, Clocolan, 1428
ERASMUS J.J., Asst. Agent, De Aar, 4407
EISELEN Dr. W.W.M., Commissioner General,
  Pietersburg, 1826
ERASMUS J.C.K., Pensioner, Port Elizabeth, 864
ERASMUS J., ex-Farmer, Rustenburg, 6975
ELLIS H.J., Furniture Manufacturer,
  Worcester, 5230
ERLANK A.E., ex-Senator, Bellville, 1566
ELOFF G., Professor, Bloemfontein, 2307
ERASMUS J.C., Defence, Pretoria, 5687
ERASMUS P., Farmer, Somerset East, 2840

FERREIRA L., Farmer, Chipinga
FOURIE P.J.V., Dentist, Randfontein
FECHTER L.F., Accountant, Knysna
FOURIE W.A.J., Dept. Prisons, Kroonstad
  (Kroonheuwel)
FERREIRA J.T., Port Elizabeth (Diaz), 7758
FOUCHE L., Pretoria (Voorslag), 7790
FOUCHE G.W., Zastron, 7801
FOURIE I.B., Ceres, 7821
FOURIE N.J., S.A. Police, Kemptonpark-North
FOURIE J., Lecturer, Paarl (Bergriver)
FRANZSEN P.J.J., Missionary, Riebeeck-West
FOURIE G.J., Teacher, Noupoort
FOURIE J., Tradesman (SAR), Bloemfontein
  (Sannaspos)
FOURIE N.P., Manager (Bookshop), Florida
  (J.G. Strydom)
FOURIE R.G., Teacher, Henneman
FOUCHE A.F., Manager, Witbank
FERREIRA G.T., SAR, Florida
FOURIE J., Defence, Pretoria
FICK J.J., Farmer, Reitz
FILMALTER L.J., Iscor (Scientist), Pretoria
FRASER H.C., Accountant, Johannesburg
FOURIE O.J., Lecturer, Wellington
FOURIE P.J., Springs
FERREIRA C.J., Koster
FOURIE D.P., Hennenman
FOURIE C.M., Hennenman
FOURIE J.S., Pk. Vivo
FOURIE J.P., Potchefstroom
FOUCHE P.J., Rouxville
FOURIE J., Defence, Tempe
FOUCHE J.J., ex-State President, 1899
FUCHS C.D., ex SABC, Johannesburg
FRANCHEN J.J., Businessman, Johannesburg
FOURIE H.C., Farmer/Teacher, Babanango
FICHARDT G.A., Director, Bloemfontein, 3401
FICK Dr. J.C., Farmer, Duiwelskloof, 5702
FERREIRA T.I.J., Farmer/Miner, Ogies, 4563
FERREIRA J.F.W., Farmer, Witbank, 5893

GROENEWALD A.P.J., Farmer, Griekwastad
GOUWS J.J., Inspector, Worcester (Drosdy)
GELDENHUYS J.N., Manager, Port Elizabeth
GREYLING J.A., Insp. Religious Studies
  (Minister) Pretoria (Pres. Kruger)
GROBLER J.H., Head Agricultural College,
  Potchefstroom East
GROBBELAAR G.J., School Principal, Kimberley
  (Vooruitsig)
GOBREGTS C., Med. Doctor, Bonnievale
GERRYTS E., (Sanlam), Bellville (Thalman)
GOUS E.P.F., Grootfontein, 7730
GRIESEL J.D., Schweizer Renecke, 7731
GERBER P., Molteno, 7759
GREYLING C.L., Wakkerstroom, 7812
GELDENHUYS J.M., Farmer, Lichtenburg
GROBLER G.H., Scientist, Strand
GROBBELAAR J.J., Med. Doctor, Benoni
GOUWS D.J., Manager (Volkskas), Piet Retief
GENADE G.J., Tradesman (SAR), Vasco
GROBLER N.J., Minister (Religion), Nelspruit
GOUGH J.P., Police, Greytown
GOUWS J.J., Police, Cape Town
GREYLING P.J., Police, Krugersdorp
GROBLER J.H.F., Bloemfontein
GILIOMEE P.J., Perdekop
GROENEWALD P.G., Worcester
GERICKE H.S., Kempton Park
GOUWS S.J.L., Pretoria
GREYLING B.C., Makwassie
GEYSER P.R., Mafeking
GRIMBEECK C.L.G., Vanderbijlpark
GROBBELAAR W.P., Ermelo
GROENEWALD M.D., Salisbury
GOOSSENS A.P., Potchefstroom
GROBLER B.R., Potchefstroom
GELDENHUYS L.P., Sanlam, East Londen
GROENEWALD B.H., Schweizer Reneke
GREWAR D.W.M., Gumtree, Ficksburg
GERICKE Dr. J.S., former Moderator N.G.K.
  Stellenbosch, 1999
GROBLER W.J.S. ex-MP and former FAK secretary
  Springs
GROVE Dr. E.L.,
GREYLING D.J., Defence, Pretoria, 9361
GRUNDLINGH A.E., ex-Mineworkers Leader
GREYLING Dr. E., Minister (Religion), Dordrecht,
  1564
GILDENHUYS B J.P., Farmer/Landboard Inspec.,
  Naboomspruit, 3680
GOUS P.N.J., Pensioner, Pretoria, 1945
GULDENPFENNING G.L., Inspec. Bantu
  Education, Pretoria, 1943
GELDENHUYS P.A., ex-Farmer, Rustenburg, 3605
GROBBELAAR P. de V., Minister (Religion),
  Strand
  1456

GROENEWALD H.J., Church Official,
  Trompsburg, 1095
GREEFF P.D.N., ex-Teacher, Ventersburg, 1116
GREYLING B.P., Farmer, Wakkerstroom, 149
GREYVENSTEIN C.P., Farmer, Barkley East, 2089
GROENEWALD E.P., Professor, Pretoria, 2118
GROENEWALD A.P., Attorney, Calvinia, 5387
GERICKE B.W., Farmer, George, 6271
GERMISHUYS J.A., Farmer, Heilbron, 2487
GEERTSEMA J., Civil Serivce Commission,
  Pretoria, 9108
GROBLER P.J., Civil Service, Pretoria, 3023
GREEFF C.J., Secr. Justice, Pretoria, 249
GROBLER Z.C., Minister Religion, Sannieshof,
  6303
GROENEWALD W.J., Horticulturist, Ventersdorp,
  207
GRUNDLINGH B.H., Farmer, Vredefort, 850
GROBLER J.M., Secretary, Stellenbosch, 5866

HOWARD W.F., Med. Doctor, Aliwal North
HEIGERS D., Secretary, Generaalsnek
HOLTZHAUSEN P.S.H.F., Pretoria (Derdepoort)
HUYSAMEN J.F.L., Supt. Prospector, Vredendal
HUMAN J.F., SAR, Windhoek West
HUMAN I.V., SAR, Residensia
HERMAN F., MP, Attorney, Warmbad
HENSTOCK J.G.J., Teacher, Knysna
HAVINGA J.F.E., Insp. of Education, Krugersdorp
  (Republiek), 4138
HAAK J.F.W., Attorney ex-Minister, Bellville
  (Tigerberg) 2916
HATTINGH M.J., School Principal, Springs
HEYNS M.L., Civil Service, Fraserburg
HOUGH D.J., Attorney, Pietersburg
HOUGH M.J., Teacher, Pietersburg (P. Joubert)
HAVENGA J.F., Dept. Prisons, Kroonstad
  (C. Cilliers)
HENDRIKZ P.J.R., Farmer, Marquard
HENNING C.B., Paarl (Bergrivier), 7733
HATTINGH A., Dewetsdorp, 7732
HORN V.P.B., Florida (Koos de la Rey), 7770
HANEKOM C., Pietersburg (P. Joubert), 7890
HUGO G.R., Farmer, Worcester
HAVINGA C., Teacher, Brits
HATTINGH A., Teacher, East London
HARMSE G.D., Teacher, Pretoria
HECHTER L.P.J., Commandant (Airforce),
  Pretoria
HOFFMAN S.S.B., Teacher, Nylstroom
HAASBROEK C.F.S. Police, Potchefstroom
HEYSTEK A.S.L., Uniestaal Corp, Vereeniging
HUGO J.P.J., Volkskas, Zeerust
HARMSE C.J.B., Police, Potgietersrust
HAASBROEK L.C.S., Minister (Religion),
  Vredefort

262

HENNING D.S., Teacher, Brakpan
HEYNS J.M., Secr. Pro Rege Press, Potchefstroom
HAUPTFLEISCH C.J.V., Secr. Hospital Komani
Queenstown
HUMAN J.J., Farmer, Warrenton
HEYNS M., Farmer, Senekal
HEYNS H.S., Fort Beaufort
HURTER D., Tsumeb
HENNING J.J., Potchefstroom
HOON J.H., MP Kimberley
HANEKOM H.A.C., Piketberg
HANEKOM F., Kempton Park
HUYSER P.B., Verwoerdburg
HATTINGH J.M., Potchefstroom
HAMERSMA P.J., Professor, Potchefstroom
HUYSER H.W., Potchefstroom
HEESE D.C., Cape Town
HAVENGA J.L.D.,
HIEMSTRA R.C. former Commandant General,
4152
HURTER J.A., Managing Director Volkskas, 3298
HERBST A.J.O., Asst. Secretary AB, 7663
HATTINGH H.J., Under Secretary, 7231
HOEK P.W., Professor, Pretoria,
HATTING J.H., Johannesburg
HORNE V., Johannesburg
HATTING C.J., Bethlehem
HENNING Dr. C.R., Farmer, Bloemfontein, 389
HECHTER L.G., Attorney, Elliott, 2561
HEUNIS J.C., Minister/Attorney, George, 8644
HUMAN J.A., Pensioner Butcher, Groblersdal
4017
HOOGENBOEZEM H., Businessman/Farmer,
Heidelberg Tvl.
HUGO P.J., ex-Farmer, Cape Town, 2391
HUGO G.F. de V., Judge, Kimberley, 2799
HURTER J.P., Senator, Kirkwood, 4251
HEYMAN H.C.F., ex-Farmer, Petrus Steyn,
1885
HERTZOG J.A.M., Businessman/Farmer, Pretoria
930
HOFFMANN J.W.S., School Principal, Umtata,
2863
HANEKOM F.v.S., Pensioner (MPC), Strand, 1454
HOFFMANN J.A.G., Farmer, Trompsburg, 3618
HOFMEYER J.M., Farmer, Witrivier, 309
HENNING C.R., ex-Farmer, Zastron, 3548
HATTINGH J.P.L., Farmer, Aliwal North, 4111
HATTING D.L., Attorney, Benoni, 7056
HATTING G.H., Med. Doctor, Bloemfontein
(Knysna), 3369
HEUNIS A.J., Manager, Graafwater, 8873
HARTMAN A., Conductor/Lecturer Wits,
Johannesburg, 4992
HARTZENBERG F., Farmer, Mafeking, 4984
HENNING J.M., MP, Vanderbijlpark, 6382
HUMAN J.P., Teacher/Farmer, Warden, 2688

HAASBROEK G.D., Farmer, Warrenton, 5997
HAVEMANN W.W.B., Administrator, Vierfontein,
4405
HANEKOM T.N., Professor, Stellenbosch, 5325

JOOSTE M.V., Man. Dir., Johannesburg
(Emmarentia)
JAMNECK L., Plasterer, Vanderbijlpark (Overvaal)
JANSE VAN VUUREN, (Uni. Pretoria), Pretoria
(J.J. Bosman)
JOOSTE J.A., Minister (Religion), Burgersdorp
JOUBERT I.J., Town Clerk, Brandfort
JOUBERT L.J., Teacher, Welkom (St. Helena)
JORDAAN S.T., (Sanlam), Port Elizabeth (Wel-
bedacht)
JACOBS D.J.L., School Principal, Schweizer-
Reneke
JORDAAN R.P., Alice, 7760
JOUBERT P.J.W.J., Germiston (Sonhoogte), 7735
JOUBERT J.P., Farmer, Steynsrust
JANSEN VAN RENSBURG R.J., Manager (Co-op)
Nylstroom
JOOSTE J.A., Med. Doctor, Warden
JANSE VAN VUUREN T.J.J., SAR, Alberton
JACOBS P.T., Minister (Religion), Welkom
JOUBERT F.P., Teacher, Dullstroom
JOUBERT J.J., Farmer, Ladybrand
JOUBERT W.N., Otjiwarongo
JOOSTE Dr. C.J., Sabra, Pretoria
JOOSTE J.A., Upington
JOUBERT A.J., Springs
JACOBS T.K., Postmasburg
JOUBERT B.J. le R., Hermanus
JORDAAN S.J., Chairman National Educational
Council
JOUBERT S.J., Brigadier
JOOSTE T., Teacher, Bronkhorstspruit, 1307
JOOSTE S., Teacher, De Aar, 2336
JOUBERT, Pensioner, De Aar, 4406
JOUBERT N.L., Stationmaster, Pretoria, 5038
JORDAAN T.B., ex-Farmer, Somerset East, 2841
JOUBERT Dr. G.J., ex-School Inspector,
Stellenbosch, 1418
JOUBERT J.J., Med. Doctor, Vereeniging, 3131
JONKER N.H., Farmer/Agent Meatmarket,
Vryburg, 3970
JACOBZ F.P., Union Steel Corp. Manager,
Vereeniging, 7055
JORDAAN G.J. Nas. Adv. Educational Board
Vice Chairman, Pretoria, 2631
JOUBERT D.J., Secr. Transport, Pretoria, 2231
JORDAAN J.P., Farmer, Theunissen, 1714
JOOSTE J.P., MPC, Wolmaranstad, 7058
KRIEL C.M., Farmer, Ladybrand
KLEYNHANS J.W., Clerk (Municipality), Port
Elizabeth North

KRUGER A.J., Sr. Adm. Officer (Tvl Educ. Dept)
Pretoria (Derdepoort)
KRUGER J.T., Minister, Pretoria (Libertas), 8048
KOTZE G.D., Farmer, Vaalharts
KRUGER J.A., Deputy Chief Manager, Florida
(J.G. Strydom), 1865
KEEVY J.M.,ex Commissioner Police,
Pretoria, 8125
KEMP K.G., Lecturer Teacher Training, Pretoria,
(Elandspoort)
KLOPPER J.H., Farmer, Utrecht
KRUGER H.W., Attorney, Boshof
KIRSTEIN F.E., Mine Manager, Ogies
KOK J.H.C., Principal, Nylstroom
KEULER D.A., Sutherland, 7736
KOTZE F.G., Vaalharts, 7766
KRUGER T.L., Ermelo (Uitkomst), 7780
KOTZE W.D., Bloemfontein (Kruitberg), 7788
KOCK L.C., Memel, 7814
KRUGER H.L., Pietersburg, 7823
KRUGER A.S., Farmer, Venterstad
KRUGER P.W., Major (Police), Vereeniging North
KOTZE E.C.B., Minister (Religion), Venterspos
KNOETZE C., Teacher, Port Elizabeth North
KOTZE N.J., Farmer, Naboomspruit
KOTZÉ J.N.E., S.A. Navy, Durban
KRUGER G.P., Ou Mutual, Benoni
KOTZEE A.L., Educ. Dept., Pretoria
KRUGER A.J.P., Teacher, Johannesburg
KOTZE A.B., Teacher, Kroonstad
KOTZÉ F.J., Teacher, Randfontein
KRIEK J.G., Municipality, Rosendal
KOTZÉ G.J., Farmer, Springbok
KOTZE L.E., Municipality, Barberton
KOCH A.C.F., Bellville
KLOPPERS B., Hendrina
KOTZÉ H.A., Pretoria
KNIEP L.L., Ventersdorp
KNOESEN C., Germiston
KLOPPERS G.J., Pretoria
KOCK C.D., Paarl
KRUGER W. de K., Potchefstroom
KRUGER T.G., Potchefstroom
KRUGER D.W., Professor, Potchefstroom
KUUN C. du P., former official AB, Johannesburg,
6158
KRIEK H.J., Ladybrand
KRIGE W.A., Minister (Religion), Kleinmondstrand
KOTZE W. de V., Bloemfontein
KOORNHOF Dr. P.G.J., Cabinet Minister and
former chief secretary AB, 6844
KRUGER M.J., Under Secretary AB, 6086
KROGH G.
KNOETZE A.A.N.
KRUGER J.P., Liaison Officer, Bellville, 4462
KATZKE J.J.R., Farmer, Blyderivier, 5234
KOTZE J.H., Farmer, Burgersdorp, 2319

KIRSTEN J.F., Farmer, Alice, 3362
KOTZÉ J.B., ex-Teacher, Moorreesburg-Koringberg
117
KRÜGER Dr. C.M., Iscor, Pretoria, 3206
KRITZINGER Dr. J.H., Professor, Pretoria, 3846
KOK J.A., Manager K.W.V., Robertson, 4043
KACHELHOFFER A.J., Pensioner, Sannieshof,
251
KRUGER C.H., ex-Farmer, Steynsrust, 2907
KRUGER G.J., ex-Bank Manager, Venterstad, 3650
KRITZINGER P.H., Clerk, Nelspruit, 3296
KOEN A.J., Director of Education, Pretoria, 2162
KRUGER J.M.N., Priv. Secr. of Minister, Bellville
9192
KEYTER H.C.A., MP, Clocolan, 1699
KLINGBIEL J.F.G., Works Foreman, Lydenburg,
3696
KRIEL G.J.P., Minister (Religion), Moorreesburg-
Koringberg, 6729
KEISER L.M., Farmer, Leeudoringstad, 3653
KORSTEN Gé, Singer Businessman, Pretoria, 6747
KOTZENBERG H., Secretary, Pretoria, 6362
KIESER A., Director, Pretoria, 2450
KRIEL Dr. F.H.J., Minister (Religion) Standerton,
2517
KIRSTEN J.F., Professor, Stellenbosch, 1998

LE ROUX F.S., Teacher, Durban (Port Natal)
LOUW H.J., Teacher, Reitz
LE ROUX A.A.J., Accountant, Worcester
LE ROUX C.J.P., School Principal,
Hartebeesfontein
LE ROUX P.J., Magistrate, Laingsburg
LINDE J.F., Minister (Religion) Pretoria (Voorslag)
3818
LAMPRECHT H.L.J., Manager (Volkskas), Vrede
LE ROUX P.J., Chemist, Burgersdorp
LE GRANGE J.A., Police, Komati
LE GRANGE J.H.B., Police, Kingwilliamstown
LUBBE F.C., Farmer, Eshowe
LOUW J.W., Dept. Head, Pretoria (Waterkloof)
LOXTON A.J., Kingwilliamstown, 7739
LOOTS J.M., Barkly West, 7763
LANGLEY T., MP Pretoria (Klapperkop), 7755
LOURENS J.P., Pretoria (Kwaggarand), 7774
LIEBENBERG C.J., Pretoria (Meintjieskop), 7737
LOUBSER J., Springbok, 7738
LIEBENBERG W.H.M., Vryheid, 7792
LE ROUX P.J., Kakamas, 7824
LOMBARD W.A., Major (Defence), Pretoria
(Harmonie)
LANGE J., Teacher, Bethal
LUBBE A.M., Veterinary, Vanderbijlpark (Overvaal)
LE ROUX D.J. (J.F. sn)., Farmer, Wellington
LOMBAARD E.R., Iscor (Personnel), Pretoria
LOUW C.F.M., Farmer, Hendrina

264

LOUW J.P., Iscor (Librarian), Pretoria
LIEBENBERG F.J., Government Printers, Pretoria
LÖTTER D.C., Manager Letaba Estate, Tzaneen
LANDMAN K.P., Farmer, Wakkerstroom
LLOYD J., Post Office, Potgietersrust
LABUSCHAGNE J.H., Teacher, Middelburg (Tvl)
LOOTS F.W., Defence, Windhoek
LOUW G.N., Researcher Agric. College, Middelburg
(Cape)
LE ROUX F.P.J., Med. Doctor, Welkom
LAUBSCHER H.W., Springs
LOUW J.L., Oudtshoorn
LIGTHELM C.J., Alberton
LIEBENBERG D.A., Ceres
LOUBSER P.E., Durbanville
LOMBAARD J.F., School Inspector, Potchefstroom
LESSING F.J., Teacher, Potchefstroom, 2091
LOURENS J.H., Potchefstroom
LE ROUX A.J., Potchefstroom
LABUSCHAGNE F.J., Potchefstroom
LIGHTHART N., Volkskas, Mosselbaai
LAMPRECHT J.C., Warrenton
LLOYD H.B., Springs
LOMBARD H.L., Fouriesburg, Boshoff
LOEST P.B., Alice
LOUW J.H.P., Springbok
LE ROUX J.M., Med. Doctor, Stellenbosch
LANGE H.O., Volkskas, Kimberley
LAMBRECHTS P.H.S., Petrusburg
LOUW J.F., Pretoria
LOUW Dr. M.S., Actuary, Kaapstad, 764
LE GRANGE L.
LOUBSER P., Boland
LAURIE H. de G. Perskor, Johannesburg
LE ROUX D.P., Farmer, Bonnievale, 2430
LE ROUX P.M.K., ex-Minister, De Rust, 1633
LE ROUX S.D.P., Farmer, De Rust, 3158
LOMBARD J.S., Chairman Rent Board,
Elandsfontein, 1775
LOUW J.H., School Principal Krugersdorp, 4734
LOMBARD A.v.A., Town Clerk, Krugersdorp, 4092
LUBBE W.J.G., Minister (Religion), Napier, 2400
LE ROUX J.H.J., Farmer, Oudtshoorn, 3674
LUTZ F.T., Dir. of Comp., Paarl, 2393
LUTZ G.P., Farmer/Businessman, Paarl, 2055
LE ROUX A.J., ex-Teacher, Potchefstroom, 1410
LUTZ F.G., ex Farmer, Pretoria, 355
LOURENS J.H., Emeritus Minister (Religion),
Randburg, 2315
LA GRANGE J.C.H., Pensioner, Rustenburg, 1388
LE ROUX P.J., Pensioner, Stellenbosch, 4329
LOTZ E. de V. ex-Attorney, Stellenbosch, 4329
LUBBE W.J., Church Official, Strand, 1519
LOUW J.A., Attorney, Vryburg, 3689
LEHMAN J.P., Pensioner, White River, 812
LUTZ J.J., Manager F.V.B., Kaapstad, 9580
LE ROUX J.Z., Attorney, Johannesburg, 6703

LOUBSER J.A., Attorney, Kakamas, 2438
LE ROUX F.J.H., Farmer, Laingsburg, 5393
LOUBSER W.A., Farmer, Loeriesfontein, 6587
LÖTTER G.J., Emeritus Minister (Religion),
Pearston, 2695
LINDEQUE P., Regional Magistrate, Pretoria, 5386
LE ROUX F.J., Pretoria, 3898
LE ROUX J.B., Farmer, Paarl, 3875
LANDMAN J.P., Magistrate, Queenstown, 4766
LOOTS J.J., Speaker, Queenstown, 3079
LABUSCHAGNE J.S., Farmer, Sannieshof, 4983
LOUW W.P., Senator, Walvisbaai, 6316

MIDDEL G.P., Farmer, Devon
MOOLMAN D.T.du P., Minister (Religion), Graaff-
Reinet
MULLER D., Secretary, Vasco (Ruyterwacht)
MARAIS N.B., Farmer, Alice
MALAN D., Captain (Police), Welkom, (Dagbreek)
MALAN E.S., Teacher, Clanwilliam
MALAN P.J., Med. Doctor, Clocolan
MARAIS P.G., Attorney, Bellville, (Loevenstein)
MEYER P.J., Chairman SABC, Johannesburg
(Emmarentia), 787
MULLER S.L., Minister, Robertson, 4970
MEYER T.C., Med. Doctor MP, Bothaville, 1348
MÖLLER H.F.S., Farmer/Businessman, Wolseley
MARAIS A.I., Agent (W.G.A.), Steytlerville-
Jansenville
MYBURGH A.J., Asst. Director (R.O.N.H.),
Pretoria (Waterkloof)
MEYER I.A., Attorney, Johannesburg, 8410
MUDGE P.S., Farmer, Otjiwarongo
MEISENHOLL F.S., Researcher (N.O.K.),
Johannesburg (Ciskei)
MALHERBE S.G., Missionary, Goudini-Breërivier
MALHERBE W.P.M., Med. Doctor, Pretoria
(D.F. Malan)
MARAIS W.J. v.d. M., Engineer, Pretoria
(Voorslag)
MEYBURGH C.J., Springs, 7771
MOUTON F.D., Fraserburg, 7702
MULLER J.H., Benoni, 7815
MARAIS J.F., Accountant (Volkskas), Strand
MÖLLER H.F., Accountant, Strand
MALAN A.J., Chemist, Heidelberg South
MARAIS P.B.M., Secretary (Santam), Cape Town
(Oranjezicht)
MÖLLER J., Businessman, Dewetsdorp
MULLER H.C., Auditor, Kaapstad, (Oude Molen)
MULLER G.L., (Jnr.), Farmer, Lindley
MEYER A.C., Teacher, Boksburg (Genl. Alberts)
MUSSMANN L.E.L., Teacher, Carletonville
MARÉ J.P., Teacher, Springs
MEYER J.H., Med. Doctor, Alexandria
MAREE A., Insurance, Generaalsnek
MOCKE C.H., Divisional Council, Kenhardt

265

MALAN J. de L., Civil Servant, Pretoria
MARAIS W.T., Director, (Omnia), Pretoria
MEYER J.P.C., Teacher, Pretoria
MALHERBE F.J., Volkskas, Swellendam
MOOLMAN J.N., Air Force, Vasco
MATTHEE C.J., Farmer, Willowmore
MARAIS F.A.J., Teacher, Pretoria
MARAIS J.C., Volkskas, Brandfort
MEYER R.F. v.d.W., Farmer, Humansdorp
MOOLMAN H.J., SAR, Klerksdorp
MARAIS I.J., Lecturer (Teacher Training),
   Durban
MARAIS B., Farmer, Kroonstad
MISCHKE E.v.H.E., SABC, Johannesburg
MARAIS J.I.F., Civil Service Commission, Pretoria
MEYER A.M., Magistrate, Somerset-East
MYBURGH B.J., Volkskas, Vredefort
MARX C.B., Teacher, Postmasburg
MOOLMAN H.J., Farmer, Vierfontein
MOSTERT J.P., Empangeni
MÜLLER H.W.S., Marquard
MAREE H.O., Pretoria
MALAN M.A., Windhoek
McLACHLAN R., ex-MP/Commissioner General,
   Randburg, 3352
MALAN J.A., Kaapstad
MEYER B.C., Middelburg (Tvl)
MENTZ P.K., Minister (Religion), Middelburg
   (C.P.)
MEYER J.S., Bloemfontein
MATTHEE C.F., Stutterheim
MALAN J.P., Potchefstroom
MEYER H.B., Jeffreysbaai
MALAN George, Patensie
MAREE C.G., Kleinmondstrand
MALAN L. du P., Pretoria, 7832
MULLER Tommy, Johannesburg
MOOLMAN H.J., Johannesburg
MARAIS E.J., Rector University, Port Elizabeth,
   4955
MALHERBE R.C., Pretoria
MALAN D.G., Attorney, Johannesburg
MALAN D.S., Publications, Johannesburg
MARAIS Dr. M.D., Business leader
MASSYN W.C.
MINNAAR H., Pensioner, Bellville, 2440
MARAIS J.P.A., Pensioner Teacher, Ceres, 1607
MAREE S.A., Farmer, Harrismith, 1637
MARTIN H., Farmer, Hartbeesfontein 1105
MULLER C.J., Dir. of Companies, Johannesburg
   3035
MEIRING P.G.J., Journalist, Johannesburg, 3494
MALAN J.N., ex-Administrator, Cape Town, 3600
MEIRING J.A.S., Inspector Educ., Kroonstad, 3139
MYNHARDT I., Pensioner, Kroonstad, 928
MEYBURGH P.J., Secr. Mineworkers Union,
   Krugersdorp, 4629

MARITZ J.S., Welder, Lydenburg, 3028
MINNAAR A.J., Farmer, Letsitele, 4093
MARAIS W.J.E., Restaurant Manager, Paarl, 4289
MAREE C.J., Ex-School Principal, Parys, 1129
MARAIS ADV. J., Pensioner, Pretoria, 2677
MÖNNIG Dr. H.O., Pensioner, Pretoria, 665
MAREE W.A., ex-Minister, Pretoria, 3669
MULLER Dr. H., ex-Minister, Pretoria, 3380
MARAIS D., Farmer, Pretoria, 1274
MAREE J.B., Farmer, Schweizer-Reneke, 2292
MUSSMAN P., Farmer/Schoolboard secre.,
   Schweizer-Reneke, 2293
MULLER H., Farmer, Vanderbijlpark, 1431
MALAN S.P., Farmer/Chairman Meatboard,
   Wakkerstroom, 1891
MALAN G.S., Building Contractor, Wellington,
   2767
MARTINS Theo F., Farmer (MPC), Volksrust, 4943
MULDER C.P., Minister, Randfontein, 4750
MEYER A.S., Manager, Malmesbury, 3090
MARAIS P.S., MP, Bellville, 7022
MEYER P.H., Ambassador, 6273
MOSTERT M.C., Farmer, Bothaville, 3716
MARAIS B.P., Manager, Johannesburg, 3803
MARAIS J.C., Manager Santam, Cape Town, 1869
MUDGE H.F., Farmer, Paarl, 5483
MALAN J.P., Professor, Pretoria, 3912
MARTINS H.E., ex-Deputy Minister, Pretoria, 4425
MARAIS J.N., Magistrate, Standerton, 2903

NEL C.P., Attorney, Bellville (Voorpos)
NORTJE R., Chemist, Harrismith
NAUDE S.J., Church Official, Bloemfontein
   (Spitskop) 788
NAUDE, S.J., Attorney, Bloemfontein
   (Spitskop)
NEL A., Professor Dept. Geography, Stellenbosch
   (Die Pieke)
NORTJE J.H., Farmer, Fraserburg
NIEMAN W.A., Manager (Volkskas), Warden
NEL B.J., Storekeeper, Kingwilliamstown, 7761
NEL J.G., Secretary (Hospital Saulspoort)
   Northam
NEL M.J., Brigadier (Prisons), Pretoria
NIEWOUDT G.G., Civil Servant, Springbok
NEL H. du P., Mealie Board, Pretoria
NEL T.C., Teacher, Pietermaritzburg
NEL J.H., Miner, Randfontein
NEL D.S., Vanderbijlpark
NAUDE W.L.E., Vrede
NEL F., Durban
NEL J.W., Potchefstroom
NEL P.F., Durban
NIEUWOUDT J.H.M., Potchefstroom
NAGEL R., AB Auditor, Johannesburg
NAUDÉ S. Meiring, Pretoria

266

NIENABER P.J., Professor, Bloemfontein
NAUDE C.D., Farmer, Bethlehem, 1976
NEVELING B.C., Attorney, Harrismith, 1173
NIENABER Dr. G.S., Professor, Pietermaritzburg 2665
NORTJÉ J.G.F., Farmer, Willowmore, 5143
NEL Dr. F.J., Med. Doctor, Bellville, 5908
NAUDE P.J., SABC, Johannesburg, 5326
NEL I.D.M., Humansdorp, 4439
NEL A.S., Farmer, Fort Beaufort, 6486
NEL G.J.M., Storekeeper, Kingwilliamstown, 6945
NEETHLING P.J., Farmer, Kimberley, 6218
NORTIER W.H., Farmer, Langkloof, 6935
NEL T.C., Pretoria, 4447
NEL B.F., Professor, Pretoria, 1995
NIEMAND J.H., Secr. Pretoria, 5764
NEL J.C.D., Med. Doctor., Tzaneen, 5458

ODENDAL J.S., Manager, Bonnievale
OOSTHUIZEN L.M., Med. Doctor, Kirkwood
OOSTHUIZEN N.J., General Dealer, Albertinia
OOSTHUIZEN H.J., Market Researcher (Unie-staalkorp) Vereeniging North
ORFFER C.J., Adm. Official, Pretoria (Meintjieskop)
ODENDAAL J.G., Roodepoort, 7740
OPPERMAN J.M., Potgietersrus, 7802
OOSTHUIZEN G.L., Boksburg, 7896
OELOFSE L.J., Farmer, Sterkstroom
OLIVIER J.J., Miner, Welkom (Dagbreek)
OOSTHUIZEN W.J., Farmer, Albertinia
OOSTHUIZEN R.K., Farmer, Kakamas
OOSTHUIZEN G.C.I, Landbank, Lichtenburg East
OLIVIER F.B., Inspector (Bantu Educ.), Tzaneen
OOSTHUIZEN G.F.,Teacher, Steynsburg
ODENDAAL D.C., Farmer, Queenstown
OBERKOLZER J.F., Med. Doctor, Koedoesrand
OTTO D.J., Volkskas, Alberton
OLIVIER M.J.P., Minister (Religion), Potchefstroom
OELOFSE J.C., Attorney, Pretoria
OPENSHAW L.J., Benoni
OBERHOLZER S.O., Bethlehem
OPPERMAN D.P.J., Outjo
OBERHOLZER J., Bloemfontein
OPPERMAN R.W.J., Perskor, Johannesburg
OOSTHUIZEN A.J.G., Minister (Religion), Pretoria 362
OELOFSE I.D.
OLIVIER B.J., Farmer, Burgersdorp, 1311
OPPERMAN H.C., Dir. of Companies, Johannesburg, 3438
O'GRADY Dr. J.F., Dir. of Education, Potchefstroom, 308
OBERHOLZER Dr. C.K., Professor, Pretoria, 2074

OPPERMAN P.A., Farmer, Pretoria, 4382
OOSTHUIZEN W.P., Farmer, Reitz, 1451
OLIVIER J.S., ex-Teacher, White River, 225
OLIVIER S.P., Rector Indian College, Durban, 6991
ODENDAAL A.A., Missionary/Rector, Kestell, 4098
OOSTHUIZEN Dr. P., Dentist, Bellville, 2698
OOSTHUIZEN B.P., Mine Manager, Duiwelskloof, 4244

POTGIETER D.S., Teacher, Pretoria (Eloffsdal)
PRINSLOO G.D.P., School Principal, Pretoria (Gezina)
PRETORIUS J.J.L., Teacher, Pretoria (Voorslag)
POTGIETER E.F., Manager, Windhoek
PRETORIUS M. de W., Clerk (SAR & H), Kempton Park
POGGENPOEL J.D., Manager, Kenhardt
PRETORIUS F.H., Captain (S.A. Police), Windhoek
PALM A.P., Farmer, De Doorns
PIENAAR G.G., Farmer, Tulbagh
PIENAAR G.E., Clerk (SAR) Pietermaritzburg
PRINSLOO H.F., Farmer, Smithfield
POTGIETER J.F., Minister of Religion, Pretoria (Boerefort)
PRETORIUS W.P.J.P., Barkly East, 7744
PRETORIUS A.L.P., Pretoria (Meintjieskop), 7743
PIETERSEN H.P., Alberton, 7742
PIENAAR L.D., Kingwilliamstown, 7762
PIENAAR D.C., Oudtshoorn, 7741
PRINSLOO M.J., Johannesburg (Linden North), 7793
PELSER F.P., Bethlehem (Witteberge), 7809
PRETORIUS J.H., Tiervlei, 7816
PRETORIUS P.G., Witbank, 7810
PIENAAR A.J., Inspector, Bloemfontein East, 1771
POTGIETER L.M., Iscor, Vanderbijlpark (Overvaal)
PRINSLOO J.P.N., Minister (Religion), Venterspos
PARSONS E.J.H., Magistrate, Morgenzon
PIETERS W.J., Manager (Volkskas), Zastron
PELSER P.J., Minister (Religion), Heidelberg (Tvl)
PIETERS M.H., Minister (Religion), Krugersdorp
PAPENDORF O.L., Consultant Engineer, Krugersdorp
PIENAAR A.E., Farmer & Agent (Sanlam), Chrissiesmeer
POTGIETER D., Iscor, Pretoria
POTGIETER H.H.J., Teacher, Kirkwood
PIETERSE P.J.S., Dept. Agriculture, Potchefstroom
PIETERS H.N., Teacher, Magaliesburg
PELSER G.M.M., Minister (Religion), Pretoria

PIETERSE J.L., Municipality (Non-European Affairs), Rustenburg
PIENAAR D.J., Chipinga
PIETERSE H.J.C., Pretoria
POTGIETER J.J., Komatiepoort
PRINSLOO F.J., Potgietersrust
PRETORIUS M., Pretoria
PRINSLOO P.M., Westonaria
PELSER J.C., Virginia
PRETORIUS J.v. H., Vanderbijlpark
POTGIETER T.D., Attorney, Bloemfontein
PRETORIUS C.F.S., Pk. Bingley
PELSER P.C., Rosendal
PAUW J.G., Stellenbosch
POTGIETER M.J.L., Utrecht
PIETERSE J.J.G., Johannesburg
PIENAAR P.F., Pk. Scandinavia
PRELLER J.H., Potchefstroom
PRETORIUS D.W.A., Minister (Religion), Gansbaai
PRELLER J.E.L., Kimberley
PELSER A.N.P., Professor, Pretoria, 3381
POTGIETER E.F., Prof. & Commissioner General
PRINSLOO, Brigadier, Johannesburg
POTGIETER D.H., Farmer ex-Senator, Barkley East 5376
PREIS D.P., Bookkeeper, Bethal, 226
PRETORIUS J.H., Farmer, Bethulie, 3305
POTGIETER J.E., Farmer & MP, Brits, 3702
PIENAAR J.F., Butcher, Colesberg, 2473
PIENAAR J.A., Med. Doctor, Bultfontein, 3573
PIENAAR Dr. S.W., Pensioner/School Inspector Ceres, 1405
POTGIETER M.G., Farmer, Coligny, 4207
PRETORIUS J.S., Farmer, Jamestown, 2240
PAPENFUS S.F., Commissioner-General, Kestell, 1223
POTGIETER A.H.J., Teacher, Loeriesfontein, 9293
PRINSLOO I.M., Farmer, Messina, 2221
PRETORIUS A.L., ex-Secr. State President, Pretoria, 7743
PIETERSE P.W.A., Farmer/Senator, Schweizer-Reneke, 2247
PAINTER B.A., ex-Farmer, Tulbagh, 1657
POSTHUMUS D.J., Liaison Officer, Worcester, 2982
POTGIETER F.J.M., Professor, Stellenbosch, 2757
PIENAAR H., Ambassador, 2440
PRETORIUS P.J., Farmer/MPC, Bethlehem, 7526
PRETORIUS J.L., Minister (Religion), Bloemfontein, 2975
POTGIETER L.B., Works Manager, Johannesburg, 3726
PIENAAR S.W., Med. Doctor., Lindley, 5599
PRETORIUS W.L.A., Farmer, Odendaalsrus, 4701
PELLISSIER S.H., Pensioner, Pretoria, 567

PRINSLOO J.J., Supt. Iscor, Pretoria, 4261
PIETERSE M.D., Businessman, Stellenbosch, 7245

ROBERTS T.P., Magistrate, Swartruggens
RALL W.H.B., Teacher, Bethlehem
ROTHWELL T.W., Dentist, Durban
ROOS J.H., Minister Religion, Bellville (Voorpos) 3831
RUST H.E., Med. Doctor, Wellington (Wamakers-vlei)
ROUX D.J., Teacher, Stilfontein
RICHTER G.J., Police, Komati
RAUTENBACH G.S., Teacher, Winburg
ROSSOUW J.P.H., Springbok, 7745
ROOS T.J., Somerset West (Hottentots-Holland) 7772
ROUX J.V., Waterpoort (H. Potgieter), 7746
RIEKERT P.J., Pretoria (Bronberg), 7803
RIEDEMAN C.S.G., Cape Town, 7794
RAUBENHEIMER J., Attorney, Vereeniging North
ROSS W., Manager (Wheat Co-op), Brits
RAATH R.J., Minister (Religion), Pretoria (Meintjieskop)
REYNEKE J.P.A., Teachers, Boksburg North
ROBBERTSE N.J., Information Official (Dept. Agriculture) Brits, (Krokodilriver)
ROUX G.J., Farmer, Franschhoek
ROELOFSE E.B., Managing Director, Strand North
ROUX J.P., SAR (Engineer), Johannesburg
RAUBENHEIMER J.G., Accountant (Fruit Co-op) Villiersdorp
REYNEKE F.J., Police, Aliwal North
ROOS J.J., Farmer, Brits
ROUX A.P., Secretary (Senator Wes Co-op), Klerksdorp
ROUX P.D.A., Teacher, Vereeniging
ROSSOUX P.A.G., Health Inspector, Piketberg
ROETS F.C., Secr. South Rand Hospital, Johannesburg
RICHTER C.J.S., Kuruman
ROODT E.J., Parys
RICHTER J.G.M., Zeerust
RAUBENHEIMER J.J.M., Minister (Religion), Bloemfontein
RAS J.M.N., Benoni
ROETS J.B.S., State Attorney, Verwoerdburg
RICHTER J., Johannesburg
REINEKE C.C., Verwoerdburg
ROOS de F., Potchefstroom
ROODE M.C., Potchefstroom
ROBBERTZE W.P., Professor, Potchefstroom
RETIEF F.P.le R., Johannesburg 4071
REYNEKE J., Evander
ROUX W.P., Med. Doctor, Carletonville
REINECKE C.J., ex-MP, Pretoria (Swartkop), 7842
ROUSSEAU P.E., Business Leader, 2712

268

RÁUTENBACH N.J., Middelburg (C.P.)
ROUX S.N., Middelburg C.P., 8668
RIEKERT P.J., Nelspruit
RADYN J.P.
ROBBERTSE J.A.
RAUTENBACH Dr. P.S., Senior Civil Servant, Pretoria, 6142
RETIEF P.T., Farmer, De Aar, 3521
ROBERTS B.S., Pensioner School Principal, Ermelo 791
RAUTENBACH D., Farmer, Lindley, 1567
RALL J.W., Farmer/MP, Newcastle, 5206
REYNEKE T.I., Farmer/Businessman, Port Elizabeth, 2716
RAUTENBACH Prof. C.H., ex-Rector, Pretoria, 1825

RETIEF G.J., ex-Supt. Voortrekker Monument, Pretoria, 26
ROUX J.D.J., Advisory Council, Pretoria, 869
REITZ G.D., ex-Med. Doctor, Stellenbosch, 1194
RENS R.D., Emeritus Minister (Religion), Strand, 1947
RENS A.M., Farmer, Uitenhage, 2127
ROBBERTSE P.M., Academic, Pretoria, 6546
ROSSOUW H.C.J., Bellville, 4610
ROUX A., Farmer, Dewetsdorp, 1573
RIBBENS H., Agent, Durban, 5190
ROUX J.P., Minister (Religion), Edenburg, 2759
RAATS A.D., Emeritus Minister (Religion), Grabouw, 1154
RAUBENHEIMER O.S.H., Minister (Religion), Pretoria, 5583
RUPERT A., Director, Stellenbosch, 3088
SCHEEPERS G.P., Minister (Religion), Thabazimbi
STEYN J.W., Hoofbosbewaarder, Knysna
SEYFFERT J.F., Boer, Nelspruit
SCHEEPERS H.P., Bestuurder, Welkom, (Doorn)
STEENKAMP A.J., Clerk, Benoni North
SCHOEMAN P.C., Adj. Officer (Police), Groblersdal
SCHOLTZ W. du T., Farmer, Jacobsdal
STEEL H.R., Lecturer (Goudstad Onderwys Kollege), Johannesburg (Oom Paul)
SMIT E., Teacher, Cape Town (Wynberg)
SNYMAN G.J., Minister (Religion), Klerksdorp (Schoonspruit)
SIERTSEMA H.H., Superintendent, Krugersdorp (Republiek)
SCHOEMAN S.J., Manager, Pretoria (Silverton), 8097
SCHOEMAN A.D., Asst. Buyer (Iscor), Pretoria (Skanskop)
SNYMAN F.L., Editor in Chief, Stellenbosch (Simon v.d. Stel)
SCHOLTZ P.L., Lecturer, Graaff-Reinet

SANS P.J., Teacher, Kakamas
SMIT A.P., Teacher, Middelburg-Suid
SMITH P.M., Minister (Religion), Pretoria (Rietendal), 3219
SIEBERHAGEN N., Insp. of Schools, Graaff-Reinet, 4247
STANDER A.H., Farmer & MP, Prieska, 1537
STANDER J.H., Deputy Director of Education, Pietermaritzburg, 770
SCHURINK R.W., Farmer, Lydenburg
STRYDOM S., Snr. Lecturer, Pretoria (Waterkloof)
STRYDOM S.J., Vice Principal, Stilfontein
SCHUTTE P.J., Farmer, Sannieshof
STRYDOM H.F., Chief Veterinary Surgeon, Vryheid
SCHEEPERS J.J., Farmer, Bethlehem (Witteberg)
SNYMAN J.J., Architect, Pietersburg (P. Joubert)
SMITH H.J., Farmer, Rouxville
SWANEPOEL G.J., Teacher, Somerset West (Hottentots-Holland)
STEYN G.F., Manager (Volkskas), Bronkhorstspruit
STRUWIG J.H.G., Teacher, Belfast
SCHOLTZ H.J.S., Teacher, Ottosdal
SCHICKERLING J.K., Farmer, Delareyville
SCHEEPERS T., School Principal, Swartruggens
SCHOOMBIE P.J., Clerk, Marquard
SCHUTTE F.R.P., Chemist, Witbank
SMITH M.E., Vanderbijlpark, 7764
STEYN H.H., Bloemfontein (De Bloem), 7747
SLOET H.A., Johannesburg North, 7767
SMITH P.J., Queenstown, 7795
SMIT P.A., Groblersdal, 7804
STRYDOM A.H.J.J., Heilbron, 7805
SWANEPOEL W.J., Calvinia, 7811
SCHUTTE S.H., Lieutenant (Police), Johannesburg, 8240
SWART P.J., Teacher, Vryheid
SNYMAN P.A., Farmer, Warrenton
SCHREUDER P.v. L., Farmer, Vredenburg
SPAMMER S.J., Personnel Clerk (SAR), Vryheid East
SMITH C.M. (Nelie), Businessman, Bloemfontein (De Bloem)
STEENEKAMP J.H., Minister (Religion), Johannesburg (Abr. Kriel)
SMITH F.W., Teacher, Cedarville
SHERMAN T.W.W., Secretary (Bonuskor), Cape Town
SWARTS C.C., Works Director, Benoni
SCHOEMAN P.S.J.A., Teacher, Graskop
SCHOEVERS J.E., Farmer, Victoria West
STRYDOM W.A., Teacher, Kakamas
SCHOEMAN S.J., Lecturer (Univ.), Pretoria
STEENKAMP P.E., Agricultural Official, Swellendam
STOKER P.H., Professor, Potchefstroom

269

SMIT Z.L., Businessman, Pretoria
SLABBER J.D., Dept. Agriculture, Queenstown
SNYMAN G.J., Volkskas, Kempton Park
SPAMER F.J., Auditor, Bredasdorp
SCHOLTZ J.A.C., Minister (Religion), Zeerust
STRYDOM A., Minister (Religion), Vredenburg
SCHUTTE G.P., Unie Railway Funeral Undertaker
  Germiston
SPIES A.J., Minister (Religion), Vanderbijlpark
STANDER F.W., Teacher, Cape Town
STANDER K., Architect, Cape Town
SCHEEPERS D.J.J., Minister (Religion),
  Wesselsbron
STAPELBERG J.J., Defence, Bloemfontein
SCHOLTZ J.W.K., Schoolboard Secr., Kokstad
SAAIMAN P.J., Volkskas, Krugersdorp
SNYMAN B.J., Magistrate, Lydenburg
STEENEKAMP J.C., Farmer, Magaliesburg
SCHOOMBIE J.C., Minister (Religion), Uitenhage
SNIJDERS J.F.A., Accountant Nedbank, Vasco
SMIT O.J., Volkskas, Schweizer-Reneke
STEENKAMP D.F., Teacher, Dewetsdorp
SWIEGERS G.J., Farmer, Griekwastad
SWART H.J., Devon
STEYN J.H., Phalaborwa
SPIES M.P.D., Welkom
STRUMPFER P.S.H.F., Belfast
STULTING J.D., Johannesburg
STEYN J.P.S., Pretoria
STEYN S.J., Johannesburg
STEYN F.S., Benoni
SCHUTTE P.J., Vanderbijlpark
SWANEPOEL G., Pretoria
SMIT H.C., Pretoria
STEYN W.J.A., Venterstad
SWANEPOEL J.A., Delareyville
SMIT E.J., Potchefstroom
STANDER A.H., Touwsrivier
STRYDOM P.J., Potchefstroom
SCHUTTE B.C., Professor, Potchefstroom
STOKER H.G., Professor, Potchefstrooom 179
SMITH D.P.J., Potchefstroom
SCHOEMAN D.F.N., Farmer/Businessman,
  Potchefstroom, 3389
SNYMAN W.J., Professor, Potchefstroom
STEYN H.G., Potchefstroom
SCHOEMAN G.P., Potchefstroom
SCHULZE H.G., Potchefstroom
SCHOLTZ G.D. Dr., ex Editor, Johannesburg
STRYDOM G.S.R., Burgersdorp
STEENKAMP J.J., Breyten
SCHUMANN Dr. T.E.W., Pretoria
SCHOLTZ C.F., Victoria West
SMALBERGER L.C., Petrusburg
SMIT J.D., Pretoria, 6082
SCHOEMAN S.J., 8097
STANDER J.H., Natal, 770

SWART J.H., Official AB, 1843
STOCKENSTRÖM G.P., Cape Town
SMIT J.P.S., Middelburg CP.
SMIT G.J.J., Cape Town, 2644
SWART C.R., ex-State President
SCHUMANN C.G.W., Professor, Stellenbosch
STEYL J.H., Senator & Chief Secr. of N.P. in
  Transvaal
STRYDOM Dr. N.B., Johannesburg
SCHUTTE Dr. J.H., SABC, Johannesburg
SMITH Col. P.W., A.T.K.V., Johannesburg
SNYMAN Dr. P.G., Lecturer, Potchefstroom
SCHOLTZ P.L., Johannesburg
SMITH J.A., Architect, Bellville, 1854
SWANEVELDER H.S., Pensioner/ex MP, Bellville
  1936
SCHULZE M.R., Pensioner, Benoni, 1424
STEGMANN J.A., Dentist, Bloemfontein, 605
SCHOLTEMEYER H., Farmer, Devon, 2911
SCHEEPERS W.H., Pensioner Farmer, Ermelo,
  608
STRYDOM D.P., Farmer, Groblersdal, 595
SCHEFFER C.J., SAR, Germiston, 2425
SCHOLTZ J. du P., Professor, Cape Town, 1629
STANDER H.J., Attorney, Kimberley, 2607
STEENKAMP J.R., Farmer, Kimberley, 3937
SERFONTEIN S.J., Farmer/Director, Koppies,
  1273
SLABBERT B., Miner, Letsitele, 6405
SMIT D.A., Farmer, Mariental 4830
STRAUSS A., Inspec. of Schools, Kroonstad, 7217
STOLTZ B.J., Farmer, Nelspruit, 2458
SCHUTTE A.G., Farmer, Ogies, 352
SCHOEMAN P.C., Population Registration
  Official Parow, 7958
STEENKAMP P.A., Farmer, Petrusburg, 2852
SMIT O.J., Volkskas, Pretoria, 8754
SCHOEMAN B.J., ex-Minister, Pretoria, 3613
SCHWEIKERDT E.C.G., Art Dealer, Pretoria, 4853
STEYN Dr. D.H., ex-Financial Adv. Prime Minister,
  Pretoria, 1399
SEPHTON A.C., Minister (Religion), Pretoria,
  7640
SNYMAN T.W., Pensioner, Rustenburg, 792
STEENKAMP J.A., Farmer, Stellenbosch, 2851
STEYN R.D.J., Chief Clerk, Swellendam, 5002
SWART J.N., Manager, White River, 2433
SNYMAN H.W., Physician, Pretoria, 5574
STANDER C.B., Inspector, Aliwal North, 4007
SCHABORT G.C., Farmer, Balfour, 2396
SCHRAADER L.B., Med. Doctor, Bellville, 6982
SIMES H.J.R., MPC, Bloemfontein, 5790
SCHOOMBIE J.F., Farmer/ex MP, Bronkhorst-
  spruit, 1075
SCHOEMAN H.S., Minister, Delmas, 5577
SCHOOMBEE J., Teacher, Durbanville, 7560
SONNEKUS A.J.H., Police, Johannesburg, 8528

SCHOOMBEE W.S.P., Manager, Johannesburg, 8650
SCHOLTZ P.J.F., Sanlam, Cape Town, 7052
STOFBERG P.J.R., ex-Teacher, Lydenburg, 698
SMITH P.J., Minister (Religion), Piketberg, 7795
STEYN D.J.C., Civil Service Commission, Pretoria, 4349
STEGMAN F.A., Businessman, Pretoria, 4234
SNYMAN H., Professor, Pretoria, 5574
SMIT J.M.C., Managing Director, Pretoria, 4301
STEYN J.C., Commissioner Prisons, Pretoria, 7364
STANDER Dr. G.J., C.S.I.R., Pretoria, 5276
STANDER H.J., Med. Doctor. Vereeniging 5688
SADIE N.C., MP, Winburg, 3323
STEYN A.N., MP, Willowmore, 3816

THEART J.N.J., Clerk (SAR & H), Bellville (Thalman)
TALJAARD C.J., City Engineer, Middelburg (Tvl)
THERON J.F., Farmer, Tulbagh
THERON L.F., Accountant, Virginia
TALJAARD C.M.L., Managing Director, Johannesburg (Joon van Rooy)
THOM H.B., Rector Univ. Stellenbosch, Stellenbosch (Simonsberg), 1773
TROSKIE G.F.C., Med. Doctor, Kroonstad, 2895
THERON D.C., Teacher, Belfast
TERBLANCHE J.P., Teacher, Robertson
TRUTER H.F.G., Springbok, 7775
TALJAARD J.A.L., Potchefstroom East, 7781
TRUTER De V.J.D., Attorney, Cape Town
TERBLANCHE H.M., Civil Servant, Pretoria (Elandspoort)
TRUTER M.H.G., Manager (Farmers Co-op) Beaufort West
THERON J.C., Doctor, Thabazimbi
TRIEGAARDT L.G., Accountant (Foskor), Phalaborwa
TERBLANCHE A.B., Police, Pretoria
THERON J.J., Farmer, Ottosdal
THEUNISSEN M.P., Manager Gen. Chem. Corp., Durban
TERBLANCH F.,George
TREURNICHT Dr. A.P., Deputy Cabinet Minister, 4240
THERON S., Cape Town
TRENGROVE J., Judge, Pretoria
THERON H.S., Church Official, Hennenman, 618
TOERIEN D.F., Pensioner, Johannesburg, 51
THERON J.C.H., ex-Farmer, Parys, 3032
THERON J.D., Insp. of Educ., Barkly West, 2380
TALJAARDT C.H., ex-Businessman, Phillippolis, 3508
TERBLANCHE H.M., Bantu Affairs, Pretoria, 8237
TRUTER H.H., Businessman, Pretoria, 4979

UYS C. v.d. Berg., Machinist, Tiervlei
UYS D.C., Farmer, Bethal
UECKERMANN E.C., Fitter, Messina
UECKERMANN S.J., Bethal
UYS H.J., Barrydale
UYS D.C.H., ex Cabinet Minister, Bredasdorp, 1414
UYS J.J., Farmer, Memel, 3570
UYS M.J., Farmer, Memel, 3991

VILJOEN M., ex-Minister, Pretoria, 3226
VOSLOO A.H., ex-Deputy Minister, Somerset East, 2510
VAN VELDEN A.G.E., Emeritus Minister (Religion) Somerset West, 3695
VERMEULEN S.W., Farmer, Springbok, 7279
VAN DER WALT L.S., Farmer, Steynsburg, 1791
VERSTER J. de K., Attorney, Theunissen, 4397
VLOK A.J.L., Farmer, Upington, 4845
VAN WYK H.J., ex-MP, Ventersburg, 1020
VAN RENSBURG D.G.J., Senator, Wepener, 4237
VAN DER BERG G.P., MP, Wolmaranstad, 6075
VERMEULEN D.J., Inspector, Worcester, 7856
VAN RENSBURG H., Farmer, Babanango, 8179
VERMAAK C.J., Businessman, Babanango, 7163
VERSLUIS R.C., Digger/Businessman, Barkley-West, 4571
DE VILLIERS J.H., Med. Doctor, Bellville, 6456
VAN VUUREN P.Z.J., Senator, Benoni, 6210
VAN ZYL F.J., Businessman, Bellville, 4069
VICTOR S.F., Farmer, Bethlehem, 6214
VILJOEN M.J., MPC/Farmer, Bethlehem, 3787
VENTER E.A., Professor, Bloemfontein, 4118
VENTER R.S., Med. Doctor, Bloemfontein, 562
VAN DER MERWE C.V., Med. Doctor/MP, Bloemfontein, 4079
VERMAAK N.J., Farmer, Dewetsdorp, 1019
VAN CITTERT H., Farmer, Devon, 3419
VAN DER SCHYFF A., Businessman, Griekwastad, 8020
VISSER A.M., Pensioner, Johannesburg, 93
VAN JAARSVELD S.R., Manager, Johannesburg, 9052
VAN NIEKERK S.C.J., Med. Doctorr., Cape Town, 8445
VAN DER WALT J.H., Chemist, Cape Town, 8926
VAN DER MERWE S.W., Cabinet Minister, Keimoes, 6571
VAN DER WALT C.T., School Principal, Klerksdorp, 4116
VAN NIEKERK M., Businessman, Ladybrand, 4653
VAN SCHALKWYK J.F. v.d. M., Farmer, Lindley 3281
VERMEULEN S.O., Farmer, Luckhoff, 1712
VAN ZYL P.G.J., Farmer, Mogol, 4202
VAN STADEN W.H., Med. Doctor. , Nigel, 4654
VAN VUUREN T.H.J., Supt. SAR, Pretoria, 6222

VAN RENSBURG N.J., Med. Doctor, Pretoria, 3699
VILJOEN F.T., Industrial Court, Pretoria, 4151
VISSE J.H., ex MP, Pretoria, 3957
VORSTER B.J., State President, Pretoria, 3737
VORSTER P.W., Secretary, Pretoria, 4431
VAN VUUREN H.P.T., Secr. Justice, Pretoria, 5277
VERSTER J.P., Secr. SAR Board, Pretoria, 4595
VISAGIE W., Farmer, Calvinia
VENTER L.T.P., Teacher, Kimberley, 1850
VAN DER MERWE Dr. A., Minister (Religion), Kroonstad, 2331
VAN DER MERWE H.W., General Agent, Kroonstad, 33
VAN HUYSSTEEN G.F.Z., Farmer, Lindley, 2346
VAN SCHALKWYK J.F. v.d. M., Farmer Lindley, 3281
VAN AARDE A.M., Teacher, Nylstroom, 8559
VENTER A.A.J., SAR, Ontdekkers, 7565
VAN DER MERWE J.H.J., Inspec. of Schools, Oudtshoorn, 1463
VAN RENSBURG N.J.J., Lecturer, Potchefstroom, 5604
VENTER J.J., Rentboard, Port Elizabeth, 514
VENTER D.G., Emeritus Minister (Religion), Potchefstroom 1175
VAN DER WALT C.P., Farmer, Potchefstroom, 3682
VAN RENSBURG S.P.J.J., Professor, Pretoria, 3014
VAN DER WALT H.J., Magistrate, Pretoria, 2061
VELDMAN H.P., Teacher, Pretoria, 2534
VERMAAS M., Farmer, Pretoria, 376
VENTER D.J., ex Teacher/Farmer, Pretoria, 2542
VAN RENSBURG C.J.J., Missionary, Pretoria, 1294
VENTER W.F., Emeritus Minister (Religion), Pretoria, 1145
VILJOEN P.G., ex-Bank Manager, Robertson, 2121
VENTER C.R., Pensioner, Stellenbosch, 1608
VIVIER C.L., Pensioner, Stellenbosch, 2601
VAN DER WALT L.S., Farmer, Steynsrust, 1523
VAN ZYL F.J., Swellendam, 4537
VILJOEN D.A., Farmer, Tulbagh, 1386
VILJOEN J.P., ex-Farmer, Tulbagh, 3437
VAN DER SPUY H.H., General Dealer, Uniondale 2478
VAN DER SPUY H.H., Farmer, Uniondale, 2476
VAN EYSSEN J.C., ex-Teacher, White River, 92
VAN DYK J.H., Secr. Bantu Educ., Pretoria, 1784
VILJOEN F., ex-School Principal, Johannesburg, 365
VAN DER VYVER G.J., MPC, Adelaide, 3291
VENTER P.J., Major, Johannesburg
VAN WYK S.J., Brigadier
VAN VUUREN M., Brigadier
VAN DER WALT D.J., Minister (Religion)
VAN ROOYEN B.D.C.

VAN WYK A.J., Pietermaritzburg
VAN DEN BERGH H.J., Genl. former head of CID, Pretoria, 6745
VILJOEN Dr. Stefaan
VAN LOGGERENBERG D.C.S.
VOSLOO C.F.
VERSTER J.J.
VAN JAARSVELD F.A., Professor, Pretoria
VAN DYK Dr. P.R., Lecturer, Babanango, 7313
VERMAAK I.L., Shopkeeper, Babanango, 5578
VAN DER POEL H.R., Auditor, Bellville, 935
VAN DER POEL A.P.J., Pensioner, Bloemfontein, 4664
VAN BLERK P.J., Appeal Judge, Bloemfontein, 1841
VAN DER MERWE S.W., Farmer, Boshof, 1031
VENTER D.J., Farmer Businessman, Colesberg, 3691
VENTER S., Shopkeeper Farmer, Danielskuil, 4949
VAN FELIVELDT J.C.J., Farmer, De Aar, 4290
VENTER P.A., Farmer, Dealesville, 652
VILJOEN H.P.M., Farmer, Estcourt, 3871
VAN DER WALT M.J., Pensioner Police Major, Germiston, 4171
VAN NIEKERK A.J., Farmer, Grootfontein, 4989
VAN TONDER J.P., School Principal, Harrismith, 1811
VAN DER MERWE J.G.F., Attorney, Heilbron, 704
VILJOEN D.J., Clerk, Jacobsdal, 5405
VAN DER WESTHUYSEN J.C.J., Proof Reader, Johannesburg, 2649
VENTER D.J., Police Captain, Johannesburg, 6281
VAN DER MERWE S.W., SAR Chairman Appeal Board, Johannesburg, 1669
VAN WYK A.J., Chairman Censor Board, Cape Town, 4165
VAN NIEKERK O.W., Doctor, Mafeking
VILJOEN P.J. v. B., Med. Doctor, Newcastle
VAN DEN HEEVER F.A., Med. Doctor, Springbok
VAN REENEN C.D.D., Vryheid
VON BRATT W.P., Noupoort
VAN DER MERWE W.L., MP Meyerton, 7828
VAN VUUREN H.J., Pretoria (Wesmoot), 7827
VAN DEN BERGH G.P., Minister (Religion), Hermanus
VAN DER MERWE W.K., Stellenbosch, 7902
VAN NIEKERK J.O., Krugersdorp, 7866
VAN HEERDEN C.J., Witbank, 7872
VAN DER WALT H.S., Vanderbijlpark, 7865
VORSTER C.G., Volkskas, Durban
VAN TONDER L.G., Durban
VAN DEVENTER B., Riversdal
VAN WYK J.A., 5582
VAN DER MERWE P.S., ex MP, Windhoek, 7494
VAN DER WALT L.S., former organizer & Boss official
VENTER W., Middelburg C.P.

272

VAN DER WALT J.C., Graaff-Reinet
VAN ZYL J.P., Graaff-Reinet
VENTER S.J., Graaff-Reinet
VAN DER WESTHUIZEN J.H., Cape Town
VAN ZYL S.J., Cape Town
VAN WYK de Vries P., Johannesburg
VILJOEN D.J., Bloemfontein
VAN DER SPUY, J.P. ex-Cabinet Minister 2985
VENTER S. de K., Pretoria
VAN WYK P., Bapsfontein
VAN SCHOOR A.M., Senator ex-editor,
Johannesburg
VAN DYL L.
VENTER H.J.J., Brigadier, Johannesburg
VAN NIEKERK W.P., Dullstroom
VAN TONDER P.C., Marandellas
VERSTER A.A., Alexanderbaai
VLOTMAN G.C., Brandfort
VAN RENSBURG W.C.J., Glencoe
VAN WYK G.E., Florida
VENTER G.H., Kimberley
VAN AARDE J.J., Rustenburg
VAN DER WALT H.J., Odendaalsrus
VAN TONDER P.J.H., Potgietersrus
VAN RENSBURG D.J., Sabie
VAN ZYL D.R., Trompsburg
VAN DEN BERGH J.P.J., Welkom
VAN TONDER H.P., Bloemfontein
VENTER J.A., Minister (Religion), Elliot
VAN VUUREN D.M.J., Evander
VAN RENSBURG W.L.D.M.J., Jamestown
VAN WYK A.J., Sutherland
VAN ZYL P.A., Cape Town
VAN ROOYEN M.M., Ladybrand
VAN ASWEGEN G.J., Bloemfontein
VAN NIEKERK A. Minister (Religion), Pietersburg
VAN ZYL W.I, Minister (Religion), Port Elizabeth
VAN EEDEN D.P.W., Police, Robertsham
VAN EEDEN J.J., Secr. National Party, Alberton
VAN ZYL J.P., Med. Doctor, Messina
VILJOEN T.A., Verwoerdburg
VAN ROOYEN M.S., Empangeni
VAN DER MERWE S.J., Touwsrivier
VAN ZYL F.L., Windhoek
VOSLOO P.C., Johannesburg
VAN WYK A., Pretoria
VENTER L.J., Salisbury
VAN DER MERWE J.M., Chemist, Glencoe
VAN DER SCHYFF D.H., Secretary, Griekwastad
VAN RENSBURG B.W.J., Farmer, Babanango
VAN DYK W.J., Farmer, Bredasdorp
VAN DER WESTHUYSEN D.B., Farmer,
Kenhardt
VERMEULEN A., Teacher, Kimberley
VENTER S.G., Farmer, Otjiwarongo
VAN SCHALKWYK O.D., Manager, Potch.
(Mooirivier)

VAN DER MERWE J.H., Teacher, Pretoria
(Swartkop)
VAN TONDER P., Teacher, Somerset West,
(Hottentotholland)
VAN ZYL M.C., Asst. Personnel Manager,
Vereeniging North
VAN NIEKERK F., Accountant, Brits
(Krokodilrivier)
VAN DER WALT B.J., Ind. Official (SAR & H),
Johannesburg (Iwan Lombard)
VENTER M., Minister (Religion), Johannesburg,
(Oorwinning)
VAN ZYL J.C., Teacher, Kuilsrivier
VAN DER WALT J.H.P., Teacher, Petrusburg
VERHOEF L.H., Geologist, Phalaborwa
VAN WYK W.L., Geologist, Pietermaritzburg
VAN HUYSTEEN S., Representative (Sanlam)
Port Elizabeth, (Diaz)
VAN DER MERWE S.W., Farmer, Porterville
VAN DER MERWE W.K., Regional Organizer,
Vanderbijlpark
VAN WYK M.C., Teacher, Vasco,
(Ruyterwacht)
VAN DE WALL M., Minister (Religion), Vryburg
VAN DER WALT N.S.T., Architect, Bloemfontein
(Louw Wepener)
VERMAARK H.D.S., Manager (Volkskas), Louis
Trichardt
VAN AARDE J.A., Head Dept., Psycology
Dept. of Education, Port Elizabeth North
VAN DEN BERG A., Teacher, Port Elizabeth
West
VAN ROOYEN G.P., Inspec. of Education v.
Onderwys, Krugersdorp (Republiek), 265
VAN WYK de V.J., Adv., Johannesburg (Iwan
Lombaard) 2301
VISSER G.J.F., Businessman, Johannesburg North,
3571
VAN JAARSVELD J.G.P., Grootfontein
VAN ASWEGEN C.H.J., Manager. SANTAM,
Cape Town, 4223
VENTER W.L., Minister (Religion), MP, Barkly
West, 3235
VAN ZYL N.J., S.A. Police Lieutenant, Potchef-
stroom Central
VAN DER LINDEN F.J., Farmer, Sannieshof
VAN ZYL H.J.P., Lieutenant (Police), Johannesburg
(Christo Beyers)
VAN RENSBURG C.J.J., Farmer, Kestell
VAN ZYL W.A., Lieutenant (Police), Oudtshoorn
VAN JAARSVELD A.A., Farmer, Grootfontein
VAN ROOY H.F. de W. Farmer, Krugersdorp
(Paardekraal), 8129
VAN RENSBURG JANSE S.W., Chemist,
Newcastle
VERMEULEN J.U., Farmer, Philipstown
VAN DEN BERG J.C., Teacher, Warden

273

VAN NIEKERK S.C.J., Med. Doctor, Malmesbury (Swartland)
VAN DER MERWE I.S., Commander, Vaalharts
VAN WYK G.J., Detective Sergeant (Police), Springbok
VERMAAK D., Headmaster, Calitzdorp
VAN WYK L.J., Teacher, Calvinia
VAN DER WALT J.P., Teacher, Carletonville North
VAN DEN HEEVER D.J., Representative SANLAM, Johannesburg, (Klipriviersberg)
VENTER A.A., MP Attorney, Klerksdorp North
VAN DER WALT H.J.D., Attorney, Klerksdorp North
VENTER J.C., Med. Doctor, Knapdaar
VAN DER WESTHUIZEN, H.I., Representative (Sanlam), Mafeking
VAN WYK J.K., Businessman, Springbok
VAN RENSBURG H.M.J., Missionary, Wellington (Groenberg)
VAN DER WALT G.M., Director, Johannesburg
VENTER A.J., Branch Manager (Co-op), Postmasburg
VAN NIEKERK D.H., Attorneys Clerk, Klerksdorp Schoonspruit)
VAN ZYL D.P., School Principal, Vryheid-East
VAN DER MERWE D.B., Minister of Religion, Langkloof
VAN WYK D.J.O., Regional Manager (Sanlam) Witbank
VAN WYK D.F.H., Farmer, Danielskuil
VENTER S.J.J., Farmer, Danielskuil
VAN VUUREN J.J.M.J., Heilbron, 7754
VAN DER MERWE J.P., Springbok, 7750
VAN DER WALT M.P.A., Christiana, 7751
VAN COLLER C.P., Johannesburg (A. Kriel), 7749
VAN BILJON W.J., Johannesburg (Linden North), 7748
VAN EYK D.J.M., Stellenbosch (Helderberg), 7765
VAN NIEKERK A.A., Johannesburg (J. v. Rooy), 7753
VAN EEDEN J.A., Potchefstroom West, 7752
VAN LOGGERENBERG P.H., Winburg, 7773
VAN DER MERWE W.A.H, Aliwal North, 7776
VAN RENSBURG M.C.G.J., Bloemfontein (Bergendal), 7734
VAN DER WALT B., Kimberley (Vooruitsig), 7777
VAN DER SPUY M.T., Humansdorp, 7721
VILJOEN G., Pretoria (Andries Pretorius), 7785
VILJOEN F.D., Standerton, 7782
VAN RENSBURG M.T.S.J., Hennenman, 7784
VAN VUUREN D.C.L.J., Nelspruit, 7806
VAN DER WALT E., Potchefstroom Central 7789
VAN STADEN A.J.C., Pretoria (Totiusdal), 7868
VORSTER S.J., Lecturer (Teachers Training Col) Pretoria (Klipkoppies)
VAN NIEKERK B., Farmer, Springbok
VORSTER J.D., Minister (Religion), Cape Town

VAN ZYL C.J.J., Teacher, Natalspruit
VAN NIEKERK J.C.H., Health Inspector (SAR), Beaufort-Wes)
VAN ROOYEN G.R., Minister (Religion), Estcourt (Saailaer)
VAN DER BERG P.J., Manager, Kuilsrivier
VAN NIEKERK P.J., Manager (Volkskas), Christiana
VAN NIEKERK S.G., Farmer, Ficksburg
VAN NIEKERK H.G., Lecturer (University), Stellenbosch (Helderberg)
VAN DER WESTHUIZEN I.J.O., Farmer, Uniondale
VAN TONDER J., Clerk to City Council, Ermelo
VAN DER BURGH C., Manager (Saambou), Pietersburg
VAN DER MERWE S.D., Minister (Religion), Vanderbijlpark
VAN DER MERWE D.S., Teacher, Pretoria
VAN DER MERWE J.S., Farmer Architect, Graskop
VENTER J.L., Teacher, Phalaborwa
VAN ROOYEN L., Farmer, Vryheid East
VAN DER MERWE M.J., Farmer, Bray
VAN ROOYEN M., Professor (Univ.), Pretoria
VENTER J.D., National Bureau Educational Research, Pretoria
VAN VUUREN P.J.J., Researcher (Agricura), Pretoria
VAN DER MERWE C.M., Teacher, Steynsrus
VAN HUYSTEEN G.F., Farmer, Steynsrus
VAN NIEKERK J.S., Chemist, Vryburg
VISAGIE J.H., S A R Police, Pretoria
VAN DEN HEEVER S., Volkskas, Smithfield
VAN DER MERWE F.H.H., Farmer, Bothaville
VAN HEERDEN W.J.S., Consultant Engineer, Pretoria
VAN DYK T.A., Defence, Pretoria
VAN EEDEN J.A., Superintendent (Non-European Affairs) Pretoria
VAN NIEKERK I.J.M., Police, Vasco
VAN NIEKERK H.J., Farmer, Dewetsdorp
VAN DER LINDE J.A., Businessman, Postmasburg
VILJOEN J.T.B., Costing Accountant, Pretoria
VAN ZYL J.H., Med. Doctor, Rustenburg
VILJOEN M.D., Farmer, Schweizer-Reneke
VAN WYK R.R. Minister (Religion), Springs
VAN ZYL A.H., Minister (Religion), Pretoria
VENTER J.H., Teacher, Tweeling
VAN ZYL J.W., Magistrate, Christiana
VAN DEN BERGH B.H., Volkskas, Jansenville
VAN HEERDEN W.F.P., Teacher, Vereeniging
VAN DER MERWE C.I., Farmer, Coligny
VAN WYK L.A.S., Minister (Religion), Naboomspruit
VAN DER WESTHUIZEN, Chemist, Naboomspruit
VAN DER WALT D.J., Municipality (Engineer), Alberton

274

VAN AARDT B., K.W.B., Ermelo
VENTER H.J., Farmer, Ermelo
VISSER H.J., Teacher, Greytown
VAN HEERDEN P.J., Teacher, Johannesburg
VAN DER VYVER M.J., Teacher, Welkom
VAN ZYL J.D., Chemist, Bellville
VAN SCHALKWYK W.V.L., Police, Benoni
VAN DER MESCHT, African Life Ins. Agent,
Port Elizabeth
VAN ASWEGEN A.M., Farmer, Noupoort
VAN WYK J.P.R., Secr. S.A. Wool Commission,
Port Elizabeth
VAN VUUREN S.M., Minister (Religion),
Johannesburg
VAN WYK P.J.R., Volkskas, Kirkwood
VILJOEN F.J.,Med. Doctor, Nelspruit
VOS L.P.G., Municipality, Pretoria
VAN WYK J.A. du P., Police, Randburg
VAN STADEN M.J., Police, Riviersonderend
VAN DYK J.J., Teacher, Rustenburg
VAN WYK H.A., Missionary, Springbok
VAN WYK J.M., Director (Warmbaths Retreading
Works), Warmbad
VAN VUUREN J.H., Farmer, Dewetsdorp
VAN DER MERWE M.A., Farmer,/Businessman,
Kakamas
VAN WIJK S.J., Rembrandt, Paarl
VAN DER SPUY, Med. Doctor, Worcester,
VENTER L., Windhoek
VAN ZYL J.A., Bloemfontein
VAN WYK M.J., Harrismith
VAN RENSBURG H.I.J., Kroonstad
VAN DER MERWE J.L., Kroonstad
VAN DER MERWE W.J., Vereeniging
VAN STADEN P.R., Verkeerdevlei
VAN WYK W.A., Potchefstroom
VENTER D.G., Potchefstroom
VAN ROOY H.C., Professor, Potchefstroom
VAN DER WALT C.P., Potchefstroom
VAN DER WALT S.P., Professor, Potchefstroom
VAN DER WALT P.J., Potchefstroom
VENTER T.B., Potchefstroom
VAN DER WALT M.P.A., Teacher, Potchefstroom
VORSTER R.J., Potchefstroom
VIVIERS, H.J.B., Potchefstroom
VILJOEN D.J., Potchefstroom
VAN ROOY D.J., Professor, Potchefstroom
VAN ROOYEN A., Potchefstroom
VENTER C.N. Potchefstroom
VAN DEN BERG J.A., Potchefstroom
VERBEEK W.A, Potchefstroom
VENTER H.L., Potchefstroom
VAN DER WALT J.P., Potchefstroom
VENTER H., Professor, Potchefstroom
VAN WYK H.P.D., Agric. College, Potchefstroom
VENTER N.G., Potchefstroom
VAN DER WALT J.A., Potchefstroom

VAN DER MERWE J.S., Professor, Potchefstroom
VENTER H., Sanlam, East London
VAN RENSBURG Fanie, Waterkloof, Pretoria
VAN ZYL W.H., Volkskas, George
VAN WYK A.M., Hermanus
VISSER J.C., Calvinia

WESSELS J.H.W., Optician, Bloemfontein North
WEIDEMAN W.J., Admin. Official, Windhoek West
WIESE T.J., Farmer, Hertzogville
WILBERS P.J.E., Vice-Principal, Pretoria (Eloffsdal)
WILCOCKS M.S., Asst. Manager, Bloemfontein
(Pres. Steyn)
WELMAN H., Farmer, Koster
WÜST W.G.C., Head Master, Johannesburg
(Anthonie Moll), 4560
WILCOCKS C.T.M., Senator-Businessman,
Bloemfontein North, 1041
WHITEMAN M.G., Foreman Electrician,
Vereeniging
WIENAND v. M., Clerk (Dept. of Immigration)
Komati
WEIDEMAN W.J., Clerk (SAR), Alberton
WIUM D.J.W., Farmer, De Doorns
WEIDEMAN P.J., Police, Pietermaritzburg
WILMS C.A., Med. Doctor, Bethal, 8591
WOLMARANS J.B., Iscor, Vanderbijlpark
WOHLITZ J.F., Minister (Religion), Delareyville
WARNICH P.G., Minister (Religion), Port Elizabeth
WEBER P.C.H., Butcher, Ugie
WESSELS B.H.J., Sanlam, Port Elizabeth
WOLMARANS C.F., Tweeling
WARMENHOVEN W.J.M., Tzaneen
WARMENHOVEN H.W., Tzaneen
WESSELS J.S.O., Mosselrivier
WOLMARANS H.P., Bronkhorstspruit
WOLMARANS J.N., Minister (Religion),
Johannesburg
WASSENAAR A.D., Business Leader, Cape Town,
3947
WESSELS Louis, Brigadier, Johannesburg
WEIDEMAN H.J., Attorney
WILLEMSE P.E., Chemist, Bethlehem, 3244
WENTZEL L.F.J., ex-Farmer, Klerksdorp, 890
WESSELS P.J., Farmer, Memel, 385
WESSELS A.J. de V. Farmer, Napier, 6256
WESSELS P.L.J., Pensioner, Pretoria East, 5363
WELGEMOED C.A., Dentist, Pretoria, 2461
WICHT Dr. C.L., Med. Doctor, Bellville, 7885
WESSELS P.J., School Principal, Heilbron, 9716
WEYERS F.D., Auctioneer, Kroonstad, 3656
WALTERS S.W., Stellenbosch, 6324
WEIDEMAN L.H., Farmer, Tromspburg, 3619

ZAAIMAN S.F., Journalist, Bloemfontein
ZWIEGERS W.A., SA' Police, Florida
ZERWICH J.L., Pensioner Farmer, Clocolan, 4047

275

Index

277